Exploring Social Psychology

Exploring Social Psychology

THIRD EDITION

Robert A. Baron Rensselaer Polytechnic Institute

Donn Byrne State University of New York at Albany

Jerry Suls State University of New York at Albany

Allyn and Bacon

BOSTON   LONDON   SYDNEY   TORONTO

Series Editor   John-Paul Lenney
Cover Coordinator   Linda Dickinson
Manufacturing Buyer   William Alberti
Cover Designer   Susan Slovinsky
Text Design/Editorial/Production Services   The Book Department

Copyright © 1989, 1982, 1979 by Allyn and Bacon
A Division of Simon & Schuster
160 Gould Street
Needham, Massachusetts 02194

Library of Congress Cataloging-in-Publication Data

Baron, Robert A.
    Exploring social psychology.

    Includes index.
    1. Social psychology.   I. Byrne, Donn Erwin.
II. Suls, Jerry M.   III. Title.
HM251.B435   1988   302   88-7908
ISBN 0-205-11908-5

Printed in the United States of America
10   9   8   7   93

To our children:

Jessica

Lindsey, Robin, and Keven

Robert

Brief Contents

Contents

Preface
Why The Third Time Just Might Be Charmed

There seems to be something almost magical about the number *three*. Plays usually have three acts; it takes three items to make a list; three strikes and one is out. Even wishes, it seems, are granted in three's! The number three seems to have special significance for textbooks, too: it is the third edition that often decides their future fate. At this point many texts seem to slide into a rigid "middle-age." They become locked into content that was useful at the start, but no longer reflects major shifts in the fields they represent. The result: they lose a portion of their usefulness and begin to fade from the scene. In contrast, a smaller number of texts opt for flexibility; they undergo major changes in form and content, and so retain their currency and value.

If the third edition of a text does indeed mark an important turning point or crossroads, we can honestly state that we have done everything in our power to assure the survival of *Exploring Social Psychology*. This edition is definitely *not* a stand-pat, surface revision. On the contrary, we have rewritten the book from the ground up in a concerted effort to keep abreast of the ever-changing and ever-advancing field we know as social psychology. In order to achieve this goal, we have made many changes, including the following:

CHANGES IN CONTENT: Reflecting Major Trends

In our view, one of the most significant trends in social psychology in recent years has been the growing interest in, and emphasis on, cognitive processes. To reflect this major development, we have added a new chapter on *Social Cognition*. This chapter describes important advances in our understanding of the manner in which we interpret, process, remember, and use social information. We believe that it constitutes a major addition to the text, and hope that you, our colleagues and readers, will agree.

A second, concurrent trend within the field has involved growing interest in *application*— in applying the knowledge and findings of social psychology to a wide range of human activities in diverse practical settings. The relationship of social psychology to the legal process, to health issues, and to business—these are a few of the topics that have captured the attention and research activities of many social psychologists in recent years. This trend is reflected in the expanded chapter on *Applying Social Psychology*. In addition, it is represented throughout the text, in discussions of the practical significance and applications of social psychological knowledge.

CHANGES IN CONTENT: Reflecting Recent Research

In addition to the major changes outlined above, we have attempted to keep abreast of, and describe, many new lines of research. As a result, literally dozens of topics not covered in the previous edition are now included. Among these are the following:

Detection of deception: does experience help?

Social consensus and moral judgment

Effects of competence feedback on intrinsic motivation

Attributional approaches to depression

Social cognition and illness

Effects of mood on social judgments

Effects of audience responses on persuasion

The accessibility model of attitude-behavior relationships

Minimal group paradigm and ingroup favoritism

Prejudice and AIDS

Illusion of in-group homogeneity

Self-esteem maintenance

Liking and the self-fulfilling prophecy

The "that's not all" technique

Ways to reduce social loafing

Status, type of task, and group influence

Computers and group decision-making

Self-disclosure and health

Social perceptions of smoking

Roommate choice and recovery from surgery

Effects of TV in the courtroom

Effects of destructive and constructive criticism in work settings

CHANGES IN SPECIAL INSERTS

Social psychology is ever-changing; yet, at the same time, it *has* established a firm store of lasting knowledge. To reflect this fact, we have included two types of special inserts throughout the text. The first, which represents the lasting knowledge-base of our field, is titled FOCUS ON RESEARCH/*Classic Contributions*. Such inserts describe studies that are generally viewed as "classics" in social psychology—investigations

that changed our way of thinking about various aspects of social behavior, or which started long and fruitful lines of research.

The second type, which is labeled FOCUS ON RESEARCH/*The Cutting Edge,* describes studies and findings that seem, to us, to fall at the very edge of expanding knowledge in social psychology—at the "cutting edge" of our field, so to speak. Together, these two groups of inserts should help students acquire a balanced grasp of the research endeavor in social psychology—how our field progresses, and how it has already added much to human knowledge.

In addition, we have retained a third type of insert labeled ON THE APPLIED SIDE. As the title suggests, these are designed to highlight the practical implications and applications of the findings of social psychology.

One final point: all special inserts are introduced at points where they make good sense. They are *not* merely appended, and do not interrupt the logical flow and development of each chapter. Moreover, each one is clearly cited in the text, so that students will know just when they should read them.

CONTINUITY: What Has Remained the Same

As our comments above suggest, there is indeed much that is new about the content of the third edition. Yet, we have retained several important features or perspectives. First, as in the previous edition, we have tried to be as eclectic, accurate, and up-to-date as possible in our presentation of social psychology. We perceive our role as that of describing our field as it currently exists—*not* expounding our own approaches or interests.

Second, the length is comparable to that of the second edition. The book is relatively short, and this should make it especially useful for colleagues who wish to assign additional outside readings, or who feel that a briefer text is most appropriate to their time-frame or students.

Third, the style of writing and presentation remains unchanged. As in the past, we have striven for *clarity,* softened, here and there, by a touch of humor. Research evidence suggests that an occasional smile can indeed be helpful in the learning process (as well as in many other contexts), so we have retained this as a feature of our general approach.

ACKNOWLEDGMENTS: Some Words of Thanks

In preparing this third edition of our text, we have been assisted by many hard-working, talented people.

First, our thanks to Choi K. Wan, who helped greatly with the references. Second, we wish to thank the persons listed below, who read and commented upon various portions of the manuscript. Their suggestions were thoughtful and informative, and we have tried to follow them as closely as possible: Ronald K. Barrett, Loyola Marymount College; Sue S. Schmitt, North Seattle Community College; Jack S. Croxton, State University of New York at Fredonia; and Herbert C. Fink, State University of New York at Brockport.

Third, our special thanks to Sandra Rigney for her excellent design and Margaret Kearney for her copy editing. It was a pleasure working with you.

Fourth, we want to thank Elaine Ober at Allyn and Bacon for her outstanding efforts as produc-tion administrator, to Linda Dickinson for devising the striking cover, and to Susan Brody for helping to facilitate and coordinate our efforts.

Fifth, warm thanks to our supportive editor, John-Paul Lenney, for his advice and support.

Finally, our thanks to Gene F. Smith of Western Illinois University for preparing the excellent set of ancillaries to accompany our text (a comprehensive instructor's manual and an extensive test bank).

To all of these outstanding people, a warm "Thank you."

A CONCLUDING COMMENT

It is our hope that you, our colleagues and readers, will find the third edition changes to be helpful ones. We have spared no effort in preparing this new edition. Yet we are certain that now, as in the past, there is still room for improvement. We would appreciate it greatly, therefore, if you would share your reactions with us. We *do* pay close attention to such feedback and always find it helpful. So please don't hesitate—send us your comments and suggestions whenever you can and as often as you wish.

ROBERT A. BARON
Department of Psychology
Rensselaer Polytechnic Institute
Troy, New York 12180

DONN BYRNE
Department of Psychology
State University of New York
   at Albany
Albany, New York 12222

JERRY SULS
Department of Psychology
State University of New York
   at Albany
Albany, New York 12222

About the Authors

ROBERT A. BARON is currently Professor of Psychology and Chair of the Department of Psychology at Rensselaer Polytechnic Institute. A 1968 Ph.D. (University of Iowa) he has also held academic positions at Purdue University, the University of Washington, Oxford University, Princeton University, the University of Texas, the University of Minnesota, and the University of South Carolina. Winner of numerous awards for teaching excellence, he is the author of seventeen books and more than eighty articles in professional journals. From 1979 to 1981, Professor Baron was the Program Director for Social and Developmental Psychology at the National Science Foundation. A fellow of the American Psychological Association, he has served as an Editor or member of the Editorial Board for several journals (e.g., *Journal of Personality and Social Psychology, Journal of Applied Social Psychology, Aggressive Behavior*). His current research interests are focused on applying the principles and findings of social psychology to key aspects of organizational behavior (e.g., organizational conflict, employment interviews). A long-time runner, his hobbies include woodworking and music.

DONN BYRNE is currently Professor of Psychology and Chairman of the Department of Psychology at the University at Albany, State University of New York. He received his Ph.D. degree in 1958 from Stanford University and has held academic positions at the California State University at San Francisco, the University of Texas, Stanford University, the University of Hawaii, and Purdue University. A past president of the Midwestern Psychological Association and a Fellow of three divisions of the American Psychological Association, he has written more than twenty books, twenty-five invited chapters, and one-hundred thirty articles. He was invited to deliver a G. Stanley Hall lecture at the 1981 meeting of the American Psychological Association in Los Angeles and a State of the Science address at the 1981 meeting of the Society for the Scientific Study of Sex. In 1987, he received an Excellence in Research Award from the University at Albany. He has served on the Editorial Boards of thirteen journals, including *Psychological Monographs, Journal of Experimental Social Psychology, Journal of Research in Personality, Journal of Applied Social Psychology, Journal of Personality,* and *Motivation and Emotion.* His current research interests include interpersonal attraction and the prediction of sexually coercive behavior. Leisure-time activities include literature, the theater, and landscaping.

 JERRY SULS is currently Professor of Psychology and Director of the Social-Personality Program at the State University of New York at Albany. A 1973 Ph.D. (Temple University), he has also held an academic position at Georgetown University. He is the author of more than fifty articles in professional journals, twelve invited chapters, and the editor of five books. He has served on the editorial boards of the *Journal of Personality and Social Psychology, Journal of Applied Social Psychology, Journal of Personality, Health Psychology,* and the *Journal of Behavioral Medicine,* and is a Fellow of the American Psychological Association. From 1983 to 1986, he served as a member of the Behavioral Medicine Study Section of the National Institutes of Health, and in 1987 was a National Science Foundation Fellow in Social Psychophysiology at the University of Iowa. His current research interests focus on how people use social comparisons to evaluate their traits and abilities and the study of social psychological factors influencing physical health. Playing jazz piano is his main leisure-time activity.

Chapter One
Understanding Social Behavior: An Introduction

The scene is a two-person dormitory room, somewhat cluttered with books, clothing, a stereo, and other accompaniments of campus life. It is evening, and Greg is sitting alone, studying, with music playing softly in the background. There is a knock on the door.

GREG: [*shouting*] Come on in. It's not locked.

The door opens, and a young woman tentatively sticks her head inside the room.

SARAH: Excuse me. I'm sorry to bother you, but I saw that your light was on. My name's Sarah.

GREG: That's alright. Come in. I'm Greg.

She enters, carrying a case. She places it gently on the floor.

SARAH: It's just that I have a problem. I can't pay this month's dorm rent unless I raise some extra money. I made a deal to sell candy on campus, and I get a small commission for each box I sell. Could you possibly help me out by buying a dozen boxes of chocolates? They're only $5 a box.

GREG: If you were looking for someone with $60 to spend, you came to the wrong room. I'd like to help, honest, but I'm not exactly rolling in dough either.

SARAH: [*her voice breaks as though she were about to cry*] Oh, that's O.K. I just hoped that I might be lucky tonight. Once I sell these last twelve boxes, I can make my payment. Then I can get back to hitting the books. [*she hesitates*] I don't suppose that you could take just one box, could you?

GREG: [*sighing*] Oh, I guess so. I buy candy from time to time anyway.

He pulls out a five dollar bill, and she opens the case to give him a box of candy.

SARAH: Thanks. This really means a lot to me. 'Bye.

She leaves. A few minutes later, Greg's roommate, Rob, returns. He throws his books on the bed.

ROB: [*yawning*] Nothing like a night at the library to make you sleepy. Wasn't that Sweet Sarah, the candy kid, who just left here?

GREG: Yeah. Do you know her?

ROB: Well, most of us have done business with her at one time or another. She didn't hook you with her old trick of trying to sell a dozen boxes and settling for one, did she?

GREG: [*embarrassed, looking at the box of candy on his desk*] Yeah, I guess, she did.

ROB: I told you that you should have signed up for social psych this semester when I did. We learned all about that.

GREG: Where were you when I needed you?

Each of us spends a large portion of our lives dealing with other people. Various individuals play a central role in our everyday activities. We express prejudice toward others, we get angry at someone, we make friends, we help select leaders or become leaders ourselves. Sometimes, like Sarah in the story, we try to influence the behavior of others, attempting to convince them to do as we wish. At other times, like Greg and Rob, we would like to protect ourselves against those who are trying to persuade us to do something. Furthermore, most of us agree that people usually provide our most important forms of pleasure, and our most upsetting types of pain (see Figure 1.1).

For these reasons, most of of us think about other persons and our relations with them on a fairly regular basis. In this respect, we are in excellent company. Over the centuries, poets, philosophers, playwrights, and novelists have filled countless volumes with their thoughts about human social affairs. Since many of these thinkers were brilliant and talented, their work is often insightful. Thus, there seem to be basic truths in such age-old clichés as "Misery loves company," "Revenge is sweet," and "It is better to give than to receive."

In many cases, though, such informal knowledge seems both confusing and inconsistent. Think of a statement such as "Birds of a feather flock together." This ancient bit of wisdom implies that friendship and perhaps romantic attraction are based on similarities. That seems reasonable enough, until you remember another equally reasonable truism: "Opposites attract." Which view is correct? Can both be true? Common sense offers no clear-cut answers (see Figure 1.2). Consider another example. How can we best deal with someone who is aggressive toward us? On the one hand, we are urged to "Turn the other cheek." On the other, we are told to return the aggression in kind: "An eye for

Figure 1.1 Other people are probably our biggest source of pleasure and also our biggest source of pain. Ziggy can certainly attest to the latter, at least on this day. (Source: Ziggy. Copyright 1987 Universal Press Syndicate. Reprinted with permission. All rights reserved.)

People: A source of pleasure and pain!

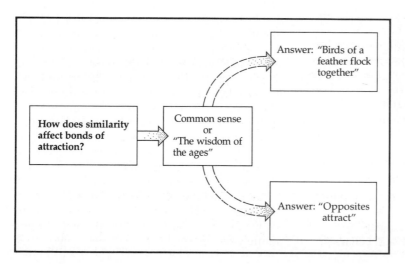

Figure 1.2 Common sense or "the wisdom of the ages" frequently offers contradictory answers to questions about human social relations.

Common sense: An imperfect guide to human social behavior

an eye, a tooth for a tooth." Again, the wisdom of the ages lets us down if we are looking for a guide to effective behavior or for an explanation of the behavior that we observe.

At this point, we should hasten to insert a word of caution: we certainly do not mean to imply that such information is totally useless. On the contrary, it can serve as a rich source of suggestions for further study, and often provides reasonable explanations for social phenomena after the fact—after they have occurred. By itself, though, informal knowledge cannot stand alone; it fails to provide an adequate basis for fully understanding the complex nature of our social relations with others.

Of course, it is one thing to reject these traditional sources of knowledge about social behavior, and quite another to offer alternative means of acquiring such information. How, aside from speculation, insight, and intuition, can this crucial task be accomplished? One answer—and a successful one, we believe—is provided by the field of **social psychology**. In simplest terms, this answer rests on the following assertion: accurate and useful information about human social relations can be readily acquired through the use of scientific methods. In short, social psychologists contend that we can indeed come to understand even complex aspects of social behavior, provided we are willing to study them in an essentially scientific manner.

Though this suggestion might seem both reasonable and obvious, you may be surprised to learn that a science-oriented approach to the study of social relations is quite new. Only at the end of the last century were social psychological methods initially developed, and the field has been an active one primarily in the decades since World War II. Despite its recent arrival on the scene, however, social psychology has provided some very valuable knowledge about behavior. Perhaps the breadth of its contribution is best suggested by the following list, which offers a small sample of the topics currently under investigation by social psychologists:

1. Why do we only remember some things about other people?

2. Is there a way to resist attempts by others to influence our attitudes and behavior?

3. What is the difference between an effective leader and an ineffective one?

4. How do intimate relationships form, develop, and sometimes dissolve?

5. What makes an individual satisfied with his or her job?

6. Does having friends provide protection against the effects of stress?

7. Why do some individuals behave consistently across a wide range of social situations, while others seem to change their behavior (and even their personalities) as they move from one setting to another?

8. Why are the members of large crowds often willing to engage in actions they would never perform as individuals?

9. Are some people aggressive by nature?

10. How are stereotypes formed? How can they be changed?

11. Does our present mood affect our evaluations of others?

12. Does exposure to pornography—especially violent pornography—contribute to the occurrence of sexual assaults and related crimes?

As even this short list suggests, social psychologists have turned their attention to a wide range of issues. Indeed, if modern social psychology has a "middle name," *diversity* is it! Before we turn to these intriguing topics, however, we believe it will be useful to pause briefly in order to provide you with certain background information. In the remainder of this chapter, then, we will focus on completing three preliminary tasks. First, we will present a formal *definition* of social psychology—our view of what it is and what it seeks to accomplish. Second, we will offer a capsule summary of social psychology's *history*—how it began, how it developed, and where it is today. Finally, we will examine some of the basic methods used by social psychologists in their *research*. Our goal here is simple: helping you to understand just how the facts and principles presented throughout this text were obtained. Before proceeding, you may find it useful to read the "On the Applied Side" insert (opposite). This indicates why the systematic study of social behavior is an important task and a timely one.

ON THE APPLIED SIDE

SOLVING SOCIETY'S PROBLEMS: TECHNOLOGY IS NOT ENOUGH

Think for a moment about what you consider to be the most serious social problems we face as human beings, problems that threaten our very survival. Each of us might provide slightly different lists, but surely there is fairly good agreement with respect to the threat of nuclear war, the consequences of a steadily increasing world population, the AIDS epidemic, the incidence of violent crime, air pollution, and many more (see Figure 1.3). Though we might be able to agree on identifying such problems and about the desirability of solving them, *how* do we do so?

One possibility is to develop improved technology that will enable us to eliminate these pressing problems. Thus, the creation of an impregnable nuclear defense, the

distribution of safe and effective contraceptives, an AIDS vaccine, the application of improved crime fighting devices, and the use of air cleansing equipment in factories and cars might be expected to yield a safer, healthier, cleaner, and more pleasant world. Yet, there are two major difficulties in pursuing purely technological solutions. One is that the appropriate technology needed to solve some problems simply may not be available in the foreseeable future. The other difficulty is that human beings are involved at each step of the process. People must decide to spend the time, money, and effort to create and to use the necessary products. Beyond that, it is obvious that wars are instigated or not, contraceptives are used or not, preventive health measures are

taken or not, crimes are committed or not, and antipollution equipment is installed or not *by people*.

We have already discussed the fact that reliance on common sense and the wisdom of the ages as guides to predicting or explaining behavior can be both confusing and inaccurate. Because social psychology uses scientific procedures to study behavior, it might be assumed that most social psychologists would propose that we are now able to provide immediate solutions to all of the problems listed above and to many others as well. Is that reasonable? Can we turn to the findings of social psychologists and learn how to stop war, bring about zero population growth, eliminate AIDS, stop all crime, and restore a clean and safe environment?

Figure 1.3 Problems such as nuclear war, the AIDS epidemic, overpopulation, violent crime, and air pollution probably cannot be solved by technological advances alone. Effective solutions will also require the ability to understand the behavior of individuals and devise means to change that behavior in desirable ways.

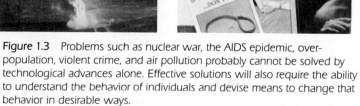

Needed for survival: A marriage of psychology and technology

The answer, of course, is "no," but the situation is far from hopeless. If we can visualize each major problem as consisting of a large number of small elements, there is reason to believe that even now many aspects of the larger issues are well understood by behavioral scientists. As you will learn in the following chapters, social psychology can tell us more today about such things as controlling violent behavior, encouraging preventive health practices, and inducing environmentally responsible behavior than was possible 20 years ago—or even 10 years ago. Future prospects are bright, and there is good reason to believe that the application of the scientific method to understanding, predicting, and altering behavior is one of the great hopes of humankind.

Many of us are willing to conclude that there are powerful reasons to seek increased scientific knowledge about human social behavior. Advances in such knowledge may be as essential as advances in technology (perhaps more so) in guaranteeing the survival of our species in the decades ahead. If anything, the combined advances of behavioral science and technology are one of our best bets.

SOCIAL PSYCHOLOGY: A Working Definition

Suggesting a formal definition of almost any field is a complex task. In the case of social psychology, these difficulties are intensified by two factors: the field's diversity and its rapid rate of change. Despite the broad sweep of topics they choose to study, though, most social psychologists seem to focus the bulk of their attention on the following central task: understanding the behavior of individuals in social contexts. In short, they are primarily concerned with comprehending how and why individuals behave, think, and feel as they do in situations involving the presence (actual or symbolic) of others. Taking this central focus into account, our working definition of social psychology is as follows: *Social psychology is the scientific field that seeks to understand the nature and causes of individual behavior in social situations.* (Note that by the term "behavior" we mean feelings and thoughts as well as overt actions.) Since this definition, like all others, is a bit abstract, please bear with us for a few moments while we clarify several of its major features.

Social Psychology Is Scientific in Orientation

In the minds of many persons, the term "science" refers primarily (or more exclusively) to specific fields such as chemistry, physics, and biology. Such individuals, of course, will find somewhat puzzling our suggestion that social psychology, too, is scientific. How, they wonder, can a field that seeks to investigate the nature of love, the causes of interpersonal violence, and everything in between be scientific in the same sense as nuclear physics or neuroscience? The answer is surprisingly simple. In reality, the term "science" does *not* refer to a select group of highly advanced fields. Rather, "science" refers to a general set of methods—techniques that can be used to study a wide range of topics. In deciding whether a given field is scientific, therefore, the crucial question is this: does it make use of such procedures? To the extent that it does, it can be viewed as scientific in orientation; to the extent it does not, it can be perceived as falling outside the realm of science. When this basic criterion is applied to social psychology, there can be little doubt that it fits into the first of these two categories. In their efforts to understand social behavior, social psychologists rely heavily on the same methods of other scientists. Thus, while the topics they study are certainly different from those in older and more established fields, their overall approach—and so social psychology itself—is clearly a scientific one (see Figure 1.4).

Social Psychology Focuses on the Behavior of Individuals

Societies may differ in terms of their overall level of bigotry, but it is individual persons who hold stereotypes about specific groups, experience negative feelings toward them, and seek to exclude them from their neighborhoods, jobs, and schools. Similarly, it is specific persons who give aid to others, who commit acts of violence, and who fall in or out of love. In short, social

"I'm a social scientist, Michael. That means I can't explain electricity or anything like that, but if you ever want to know about people I'm your man."

Figure 1.4 Social psychologists study topics that are quite different from those of the older, established sciences such as chemistry or physics. However, social psychology falls within the realm of the sciences because it uses the same general set of methods or techniques. (Source: Drawing by Handelsman; © 1986 The New Yorker Magazine, Inc.)

Social psychology: Scientific in orientation

behavior, ultimately, is performed by individual persons. With this basic fact firmly in mind, social psychologists have chosen to focus the bulk of their attention upon the actions and thoughts of individuals in social situations (ones involving the real or symbolic presence of others). They realize, of course, that such behavior always occurs against a backdrop of sociocultural factors (e.g., group membership, culturally shared standards and values). But their major interest is that of understanding the factors that shape and direct the actions of individual human beings in a wide range of social settings.

Social Psychology Seeks to Comprehend the Causes of Social Behavior

In a key sense, this is the most central aspect of our definition: it specifies the very essence of our field. What it means is this: social psychologists are primarily concerned with understanding the wide range of conditions that shape the social behavior of individuals—their actions, feelings, and thoughts with respect to other persons. Interest in this issue, in turn, stems from a basic belief: knowledge about these conditions will permit us both to predict social behavior and, perhaps, to change it in desirable ways. Thus, it may have important practical as well as scientific outcomes.

As you can readily guess, the task of identifying all of the factors that affect our behavior with respect to others is one of huge proportions. Social behavior is shaped by a seemingly endless list of variables, so in this sense social psychologists truly have their work cut out for them! While the number of specific factors influencing social reactions is large, however, it appears that most fall into five major categories. These involve: (1) the behavior and characteristics of other persons, (2) social cognition, (3) ecological variables (direct and indirect influences of the physical environment), (4) the sociocultural context in which social behavior occurs, and (5) aspects of our biological nature relevant to social behavior (Georgoudi and Rosnow, 1985). Perhaps a few words on each of these categories will clarify their basic nature. (Also, see Figure 1.5.)

That social behavior is strongly affected by the actions and characteristics of others is obvious. For example, imagine how you would respond if, while eating in a crowded restaurant, one of the waiters began to shout "Fire! Fire!" Almost instantaneously your overt actions, your emotional state, and your thoughts would be strongly altered. Similarly, imagine that you are at a party and a stranger of the opposite sex walks up to you and says, "I've been looking at you all evening. I've never seen a more attractive person than you." Again, you could expect to experience a powerful series of reactions.

In a similar manner, the observable characteristics of others, too, strongly affect our feelings, thoughts, and subsequent behavior (e.g., Warner and Sugarman, 1986). We often react differently to highly attractive persons than to unattractive ones; we treat well-dressed and well-groomed people differently from those who are not so well turned out; and we even respond to others' style of speech, apparent age, and ethnic background.

The external aspects of others represent only part of the total picture. We also may be strongly affected by *social cognition*—our own thoughts, beliefs, attitudes, and memories concerning those around us. Consider the situation in which you must decide between two individuals who have applied for a position in your organization. You might well consider the qualifications, training, experience, and references of both candidates. The way in which you remember, evaluate, combine, and give weight to each element of information would affect your final decision. As another example, imagine that you are having a friendly conversation with a neighbor, and she says something nasty about the way you look. How will you react? Cognitions play a major role, because you have to decide whether this was an

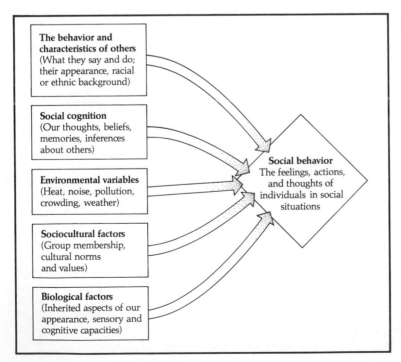

Figure 1.5 Social behavior stems from many different causes. Among the most important of these are (1) the behavior and characteristics of others, (2) social cognition, (3) ecological (environmental) variables, (4) sociocultural factors, and (5) biological factors.

Social behavior: A summary of its major causes

The behavior and characteristics of others
(What they say and do; their appearance, racial or ethnic background)

Social cognition
(Our thoughts, beliefs, memories, inferences about others)

Environmental variables
(Heat, noise, pollution, crowding, weather)

Sociocultural factors
(Group membership, cultural norms and values)

Biological factors
(Inherited aspects of our appearance, sensory and cognitive capacities)

Social behavior
The feelings, actions, and thoughts of individuals in social situations

intentional insult or a clumsy attempt to be helpful. If you believe an insult was involved, you are likely to become angry and counterattack in some way. If you believe the person was trying to be helpful, you are likely to overlook the insult. Because such perceptions and interpretations of behavior are important predictors of what we do, the investigation of cognitive influences is a major part of modern social psychology.

The impact of the physical environment on social behavior, too, is readily illustrated. For some personal insight into such effects, simply recall how you have felt and behaved on hot, humid days and on cool, dry ones. If you are like most persons, you probably remember being more irritable, and perhaps harder to get along with, when uncomfortably hot than when comfortably cool. In a similar manner, many other environmental variables, such as noise, pollution, excessive crowding, and even many aspects of weather all seem to affect our moods, cognitive processes, and overt actions toward others (e.g., Rotton and Frey, 1985; Anderson, 1987).

Finally, we should note that social behavior definitely does *not* unfold in either a cultural or a biological vacuum. With respect to the former, such factors as cultural norms (rules about how people should behave in specific situations), our membership in various groups, and shifting societal standards or values can influence many aspects of our behavior—everything from our political attitudes on the one hand through our choice of marriage partner on the other. Similarly, some biological factors (e.g., inherited aspects of our physical appearance, built-in limits to our capacity to process social information) affect key aspects of our behavior in many social settings. It is probably fair to conclude that in the past, sociocultural and biological factors have received less attention from social psychologists than the other types of potential causes. However, they, too, often play a role in shaping social behavior and fall within the scope of both our field and this text.

Social Psychology: Summing Up

To conclude: social psychology focuses mainly on the task of understanding the causes of social behavior—identifying factors that shape our feelings, behavior, and thought in social situations. Further, it seeks to accomplish this goal through the use of essentially scientific methods. The remainder of this text is devoted to the task of summarizing the findings uncovered by social psychologists in their studies of social interaction. This information is intriguing, so we're sure you'll find it to be of interest. But please be warned: it is also full of surprises, and what you learn will challenge many of your current views about people and relations between them. Thus, it is probably safe to predict that after exposure to it, you'll never think about social relations in quite the same way as before. If you value such change, and look forward to new insights, read on; if not, now is the time to turn back!

SOCIAL PSYCHOLOGY: A Capsule Memoir

When, precisely, did social psychology begin? This is a difficult question to answer, for speculation about social behavior has continued since the days of antiquity (Allport, 1935). Thus, any attempt to present a complete survey of its historical roots would quickly bog us down in endless lists of names and dates. Since we definitely wish to avoid that pitfall, this discussion will be limited in scope. Specifically, we will focus on the emergence of social psychology as an independent field, its growth during the middle decades of this century, and its current status and trends.

The Early Years: Social Psychology Emerges

Few fields of science mark their beginnings with formal ceremonies and ribbon cuttings. Instead, most develop slowly and gradually as scholars begin to focus on a particular set of problems or develop new methods of investigation. This was precisely the pattern for social psychology. Though there was no specific date on which social psychology was born, the years between 1908 and 1924 seem to qualify as the period when it first emerged as an independent entity. These two dates represent years in which important texts were published with the term "social psychology" in their titles. Comparison of the two books is informative. The first, by William McDougall in 1908, was based on the view that social behavior stems mainly from a small set of innate tendencies or instincts. This general viewpoint has been generally rejected by almost all later social psychologists, so McDougall's ideas clearly did not provide the cornerstone of the field (Jones, 1985).

The second book, published in 1924 by Floyd Allport, provides a sharp contrast. Allport's orientation was much more like that of our current field than was McDougall's. In his text, Allport argued that social behavior stems from and is influenced by many different factors such as the presence of other people and the behavior of other people. In addition, Allport's book discussed actual research that had been done dealing with such topics as the ability to recognize the emotions of other people based on their facial expressions, conformity in social situations, and the impact of an audience on how a task was performed. These topics are still of interest to social psychologists and will be discussed in later chapters of this book. So, you can see that by the middle of the "Roaring Twenties" social psychology was clearly established and beginning to focus on some of the issues and topics that remain matters of active interest today.

Following the appearance of Allport's text, there was a period of rapid growth in social psychology. New and very interesting problems were investigated, and increasingly sophisticated methods were developed to conduct such research. Especially important was the work of two major pioneers in our field—Muzafer Sherif and Kurt Lewin. Sherif (1935) began the study of *social norms*—rules telling individuals how they ought to behave. We will consider these in more detail in Chapter Seven. Lewin and his colleagues (Lewin, Lippitt, and White, 1939) began the systematic study of *leadership* and the related topic of *group processes* (see Chapter Nine). They also urged the adoption of an approach in which careful scientific methods are applied to the study of social problems. That concern has persisted as a major theme of social psychology throughout its history (see Chapter Ten). By the end of the 1930s, then, social psychology was

clearly an active and growing field with some traditions that have persisted into the 1980s. As a help in placing these developments in the context of what else was happening in the world at the same time, see Figure 1.6.

The Growth Years: The 1940s, 1950s, and 1960s

Despite the disruptions caused by World War II, social psychologists actively engaged in research in the military and elsewhere during the first half of the 1940s. When the war ended, this field began a period of rapid growth and expansion. The scope of social psychology expanded in a variety of directions. One important theme, especially in the 1950s, was the influence of groups and group membership on individual behavior (Hendrick, 1987; Mullen and Goethals, 1987). Perhaps the major development of the period, however, was the development of the theory of **cognitive dissonance** (Festinger, 1957). This theory proposed that human beings dislike inconsistency and are motivated to act in such a way as to reduce or minimize it. Specifically, it argues that we find inconsistency between our attitudes—or inconsistency between our attitudes and our behavior—disturbing, and seek to eliminate it. While these ideas may not strike you as very surprising, they actually lead to many unexpected predictions. For example, they suggest that offering individuals small rewards for stating views they don't really hold may often be more effective in getting them to change their opinions than offering them large rewards for engaging in such behavior—a principle sometimes known as the "less leads to more" effect. Festinger's theory captured the interest of many social psychologists, and it remained a topic of research for several decades. (We will return to this theory in Chapter Four.)

In an important sense, the 1960s can be viewed as the time when social psychology "came into its own." During this turbulent decade the number of social psychologists rose dramatically—from less than 1,000 in 1950 to nearly 5,000 by 1970. Furthermore, the field expanded its scope to include virtually every imaginable aspect of social interaction. So many lines of research either began or developed during

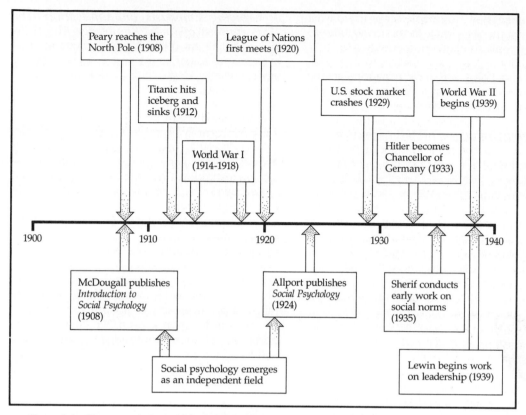

Figure 1.6 *The years during which social psychology emerged as a field of scientific inquiry and took its present form were eventful ones in world affairs.*

An historical perspective on the years when social psychology took shape

these years that we could not possibly list all of them here. Among the topics and questions receiving major attention, though, were these: *social perception* (how do we form first impressions of others? how do we determine the causes behind others' behavior?); *aggression* (what are the roots of this dangerous type of behavior? how can it be controlled?); *attraction and love* (why do individuals like or dislike others? what is the nature of romantic love?); *group decision-making* (how do groups go about making decisions? do such decisions differ from ones made by individuals?); and *prosocial behavior* (why do people sometimes fail to come to the aid of others during emergencies?) As you can see from this brief list, social psychology moved into many new areas during the 1960s.

The 1970s, 1980s and Beyond: Where We Are and Where We're Going

The period of rapid growth and change did not slacken in the most recent years of social psychological activity. If anything, there was an acceleration. Many lines of investigation begun in the 1960s were continued and expanded. In addition, several new topics rose to prominence, or were investigated from a more sophisticated perspective. Among these were *attribution* (how do we infer the causes of behavior behind others'—and our own—behavior?); *sex roles and sex discrimination* (how are sex roles and sexual stereotypes acquired? what forces work against full equality for females in many societies?); *so-*

cial influence (how do people get us to do what they want?); the *self* (what factors contribute to the ways people think about themselves?).

In addition, two larger-scale trends took shape in the 1970s and have expanded in the 1980s. Since these are of great importance, we will consider them separately here.

Growing Influence of the Cognitive Perspective. As we noted earlier, social psychologists have long been aware of the fact that cognitive factors—attitudes, beliefs, values, and inferences—play a key role in social behavior. Starting in the late 1970s, however, interest in such topics has taken an exciting new form. At present, many of our colleagues believe that our understanding of a wide range of social phenomena can be greatly enhanced through adoption of a strategy in which we first seek to comprehend the basic cognitive processes that underlie them (Markus and Zajonc, 1985). Consistent with this view, they have investigated a wide range of social processes, including stereotypes (Anderson and Klatsky, 1987), self-evaluation (Markus and Wurf, 1987), group decision-making (Kaplan and Miller, 1987), and persuasion (Petty and Cacioppo, 1986) from a **cognitive perspective**. What this involves, in essence, are efforts to apply basic knowledge about such issues as these to complex social processes: (1) how memory operates, (2) how reasoning occurs, and (3) how information is integrated by the human mind, to complex social processes. Thus, to mention just one example, the formation and persistence of beliefs about oneself are understood in the context of certain aspects of memory (which lead us to recall only certain types of information), and several aspects of social inference or reasoning (ones that lead us on some occasions to jump to false conclusions about ourselves).

The results of research conducted within this general perspective have been impressive, to say the least. Major insights into key aspects of social behavior have been gained, and new phenomena previously overlooked have been brought sharply into focus (Fiske and Taylor, 1984; Wyer and Srull, 1986). Thus, it is far from surprising that the volume of work concerned with cognitive factors has risen sharply in recent years.

Growing Emphasis on Application: The "Exportation" of Social Knowledge. The 1970s and especially the 1980s have also been marked by a second major trend where social psychology is concerned: growing interest in the application of social knowledge (Oskamp and Spacapan, 1987). An increasing number of social psychologists have turned their attention to questions concerning *personal health* (what factors help individuals resist the harmful effects of stress?), the *legal process* (e.g., how valid is eyewitness testimony?), and the functioning of large *organizations* (e.g., how can performance in various jobs best be evaluated or appraised?). In addition, many other social psychologists have actually moved from positions within departments of psychology to jobs in business, law, and medicine, or to posts in government agencies or private corporations. In such locations, they apply their unique skills and knowledge to a wide range of practical issues, and also serve a major educational function as well. We view this "exportation" of social knowledge to other fields, and to society as a whole, as a healthy development; further, we look forward to many practical benefits from it in the years ahead.

So Where Do We Go from Here? A Brief Glance at the Future. Earlier in this chapter, we noted that *diversity* is social psychology's "middle name." For this reason, guesses about its future development are risky—perhaps as risky as trying to predict the up-and-down motions of the stock market! Even with this warning firmly in mind, though, we are still willing to make several predictions about where social psychology may, perhaps, go from here.

First, we believe that the cognitive perspective described above will continue to grow and prosper. Indeed, we expect it to spread to all areas of the field, and to provide it with a degree of conceptual unity it has not enjoyed before. Second, we believe that the shift toward application, too, will continue. This will be the case because of economic necessity (sources of financial support for "pure" social research have decreased sharply in recent years), and also because increasing maturity in any field of science tends to foster growing interest in application of the knowledge it possesses. Third, and probably riskiest of all, we predict that social psychologists will gradually direct increasing attention to the study of social behavior in natural settings, and to the impact of sociocultural factors (e.g., cultural norms, socioeconomic status [Sears, 1986]). The major basis for this belief is the recent emergence of what has been termed the **contextualist view**—a perspective suggesting that no form of social behavior can be understood apart from the context in which it occurs (Georgoudi and Rosnow, 1985). Since sociocultural factors form a backdrop for much of social behavior, it seems only reasonable to expect that greater attention will be focused on such variables in the years ahead.

These, then, are our predictions. Only time will tell whether and to what extent they will be confirmed. Regardless of their fate, however, there is one additional prediction we are willing to make with considerably greater conviction: no matter how social psychology changes in the years ahead, it will remain an active, vital field—one with considerable potential for contributing in essential ways to overall human welfare.

HOW DOES SOCIAL PSYCHOLOGY ANSWER QUESTIONS? Conducting Research and Building Theories

Now that you have a general idea of the kinds of problems on which social psychologists focus, we need to describe just what it means to conduct research on social behavior. Answering this question will require three steps. First we will describe the major *methods* in social psychological research: the **experimental** and **correlational** approaches. Next we will examine the role of *theory* in such research. Finally, we will consider some of the complex *ethical issues* that often arise in the context of systematic research on human social behavior.

The Experimental Method: Manipulating Variables to Determine Effects

Because it is the research method preferred by most social psychologists, we will begin with **experimentation**. If you have the idea that experimentation is mysterious and complex, you can relax; in its basic form, it is surprisingly simple. To help you understand its use in social research, we will first describe its basic nature—how it actually proceeds. Then we will describe two conditions that are essential for its successful use.

Experimentation: Its Basic Nature. There is generally a clear-cut goal in a social psychological experiment: determining whether a given factor (variable) influences some specific form of social behavior. To find out about such influence, the experimenter (1) varies the presence or the strength of this factor and (2) determines whether these variations have any impact on the aspect of social behavior under investigation. The central idea underlying this approach is: if the factor does have any effect, individuals exposed to different levels or amounts should behave differently. That is, exposure to a small amount of the factor should lead to one level of behavior, exposure to a larger amount should result in another level, and so on.

The factor that is systematically varied by the researcher is known as the *independent variable,* while the behavior (or aspect of behavior) in question is known as the *dependent variable.* In a simple experiment, then, subjects in different groups are exposed to contrasting levels of the independent variable (e.g., low, moderate, high). The behavior of these individuals is then carefully examined and compared to determine whether it does in fact vary with different levels or amounts of the independent variable. If it does—and if two other conditions we shall mention below are met—it can be tentatively concluded that the independent variable does indeed affect the form of behavior being studied.

Since our discussion has been a little abstract, a concrete example should make the process a bit easier to understand. Let's consider an experiment designed to test the *hypothesis* (an as yet unverified suggestion) that individuals who feel anxious respond more positively to an opposite-sex stranger than do individuals who feel calm and relaxed. In Chapter Six, we'll discuss *why* such a prediction might be made, but for now just assume that there is a good reason to hypothesize that effect. We might decide to make some subjects (that is, the people participating in the experiment) feel mildly anxious by asking them to sing the "Star Spangled Banner" in front of a video camera. A much lower level of anxiety could be created by asking other subjects simply to write the words of that song on a piece of paper. Subjects in both conditions would be asked to respond in some way to an opposite-sex stranger (an accomplice of the experimenter; also sometimes called a confederate) just after the task was completed. (This is a common arrangement in many social psychological experiments; social psychologists often need the aid of other persons in carrying out their research.) We could ask how much they liked this person, how attractive he or she is, and how desirable it would be to date this individual. In this experiment, anxiety is the *independent variable* and attraction is the *dependent variable*. A crucial step in the procedure would be to measure the anxiety level of our subjects to determine whether we actually did create two levels of this emotional state; such verification is known as a **manipulation check**. If we found that one group was more anxious than the other and that those in the anxious condition were more attracted to the stranger than those in the nonanxious condition (see Figure 1.7), we could say that the hypothe-

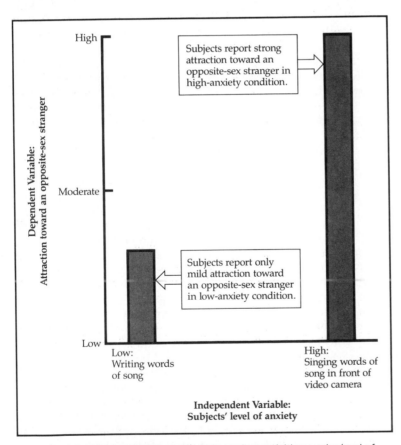

Figure 1.7   In this experiment, the *independent variable* was the level of anxiety induced in each subject. The *dependent variable* was the subject's subsequent attraction toward an opposite-sex confederate. Attraction was greater when the anxiety level was high than when it was low.

An example of experimental research

sis was confirmed. On the basis of such results, one would tentatively conclude that as anxiety increases, attraction toward an opposite-sex stranger increases. Actually, several such experiments have been performed (for example, Murnen, Byrne, and Przybyla, 1985), and generally do support the hypothesis (related research is discussed in Chapter Six).

At this point we should note that the example just presented involves an extremely simple case—the effect of one independent variable on one dependent variable. Often, an experimenter wishes to examine the effect of several independent variables at once. For example, in the study just described, it would have been possible to examine the effects of such factors as the attractiveness of the opposite-sex stranger (unattractive, moderately attractive, and extremely attractive), as well as the degree of anxiety experienced by the subject. Other factors, termed **dispositional variables**, are also often included in experimental designs. They function like independent variables but are not actually manipulated by the experimenter; examples are sex of the subject, race of subject, and any personality variables that might be relevant. When several such variables are included in a single experiment, an increased amount of information about the determinants of the behavior can be obtained. Of even greater importance, potential **interactions** between or among variables can be examined. That is, we can find out whether the effect of one independent variable is affected in some way by other independent variables. For example, we might find that anxiety leads to increased attraction toward very attractive strangers, but not toward unattractive ones. Or, we might find that males are more responsive to the anxiety-attraction effect than females. Because social behavior is usually affected by many factors operating at the same time, knowledge of such interactions is necessary in order to be able to make accurate predictions. In the chapters that follow, you will notice many instances in which interactions are described.

Successful Experimentation: Two Basic Requirements. Earlier we mentioned that two conditions must be met before we can conclude that an independent variable has an effect on a de-

pendent variable. What are these conditions? They are related, but we will describe them separately.

The first involves what is generally termed **random assignment of subjects to groups.** According to this principle, each person taking part in a study must have an equal chance of being exposed to each level of the independent variable. The reason for this is simple: if subjects are *not* randomly assigned to each group, it may prove impossible to determine whether differences in their later behavior stem from differences they brought with them to the study, or from the impact of the independent variable. Suppose, in the study we described, the subjects were given a choice of being in the high- or low-anxiety condition. Under those circumstances, any differences in attraction toward the opposite-sex stranger might be a function of existing anxiety differences or differences in the kind of people who choose high- versus low-anxiety experiences or some combination of the two. So, if subjects are not randomly assigned to the various conditions of the experiment, any results obtained can be ambiguous in their meaning.

The second essential condition is that, insofar as possible, all factors that might affect the behavior in question (in addition to the independent variable) must be held constant. Otherwise, the effects of the independent variable and some other variable are **confounded,** and we cannot determine which one was responsible for the differences in behavior. Returning to our example, what if the low-anxiety portion of the experiment took place during midterms, while the high-anxiety portion took place just before Thanksgiving vacation? Any mood differences among students during the two different time periods would be *confounded,* with differences in anxiety created by the experimenter. There would be no way of knowing whether differences in responding to the stranger were brought about by the independent variable, by the general mood differences at the two time periods, or some combination of the two. In Figure 1.8, you can see how confounding makes it impossible to separate or disentangle the effects of different variables.

In the case we have just described, confounding between variables is relatively easy to spot.

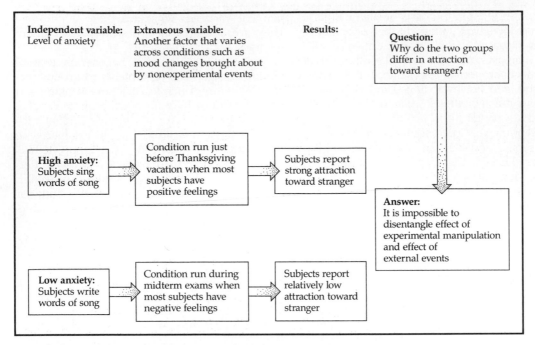

Figure 1.8 *Factors other than the independent variable must be held constant across experimental conditions, or it will be impossible to interpret one's results. In the example here, if the experimental manipulation (anxiety level) and some emotion-arousing external events (Thanksgiving vacation versus exams) both vary across conditions, it is impossible to determine which one affected subjects' attraction toward a stranger.*

Confounding of variables: A trap to be avoided

Often, though, it can enter in more subtle and hidden ways. For this reason, researchers wishing to conduct successful experiments must always be on guard against it. Only when such confounding is prevented can the results of an experiment be interpreted with confidence.

The experiment we just described took place in a laboratory setting. Some people have suggested that such studies are too artificial to have any meaning in the real world. One answer is to conduct experiments outside of the laboratory, in a real-life setting. Such studies are termed **field experiments**. Actually, there are advantages and disadvantages to each type of experiment. Before you go any further, you might find it helpful to read the "Focus on Research" insert (opposite).

The Correlational Method: Knowledge Through Systematic Observation

Earlier, we noted that experimentation is usually the preferred method of research in social psychology. (We will comment on why this is so shortly.) Sometimes, though, it simply cannot be used. This can be true for either of two general reasons. First, systematic variation of some factor of interest may simply lie beyond a researcher's control. For example, imagine that a would-be experimenter has reason to believe that height plays a major role in political elections: taller candidates have an important edge and usually win. Clearly, he or she could not vary the stature of persons running for public

LABORATORY EXPERIMENTS VERSUS FIELD EXPERIMENTS: WHICH TYPE IS BETTER? (MUST WE CHOOSE?)

For most of us, the word "experiment" suggests procedures conducted in a laboratory. Generally, that is a reasonable assumption because most scientific experiments take place in that setting. This is so because such research has several advantages. It is possible to maintain a great deal of control over what occurs and also to exert control over extraneous variables in order to avoid the problem of confounding (described earlier). When human subjects are the object of research, as in social psychology, laboratory experimentation is a very efficient way to obtain data. Research participants report directly to the lab for their appointments—an arrangement which saves much time for experimenters. Further-more, it is possible to use only volunteers who have given their prior consent to participate and who can receive a full explanation of the study afterward, to answer any questions they may have and resolve any worries that may have been created by the experiment.

Despite these very important advantages, laboratory research with humans also raises some

	Laboratory experiments	Field experiments
Advantages +	Independent variables can be well controlled	Demand characteristics are less likely to operate
	Subjects can be scheduled for maximum efficiency	Realism is enhanced because subject can be studied in natural settings
	There is less likelihood for confounding of variables	Usually a wider range of subjects can be studied
	Informed consent and debriefing can protect rights of subjects	
Disadvantages −	Conditions are often artificial and quite different from the outside world	It is much more difficult to control the independent variables
	Demand characteristics are a potential problem	There are many more extraneous variables, so confounding is more difficult to avoid
	If subjects are restricted to a specific group (such as college students), results may not generalize to others in the population	Because subjects may not have the opportunity to decide beforehand about being research participants or be provided afterward with a full explanation of the study's true goals and the need for temporary deception, it is difficult to protect the rights of subjects

Figure 1.9 Both field and laboratory experiments offer important advantages to the investigator. It is also true that each type of research has drawbacks.

Laboratory and field experiments: Advantages and disadvantages

problems. The conditions are often artificial and not like what is encountered in our everyday lives. Thinking back to the experiment we described earlier, were you ever asked to sing the U.S. national anthem in front of a video camera or to write the words of that song and then to indicate on paper how much you like a stranger? None of the authors has been faced with just that experience in real life. Another problem in such a special setting is that subjects *know* they are subjects. They frequently try to guess what the experiment is about and to behave in ways that will help or hurt the experimenter. Any cues that reveal the hypothesis being tested are known as **demand characteristics,** and it is sometimes difficult to avoid them in laboratory experiments. Finally, because it is almost impossible to get a random sample of the population to report to a laboratory to take part in a research project, most social psychological experiments involve a restricted subject population such as introductory psychology students. It is not always accurate to generalize from the behavior of this specific group of individuals to other, very different groups of people. Figure 1.9 illustrates and

summarizes some of these positive and negative aspects of laboratory experimentation.

In response to the problems created by such research, many social psychologists have gone into everyday settings to conduct experiments. In recent years, field experiments have been conducted in busy shopping malls, train stations (Milgram et al., 1986), jogging tracks (Strube, Miles, and French, 1981), restrooms (Middlemist, Knowles, and Matter, 1976), taverns (Sprecher et al., 1984), residential neighborhoods (Weyant and Smith, 1987), and even prisons (Cox, Paulus, and McCain, 1984). The advantages of these field experiments are clear. A diverse sample of subjects participate, and their behavior is presumably representative of how they actually respond in real life. Because the participants do not know that they are part of an experiment, the possibility of demand characteristics is greatly reduced. It might seem that this type of research solves all of our problems, but actually new problems are created.

Out in shopping malls, taverns, and so forth, it becomes very difficult to control independent variables. By its very nature, this kind of research is often viewed as

more "sloppy" than laboratory experimentation. Similarly, it is much more difficult to avoid confounding variables in such settings. Still another problem concerns the ethics of field research. Is it right to expose subjects to selected experimental conditions (for example, a scene indicating there is a medical emergency) without informing them they are subjects in an experiment and without obtaining their prior consent to participate? There is no simple answer to such questions, and we discuss this and related issues on page 22.

Altogether, there is a definite trade-off involved in choosing between laboratory and field experimentation. Because each has its advantages and drawbacks, there is no answer as to which is better. Both techniques are useful, and both can add substantially to our knowledge of human social behavior. In fact, the ideal situation occurs when the same variables have been investigated in *both* laboratory and field settings. When the results are the same in these very different kinds of experiments, we feel much more confident in our conclusions about how a particular variable affects a particular behavior.

office or arrange to have candidates of different height compete against each other in the same elections.

Second, ethical constraints may prevent a researcher from conducting what might otherwise be a feasible experiment. It may be possible to vary some factor of interest, but doing so would violate basic ethical standards accepted by all social psychologists. Suppose there is reason to believe that violent, aggressive behavior in adolescence was brought about by child abuse. You obviously would not randomly assign one group of children to a condition in which they

were abused and other children were not, and then examine the subsequent aggressive activity of both groups.

Though some factors remain beyond an experimenter's control and ethical constraints prevent experimental studies of some topics, researchers can adopt an alternative technique known as the **correlational method.** For example, it *is* possible to measure the relative heights of various candidates and to get a tally of their votes. This would determine whether there is an *association* between height and votes. Similarly, you *could* look for an association between self-reports of having been abused as a child and current indications of committing violent acts.

When changes in one variable are consistently found to be associated with changes in another, this *correlation* suggests there is some sort of link between them. Unlike experimentation, there is *no attempt to vary one factor in a systematic fashion.* Instead, naturally occurring variations are simply observed and measured to determine whether changes in one are consistently associated with changes in the other.

Correlation Doesn't Necessarily Indicate Causation. Unlike an experimental finding, the establishment of a correlation between two variables tells us nothing conclusive about a direct causal (cause-effect) relationship between them. For an example of how one might reach an incorrect conclusion in this respect, examine the cartoon in Figure 1.10.

To take another example, imagine a hardworking but not very bright investigator who decided to study the relationship between the number of refrigerators sold in the United States and the number of bank robberies committed. Let's say that he gathered careful data spanning several decades from 1940 to 1986: number of refrigerators sold each year and the number of bank robberies committed each year. He would find over this period that there was a substantial relationship between these two variables. As refrigerator sales increased, bank robberies increased.

Should the investigator conclude that the presence of refrigerators in homes and in restaurants *causes* bank robberies? Or should he conclude that bank robberies bring about the purchase of refrigerators? Actually, the second suggestion is slightly more sensible than the first (perhaps people steal money in order to buy appliances), but neither suggestion is likely to be correct as to cause and effect. The best guess is that both refrigerator sales and bank robberies have increased over the years because the population of the country also increased during this period. As a result, there were more refrigerators purchased and more bank branches opened—thereby increasing the opportunity for

"Yee yee hee hee haw haw yip yip!"

Figure 1.10 As this cartoon suggests, it is easy to assume that because two events occur in association (such as throwing the rock and the eruption of the volcano) that one was the cause of the other. This assumption that correlation means causation is often incorrect. (Source: Drawing by Booth; © 1981 The New Yorker Magazine, Inc.)

Correlation does not necessarily indicate causation.

more robberies (see Figure 1.11). The major point is that a correlation between two variables—the tendency for them to rise or fall together—may reflect the fact that both are caused by a third, perhaps less visible, factor. We hope you can now appreciate why a correlation cannot be interpreted as a definite indication that two factors are causally linked. Such conclusions are justified only in the presence of additional confirming evidence.

Theory: Essential Guide to Research

"How do social psychologists come up with the ideas for their studies?" This is a question we often hear from students in our classes. Our reply touches on several points. First, we note that ideas for research projects are often suggested by the observation of the social world around us. Researchers often notice some aspect of social behavior that is puzzling or surprising, and plan investigations to shed new light upon it. Second, we call attention to the fact that successful experiments tend to raise more questions than they answer. Thus, the problem facing social psychologists is usually not that of coming up with interesting ideas for further study; rather, it is choosing among the many enticing possibilities. Third, and most central of all, we point to the essential role of **theory**. In our view, this is the most important source of research in social

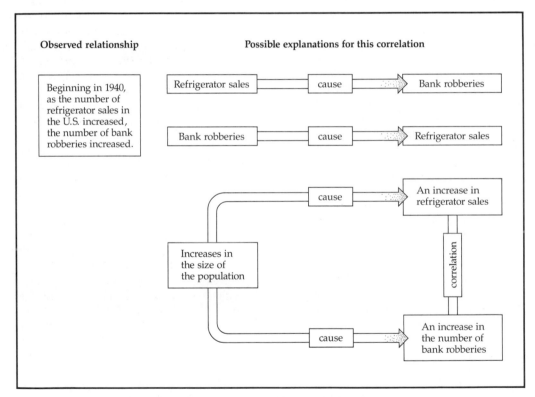

Figure 1.11 The fact that two variables increase or decrease in the same manner does not always indicate that either functions as a cause of the other. Sometimes a third factor is causing both of the other factors to vary, as in the example here.

Correlations can occur for three major reasons.

psychology. For this reason alone, it is worthy of our careful attention here.

Put very simply, theory represents efforts, by scientists in any field, to answer the question "why?" In short, it involves attempts to understand precisely *why* certain events or processes occur as they do. In this sense, theory goes beyond mere observation or description of various aspects of social behavior; it seeks to *explain* them. The development of comprehensive, accurate theories is a major goal of all science, and social psychology is no exception to this basic rule. Thus, a great deal of research in our field is concerned with efforts to construct, refine, and test such frameworks. But what precisely are theories? And what is their value in social psychology? Perhaps the best means of answering such questions is, again, through a concrete example.

Imagine that we observe the following: when people work together in a group, each member exerts less effort on the joint task than when they work alone. (This is known as *social loafing,* and is discussed in Chapter Nine.) The observation just described is certainly useful by itself. After all, it allows us to predict what will happen when individuals work together, and it also suggests the possibility of intervening in some manner to prevent such outcomes. These two accomplishments—*prediction* and *intervention* (sometimes known as *control*)—are major goals of science. Yet, the fact that social loafing occurs does not explain *why* it takes place. It is at this point that theory enters the picture.

In older and more advanced fields such as physics or chemistry, theories are often phrased as mathematical equations. In social psychology, however, they are usually verbal statements or assertions. For example, a theory designed to account for social loafing might read as follows: When persons work together, they realize that their outputs will not be individually identifiable, and that all participants will share in the responsibility for the final outcome. As a result, they conclude that they can get away with "taking it easy," and so exert less effort on the task. Note that this theory, like all others, consists of two parts: several basic concepts (e.g., individual effort, shared responsibility) and statements concerning the relationships between these con-

cepts (e.g., as belief in shared responsibility increases, individual effort decreases).

Once a theory has been formulated, a crucial process begins. First, predictions are derived from the theory. These are formulated in accordance with the basic principles of logic, and are known as *hypotheses.* For example, one such prediction that might be derived from the theory of social loafing outlined above would be as follows: to the extent members of a group believe their work will be identifiable, social loafing will decrease.

Next, such predictions are tested in actual research. If they are confirmed, confidence in the accuracy of the theory is increased: it is viewed as providing an adequate explanation for the phenomena with which it deals. If, instead, such predictions are disconfirmed, confidence in the theory is weakened. Then, the theory itself may be altered so as to generate new predictions, and these, in turn, can be subjected to testing. In short, the process is a continuous one, involving the free flow of information between a theory, predictions derived from it, and the findings of ongoing research. (See Figure 1.12 for a summary of this process.)

Please note, by the way, that theories are useful, from a scientific point of view, only to the extent that they lead to testable predictions. Indeed, if they do not generate hypotheses that can be examined in actual research, they should not be viewed as scientific in nature. For example, consider the following "theory": the reason you recently had a run of bad luck (lost your job, had a minor traffic accident, caught the flu) is that one of your ex-lovers has put a hex on you. Obviously, hexes, evil spells, and similar events lie outside the realm of science. Thus, such a "theory" is not a theory at all; it does not generate predictions testable by scientific means (i.e., by the experimental or correlational methods described earlier).

In sum, theories serve as important guides to research in social psychology, just as they do in other branches of science. Thus, we will have reason to consider many theories in the pages that follow. As each theory is presented, try to keep the following points in mind: (1) theories are designed to explain key aspects of social behavior,

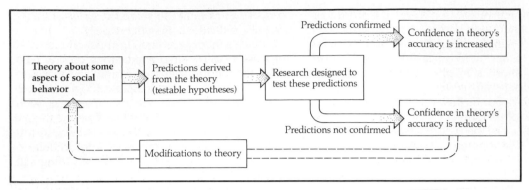

Figure 1.12   *Once theories are formulated in social psychology (or any other branch of science), they are put to an empirical test. This involves a process in which predictions derived from the theory are examined in actual research. If these predictions are confirmed, confidence in the theory's accuracy is increased. If they are disconfirmed, confidence in the theory's accuracy is reduced. In the latter case, the theory may be modified so as to generate new predictions, and these, in turn, may be tested.*

Putting theories to the test: An ongoing process

and (2) they should be accepted as valid or useful only to the extent that the predictions they generate are confirmed by research findings.

The Quest for Knowledge and the Rights of Individuals: In Search of an Appropriate Balance

In their use of experimentation and systematic observation, and in their reliance on comprehensive theories, social psychologists do not differ from researchers in many other fields. There is one technique, however, that seems to be unique to research in our field: **deception.** Basically, this involves efforts by researchers to conceal the true purpose of their studies from persons participating in them. The reason behind this procedure can be simply stated: many social psychologists are convinced that if subjects know the true purposes behind an investigation, their behavior will be changed by such knowledge. Then, the research itself will be doomed to fail; it will have little chance of adding to our knowledge of human social behavior.

On the face of it, this is an eminently reasonable suggestion. For example, imagine that in a study to examine the impact of anxiety upon liking for a stranger, subjects are informed of this purpose. Clearly, they may react differently to the stranger than would otherwise be the case. Similarly, imagine that subjects taking part in a study of racial prejudice are told that this is the topic under investigation. With this information in their possession, they may lean over backward to avoid showing any trace of prejudice whatsoever. Because of such considerations, many social psychologists feel that deception—at least on a temporary basis—is essential for the research (Suls and Rosnow, 1988). Thus, deception is common in social psychological research (Gross and Fleming, 1982). The adoption of this technique, though, is not without its costs. Deceiving or misleading research participants, no matter how justified this may seem, raises important ethical issues that should not be overlooked.

First, it is possible that at least some persons exposed to such treatment will resent having been led astray. As a result, they may adopt a negative attitude toward social research generally. Second, deception, even when temporary, may result in some type of harmful outcome for the persons exposed to it (Kelman, 1967). For example, they may experience discomfort, stress, negative shifts in their self-esteem, or related effects. Finally, there is the very real question of whether scientists, committed to the search for knowledge, should place themselves in the position of deceiving persons kind enough to assist them in this undertaking.

In short, the use of deception does pose something of a dilemma to social psychologists. On the one hand, it seems essential to their research. On the other, its use raises serious problems. How can this issue be resolved? At present, opinion remains somewhat divided. Some of our colleagues believe that deception, no matter how useful, is inappropriate and must be abandoned (Baumrind, 1979). In contrast, many others (perhaps a large majority) believe that temporary deception *is* acceptable provided certain safeguards are followed (Baron, 1981). The most important of these are **informed consent** and thorough **debriefing.**

Informed consent involves providing research participants with as full a description of the procedures to be followed as feasible, prior to their decision to take part in a given study. In short, the guiding principle is "Research partici-pants should know what they are getting into be-fore they make a commitment to assist." In contrast, thorough debriefing *follows* rather than precedes each experimental session. It consists of providing participants with a full explanation of all major aspects of the study, including its true goals, the hypotheses under investigation, and an explanation of the need for temporary deception. The basic principle here is that all research participants should leave the session in *at least* as favorable or positive a state as when they arrived (see Figure 1.13).

That informed consent and thorough debriefing go a long way toward eliminating the potential dangers of deception is suggested by several studies concerned with this issue. First, an overwhelming majority of subjects view temporary deception as acceptable and do not resent its use (Rogers, 1980). Second, there is some indication that individuals who have participated in studies involving deception actually report more positive feelings about the value of psychological research than subjects who have not taken part in such research (Smith and Richardson, 1983). Third, it appears that effective de-

Figure 1.13 At the end of an experimental session, subjects are debriefed by the experimenter. At this time, all aspects of the experiment are accurately described. Subjects learn what the experimenter hoped to find, how his or her group fit into the design, and why there was deception. Ideally, subjects leave the experiment with more knowledge than when they began and with feelings at least as positive as they were prior to taking part.

Debriefing: One of the safeguards in social psychological research

briefing does eliminate many negative aspects experienced by subjects as a result of temporary deception (Smith and Richardson, 1985). Of course, even in light of such results, it is unwise to take the safety or appropriateness of deception for granted. As noted recently by Rubin (1985), this would be a serious error indeed. Rather, it appears the key phrase for all researchers wishing to use deception in their studies must remain: "Danger: Complex ethical issues ahead. Proceed with extreme caution."

USING THIS BOOK: A Displaced Preface

Before concluding, we would like to comment briefly on several features of this text. Often, such information is included in the preface, but since many readers seem to skip such messages from authors, presenting it here seems to make good sense.

First, we should mention several steps we've taken to make our text easier and more convenient for you to use. Each chapter begins with an outline of the major topics covered, and each ends with a summary. Key terms are printed in **boldface type** and are defined in a glossary that follows each chapter. All figures and graphs contain special labels designed to call your attention to the key findings they present. Finally, a list of sources for further information is offered at the end of each chapter.

Second, we wish to call your attention to the fact that we've included two distinct types of special inserts throughout the text. The first of these, called "Focus on Research," examines specific studies performed by social psychologists. Such inserts appear in two basic forms. The first is subtitled "Classic Contributions," and describes investigations now widely considered to be "classics" in our field—ones that initiated new lines of research or changed the thinking about important social phenomena (see pages 17–18 for an example). The second type is subtitled "The Cutting Edge" and focuses on recent projects carried out at the frontiers of our field. The presence of two types of "Focus" inserts reflects our desire to maintain a balance between con-

temporary trends in social psychology and its past history and progress.

The second type of insert is titled "On the Applied Side" (see pages 5–6 for an example). These focus primarily on the practical implications of social psychology—ways in which the knowledge it yields can contribute to the solution of a broad range of practical problems.

It is our hope that these and other features of our text will help us communicate knowledge about social behavior in a manner you will find interesting and enlightening. We also hope that they will permit some of our own excitement about the field to come through in an undistorted way. To the extent we succeed in these basic tasks—and only to that extent—will we be satisfied that as authors, teachers, and representatives of social psychology, we have done our part.

SUMMARY

Social psychology is defined as the scientific field that seeks to understand the nature and causes of individual behavior in social situations. Informal speculation about social interaction has gone on since ancient times, but a science-oriented field of social psychology emerged only in the early decades of this century. Once established, it grew rapidly and today seeks to examine every conceivable aspect of social behavior. Two recent trends have involved the growing influence of a *cognitive perspective*—efforts to understand complex social behaviors in terms of the basic cognitive processes that underlie them, and an increasing emphasis on *application*—applying the knowledge and principles of social psychology to many practical problems.

In conducting their research, social psychologists generally employ either the **experimental** or the **correlational method**. The first involves procedures in which one or more factors are systematically varied in order to examine the impact of such changes on one or more aspects of social behavior. Social psychologists conduct experiments in the laboratory, but also conduct **field experiments** in real-life settings. The correlational method involves careful observation of existing relationships between two or more variables. In selecting the topics of their research and planning specific studies, social psychologists are often guided by **theories**. These are logical frameworks designed to explain why certain events or processes occur as they do. Predictions derived from theories are tested in ongoing research. If they are confirmed, confidence in the accuracy of the theory is increased. If they are disconfirmed, such confidence is reduced.

Social psychologists often attempt to conceal the true purpose of their studies from the persons participating in them. That is, they make use of temporary **deception**. Use of this technique stems from the belief that if subjects know the true purpose of a research project, their behavior may be altered, thus rendering the results invalid. Use of deception raises important ethical issues, but most social psychologists believe it is permissible, provided proper safeguards (e.g., **informed consent** and thorough **debriefing**) are adopted.

GLOSSARY

cognitive dissonance An unpleasant state that occurs when individuals notice inconsistency between their attitudes and their overt behavior.

cognitive perspective The view that many complex social phenomena can best be understood in terms of the cognitive processes (e.g., memory, social inference) that underlie them.

confounding (of variables) Occurs in situations where factors other than the independent variable under investigation in an experiment are permitted to vary. Confounding makes it impossible to determine whether results stem from the independent variable or from other factors.

contextualist view A new perspective on social behavior suggesting no action can be adequately interpreted or understood apart from the context in which it occurs.

correlational method A method of research based on careful observation of two or more variables. If changes in one are consistently associated with changes in another, evidence for a link between them is obtained.

debriefing Procedures at the end of an experimental session in which research participants are informed about the true purpose of the study and the major hypotheses under investigation.

deception Efforts by researchers to conceal the true purpose of their studies from persons participating in them. Use of this technique stems from the belief that if subjects know the purpose of a study, their behavior may be changed by this knowledge.

demand characteristics Any cues serving to communicate the experimenter's hypothesis to a subject in an experiment. To the extent that demand characteristics are present, the results of an experiment may be invalid.

dispositional variables Some aspect of individuals (including sex, race, and personality traits) whose effect can be investigated as part of an experimental design. Though such dispositions cannot be manipulated, they can be treated in the same fashion as independent variables.

experimentation (experimental method) A method of research in which one factor (the independent variable) is systematically changed or adjusted in order to determine whether such variations affect a second factor (the dependent variable).

field experiments In this type of experiment, subjects are randomly assigned to experimental and control groups in real-life settings. Since subjects are generally unaware they are being studied and the settings are realistic, problems associated with demand characteristics and the artificiality of the laboratory setting may be reduced.

informed consent Procedures in which subjects are told, in advance, about the activities they will perform during an experiment. They then participate in the study only if they are willing to engage in such activities.

interaction (between variables) Occurs when the impact of one variable is affected by one or more other variables. For example, anxiety may lead to increased liking for an attractive stranger, but not toward an unattractive stranger.

manipulation check A procedure in an experiment to determine whether the manipulation of an independent variable was effective.

random assignment of subjects to groups A basic requirement for an experiment to be valid. According to this principle, research participants should have an equal chance of being exposed to each level of the independent variable. In short, they should be randomly assigned to various conditions within the study.

social psychology The scientific field that seeks to comprehend the nature and causes of individual behavior in social situations.

theory Systematic efforts by scientists to explain natural phenomena. Theories generally consist of two major parts: basic concepts and assertions regarding the relationships between these concepts.

FOR MORE INFORMATION

BARON, R. A. (1986). *Behavior in organizations: Understanding and managing the human side of work,* 2nd ed. Boston: Allyn & Bacon.

This text provides a broad survey of the field of organizational behavior. By skimming through it, you can get an idea of how the findings of social psychology have been applied to the solution of many practical problems in businesses and other organizations (e.g., enhancing employee morale, providing effective leadership).

DREW, C. J., and HARDMAN, M. L. (1985). *Designing and conducting behavioral research.* New York: Pergamon Press.

A clear and relatively brief description of how psychologists and other behavioral scientists actually conduct their research. If you'd like to learn more about this topic, this is a good source to consult.

JONES, E. E. (1985). Major developments in social psychology during the past five decades. In G. Lindzey and E. Aronson (Eds.), *Handbook of social psychology* (Vol. 1). New York: Random House.

A summary of important theoretical and experimental trends in social psychology over the last 50 years or so. This chapter provides an excellent overview of social psychology's recent history.

SAKS, M. J., and SAXE, L. (Eds.). (1986). *Advances in applied social psychology* (Vol. 3). Hillsdale, N.J.: Erlbaum.

The latest in a series of volumes representing important applications of social psychological knowledge to practical problems. This volume has chapters on using social psychology to increase blood donations, to study the effects of school desegregation, and to explain alcohol abuse to name just a few of the topics covered.

Chapter Two
Social Perception: Knowing Others— and Ourselves

"Linda, what's wrong?" Terry Spiak asks her friend Linda Barton. "You look like you haven't slept in days!"

"I haven't, and I feel rotten, plain rotten."

"Well, don't keep me guessing. What's the problem?"

"It's Tony. Isn't it always?"

"But I thought you were getting along so well. What's up?"

"The usual. I think he's been seeing another woman . . . or maybe its two or three other women."

"But why would he? You're so good to him, it makes me nervous. If Jeff ever found out about all the stuff you do for Tony, I'd have it rough."

"That's just what I keep wondering about. *Why* does he do it? I love him so much it hurts, and I know that I make him happy. But then he goes out and meets these other people . . . I just can't stand it!"

"What makes you so sure he's still doing it? Didn't he promise you that he'd stop?"

"Oh sure. But I can tell; I can always tell. It's lots of little things. Like the other day. He was supposed to be over at 6:00, but didn't show up until 7:30. I asked why he was late, and it was as though he had the whole thing rehearsed. It was so smooth. One good excuse after another. Yet . . . the way he paused, and that look in his eye . . . I just knew he'd been doing something he didn't want me to know about."

"Yeah, I guess that when you get to know someone real well, you can read the little signs . . . I can always tell when Jeff is lying, or at least not telling me everything. But what are you going to do?"

"I don't know. I'm really crazy about him, and I don't know what I'd do if I lost him. If only I could figure out what makes him do it . . . He knows how it hurts me, and how jealous I get. And I don't think he even *likes* some of these other women."

"Maybe he just wants to prove that he's attractive—that he can still have his pick."

"Could be. And sometimes I think it's just that he's afraid of getting *too* close; you know, so that he'd be dependent on me, and really need me."

"It's strange, all right," Terry remarks, stroking her chin. "But then, men are always a puzzle. Who can figure out why they do what they do? Not me!"

Admit it. Other people are often something of a mystery. They say and do things we don't expect, have motives we don't readily understand, and seem to perceive the world in ways very different from ourselves. Yet, because they play such a key role in our lives, this is one mystery we cannot afford to leave unresolved (see Figure 2.1). Thus, we often engage in efforts to understand other persons—to comprehend their major motives and traits. Like Linda, in the opening story, we try to figure out what they are *really* like, and

HERMAN®

"You're quite a puzzle, aren't you?"

Figure 2.1 We often engage in efforts to understand other people. "Social perception" is the term social psychologists use to describe how people seek knowledge of others. (Source: Herman. Copyright 1987 Universal Press Syndicate. Reprinted with permission. All rights reserved.)

People: Often something of a mystery

why they behave in the ways they do. Social psychologists generally term the processes through which we seek such knowledge about others as **social perception**, the major focus of the present chapter.

While our efforts to understand the people around us (and ourselves too) focus on many different issues, two of these are most important. First, we often seek to grasp the current, temporary causes behind others' behavior—their present moods, feelings, and emotions. Information on this issue is often provided by *nonverbal cues* relating to others' facial expressions, eye contact, and body posture or movements. Second, we attempt to comprehend the more lasting causes behind others' actions—their stable traits, motives, and intentions. Information pertaining to this second task is usually gained through a complex process known as **attribution**, in which we observe others' behavior and then try to *infer* the causes behind it in a relatively systematic way (Harvey and Weary, 1985). Because nonverbal communication and attribution provide us with somewhat different kinds of information about others, we will consider them separately here. But please note: they usually proceed simultaneously in actual social settings.

NONVERBAL COMMUNICATION: The Silent—but Often Eloquent— Language of Gestures, Gazes, and Expressions

In many situations, behavior is strongly affected by temporary factors or causes. Shifting moods, fleeting emotions, fatigue, and various drugs can all exert strong effects on individual behavior. To mention just a few examples, most persons are more willing to do favors for others when in a good mood than in a bad one (Isen, 1984), and many are more likely to lose their tempers and lash out at others when feeling irritable than when feeling mellow (Geen and Donnerstein, 1983). Because these temporary factors produce important effects on social behavior, it is useful to know something more about them. How can we know others are in a good or bad mood,

whether they are experiencing anger, joy, or sorrow, and whether they are calm or tense? One answer is deceptively simple: we can ask them directly. Unfortunately, this strategy doesn't always work. Sometimes people are willing to reveal their inner feelings or moods, and sometimes they are not. Indeed, they may actively seek to deceive or mislead us in this regard (e.g., DePaulo, Stone, and Lassiter, 1985). (If you've ever tried to conceal your own anger, or your own attraction to another individual, you are already well aware of this basic fact.) In such cases, it is not necessary for us to give up in despair, for there is another source of information about temporary causes of behavior: *nonverbal cues.* In short, we can learn about others' current moods and feelings from a silent language that often accompanies, but exists independently from, their spoken words. Such **nonverbal communication** is quite complex and has been studied from many perspectives. For purposes of this discussion, however, we will focus on two major issues: (1) the basic channels through which such communication takes place and (2) how well people send and interpret nonverbal cues.

Nonverbal Communication: The Basic Channels

How do individuals communicate nonverbally? Several decades of research suggest they do so in many different ways. The most important of these seem to involve touching, body movements and posture (**body language**), eye contact, and facial expressions.

Touching: Physical Contact as a Nonverbal Cue. Suppose that while you are conversing with another person, she or he touches you briefly. How would you react? And what information would you view this behavior as conveying? The answer to both questions is, "It depends." And what it depends on is several factors relating to who does the touching (a friend or stranger; a member of your own or the opposite sex), the nature of this physical contact (is it brief or prolonged, gentle or rough, what part of your body is involved), and the context in which it takes place (a business or social setting; a public or private location). Thus, depending on such factors, touch can suggest affection, sexual interest, dominance, or even aggression (Knapp, 1978; see Figure 2.2). Further, it has been found that touching does not occur in a random manner. On the contrary, it follows clear-cut patterns. Thus, males touch females more than twice as often as females touch males, and high-status persons touch low-status ones much more often than vice versa (Henley, 1973).

Despite these and other complexities, however, a growing body of evidence points to the following conclusion: when one person touches another in a noncontroversial manner (i.e., gently, briefly, and on a nonsensitive part of the body), positive reactions generally result

Figure 2.2   The meaning of physical touching can vary, depending on how and where it takes place. At different times and different conditions, touching can signify affection, sexual interest, dominance, or even aggression.

Touching: Different contexts, different meanings

(Alagna, Whitcher, and Fisher, 1979; Smith, Gier, and Willis, 1982; Crusco and Wetzel, 1984).

We should emphasize, once again, that touching does not always produce such effects. Indeed, when it is perceived as a status or power play, or when it is too prolonged or intimate, it may evoke anxiety, anger, or other negative reactions. Thus, in most cases, it is a form of nonverbal cue that should be used sparingly, and with great restraint.

Body Language: Gestures, Movements, and Posture. Our current moods or emotions are often reflected in the posture, position, and movement of our bodies. Nonverbal cues from such sources, usually termed "body language," can provide us with several useful types of information about others.

First, body language often reveals much about other persons' emotional states. Large numbers of movements—especially ones in which a particular part of the body does something to another (e.g., scratching, stroking)—suggest emotional arousal. The greater the frequency of such behavior, the higher the others' level of arousal or nervousness seems to be (Knapp, 1978).

Second, more specific information about others' feelings is often provided by gestures. These fall into several different categories, but perhaps the most important are *emblems*—that is, body movements that carry a highly specific meaning in a given culture. For example, in the United States (and elsewhere), rubbing one's stomach with an open hand signifies a favorable response to food or other items (yum-yum!). In contrast, seizing one's nose with the thumb and index finger indicates disgust. Although emblems vary greatly from culture to culture (Morris et al., 1979; see Figure 2.3), all human societies appear to have at least some signals of this type for greetings, departures, insults, and the description of various physical states (hunger, thirst, fatigue).

Finally, body language can also reveal others' reactions to *us*. Certain body movements or postures signify liking, while others signal disliking or rejection (Mehrabian, 1968). For example, research on this topic reveals that when others sit

Figure 2.3 *Gestures that carry a specific meaning in a specific culture (known as* emblems*) may carry quite different meanings in a different culture. For example, the man with the finger on the side of his head is indicating a common European message that the person under discussion is "stupid." In the United States, we may take it to mean that the person under discussion is crazy.*

Emblems: Different meanings across cultures

facing us directly, lean in our direction, or nod frequently while we speak, we conclude that they like us. When, in contrast, they sit so as to avoid staring at us directly, lean away, or look at the ceiling while we speak, we may reach the opposite conclusion (Clore, Wiggins, and Itkin, 1975). Clearly, then, we can often learn much from carefully watching others' body language.

Gazes and Stares: The Language of the Eyes. Have you ever had a conversation with someone who was wearing dark glasses? If so, you may remember that this was an uncomfortable situation. The reason for your discomfort is simple: you could not see the person's eyes, and so you were denied access to an important source of information concerning her or his feelings. Ancient poets often described the eyes as "windows to the soul," and in an important sense, they were correct. We *do* often learn a great deal about others' internal states—and so the causes behind their behavior—from their eye contact with us. For example, we often interpret a high level of gazing from another as a sign of liking or friendliness (Kleinke, Meeker, and LaFong, 1974; Kleinke, 1986). In contrast, if others avoid eye contact with us, we usually conclude that they are unfriendly, don't like us, or, perhaps, are simply shy (Zimbardo, 1977).

While a high level of eye contact from others is usually interpreted as a sign of liking or positive feelings, there is one important exception to this general rule. If another person gazes at us in a continuous manner, and maintains such contact regardless of any actions we perform, he or she may be said to be **staring**. As you probably know from your own experience, this is a decidedly unpleasant experience—one that makes us feel nervous or tense (Strom and Buck, 1979). Thus, it is not surprising that when confronted with such treatment by a stranger, many individuals seek to withdraw from the situation in which the staring occurs (Greenbaum and Rosenfield, 1978). Even worse, some evidence suggests that stares are often interpreted as a sign of hostility or anger, both by people and animals (Ellsworth and Carlsmith, 1973).

Together, these findings seem to imply that staring always produces negative effects. Additional evidence suggests, however, that occasionally staring can yield more positive outcomes. For example, it can sometimes increase offers of aid from passersby (Ellsworth and Langer, 1976). Recall how much harder it is to walk past persons collecting for various charities without making a donation once they have stared at you and caught your eye. It is for this reason that we often try to look down when approaching such individuals. These and other instances suggest that stares, while often unpleasant, are not always negative in their effects.

Unmasking the Face: Facial Expressions as Guides to the Moods and Emotions of Others. More than 2,000 years ago the Roman orator Cicero noted, "The face is the image of the soul." By this comment he meant that human feelings and emotions are often reflected on the face, and can be "read" there from various specific expressions. Modern research suggests that, in this respect, Cicero and many other observers of human behavior were correct; often it is possible to learn much about the current moods and feelings of others from their facial expressions. In fact, it appears that six different—and basic—emotions are represented clearly on the human face: happiness, sadness, surprise, fear, anger, and disgust (Buck, 1984; Izard, 1977). Please note: this does not imply that we are capable of demonstrating only six different facial expressions—far from it. Emotions come in many combinations (e.g., anger along with fear, surprise together with happiness). Further, each of these reactions can vary greatly in intensity. Thus, although there appear to be only six basic "themes" in facial expressions, the number of variations is truly huge.

The fact that facial expressions do indeed often reflect our inner feelings raises another intriguing question: are such expressions themselves universal in nature? For example, if you traveled to a remote part of the globe and visited a group of people who had never met an outsider, would their facial expressions in various situations resemble your own? Would they smile when they encountered events that made them happy, frown when exposed to conditions that upset them, and so on? Further, would you be able to recognize their facial expressions in such situations as you can readily recognize those of persons belonging to your own culture? The answer to both questions appears to be "yes." People living in widely separated geographic areas do seem to demonstrate similar facial expressions in similar, emotion-provoking situations; and they show an impressive ability to recognize each others' expressions accurately (Ekman and Friesen, 1975). For example, preliterate men and women from an isolated culture in New Guinea recognized the expressions for all of the basic emotions from photographs from eight literate cultures (e.g., Greece, Hong Kong, Turkey, United States) just as well as college students (Ekman et al., 1987; see Figure 2.4). Thus, it appears that when experiencing basic emotions, human beings all over the world tend to show similar facial expressions, and the meaning of

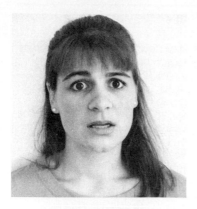

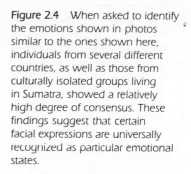

Figure 2.4 *When asked to identify the emotions shown in photos similar to the ones shown here, individuals from several different countries, as well as those from culturally isolated groups living in Sumatra, showed a relatively high degree of consensus. These findings suggest that certain facial expressions are universally recognized as particular emotional states.*

The face: A universal communicator

such expressions, too, is universal. For this reason, the language of the face, in contrast to that of spoken words, rarely requires an interpreter.

Detecting Deception: Reading the Nonverbal Signs

We can all think of cases when *what* we were saying was in conflict with how we really felt. A neighbor drops in for a favor, which we feel uncomfortable refusing. The statement "Of course, no problem, I'd be happy to . . ." may be accompanied by nonverbal cues to the contrary. How do people deal with messages that are inconsistent: the verbal message says one thing, but the nonverbal says something else? Research shows that people can detect inconsistencies between verbal and nonverbal channels of communication to some degree. For example, verbal messages that are accompanied by discrepant nonverbal cues will be incorrectly recalled more

than verbal messages presented with consistent nonverbal signals (Hertel and Narvaez, 1986).

The issue of inconsistency between verbal and nonverbal messages raises the question of how good people are at detecting deception. Freud (1959) thought that nonverbal cues would "leak" information that people might be trying to hide from others: " . . . betrayal oozes out of every pore" (p. 94). Research in the last three decades has examined how successful people are at detecting deception. In general, people can discriminate truth from lies with better than chance success (DePaulo, Stone, and Lassiter, 1985; Zuckerman, DePaulo, and Rosenthal, 1981), so we are at least moderately effective in this regard.

But how, precisely, do people detect deception? Four kinds of cues appear to be used. Fleeting facial expressions lasting only a few tenths of a second, called *microexpressions,* appear on the face very quickly after an emotion-provoking

SKILL AT DETECTING DECEPTION: DOES EXPERIENCE HELP?

Although many cues appear to be available to detect deception, as mentioned on page 35, our accuracy in detecting deception is not impressive. In studies in which lies and truths occur equally often and a chance level of accuracy would be 50 percent, overall accuracy usually ranges from 45 to 60 percent. However, this research has a drawback in that it depended on inexperienced deception detectors. Perhaps, people who are employed in jobs in which the detection of deception is important are

more accurate. Kraut and Poe (1980) considered the possibility that customs inspectors should be good at detecting deception because part of their job is to try to detect travelers who are smuggling illegal goods. But contrary to the notion that experience should make a difference, Kraut and Poe (1980) found that customs inspectors were no more successful than others at deciding, on the basis of verbal and nonverbal cues, which travelers to search.

In a more recent experiment of

the effect of experience on the detection of deceit, DePaulo and Pfeifer (1986) administered a deception-detection test to a group of undergraduates with no special experience at detecting deceit, and a group of advanced federal law enforcement officials with years of experience working at jobs in which the detection of deception is very important (such as the Secret Service and the Military Police). All subjects listened to an audiotape of undergraduates who had been asked to tell two truths

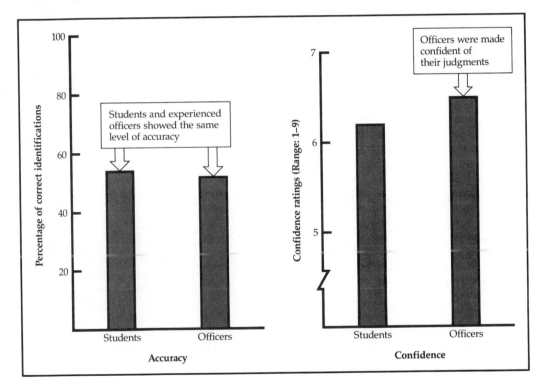

Figure 2.5   Officers with years of experience working at jobs in which the detection of deception is very important were no more accurate than a group of undergraduates in identifying when people were telling lies or telling the truth. However, although they were no more accurate, the officers were more confident of their judgments. (Source: Based on data from DePaulo and Pfeifer, 1986.)

Experience at detecting deception: Evidence that it doesn't help and two lies. The subjects recorded their judgment of deceptiveness and their confidence in that judgment after each message.

As Figure 2.5 shows, the officers were no more accurate than the students at detecting deception and truth. However, the officers were significantly more *confident* about their judgments than were the students. DePaulo and Pfeifer also looked at changes in accuracy and confidence over the course of the test. The advanced officers felt increasingly confident about their performance as they progressed through the test, although actually their accuracy did not improve. These results, along with others (Kraut and Poe, 1980), suggest that experienced individuals do no better than undergraduates at detecting deception. Why does experience fail to help? DePaulo suggests that in most law enforcement jobs, the officers do not receive feedback about whether they are right or wrong after every deception-detection attempt. Even when they do receive feedback, it may be delayed in time. Furthermore, outcome feedback in the form of success or failure does not provide information about the specific rules or cues that led them to the right or wrong answer. As a result, the inspectors may develop their own theories about what gestures or expressions are signals of deceit, but these theories may be quite erroneous. Their unwarranted confidence (shown in the DePaulo experiment) may be a result of the erroneous notions that these experienced officers have about cues to deception.

Of course, criminal investigators frequently have more to work on than the testimony of a suspect such as factual information, clues, etc., so federal officers may indeed succeed quite often at detecting deceptions and truths in their day-to-day work experiences. Nonetheless, the studies discussed above suggest that even presumed experts are frequently fooled when people want to hide the truth. Currently, training programs are being conducted in which trainees learn to focus on critical nonverbal cues; presumably, this may help them to master the skills needed for detecting deception when it occurs (DePaulo et al., 1985; Zuckerman, Koestner, and Alton, 1984).

---

event before the person can get his or her "mask" in place (Ekman and Friesen, 1975). These expressions can be quite revealing about true underlying feelings and also call attention to subsequent efforts at concealment. Voice pitch also signals possible deception. When people tell lies, the pitch of their speech rises slightly (Streeter et al., 1977). Third, we are apt to believe that people who avoid eye contact with us are engaging in deception (Kleinke, 1986). Finally, bodily movement of the limbs may signal possible deception. (For discussion of whether supposed deception-detection experts are any better at it than most of us refer to the "On the Applied Side" insert above.)

In summarizing the research in the preceding sections, we see that nonverbal communication can be an important source of information for social interaction. At the same time, it is clear that when people want to, they can successfully disguise their true feelings. At one level, this may seem unfortunate, but many social interactions are probably made easier because we are capable of disguising our true feelings. After all,

who wants to tell Aunt Gusie that her meatloaf is inedible, or tell the boss that he has terrible taste in ties?

ATTRIBUTION: Understanding the Causes of Behavior

Knowledge about others' moods or feelings can be useful, but it is usually only part of the total picture. In addition, we usually want to know something about others' lasting traits—the stable characteristics that they bring with them from situation to situation. And, more generally, we wish to understand the *causes* behind their behavior—to know precisely *why* they have acted in certain ways under certain conditions (see Figure 2.6). The process through which we attempt to gain such information is known as **attribution,** and has been of major interest to social psychologists for several decades. Because attribution is complex, several theories designed to explain its operation have been proposed (e.g., Heider, 1958). Here we will focus on two

DENNIS THE MENACE

"I always know what's going on . . . I just don't always know why."

Figure 2.6 As suggested by the cartoon, people have a strong desire to know why things occur. Attribution theory is concerned with the rules and processes used to answer the question of "why" in terms of others' behavior as well as our own behavior. (Source: DENNIS THE MENACE® used by permission of Hank Ketcham and © by North American Syndicate.)

Like everyone, "Dennis the Menace" wants to know "why?"

that have been especially influential—frameworks proposed by Jones and Davis (1965) and by Kelley (1972).

From Acts to Dispositions: Using Others' Behavior as a Guide to Their Lasting Traits

The first of these theories is concerned with a basic—and very reasonable—issue: how do we go about inferring the lasting characteristics of other persons from their behavior? Such inference is necessary because individuals do not

carry signs proclaiming their central traits. Indeed, they are often quite unaware of these, and in other cases they are unwilling to share such knowledge with us even if they possess it. (After all, how many persons would admit, openly, that they are stingy, manipulative, prejudiced, or cruel?) Thus, if we wish to understand the persons around us, we must usually observe their behavior and use the information observation provides as a basis for reaching conclusions about them.

At first glance, it might appear that our task in this regard is quite simple—others' behavior *does* provide us with a rich source of input. Actually, though, it is complicated by the following fact: often, people act in certain ways not because of their own traits or dispositions, but because of the influence of factors outside their control. For example, imagine that you observe a state trooper giving one speeding ticket after another to passing motorists. Does this mean she is a "tough cookie" who enjoys punishing hapless strangers? Not necessarily. She may have been given a high quota for tickets that week, and believes she has no choice. In cases such as this, using others' behavior as a guide to their lasting traits or motives can lead us seriously astray.

How do we cope with such complications? How do we decide either that others' actions reflect their "true" characteristics or, alternatively, that these actions stem from other factors? Jones and Davis provide an answer in their theory of **correspondent inference** (Jones and Davis, 1965; Jones and McGillis, 1976). According to this theory, we accomplish this difficult task by focusing our attention on certain types of actions—those most likely to be informative in this regard.

First, we consider only behaviors that seem to have been freely chosen; those that were somehow forced on the persons in question tend to be ignored. Second, we pay careful attention to behaviors that produce unique or *noncommon effects*—outcomes that would not be produced by any other action. The advantage offered by such behaviors is readily illustrated. For example, imagine that one of your friends has just gotten married. Further, suppose that her spouse is (1) highly attractive, (2) pleasant and friendly, and (3) incredibly rich. Would the fact that your friend married this man tell you much about her personality? Probably not. There are so many potential reasons for having married him (his good looks, charm, wealth) that it is impossible to tell which was most important to her. But now, in contrast, imagine that your friend has just married someone who is (1) highly unattractive, (2) grumpy, and (3) incredibly rich. In this case, there is only one apparent reason for your friend's decision to marry: her mate's great wealth. Under these conditions, your friend's decision *does* tell you something about her major traits or motives. Thus, you may conclude that she values money more than other things such as getting along with her spouse or a good sex life. By comparing these situations, you should be able to see why we can usually learn more about others from actions on their part that produce noncommon effects than from actions without any distinctive consequences.

Finally, Jones and Davis suggest that we also pay greater attention, in our efforts to understand others, to actions they perform that are low in *social desirability* than to actions that are high on this dimension. In short, we learn more from actions that depart from the ordinary and are not encouraged by society than from actions that *are* widely encouraged. For example, consider the state trooper mentioned previously. If you see her helping a stranded motorist, you may be reluctant to form any conclusions about her stable traits; after all, this is part of her job, and other officers would probably act in the same manner. If you see her refuse to help a motorist in distress, or observe her drinking beer while tooling down the highway in her patrol car, you may be more willing to reach such conclusions. These actions are both unusual and against rules she's supposed to follow.

In sum, the theory proposed by Jones and Davis suggests that we are most likely to conclude that others' behavior reflects their stable traits (i.e., we are likely to reach *correspondent inferences* about them) when these actions (1) occur by choice; (2) yield distinctive, noncommon effects; and (3) are low in social desirability (see Figure 2.7 for a summary of these principles).

Kelley's Theory of Causal Attribution: How We Answer the Question "Why?"

Consider the following events: you apply for membership in a social organization but are rejected; your boss announces, unexpectedly, that he is giving you a big raise; you ask someone special for a date but are refused. What questions would arise in your mind in each of these situations? If you are like most people, your answer can be stated in a single word: "Why?" You wonder *why* the organization has rejected you, *why* your boss is giving you that raise, and *why* your advances have been spurned. In countless life situations, this is the central attributional task we face. We want to know why other persons have behaved the way they have. Such knowledge is of crucial importance, for only if we understand

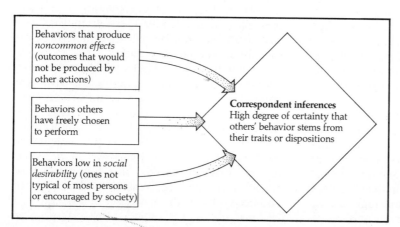

Behaviors that produce *noncommon effects* (outcomes that would not be produced by other actions)

Behaviors others have freely chosen to perform

Behaviors low in *social desirability* (ones not typical of most persons or encouraged by society)

Correspondent inferences High degree of certainty that others' behavior stems from their traits or dispositions

Figure 2.7 *According to a theory proposed by Jones and Davis, when others' behavior produces noncommon effects, appears to be freely chosen, and is low in social desirability, we attribute it to their traits or personal dispositions. (Source: Based on suggestions by Jones and Davis, 1965.)*

Correspondent inference: Attributing others' behavior to their traits and dispositions

the causes behind their actions can we adjust our own behavior accordingly and make sense out of the social world around us. Obviously, the number of specific causes behind others' behavior is very large—perhaps almost infinite. To make this task more manageable, therefore, we often begin with a preliminary question: has others' behavior stemmed mainly from *internal causes* (their own characteristics, motives, intentions), mainly from *external causes* (some aspects of the social or physical world), or from a combination of the two? For example, with respect to your raise, you might wonder whether your boss has decided to reward you in this manner because of internal causes (he is a kind, benevolent person sensitive to your dire need!), external causes (he was told to do so by *his* supervisor), or some combination of causal factors. Revealing insights into just how we carry out this initial— but central—attributional task are provided in a major theory proposed by Kelley (Kelley, 1972; Kelley and Michela, 1980).

According to Kelley, in our attempts to answer the question "why" about others' behavior, we focus on three major dimensions. First, we consider **consensus**—the extent to which others react in the same manner to some stimulus or event as the person we are considering. Second, we consider **consistency**—the extent to which this person reacts to this stimulus or event in the same way on other occasions. And third, we examine **distinctiveness**—the extent to which he or she reacts in the same manner to other, different stimuli or events. (Note: please do not confuse consistency and distinctiveness. Consistency refers to the extent to which an individual reacts similarly to the same stimulus or event at different times. Distinctiveness refers to the extent to which he or she reacts in a similar manner to different stimuli or events. If the individual reacts in the same way to a wide range of stimuli, distinctiveness is *low*.)

Kelley's theory suggests that we are most likely to attribute another's behavior to *internal* causes under conditions of low consensus, high consistency, and low distinctiveness. In contrast, we are most likely to attribute another's behavior to *external causes* under conditions of high consensus, high consistency, and high distinc-

tiveness. And we generally attribute another's behavior to a combination of these factors under conditions of low consensus, high consistency, and high distinctiveness (see Figure 2.8).

Perhaps the reasonable nature of these proposals can be best illustrated by means of a simple example. Imagine you are dining in a restaurant with some friends and one of them acts in the following manner: she takes one bite of her food and then shouts loudly for the waiter. When he appears, she claims that the dish is inedible and demands that it be replaced. Why has your friend acted in this manner—because of internal or external causes? In other words, is your friend a fussy eater, almost impossible to please, or is the dish so terrible that it deserves to be returned? According to Kelley's theory, your decision would depend on the three factors mentioned above. First, assume that the following conditions prevail: (1) no one else at your table complains (consensus is low); (2) you have seen your friend return this dish on other occasions (consistency is high); and (3) you have seen your friend complain loudly in other restaurants (distinctiveness is low). In this case, Kelley's theory indicates that you would probably attribute her behavior to internal causes. For example, you might conclude that your friend is a perfectionist, or just likes to complain.

In contrast, assume that the following conditions exist: (1) several other diners at your table also complain about the food (consensus is high); (2) you have seen your friend return the same dish on other occasions (consistency is high); and (3) you have *not* seen her complain in this manner in other restaurants (distinctiveness is high). Under these conditions, you would attribute her behavior to external causes (i.e., the food really *is* terrible).

As noted earlier, Kelley's theory is a reasonable one, and this fact becomes clear when it is applied to concrete social situations such as the one described above. Further, it has been confirmed by the findings of a large number of studies (e.g., Harvey and Weary, 1985; McArthur, 1972; Hansen and Hill, 1985). We should note, though, that research on this framework also suggests the need for certain modifications or additions. One of these is described next.

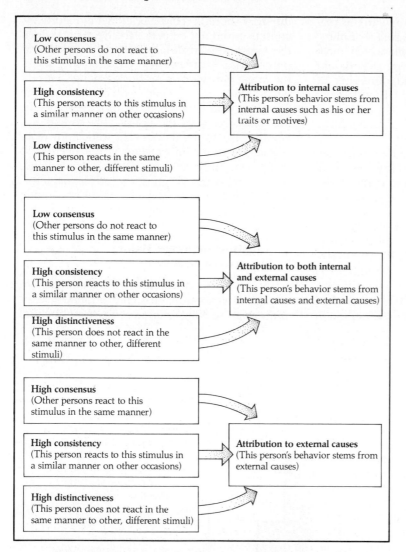

Figure 2.8 According to a theory proposed by Kelley (1972), we focus on information about three central factors when attempting to determine whether others' behavior stemmed from internal or external causes. These causes are *consensus*, *consistency*, and *distinctiveness*.

Kelley's theory of causal attribution: Its major predictions

Implicit Theories About the Relationships Between Dispositions and Behavior. In addition to the attributional rules described above, people also have implicit notions about the relationships between certain dispositions or traits and certain behaviors (Reeder and Brewer, 1979; Gilovich and Regan, 1986). One such belief is that "bad people are those who *sometimes* act bad, but good people almost always act good" (Reeder and Coovert, 1986). In a sense, good people are "restricted" to moral behaviors while

"bad people" can do both. This reasoning suggests that immoral acts will be more diagnostic or indicative of underlying character than will moral acts. The "diagnosticity" of bad versus good behavior may be an important consideration for how people go about making moral judgments. Because moral behavior is less diagnostic, perceivers may have to rely on other kinds of information in the judgment process. Consensus information—how common is the behavior in the population—may be especially useful in this regard. In accordance with this reasoning, McGraw (1987) hypothesized that information about the frequency with which most other people engage in a moral act should strongly affect how worthy and deserving of credit the source of a moral act will be judged; however, frequency of immoral acts should have little influence on judgments of blame or degree of punishment for an immoral act.

In a study to test these notions, McGraw (1987) devised a series of dilemmas involving moral or immoral acts. One of the immoral decisions concerned a man who cheated on an exam. One of the moral decisions was about a man who decided to return a wallet and money he had found. For each decision, some subjects received information about a low base rate (less than 25 percent of college students would do it) or a high base rate (75 percent would do it). After reading each scenario, subjects were asked to rate how much credit or blame the person in the story should receive. As shown in Figure 2.9, consensus did not influence the degree to which the target who made an immoral decision was perceived as blameworthy. On the other hand, the target was seen as more deserving of credit when few other people would perform the moral act than when many would. These results are consistent with the notion that certain acts (in this case immoral ones) are sufficiently diagnostic that other information is not needed to make a moral evaluation. On the other hand, moral acts are less diagnostic so additional information, such as how frequently it occurs among other people, tends to be utilized.

Attribution: Some Major Sources of Bias

So far in this discussion, we have seemed to imply that attribution is a highly rational process. Individuals seeking to unravel the causes behind

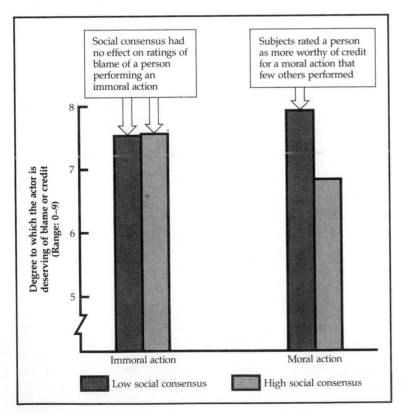

Figure 2.9 The degree to which someone is credited for a moral act is influenced by the extent to which other people also perform the behavior. In contrast, the evaluation of immoral acts is unaffected by social consensus. The reason for this is that immoral behavior is viewed as more diagnostic and informative about someone's character (or internal traits) than is moral behavior. (Source: Based on data from McGraw, 1987.)

Consensus information: More important for evaluating moral acts

others' behavior focus on certain key factors and then follow an orderly process en route to their conclusions. In general, this view is correct: attribution is logical in several respects. We should note, though, that it is subject to important types of bias—tendencies that can lead us into serious errors about the causes of behavior (or even our own). Several of these are summarized below.

The Fundamental Attribution Error: Overestimating the Role of Dispositional Causes. Suppose that during a visit to the park you witness the following scene: a young woman picks up a plate of potato salad and dumps it on the head of another woman sitting at the same picnic table. How would you explain this unusual behavior? Research evidence points to an intriguing answer: the chances are good that you would conclude (however tentatively) that the first woman has a violent temper—she is someone to avoid at all costs. This example illustrates what is often described as the **fundamental attribution error**: our tendency to explain others' actions in terms of dispositional rather than situational causes. Often, we seem to perceive others as acting as they do largely because they are "that kind of person"; the many situational factors that may have affected their behavior tend to be ignored, or at least downplayed. Thus, in the above example we tend to attribute the woman's actions to her temper, impulsiveness, or other traits; potential situational causes, such as strong provocation from the victim of her potato salad assault, are overlooked. (See the "Focus on Research" insert on pages 42–43 for discussion of a classic experimental demonstration of this bias.)

This tendency to overemphasize dispositional causes while underestimating the impact of situational ones appears to be quite strong. Indeed, it even seems to come into play in situations in which we know that others' actions were *not* under their own control. For example, if we read an essay written by a stranger, we tend to assume that it reflects this person's views, even if we are told that the author was instructed to write it in a particular way (Jones and Harris, 1967; Yandrell and Insko, 1977). One explanation of the fundamental attribution error is that when we observe another person's behavior, we tend to focus on his or her actions; the context in

which these actions occur often fades into the background. As a result, the potential influence of situational causes is not recognized. A second interpretation is that individuals do, in fact, notice situational factors but do not perceive them as being as important as they actually are (see Gilbert and Jones, 1986; Johnson, Jemmott, and Pettigrew, 1984; Ginzel, Jones, and Swann, 1987).

Whatever the precise basis for the fundamental attribution error, it has important implications. For example, it suggests that even if individuals are made aware of situational forces that adversely affect minorities and other disadvantaged groups (e.g., poor diet, broken family life), they may still perceive these persons as largely responsible for their own plight. Clearly, then, this attributional bias can have important social consequences.

The Actor-Observer Effect: You Tripped; I Was Pushed. A second and closely related type of attributional bias can be readily illustrated. Imagine that while walking along the street you see another person stumble and fall. How would you explain this behavior? Probably, in terms of the characteristics of the individual. For example, you may assume he is clumsy. But now suppose the same thing happens to you. Would you explain your own behavior in the same terms? Probably not. Instead, you may well assume that you tripped because of situational causes—uneven pavement, slippery heels on your shoes, and the like.

The tendency to attribute your own behavior to external or situational causes but that of others to internal ones is termed the **actor-observer effect** (Jones and Nisbett, 1971), and it has been demonstrated in many different studies (e.g., Eisen, 1979). It seems to stem, in part, from the fact that we are quite aware of the situational factors affecting our own behavior but less aware of these factors when we turn our attention to the actions of others. Thus, we tend to perceive our own behavior as stemming largely from situational causes but that of others as deriving more heavily from their dispositions (Fiske and Taylor, 1984).

While the actor-observer effect is both frequent and general, it can be eliminated under certain conditions. For example, if we *empathize*

THE FUNDAMENTAL ATTRIBUTION ERROR: SOCIAL ROLES AND BIASES IN SOCIAL PERCEPTION

Ross, Amabile, and Steinmetz (1977) provided a classic demonstration of the **fundamental attribution error**—the tendency to explain other people's behavior in terms of their dispositions rather than in terms of situational causes. It also showed how assigned social roles can confer advantages in social perception because observers give too little weight to the situation. Students at Stanford University were recruited for a study on how "people form impressions about general knowledge." The experimenter explained that one subject would be given the job of contestant and the other the job of questioner. The random and arbitrary nature of the role assignment was then made obvious by having them choose one of two cards ("Questioner" or "Contestant"). The subjects were then separated, and each questioner was asked to compose challenging general knowledge questions from any area in which he or she had a special interest or expertise. Then in a quiz-show-like format the quiz master asked the questions and the contestant subject tried to answer. On the average, contestants could only answer about four of the ten questions correctly. Considering the instructions given to the

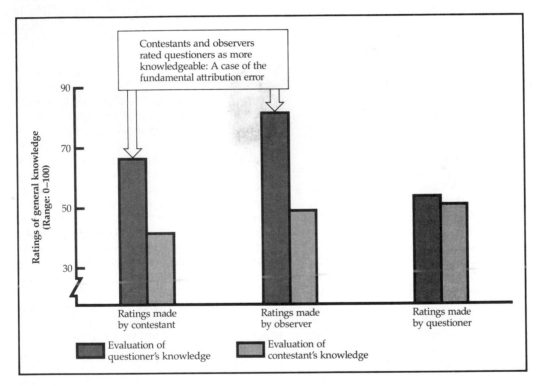

Figure 2.10   The fundamental attribution error: Contestants and noninvolved observers attributed greater knowledge to the questioners, even though they knew the role of questioner and contestant had been randomly assigned and that questioners were instructed to ask difficult questions based on their esoteric knowledge. This study indicates that people give too much weight to behavior and too little to situational constraints. (Source: Based on data from Ross, Amabile, and Steinmetz, 1977.)

Overestimating the role of dispositions and underestimating the role of the situation

questioners, it is no surprise that the questions tended to be difficult and reflected the questioners' esoteric knowledge. After the quiz, the experimenter asked both the questioners and the contestants to rate themselves and their partners in terms of their general level of knowledge compared to the average Stanford student. Despite the seemingly obvious nature of the questioners' self-presentation advantages, the questioners were rated as having more general knowledge than the contestants. As Figure 2.10 indicates, the contestants rated themselves far inferior to their questioners, and the questioners rated themselves as only slightly better than their contestants. It is also worth noting that subjects who watched a realistic reenactment of the same situation showed the same tendency to attribute more general knowledge to the arbitrarily assigned occupant of the questioner role.

It is clear that the contestants and the observers failed to make adequate allowance for the fact that had the role assignments been reversed, the contestants could just as easily have prepared questions that would have stumped their questioners and revealed their own knowledge to best advantage. Contestants and observers fell victim to the fundamental attribution error. Interestingly, the questioners did not see a wide gap in knowledge between themselves and the contestants. Why not? Unlike the contestants and observers who only had the ten questions to rely on, the questioners had a lifetime of experience to assess their own knowledge; moreover, they were aware of areas of their ignorance that they had passed over in searching for hard questions. As a result, the questioners were able to take the arbitrary role assignment into account. Given these results, it should be no surprise that your teachers seem smarter. They get to make up the questions.

with another person—try to see the world as he or she does—our attributions about his or her behavior become more situational in nature (Gould and Sigall, 1977). Similarly, if the situational causes behind others' behavior are made very clear, we may assign these more weight (Monson and Hesley, 1982). Finally, the actor-observer effect can also be overcome by yet another attributional bias, the self-serving bias, discussed next.

The Self-Serving Bias: Or the Tendency to Assume That We (Unlike Others) Can Do No Wrong. Suppose you write a report for your boss. After reading it, she provides you with glowing feedback—she's very pleased. To what will you attribute this success? The actor-observer effect seems to suggest that you will explain it in terms of situational factors (e.g., the task was easy, your boss is lenient, you had plenty of time to complete the report). But would this be the case? We doubt it. If you are like most persons, the chances are good that you will explain your success in terms of *internal* causes—your high level of intelligence, good judgment, and so on. Now, in contrast, imagine that your boss is unhappy with your report and criticizes it harshly. How will you explain *this* type of outcome? Here, the probability is high that you will focus mainly on situational factors—the difficulty of the task, your boss's unfairly high standards, and so on. In short, the actor-observer bias may well be overturned, in this context, by yet another attributional bias: our tendency to take credit for positive behaviors or outcomes but to blame external causes for negative ones (see Figure 2.11). This tendency is generally known as the **self-serving bias** (Miller and Ross, 1975), and its existence has been confirmed by the results of many experiments (e.g., Arkin, Gleason, and Johnston, 1976; O'Malley and Becker, 1984; Russell, McAuley, and Tarico, 1987; Baumgardner, Heppner, and Arkin, 1986).

The self-serving bias appears to stem from two different but related sources. First, this "tilt" in our attributions allows us to protect or enhance our self-esteem. After all, if we are responsible for positive outcomes but are not to blame for negative ones, our feelings about our own worth may be bolstered (Greenberg, Pyszcynski, and Solomon, 1982). As we will see, additional findings offer support for this possibility (see pages 45–46). Second, the self-serving bias permits us to improve our public image—to "look good" in the eyes of others (Bradley, 1978; Riess et al., 1981). Regardless of its precise origins, however, this common attributional error can be the cause of much interpersonal friction.

Figure 2.11   As suggested by this cartoon, most persons have a strong tendency to attribute favorable outcomes to internal causes (e.g., their own talent or effort), but unfavorable outcomes to external ones (e.g., unreasonable actions by others, forces beyond their control). (Source: Reprinted by permission: Tribune Media Services.)

The self-serving bias strikes again!

Consider what happens when two or more persons work together on a task. Because of the self-serving bias, each may perceive any success resulting from their joint efforts as stemming from his or her own contributions. In contrast, each may perceive failures as primarily the fault of others (Ross and Sicoly, 1979). Clearly, to the extent such reactions develop, the chance for future cooperation flies quickly out the window.

Applying What We Know: Practical Applications of Attribution Theory

In recent years, a growing understanding of this aspect of social perception has been followed, quite closely, by its application. The range of topics to which attribution principles have been applied is vast, but we will restrict ourselves to two of them: marriage and depression.

Marriage and Attributions. Knowledge of attribution has added to our understanding of the origins of serious marital difficulties (Holtzworth-Munroe and Jacobson, 1985). Couples experiencing such maladjustment are more likely than their better-adjusted counterparts to attribute negative actions by their partner to lasting

traits and characteristics rather than situational influences. Thus, they see little hope of change. The long-term effects of attributions made by marriage partners are illustrated in a study conducted by Fincham and Bradbury (1987). Thirty-four couples answered questions about marital satisfaction and made causal attributions for marital difficulties. The marital satisfaction of these couples was then reassessed 12 months later. Spouses who viewed their mates' negative behaviors as reflective of internal characteristics were more likely to be dissatisfied a year later than couples who attributed their spouses' negative behaviors to external causes. Such findings suggest that important benefits may result if couples can be induced to shift their perceptions of causes behind each other's behavior.

The Causes of Depression: An Attributional Perspective. Attribution theory has also been helpful in understanding the origins of psychological depression (see Figure 2.12). One major theory (Abramson, Seligman, and Teasdale, 1978) proposes that the predisposition to depression is associated with a **depressive attributional style.** According to the theory, when people encounter negative life events, the kinds of attributions they make about the causes of these events determine the onset and intensity of their depressive reactions. In particular, those who attribute negative events to *internal* (something about the self), *stable* (due to a factor that will persist over time), and *global* (due to factors that affect many situations) causes are more susceptible to serious depression (Brown and Siegel, 1988). The notion is that such an attributional style leads to expectations of helplessness and hopelessness about the future and anything they could do to change things.

Consistent with the theory, college students with a depressive attributional style who receive low midterm grades are more likely to become subsequently depressed than students who attribute negative outcomes to external, unstable, and specific causes (Metalsky, Halberstadt, and Abramson, 1987; Riskind et al., 1987). In related studies, patients hospitalized for depression are

Figure 2.12 *Depression may, in part, be the result of a particular attributional style.*

Depressive attributional style

more likely to exhibit this attributional style than patients in the hospital for surgery (Raps et al., 1982). And college students with a negative attributional style receive lower grades and take less initiative in their education as indicated by their making less use of academic advising and having less specific academic plans (Peterson and Barrett, 1987).

In considering the depressive attributional style, it is natural to assume that hopelessness is a highly distorted view of the world on the part of the depressives. But perhaps it is not the case that depressed people make unrealistically negative attributions, but that nondepressed normals make unrealistically positive attributions. Recall our discussion of the *self-serving bias:* in general, people attribute their successes to internal causes and their failures to external causes. Not surprisingly, depressives' attributions for successes and failures do not show a self-serving bias (Sweeney, Anderson, and Bailey, 1986). Of course, in order to assess the degree of distortion one must compare attributions against some standard of accuracy. Fortunately, such research has been done.

Alloy and Abramson (1979) programmed a computer to present subjects with a situation in which they had partial control. In one condition, whether a subject got a reward depended 75 percent on the subject's responses, but the other 25 percent was decided at random by the computer. Alloy and Abramson then asked subjects to estimate the contingency—that is, how much the outcome was due to their own efforts. Sure enough, depressed people were more likely than normals to say that failure had been a result of their own actions, consistent with the usual pattern. But it was the depressives who were closest to the true judgment (75 percent in that condition). Normal people underestimated their responsibility when the outcome was failure and overestimated their role in success. Depressives were pretty accurate and even-handed, regardless of success or failure.

Other evidence for a self-enhancing bias is the tendency for normals to overestimate the probability of their future successes and underestimate their probability of future failures relative to their peers. Depressed individuals do not show the same pattern (Alloy and Ahrens, 1987).

Thus, again, a common distortion in the way normal people process social information is reduced or absent in depressed people. Alloy, of course, is not saying that it is better to be depressed. In fact, there may be important advantages to using distorted ways of thinking. Taylor and Brown (1988) argue that the self-serving bias may actually contribute to feelings of happiness, confidence, and well-being. This may explain why the prevalence of esteem-enhancing biases appears to be more pronounced among persons with positive than negative self-attitudes. We will return to this topic in Chapter Three. In any case, the research by Alloy, Abramson, and others suggests that depressed people differ from normals in the kinds of attributions they make about life events and in the use of self-enhancing biases. Understanding the kinds of perceptions that predispose people to become depressed may help clinical psychologists to formulate therapies to re-train people regarding the kinds of attributions they make (Forsterling, 1985).

SELF-ATTRIBUTION:
Understanding Ourselves

So far in our discussion of attribution we have focused mainly on the manner in which we come to know and understand others. At this point, then, it makes sense to turn to a related question of equal importance: how do we come to know and understand *ourselves?* At first glance, you might assume that this is a simple task. After all, our own feelings, motives, and intentions are open to our direct observation; thus, it should be easy to obtain information about them by turning our attention inward (Carver, Antoni, and Scheier, 1985; Carver and Scheier, 1981). To a degree, this is true. But think again; there is at least one important complication in this process: we are often unaware of at least some of the factors that affect our own behavior (Nisbett and Ross, 1980). We may know that we acted in a given manner but are uncertain—or even wrong—about *why* we did so. Social psychologists have long been aware of this fact, but perhaps it has been stated most forcefully by Daryl Bem in an influential theory of **self-perception**.

Bem's Theory of Self-Perception: Behavior as a Source of Self-Knowledge

The central idea behind Bem's theory is this: often, we do not know our own attitudes, feelings, or emotions directly. Rather, we find it necessary to infer them from observations of our own behavior (Bem, 1972). If we have acted in some manner, we seem to reason, then we must hold an attitude or feeling consistent with such behavior. What we *do,* in short, serves as a useful guide to what is happening inside! Further, according to Bem, we draw inferences about ourselves in much the same manner as we do about other persons.

We should quickly add that Bem assumes that we use observations of our own behavior to infer our feelings or attitudes primarily in situations where internal cues concerning such matters are weak or ambiguous. For example, if we violently dislike another person, we generally don't have to infer such feelings from the fact that we usually avoid her company. Similarly, Bem suggests that we will use our behavior as a guide to our attitudes or emotions only in cases where these actions were freely chosen. If, instead, they were somehow forced upon us, we refrain from drawing such conclusions.

Although Bem's theory may strike you as being counterintuitive, it is supported both by informal observation and by research findings. To illustrate the former, try to recall incidents in your own life when you were surprised by your own actions. For example, have you ever been in a situation where, once you lost your temper, you found that you were angrier than you realized? In such cases we discover that we really don't know our own internal states as well as we think we do. And in such cases our overt actions often help us gain a more accurate picture of these hidden processes.

Turning to research findings, Bem's theory has been supported by the results of several different lines of work. For example, it has been found that when individuals perform some action consistent with an attitude they hold, they may then come to hold it even more strongly than they did before (Chaiken and Baldwin,

1981). Perhaps the most intriguing investigations deriving from Bem's theory, though, have been concerned with the topic of intrinsic motivation.

Self-Perception and Intrinsic Motivation: The Overjustification Effect. Individuals perform many activities simply because they find them enjoyable. Such activities may be described as stemming largely from **intrinsic motivation**. That is, the persons who perform them do so largely because of the pleasure they yield—not because of any hope of external rewards. But what would happen if individuals performing such behaviors were suddenly provided with extra payoffs for doing so? For example, what would happen if we were actually to pay someone for pursuing a favorite hobby? Bem's theory predicts that under at least some conditions, the persons involved would actually experience a *drop* in their intrinsic motivation. In short, they would be less motivated to engage in such activities than was the case before. The reasoning behind this prediction is as follows. Upon observing their own behavior, such "overrewarded" persons may conclude that they chose to engage in such activities partly to obtain the external rewards provided. To the extent they do, they may then perceive their own intrinsic interest as

lower than was previously the case. In short, such persons may shift from explaining their behavior in terms of intrinsic motivation ("I engage in this activity simply because I enjoy it") to accounting for their actions in terms of external rewards ("I engage in this activity partly to obtain some external reward"). In other words, such persons may have too many good reasons (the **overjustification effect**) for performing such behavior to continue to view it as intrinsically motivated (Hansen and Hill, 1985) (see Figure 2.13). Along these lines, consider the following statement by Reggie Jackson, a baseball player whose salary at the time was $975,000 a year: "A lot of it is the money, but I'd be playing if I was making $150,000" (*Newsweek,* 1986). Given the impact of external rewards on intrinsic motivation, our summary comment is: "We wonder!"

Support for the reasoning outlined above has been obtained in many experiments (e.g., Lepper and Greene, 1978; Deci and Ryan, 1987; Boggiano and Pittman, in press). In these and other studies, subjects provided with extrinsic rewards for engaging in some task they initially enjoyed later demonstrated lower quality performance and reduced tendencies to perform these activities voluntarily than did other subjects not given such rewards. Thus, it appeared that the intrinsic

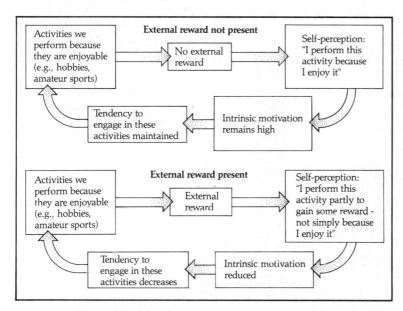

Figure 2.13 When individuals perform some activity they enjoy in the absence of external rewards, their intrinsic motivation to engage in this behavior is maintained (upper panel). When they receive extrinsic rewards for performing this activity, however, their perceptions about why they do so may change. As a result, their intrinsic motivation may be reduced (lower panel).

Self-perception: Its role in intrinsic motivation

interest of rewarded subjects in such tasks had in fact been reduced. Further, additional evidence suggests that such effects are most likely to occur under the conditions predicted by Bem's theory—when internal cues relating to the tasks at hand (e.g., attitudes toward them) are unclear or low in salience (Fazio, 1981).

Do all rewards produce the overjustification effect? Several researchers have suggested that if a reward provides information about one's competence (*performance contingency*), then actually intrinsic motivation may increase because one's feeling of competence and satisfaction may be enhanced. However, if the reward focuses on its controlling function ("you are doing it for the reward") (*task contingency*), then intrinsic motivation will decrease.

To test these hypotheses, Boggiano et al. (1985) had children complete a set of maze puzzles. Children in the condition designed to emphasize the controlling function of reward were told that if they simply worked on the

puzzles, they would receive five colorful stickers. In contrast, children in the condition designed to emphasize feedback about competence were told that they would be awarded up to five stickers depending on their success completing the puzzles. (There was also a control group who worked on the puzzles, received no rewards, and heard no mention of them.) When the children finished the puzzle series, and those in the reward groups received their stickers, the experimenter explained she would be going to another room to get things ready for a second game. The experimenter placed a stack of new mazes on the table and informed the children that while she was gone they could play with any of the different puzzles on the table, including ones like those they had just finished. The amount of time that the children spent working on the target activity (mazes) served as the measure of intrinsic motivation.

As shown in Figure 2.14, rewards providing information about task competence enhanced

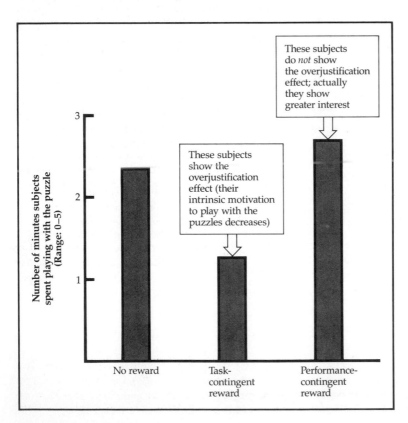

Figure 2.14 When rewards communicate information about competence ("performance-contingent"), intrinsic motivation may actually increase as compared to conditions in which no reward is received. In contrast, when rewards convey only their controlling function ("task-contingent"), we see the familiar overjustification effect: intrinsic motivation is reduced. (Source: Based on data from Boggiano et al., 1985.)

The hidden costs of certain kinds of rewards

intrinsic motivation. In contrast, children who received rewards that emphasized the controlling aspect of the reward (simply complete the mazes) showed less interest in the mazes than the control subjects. These results, along with others (Rosenfield, Folger, and Adelman, 1980; Sansone, 1986), show that when external rewards are offered as a sign of competence or effectiveness rather than as a bribe, intrinsic motivation can actually be enhanced.

Research on intrinsic motivation has obvious relevance to child rearing, and educational and work settings (Harackiewicz and Larson, 1986). For example, parents may not consider the hidden costs of certain kinds of rewards for tasks that are already held with high interest by their children. Recent research shows that parents *believe* that rewards given for simply engaging in the activity (task contingency) and feedback focusing on feelings of competence are equally effective in encouraging children's academic performance. In light of self-perception theory, however, parents who use the former type of rewards may unintentionally be undermining their children's interest in the activity (Boggiano et al., 1987).

In sum, several factors play a role in determining whether, and to what extent, external rewards will reduce or increase intrinsic motivation. Given the widespread use of such rewards in many different settings, careful attention to these factors seems justified. If they are ignored, costly rewards may reduce intrinsic motivation, and so may actually reduce the frequency of the behaviors they are designed to encourage. Clearly, this is an outcome few individuals, organizations, or societies can afford.

Self-Handicapping: When You Don't Want to Know About Yourself. According to Bem, attributions contribute to our understanding of our abilities, attitudes, and motivations. But people may not always want to know about themselves, especially if the knowledge might lead to negative conclusions about the self. Suppose a student has an important exam in an area relevant to his or her future career. The student wants to do well but is apprehensive about the outcome. If he or she fails after much preparation, the implication is clear: the student lacks the requisite ability. This possibility may be viewed with such apprehension that the person may purposely set up obstacles for success. For example, the student may go drinking or party the night before the big exam. If he or she then fails the exam, a ready excuse or *external attribution* for the failure is available: the person was too tired or not sufficiently prepared. Setting up obstacles to blame future failures on external causes (as opposed to internal causes such as ability or intelligence) is called **self-handicapping strategy**.

There have been several experimental demonstrations of the self-handicapping strategy. For example, in one laboratory experiment, subjects chose to take a drug that was described as impairing performance when they felt uncertain about how well they would perform on an upcoming performance task (Berglas and Jones, 1978). This is quite reminiscent of some students who walk into the exam saying that they're sure they'll perform poorly because they got too little sleep the night before. Notice that this strategy can serve two purposes: it protects one's own self-esteem, and it also provides an excuse to others if you perform poorly (Snyder, Higgins, and Stucky, 1983; Mehlman and Snyder, 1985).

Although the self-handicapping strategy may have some short-term benefits, as a long-term strategy it can be quite harmful. People who set up obstacles to avoid learning about their true abilities may fall back on this strategy whenever an important test of their capability arises. In fact, Jones and Berglas (1978) propose that some individuals may use alcohol as a self-handicapping strategy because it provides an external cause or excuse for performing poorly. Dependence on alcohol in this way could lead to its chronic use and to alcoholism. It should be clear that the self-handicapping strategy if used frequently could create serious problems. Thus, "users beware!"

SUMMARY

The process through which we attempt to understand the persons around us is known as **social perception**. In order to gather information on the temporary causes of others' behavior, we often focus on **nonverbal cues** provided by their facial expressions, eye contact, body posture, or movements and touching. Such cues communicate others' moods or feelings. However, when people are trying to deceive us, our detection accuracy decreases. Even people whose jobs involve detecting deception, such as law enforcement officers, have difficulty interpreting verbal and nonverbal deception attempts.

Knowledge about the more lasting causes of others' behavior is gained through the process of **attribution**. In this key aspect of social perception, we attempt to infer others' traits, motives, and intentions from observation of their overt actions. In order to determine whether others' behavior stems mainly from internal or external causes, we focus on information relating to three factors: **consensus, consistency,** and **distinctiveness.** Whether we use consensus information may be influenced by the kind of action we are evaluating. People rely less on consensus information when evaluating the blameworthiness of immoral acts than when deciding about the amount of credit to be given for a moral action. Attribution is far from a totally rational process. In fact, it is subject to a number of biases, such as the **fundamental attribution error**, the **actor-observer effect**, and the **self-serving bias**.

The task of understanding the causes of our own behavior is more difficult than might be suspected. According to Bem's theory of **self-perception**, we often infer our attitudes or emotions from our overt actions. This theory helps explain why providing individuals with external rewards for engaging in activities they enjoy often reduces their motivation to participate in these activities. The **overjustification effect** tends to occur most strongly when the external rewards are seen as *controlling.* In contrast, when rewards emphasize *performance competence,* intrinsic motivation may actually increase.

GLOSSARY

actor-observer effect Refers to our tendency to attribute our own behavior largely to situational causes, but the behavior of others to internal (dispositional) causes.

attribution The process through which we seek to determine the causes of others' behavior and gain knowledge of their stable traits and dispositions.

body language Cues provided by the position, posture, and movement of others' bodies or body parts.

consensus The extent to which actions shown by one person are also shown by others.

consistency The extent to which an individual responds to a given stimulus or situation in the same way on different occasions (i.e., across time).

correspondent inferences Inferences concerning the stable traits of others about which we have a high degree of confidence.

depressive attributional style Refers to the tendency to attribute the causes of negative events to internal (something about the self), stable (something that persists over time), and global (something that affects many situations) causes. This tendency is found among people who are predisposed to becoming depressed.

distinctiveness The extent to which an individual responds in a similar manner to different stimuli or different situations.

fundamental attribution error Our tendency to overestimate the impact of dispositional causes to others' behavior.

intrinsic motivation Motivation to perform various activities simply because they are enjoyable in themselves.

nonverbal communication Communication between individuals that does not involve the content of spoken language. It relies, instead, on a "silent language" of facial expressions, eye contact, body language, and touching.

overjustification effect Reductions in intrinsic motivation that are produced by external rewards.

self-handicapping strategy The tendency to set up obstacles to blame future failures on external causes (as opposed to internal causes such as ability or intelligence).

self-perception The process through which we seek to understand our own feelings, traits, and motives. We must often infer these from observation of our overt behavior.

self-serving bias Our tendency to view positive outcomes as stemming from internal causes (e.g., our own effort or ability) but negative outcomes as stemming largely from external factors.

social perception The process through which we seek to know and understand the persons around us.

staring Eye contact in which one person continues to gaze at another for an extended period of time regardless of what the recipient of such treatment does.

FOR MORE INFORMATION

BUCK, R. (1984). *The communication of emotion.* New York: Guilford.

　　While this excellent book considers emotion and the communication of emotion generally, it contains a wealth of valuable information about nonverbal aspects of this process. In particular, the chapter on the role of nonverbal communication in social interaction is both thought-provoking and intriguing. This is a good source to consult if you want to know more about many aspects of nonverbal communication.

HARVEY, J. H., and WEARY, G. (Eds.) (1985). *Attribution: Basic issues and applications.* San Diego: Academic Press.

　　This collection of chapters by active researchers covers the major theories, recent research, and several applications of attribution processes.

ROSS, M., and FLETCHER, G. J. O. (1985). Attribution and social perception. In G. Lindzey and E. Aronson (Eds.), *Handbook of social psychology.* New York: Random House.

　　A comprehensive, thorough discussion of many aspects of social perception by two experts in this general area. While the book is primarily intended for a professional audience, it is clearly written and contains much fascinating information.

Chapter Three
Social Cognition: Understanding the Social World

MENTAL SHORTCUTS/Heuristics, Biases, and Fallacies
Some Major Cognitive Strategies: Shortcuts to Understanding the Social
World/Exceptions to Fallacies and Biases/Affect and Cognition: How Thoughts
Shape Feelings and Feelings Shape Thoughts

SCHEMATA AND THEIR EFFECTS
Types of Schemata/How Schemata Guide Information Processing

SELF-AWARENESS/The Effects of Looking Inward
Application of Self-Awareness: Alcohol Use/Application of Self-Awareness:
Group Composition and Matching to Standards

Special Inserts
ON THE APPLIED SIDE
    Social Cognition and Illness: Being Ill Isn't Just Physical
FOCUS ON RESEARCH/Classic Contributions
    The Importance of First Impressions: Early Research on Social Cognition

"So what do you think of her?" Neil Schmitt asks his friend Herb Dorizio, with a self-satisfied grin on his face.

"Not much," Herb replies. "In fact, do me a favor: next time you think of fixing me up with a blind date like that, don't."

"What!" Neil exclaims in genuine shock. "You didn't like her? Why not? Julie's one of Sue's nicest friends."

"Well, for one thing, she was just like what I expected: a spoiled little rich girl. Nothing's too much for her: the world owes her a living. You know what I mean. Man, for me, that's a real turnoff."

"Are you for real?" Neil asks angrily. "She's *nothing*, I mean *nothing* like that! I've known her for years, and she's one of the most down-to-earth women around."

Now it's Herb's turn to look annoyed. "Are we talking about the same person? The one *I* went out with is a loser with a capital L. Looks down her nose at everything. A real snob, just like all the other people at that fancy school she goes to."

"Wait a second," Neil interrupts. "You're really starting to get to me. You mean you hold it against her because her parents have money and she goes to an expensive school? Why don't you blame her for being short, blonde, and cute, too, while you're at it."

"I don't care what you say," Herb answers angrily. "She's a brainless little twit. Hopeless, with nothing upstairs."

"You know what I think?" Neil answers sarcastically. "First, you're nuts. Second, you've got some crazy ideas about people: they aren't 'all the same' just because they go to the same school, or their parents have money. And third, you must have been in a real bad mood Friday night. I can't think of any other reason why you wouldn't like someone as sweet as Julie."

"You're entitled to your own opinions," Herb answers. "But I'm not going to stand here and debate them with you. I've got better things to do. Anyway, in my book, she's a loser, and if you think she's so hot, you must have some problems, too." And with this remark, he storms off leaving Neil alone to fume over the ingratitude of friends and the futility of fixing people up with blind dates.

How do people make judgments about others? As suggested by the example above, this task is more complex than it might at first seem. Even when we don't know someone well, we have a lot of information about them at our disposal. We know how they look, what they've said at various times, and how they've acted in different situations. Somehow, we must boil this information down into a few essential impressions and base our judgments on these. As the individuals in the above story discovered, though, different persons often interpret "facts" about others in contrasting ways, or combine them in unique ways, with the result that they reach sharply different conclusions.

In recent years, social psychologists have directed increasing attention to this issue—to the ways people sort and store information about others and then make judgments about them on the basis of such input. The study of these processes is part of the new field of **social cognition**. Social cognition evolved out of research on *attributions* which, as we saw in Chapter Two, provide important insights into the ways in which people interpret social life. Social cognition also borrowed some methods and ideas from cognitive psychology and applied them to the problems of social psychology. In general, social cognition is the study of how people interpret, analyze, remember, and use information about the social world.

One essential fact that influences many aspects of social cognition is **information overload**. Stop for a moment and think about the last time you went out with friends, or took an exam, or ate lunch in a public place. How many thousands of stimuli confronted you—all sights and sensations, all the words spoken by everyone present, and all the possible implications of everything that happened? Multiply that by a lifetime's worth of such experiences, and it becomes obvious that the normal human mind could not possibly notice—let alone analyze and use—every bit of social information we encounter. And, in fact, adults' minds are marvelously efficient at screening, sorting, and storing social information. But this efficiency sometimes means being less than fully logical, thorough, or accurate. To put it simply, the human mind uses numerous shortcuts to handle the immense amount

Calvin and Hobbes   by Bill Watterson

Figure 3.1   There is a tendency for people to be "cognitive misers"—that is, for them to think as little as necessary. (Source: Calvin & Hobbes. Copyright 1987 Universal Press Syndicate. Reprinted with permission. All rights reserved.)

Thinking as little as necessary

of information that confronts it every day. A large part of social cognition is the study of those shortcuts.

The use of shortcuts is so pervasive and so necessary that many social psychologists think the human mind is always looking for the easiest way to understand the events of social life. This view portrays the individual as a "cognitive miser" (Fiske and Taylor, 1984), which means that as a general rule people actually think as little as necessary, and that once they have a certain belief or idea they are reluctant to give it up (see Figure 3.1).

Another basic fact of social cognition is that people are often unaware of their own mental processes. Nisbett and Wilson (1977) argued that people are generally unable to report the true reasons for their behavior, and that when people do explain their behavior, their explanations are often wrong and no better than those provided by an observer. People's explanations may be incorrect because several things may be affecting one's behavior at the same time, making it difficult to pinpoint which are most influential. Furthermore, in many cases, people are not really aware of the process of thinking so much as the results. This means that in many cases people may be no more accurate in explaining their behavior than are observers.

Of course, Nisbett and Wilson's argument does not mean that people never understand their own actions at all. For example, an individual may have privileged access to "idiosyncratic theories"—that is, beliefs about cause-effect relationships which he or she has acquired or developed through personal experience, which may not be shared by members of the culture at large (Wilson and Stone, 1985; Gavanski and Hoffman, 1986; White, 1987).

In addition to the question of whether people can accurately report the causes of their behavior, another issue, too, arises: do people know *what* they are doing? This may seem like a strange question to ask. "Of course," you say, "people know what they are doing. At the moment, I'm reading a textbook." But Vallacher and Wegner (1987) point out that any behavior can potentially be described on many different levels. Are you "reading a paragraph in a psychology text"? "Learning about some new theory"? Or "looking at lines of print," "studying," "learning social psychology," "moving my eyes" or "getting an education"? All of these may be valid at the same time. Thus, the question is *not* whether people know what they are doing, but rather *how* and *in what* way people know what they are doing. **Action identification** is the process of labeling and interpreting one's behaviors.

Vallacher and Wegner have demonstrated that the way people identify their actions depends greatly on their motives and circumstances. For example, criminals tend to think about their activities in terms of mechanical, low-level details. A burglary is considered "climbing the fence" or "finding the money"—a way of allowing the perpetrators to avoid thinking about the unpleasant implications of their actions. Law-abiding citizens think about the same behaviors in more general or abstract terms: "violating the property of another human being," "being dishonest."

The fact that people's action identifications differ depending on their motives and circumstances and that people may be highly inaccurate regarding their self-reports about their mental processes have important implications for social cognition research: complex, detailed experimental studies are required to learn about how the mind makes sense of the social world.

MENTAL SHORTCUTS: Heuristics, Biases, and Fallacies

Now let's begin looking at some of the shortcuts the mind uses to reduce information overload and make sense of human social life. These shortcuts, also called **cognitive strategies**, need to have two features for people to use them. First, they must provide a quick and simple way of dealing with social information. Second, they must be reasonably accurate most of the time. If a cognitive strategy always leads us to make wrong decisions, we will probably switch to a different strategy sooner or later. Often these cognitive strategies represent a trade-off between these two features—accuracy (or reliability) and speed (or simplicity).

First, a word about terminology. Social cognition researchers often label phenomena they study as heuristics, biases, and fallacies. **Heuristics** are decision-making principles used to make inferences or to draw conclusions quickly and easily. **Fallacies** and **biases** refer to the errors and distortions that crop up in the ways people use social information and think. The terms are related, for using heuristics often involves fallacies and biases.

Some Major Cognitive Strategies: Shortcuts to Understanding the Social World

In our efforts to make sense out of the social world around us, we make use of many different shortcuts and strategies. We will describe several of the most important of these.

Representativeness Heuristic: Judging by Resemblance. The **representativeness heuristic** means making a judgment or inference based on resemblance to typical cases (Tversky and Kahneman, 1982). Imagine that you have just met your next-door neighbor for the first time. On the basis of a brief conversation with her, you ascertain that she is exceptionally neat, has a good vocabulary, reads many books, is shy, and dresses conservatively. During the conversation, though, she never got around to mentioning her occupation. Is she a business executive, a librarian, a waitress, an attorney, or a dancer? One quick way of making a guess would be to compare her traits with the typical traits that go with each of these occupations. In other words, you might simply ask yourself how well she resembles the typical or average executive, librarian, waitress, attorney, or dancer. If you proceeded in this fashion (and concluded that she was probably a librarian), you would be using the *representativeness heuristic*. This heuristic allows one to make a "best guess" based on resemblance to typical patterns or general types, but of course it is far from infallible. It might turn out that your neighbor was a dancer after all.

When people have to make judgments or inferences about the probable nature of some person or event, they tend to rely on the representativeness heuristic more than on some other kinds of information. One possible alternative way to make such judgments would be to rely on how *common* each option is in the general population. In America today there are many more lawyers than librarians, so another way to guess your neighbor's occupation would be to pick the most common occupation. In this case, you would be relying on *base-rate information*—that is, information about how common some pattern is in the general population. In practice, though, it turns out that people rarely use base-rate information in making decisions.

This common failure to make use of information about the patterns and probabilities in the general population is called the **base-rate fallacy**. (You may recall the related tendency in attribution: consensus information was not used in evaluating an immoral behavior; see Chapter Two, pages 39–40.)

A famous experiment by Tversky and Kahneman (1973) pitted representative information against base-rate information. Subjects learned that an imaginary person named Jack had been selected from a group of 100 men, and subjects had to guess the probability that Jack was an engineer. Some subjects were told that 30 of the 100 men were engineers (thus, the base rate of engineers was 30 percent), while others were told that 70 of them were engineers. Half the subjects were given no further information other than these base rates, but other subjects received a personal description of Jack. The researchers found that subjects did use the base rates (30 percent or 70 percent) when they had no other information. But if they had any other information to work with, they ignored the base rates. They gave estimates based only on whether Jack resembled their stereotype of an engineer. People apparently prefer to use representativeness information instead of base-rate information.

An important application of the base-rate fallacy concerns the impact of the mass media on individuals' personal fear of being victims of crime or accidents. It is well known that fears of victimization are often grossly out of line with the actual base rates of various crimes and accidents. For example, people tend to express great concern and fear about murder and AIDS; but, in reality, car crashes and emphysema are far more common causes of death. Tyler and Cook (1984) gave groups of experimental subjects articles from the mass media to read, such as "Drunk Driving: A License to Kill" and "A Shooting Gallery Called America." These articles were chosen because they dramatized the dangers of death or injury caused by drunk drivers and firearms, respectively. Sure enough, reading these articles made subjects more likely to see drunk drivers and guns as serious national problems. Yet personal worries about these risks were unaffected by reading these articles. Thus, once again, people appear to separate judgments about particular events (in this case, their own lives) from base-rate information about national trends and patterns (Perloff and Fetzer, 1986).

Availability Heuristic: What Comes to Mind First? Which is more common—words that start with the letter *k* (e.g., king) or words that have *k* as the third letter (e.g., awkward)? Tversky and Kahneman (1982) put this question to over 100 people in a demonstration of the **availability heuristic**, which means making judgments based on how easily instances come to mind. In English there are more than twice as many words having *k* for the third letter as words starting with *k*, but most people wrongly judge that *k* is more commonly the first letter. The reason, presumably, is that it is easy to think of words starting with *k* but harder to think of words having *k* in the third position.

Judging the frequency of words may not be a crucial part of social life, but the availability heuristic probably guides many important judgments, too. When a professor assigns grades for class participation, she may rely on how easily she can remember each student's making a comment in class. A boss who is evaluating an employee's reliability may be guided by how easy it is to remember the employee's missing a deadline. In 1987 a series of highly publicized airplane crashes made many citizens afraid to fly (see Figure 3.2). Note the base-rate fallacy involved in the airplane example: millions of people fly innumerable miles all over the world, and the base rate of accidents per miles traveled shows flying to be one of the safest modes of travel. But many people ignore these statistics and become reluctant to fly because the reports of plane crashes are so readily available in memory.

False Consensus Effect: Thinking That Others Think as We Do. Several other patterns in social cognition are related to the availability heuristic. One is the **false consensus effect**, which denotes an individual's tendency to overestimate how many other people would make the same judgments and choices and would hold the same attitudes as the individual (Ross, Greene, and House, 1977; Mullen et al., 1985; see Figure 3.3). For example, high school boys who

Figure 3.2 Highly publicized airplane crashes may make possible accidents more available in memory and hence frighten many citizens.

Mass media exposure can make certain events more available.

Figure 3.3 People tend to overestimate the degree to which others share their opinions—the false consensus effect. (Source: Drawing by Saxon; © 1986 The New Yorker Magazine, Inc.)

False consensus effect

"That's just our opinion, but I believe the public feels the same way."

smoke estimated that 51 percent of their fellow male students smoke, but nonsmoking boys estimated that only 38 percent smoke (Sherman et al., 1983). College students who sometimes think about dying estimate that 63 percent of other students think about death too, whereas students who themselves rarely think about death estimate that only 33 percent of other students think about death (Sanders and Mullen, 1983). Similarly, students tend to overestimate the proportion of other students who agree with their attitudes about drugs, abortion, seat belt use, university policies, the President's record, hamburgers, Brooke Shields, and Ritz crackers (Nisbett and Kunda, 1985; Suls, Wan, and Sanders, 1988). The false consensus effect is thus very common and broad, although it is not large. A student's estimate of the average opinion of other students will often be surprisingly accurate, although slightly distorted toward his or her own opinion (see Figure 3.4).

Why does the false consensus effect occur? There are two reasons. The *self-enhancing motivational explanation* is that people want to believe others agree with them or are in the "same boat" because that makes them feel their own actions, judgments, or circumstances are normal, correct, and appropriate (e.g., Sherman, Presson, and Chassin, 1984; Marks and Miller, 1987). A second view, the *perceptual distortion* explanation, is based on the availability heuristic. It may be easier to notice and recall examples of people

agreeing with you than people disagreeing with you. Indeed, to the extent that groups of friends have the same attitudes and preferences, each person is mostly exposed to people who agree with him or her. That alone could make agreement with your own attitudes and choices more available than disagreement, producing a false consensus effect.

The false consensus effect is common, but not universal. Sometimes the self-enhancing motivation may be stronger than the availability heuristic and lead to perceptions of uniqueness. When it comes to attitudes or undesirable attributes, people should want to perceive that there are many others like themselves. However, for highly desirable attributes, people may be motivated to perceive themselves as unique (Marks, 1984; Goethals, 1986b; Suls and Wan, 1987). Consistent with this reasoning, Campbell (1986) found that people overestimate the number of others who share their opinions and negative attributes, but underestimate the number of people who share their desirable attributes.

Illusory Correlation: Seeing Patterns That Aren't There. **Illusory correlation** refers to perceiving relationships that aren't really there, because your expectations distort the way you process information. Two clinical psychologists, Chapman and Chapman (1982), were the first to study illusory correlation. For some years a test called the *Draw-a-Person Test* was used to diag-

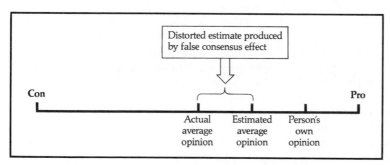

Figure 3.4 When estimating the average opinion of others, most people give an estimate that is fairly accurate but slightly distorted, being closer to their own views than is actually the case. This is the *false consensus effect.*

The false consensus effect: Its basic nature

nose mental illness. A patient would be asked to draw a human figure, and the therapist would interpret the meaning of the various features. A drawing with large eyes, for example, was taken as a sign of paranoia, or suspiciousness. A drawing of a figure with elaborate genitalia might be taken as indicative of some serious sexual delusions. Chapman and Chapman thought these supposed signs of mental illness were not valid. For example, the eyes of the figure drawn by paranoid schizophrenics were no different from the eyes of figures drawn by a normal group of student nurses. However, because clinicians tended to believe that insane persons would draw strange figures, they tended to process information in a biased fashion.

To demonstrate this point and the influence of illusory correlation, Chapman and Chapman prepared a stack of test results, randomly pairing drawings of various features (e.g., large eyes, elaborate genitals) with various symptoms of mental illness. They made sure the pairings were completely random—for example, the symptom "suspiciousness of others" was no more likely than any other symptom to be paired with drawing large eyes. Then they asked expert clinical psychologists and students in introductory psychology to go through the stacks. Though the pairs were random, most subjects who looked through the stack of test results concluded that suspiciousness had been mainly paired with large eyes. In short, their expectations led them to "see" a pattern that wasn't actually there. The Chapmans even tried preparing the stack of drawings with the opposite pattern—suspiciousness was thus less likely than other symptoms to be paired with large eyes—but people still thought they saw large eyes and suspiciousness together most often. The illusory correlation was very difficult to break.

Why do people succumb to illusory correlations? One reason has to do with what is sometimes called the **confirmation bias**: people tend to seek out, notice, and recall things that support their beliefs more than things that disconfirm their beliefs. Our later discussion of the effects of *schemata* on pages 71–73 will help to clarify the processes that contribute to the confirmation bias.

Priming: Increasing Availability. During the first year of medical school, many students experience the "medical student syndrome." They begin to suspect themselves (and their families and friends) of having various serious illnesses. An ordinary headache, for example, may cause the medical student to worry about a possible brain tumor. The medical student syndrome occurs presumably because the readings and lectures about various diseases plant the idea of those diseases in students' minds, so when a minor symptom occurs, the students' first thoughts are guided by the high availability of the disease categories. This is an example of **priming**, which is perhaps the most direct application of the availability heuristic (Gabrielcik and Fazio, 1983). Priming means exposing the person to certain ideas or categories in order to increase their availability in memory. In simpler terms, priming means planting certain ideas or categories in people's minds, causing them to use such ideas or categories to interpret subsequent events. (For example, after watching a movie or television show in which key characters act in an extremely competitive manner, we may be more likely to notice signs of competitiveness on the part of the persons with whom we subsequently interact [see Figure 3.5].)

Priming was first applied in social psychology by Higgins, Rholes, and Jones (1977). They planted various traits in subjects' minds by having them do a cognitive task that required them to memorize various trait names (e.g., adventurous, reckless, independent). Later, in what they thought was a completely separate experiment, subjects were asked to form an impression of an imaginary person named Donald based on descriptions that portrayed him climbing mountains and crossing the Atlantic in a sailboat. Subjects' impressions of Donald were shaped by the trait names they had memorized during the cognitive task. That task had made those traits highly available in the subjects' minds, so, when reading about Donald, they naturally interpreted his behavior in those terms. Moreover, their general impression of Donald was favorable if they had been primed with good traits, such as "adventurous," but it was unfavorable if they had been primed with bad traits, such as "reckless." The

Figure 3.5 *Priming may increase availability of certain thoughts or interpretations and, as a result, influence our judgments. (Source: Reprinted with special permission of King Features Syndicate.)*

Priming of sexual intent?

same information about Donald, in other words, led to quite different impressions, depending on what the subject had been thinking about earlier.

The direct effects of priming gradually wear off. Priming is more likely to influence judgments made the same day that the priming occurred than on the next day (Srull and Wyer, 1979). The indirect effects of priming may persist indefinitely. In a recent experiment, Herr (1986) primed subjects for the trait "hostile" so they would perceive their competitor in a subsequent game as more hostile and competitive than subjects primed for "nonhostile." Not only were the subjects' perceptions of their opponent different across the two conditions, but subjects primed for "hostility" made more initial moves that were competitive toward their opponents, which not too surprisingly were then reciprocated by their opponent. Thus, the subjects' "primed" expectation about the opponent led them to act in a way that produced the expected outcome. Hence, we see that priming may influence people's beliefs and subsequent behavior and produce a kind of "self-fulfilling prophecy."

Theory Perseverance: When Conclusions Outlast Their Evidence. We have seen that ideas planted in people's minds can affect their subsequent thinking. What happens if a false idea is planted in someone's mind and the person later learns that it was false? The answer is that, sadly,

the effects of that false idea may hang on. People seem to cling to their conclusions even after the supporting evidence is discredited. The durability of false beliefs has been studied under the label of **theory perseverance** (Anderson and Sechler, 1986; Ross, Lepper, and Hubbard, 1975; Slusher and Anderson, in press).

Theory perseverance was demonstrated in a well-known experiment by Anderson, Lepper, and Ross (1980). They gave half their subjects stories to read which led them to think that people who like to take risks make the best fire fighters. Their other subjects read stories suggesting the opposite—that the best fire fighters are by nature cautious people. Subjects then thought up reasons why effective fire fighting ability should be associated with the trait of riskiness or cautiousness. Anderson then informed subjects that the stories they had seen were completely untrue. Did they abandon their theories linking riskiness or caution to being a good fire fighter? Hardly! People continued to believe their theories about what made a good fire fighter, even when the basis for their theories had been destroyed. This is the cognitive miser in action—once the mind has a definite idea, it is reluctant to give it up.

Availability is one of the main reasons for theory perseverance. Thinking up reasons for a certain pattern, such as the pattern of risk-taking fire fighters being more successful, makes those reasons very available in memory. Even if you learn that the pattern is not true (fire fighters aren't necessarily risk takers), your explanation is still there in memory and may crop up in the future.

Availability isn't the only cause of theory perseverance, although it is an important one (Anderson, New, and Speer, 1985; Anderson and Sechler, 1986). Another reason is that once people have a theory, they may look for more information to support their theory. Thus, they process other information in a biased way, causing them to think their theory is generally true (Lord, Ross, and Lepper, 1979). The confirmation bias (described earlier under "illusory correlation") could produce that effect. The end result is a kind of vicious circle. A little bit of initial evidence makes someone form a general belief, which causes the person to see other evidence in a distorted fashion, which strengthens the belief. Even if the initial evidence is discredited, the person still thinks there is plenty of other evidence for the belief. Thus, once the mind draws a conclusion, it tends to disregard the basis for it. The conclusion can outlast the evidence on which it is based.

Self-Serving Theory Maintenance. People also construct theories for themselves in a self-serving manner: that is, they maintain optimistic beliefs about themselves by formulating views in which their own attributes are more likely than other attributes to facilitate desired outcomes and to hinder feared ones. When confronted with information that threatens these theories, they should be reluctant to accept it to maintain the belief that good things will happen to them and bad things will not.

To examine whether people are less likely to believe evidence linking an attribute to a negative outcome if they possess this dangerous attribute, Kunda (1987) performed several experiments. In one study, college students read an article supposedly taken from the *New York Times* about the negative effects of caffeine consumption on health. The article claimed, based on medical studies, that women who were heavy caffeine drinkers (more than three cups a day) were at serious risk of developing fibrocystic disease, which was associated in its later stages with

breast cancer. The sample of subjects was made up of males and females, some of whom were heavy caffeine consumers. The caffeine disease association in the article was deliberately made specific to women to examine the effects of self-serving bias. Male and female caffeine drinkers should hold the same prior beliefs about caffeine, but women should be more motivated to reject the evidence presented in the article because only they should be personally threatened by it.

After reading the article, subjects were asked a series of questions, including how convinced they were of the connection between caffeine and fibrocystic disease. As Figure 3.6 shows, female heavy consumers of caffeine were not as convinced as were low female consumers. Men, who should not have been threatened by the article, showed the same degree of confidence in the article regardless of whether they were a heavy caffeine user or not. This study suggests that people resist acceptance of theories and evidence that suggest they have attributes or behave in ways that might bring about negative outcomes. Thus, here, we have an example of another way in which social cognition is used to maintain positive feelings about oneself.

Counterfactual Thinking. Suppose you read an article in the newspaper about a man who was severely injured in an automobile accident while taking his usual route to work. Now, how would you react if you learned instead that the man was in a serious accident on the way to work, but he had taken a different route for a "change of pace." Evaluation of the latter incident evokes an "if only" response; that is, **counterfactual thinking**—what would have happened *if.* People respond to these incidents by thinking, "if only the man had taken his usual route, he would not have been hurt." Kahneman and Miller (1986) argue that it is easier to imagine alternatives to abnormal or unusual actions than to normal or routine actions. Furthermore, stronger reactions to an event are produced when observers can readily conceive of an alternative. Specifically, the prediction is that negative outcomes that follow abnormal actions will generate more sympathy than ones that follow normal actions.

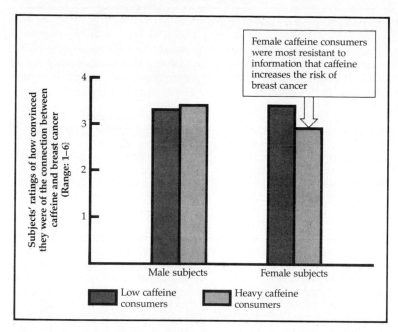

Female caffeine consumers were most resistant to information that caffeine increases the risk of breast cancer

Figure 3.6 People are reluctant to believe in theories relating their own attributes to undesirable attributes. Findings reported by Kunda (1987) indicated that female caffeine drinkers who read that caffeine is linked to a disorder that may lead to breast cancer were less convinced by the report than male caffeine drinkers or noncaffeine drinkers. (Source: Based on data from Kunda, 1987.)

People resist information linking their own attributes to feared outcomes.

In a study designed to test this suggestion, Miller and McFarland (1986) asked subjects to read a description of a victim to help decide how much monetary compensation he should receive. All subjects read about a male victim who lost the use of his right arm as the result of a gunshot wound. He had been shot when he walked in on a robbery occurring in a convenience store in his neighborhood. One group of subjects (normal condition) learned that on the night he was shot, the victim had gone to the store he most commonly frequented. Another group of subjects learned that on the night he was shot the victim had gone to the store he rarely frequented for a "change of pace." After reading the descriptions, all subjects were asked to indicate how much the victim should receive in compensation (from zero dollars to one million dollars). Subjects perceived the victim who was shot at a store he rarely visited as more deserving of compensation. Apparently, when events evoke an "only if reaction"—that is, that it almost did not happen—this makes a person's fate seem worse and sympathy for the victim greater.

Counterfactual thinking rests largely on the availability heuristic. The degree to which sub-jects can imagine "what might have been" is based on how available alternative outcomes are for them to conceive. Counterfactual thinking may be very important in understanding emotional reactions. For example, "Grief over the loss of a loved one might be especially profound when one of the events in the scenario could easily have been different in a way that would not have resulted in the loss" (Wells, Taylor, and Turtle, 1987, p. 429). Hence, we see that the ease with which people can use counterfactual thinking may have important consequences for the evaluation of victims and one's own behavior.

Exceptions to Fallacies and Biases

In our discussion of mental shortcuts, we have seen that people typically overuse some kinds of information and underuse other kinds. (See the "On the Applied Side" insert on pages 64–65 for a discussion of how these shortcuts may even influence the way people think about their physical health.) Can these fallacies be overcome? Some evidence suggests that they can (Bar-Tal and Kruglanski, 1988). For example, Tetlock and Kim (1987) found that if subjects are

SOCIAL COGNITION AND ILLNESS: BEING ILL ISN'T JUST PHYSICAL

We have seen how heuristics, biases, and fallacies can influence social judgments. It may be surprising to learn that some of the principles of social cognition also influence judgments about health and illness. The physical origins of disease are undeniable, but *judgments* about health are inherently psychological. As such, these judgments are subject to many of the same cognitive influences that affect judgments of guilt, consensus, and so forth (Meyer, Leventhal, and Gutman, 1985).

You will recall our earlier discussion of the false consensus effect in which people perceive their own characteristics as more common than do people without these characteristics. This effect also applies to the perception of the prevalence of diseases (Jemmott, Croyle, and Ditto, 1988). Furthermore, it even occurs among people with special medical expertise—practicing physicians. A sample of students and a sample of practicing physicians were asked

to report whether they ever had a long list of health disorders (e.g., colds, headache, hypertension, asthma, diabetes, etc.) and also to estimate the percentage of the population of the United States who has had these conditions. Based on research reviewed earlier, it is not surprising that college students who had a particular illness estimated there were more people like themselves than students who did not have the disease. What is interesting is that even though physicians have special expertise in the medical domain, their estimates of the commonness of particular diseases were also higher if they themselves had the illness. Physicians' susceptibility to this bias may have practical consequences. It is known that physicians are more likely to believe that a particular disease is the cause of a patient's complaints if they perceive that disease as common (Elstein, Shulman, and Sprafka, 1978). Thus, a physician with a particular health

history may be more likely to believe this illness also explains a patient's complaint, leading in some cases to a faulty diagnosis (see Figure 3.7).

People's perceptions of the seriousness of their own physical symptoms may also be distorted because of faulty judgments. The degree to which a person perceives his or her symptoms or disorders as serious may be important. Minimizing a disorder's seriousness may lead people to delay seeking medical treatment or discourage them from following their physician's recommendations. Populations have been observed in which medically significant disorders were widespread, but people did not seek treatment and evaluated their physical symptoms as benign (Zola, 1966). Why would this be? Jemmott, Ditto, and Croyle (1986) hypothesized that people tend not to see a disorder as serious if they perceive it as relatively common.

To examine this idea experi-

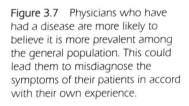

Figure 3.7 Physicians who have had a disease are more likely to believe it is more prevalent among the general population. This could lead them to misdiagnose the symptoms of their patients in accord with their own experience.

False consensus effects among physicians

mentally, the researchers "tested" a group of undergraduates for the presence of a fictitious enzyme deficiency. Subsequently, the subjects were led to believe that one in five of the people tested with them had the deficiency (low prevalence) or that four out of five of them had it (high prevalence). Ratings of the seriousness of the condition indicated that low-prevalence subjects evaluated the deficiency as more serious than did high-prevalence subjects. We might add that the researchers also manipulated whether subjects thought they had the deficiency or not. Independent of whether one had the disorder or not, perceived seriousness was lower if more people were believed to have the problem.

Why should a health disorder be judged as more serious if it is relatively low in prevalence? Jemmott and his colleagues (Jemmott, Ditto, and Croyle, 1986) speculate that people come to perceive an illusory correlation between illness prevalence and seriousness as a result of paired distinctiveness. By definition, low-prevalence disorders are distinctive; they occur infrequently. Very serious disorders, too, are distinctive by virtue of their above-average seriousness. This may lead to the belief that rare disorders are also more serious. The erroneous correlation may also be reinforced by vivid media attention to rare serious disorders instead of rare but relatively harmless disorders. Hopefully, by identifying the heuristics and biases people use to evaluate physical signs, researchers may be able to improve the accuracy of health-related judgments.

---

made to feel *accountability*—social pressures to justify one's views to others—people will show less bias. Subjects were given trait information that supposedly described a person and were asked to predict that person's responses to personality test items. Some subjects believed their responses would be anonymous (unaccountable), while others were told they would have to justify their responses (accountable condition). Those who felt accountable made more complex impressions of the target and moderated their confidence in the judgments in comparison to those who were not accountable.

Still, one should not be too optimistic about people overcoming these fallacies. Tversky and Kahneman (1971) found that even professional statisticians and mathematical psychologists were prone to some of these errors. It seems a safe bet that in normal life, many decisions and judgments are affected by the heuristics, biases, and fallacies identified by research on social cognition.

Affect and Cognition: How Thoughts Shape Feelings and Feelings Shape Thoughts

Thus far, we have concentrated on social *thinking*. As we will now see, however, thinking influences *feelings,* and *feelings* affect thought. Emotional states affect our judgment and our memory processes. For example, job interviewers who are in a good mood before the interview are more likely subsequently to forget the candidate's weaknesses and drawbacks. Similarly, interviewers in a bad mood are more likely to forget the candidate's good points (Baron, 1987).

An influential theory of emotion was originally proposed by Schachter and Singer in 1962. According to this theory, emotion has two components: *bodily arousal* and *cognitive label.* The arousal part is largely the same for all emotions. A pounding heart, a warm and flushed face, and a few tears could apply equally well to someone experiencing anger, distress, or joy. The cognitive label comes from interpreting the situation. If you are watching a horror movie, you may interpret your arousal as fear, but if you just won the lottery, you will probably interpret the same physical signs as joy. A good way to remember the two components of Schachter's theory of emotion is to think of emotion as being like a television program. The bodily arousal is the on-off (and volume) control, which decides *whether* there will be any emotion or not (and if so, how strong it will be). The cognitive part is like the channel selector, deciding *which* of the various possible emotions is taking place.

One important implication of Schachter's theory is that it is possible to switch emotions by changing the label. For example, most people experience some arousal prior to an important exam. It might help to label your arousal as "feeling excited and eager" rather than as "feeling terrified!" Research on switching emotional labels has produced mixed results. At present, the safest conclusion is that switching works best with similar emotions and with people who may be uncertain of what they are feeling. It may not work at all with very dissimilar or unambiguous emotions. If someone insults you, for example, it is unlikely that you could be persuaded to relabel your anger as joy.

A current debate in social psychology concerns whether cognition is a necessary part of emotion. Schachter's theory, for example, clearly included cognition as part of emotion. Zajonc (1984), however, argues that people form emotional preferences they cannot explain and of which they are scarcely aware. He concludes that *some* emotions occur without cognitive processes (Hansen and Hansen, 1988). A recent experiment (Robles et al., 1987) is consistent with this view. Threatening images (of monsters and bloodied faces) were shown to subjects via videotape at speeds that precluded recognition of the images. Self-rated anxiety assessed immediately afterward was higher among subjects exposed to the threatening images than subjects shown neutral or positive images (see Figure 3.8). Although

the negative stimuli were outside of conscious awareness, they nonetheless had an effect on the subjects' feelings.

Lazarus (1984) disagrees with Zajonc, claiming that a certain amount of interpretation is always involved in emotion. Probably this disagreement arises from different meanings of the word "emotion." Zajonc thinks of emotion very broadly, as something akin to mood states. He claims that everyone is always in some emotional state. Lazarus takes a more limited view of emotion, noting that preferences are not necessarily the same as emotions. Both sides agree, however, that emotion can have effects on cognitions.

Several general conclusions about the effects of feelings on social cognition emerged in a recent review by Isen (1984; 1987). Good feelings seem to have effects that are more consistent and reliable than those of bad feelings. People who feel good find it especially easy to remember good things about themselves and others. They tend to judge things in a more positive or favorable light than people with neutral or bad feelings. They tend to be optimistic about the future. Positive emotions also facilitate creative problem solving (Isen, Daubman, and No-

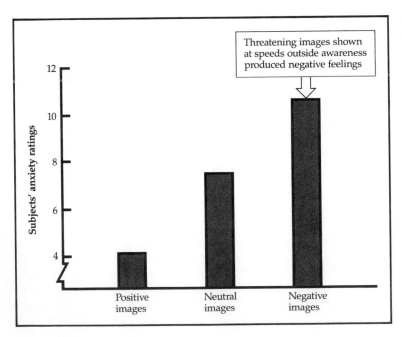

Figure 3.8 Threatening images shown at speeds that prevent conscious recognition produced more negative feelings than neutral or positive images. These data suggest that some emotions occur without conscious cognitive processes. (Source: Based on data from Robles et al., 1987.)

Emotions can occur without conscious cognitions.

wicki, 1987) and facilitate the use of quick and efficient approaches to solving problems.

Bad feelings (or "negative affect") have complex effects (Isen, 1984; 1987). One reason is that bad feelings set off conflicting tendencies. Feeling bad can cause people to see the bad side of everything, but sometimes people actively try to overcome negative feelings by deliberately looking at the good side of things or doing something to feel better. For example, subjects who are made to feel guilty may be more likely to offer help to someone else, if given the opportunity, presumably because helping is gratifying and makes the helper less depressed (Baumann, Cialdini, and Kenrick, 1981).

The effect of mood on person perception judgments has recently been studied by Forgas and Bower (1987). They reasoned that being in a particular mood will make mood-related associations and categories more salient and available in the perception of others. As a result, subjects will take less time deciding about the characteristics of another person when these are consistent with the subjects' mood. Furthermore, subjects will perceive someone else as having more traits consistent with their own mood. To test these ideas, some subjects re-

ceived negative feedback on a bogus psychological test to create a bad mood; other subjects received positive feedback to induce a good mood. Then, presumably, as part of a second independent experiment, subjects read four realistic person descriptions, each containing an equal number of positive and negative details. Subjects were asked to judge each person on a variety of dimensions, including likableness, intelligence, and so on. The exact time taken to make each judgment was also recorded.

As shown in Figure 3.9, participants in a good mood made considerably more favorable than unfavorable judgments. In contrast, negative mood had less of an effect on the number of positive versus negative judgments. Also, people who were in a good mood made positive judgments considerably faster than they made negative judgments. In contrast, people in a bad mood took longer to make judgments, regardless of whether they were positive or negative in nature. In summary, these results suggest that people are especially likely to make judgments about others that are consistent with their own mood and to make these judgments more quickly than mood-inconsistent judgments. Such results are consistent with the idea that one's mood

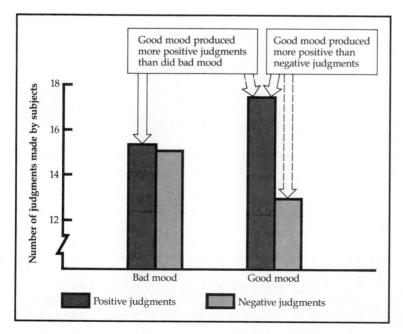

Figure 3.9 *Based on the same information, subjects in a good mood made more positive judgments about another person than did subjects in a bad mood. Furthermore, positive mood had a stronger effect on judgments than did negative mood. (Source: Based on data from Forgas and Bower, 1987.)*

Mood-consistent effects on person perception: Good mood has more effects than bad mood.

makes mood-consistent associations more salient and available. It is important to note, however, that these effects occurred only for positive moods. These findings are consistent with the notion that negative moods have more complex effects than positive moods (Clark, Milberg, and Erber, 1984; Forgas, Burnham, and Trimboli, 1988). Perhaps it is fortunate that negative mood has less power to distort our judgments of other people.

SCHEMATA AND THEIR EFFECTS

One of the main concepts in social cognition is **schema**. A schema is an organized collection of one's beliefs and feelings about something. Stereotypes, preconceptions, and generalizations are schemata (psychologists prefer the Greek plural *schemata* instead of *schemas*). The basic idea is that your mind isn't just a hodge-podge of isolated facts about everything in the world. The mind organizes its contents very carefully and elaborately. Schemata are what the mind uses to organize the wealth of its information about the world.

Types of Schemata

There are many types of schemata, including *self-schemata, person schemata, role schemata,* and *event schemata.* Let us consider each of these briefly.

Self-Schemata. What is the self? Psychologists have been studying that question from many angles, and there is no single answer (Suls, 1982; Suls and Greenwald, 1983, 1986). Social cognition has provided its own perspective on what the self is. The self is in part a schema that helps us process information (Markus and Kunda, 1986; Kihlstrom and Cantor, 1984). The self, in other words, is something that helps us interpret certain events and understand their implications.

For example, imagine failing a course, or getting the highest grade in your class. Your self-schema leaps into action to interpret that experience. What does the grade signify about your knowledge of the topic? About your intelligence in general? How will it affect what your friends

or family think of you? Does it change how you feel about yourself? And so forth.

Evidence for the importance of self-schemata for processing information has been shown in many experiments (Rogers, Kuiper, and Kirker, 1977; Markus, 1977; Markus, Hamil, and Sentis, 1987). In a recent study, Katz (1987) had subjects who scored either high or low on creativity on a test of creativity make one of three decisions about trait terms: (1) is it written in upper or lower case? (2) does the word mean the same as another word? or (3) does the word describe you? In each condition of the experiment, half of the words were descriptors of creative persons (e.g., "curious," "unconventional") and half were irrelevant as descriptors of creativity. After the decision-making task, the experimenter popped a surprise quiz to the subjects, who were asked to write down as many words as they could remember. Which words do you think were remembered best? The principle is that the more deeply the subject thinks about a word, the more likely it is to be remembered. Katz found subjects remembered best the words paired with the question, "Does this word describe you?" (see Figure 3.10). In order to answer that question, unlike the other questions, the subjects had to use his or her self-schema. But these results also show something else. Creative subjects (who presumably have a self-schema regarding the creativity domain) recalled more creative-relevant trait words than did low creatives. When the words were not relevant to creativity, however, the recall of the creative subjects was similar to that of the uncreative subjects. Thus, bringing the self-schema into play resulted in superior memory for words relevant to the self.

Person Schemata. Obviously, the self is not the only person about whom an organized impression is formed. For each person whom we know well, we have a *person schema* that organizes what we know and feel about this individual. Sometimes a person will behave in a way that surprises you, even though that same behavior would not be so surprising if done by someone else. The surprise occurs because that behavior violates the way you have come to expect that person to act—in other words, it doesn't fit your schema for that person. (Please read the

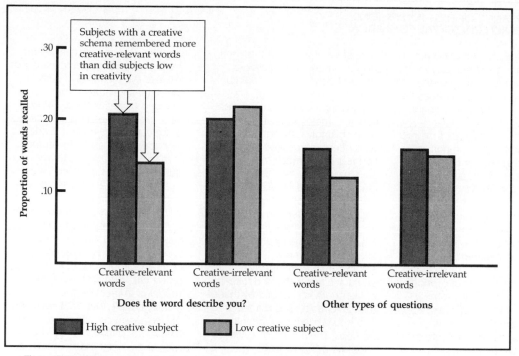

Figure 3.10 *When subjects' schemata were activated, their memory was enhanced. They remembered more words when the words were paired with the question "Does this word describe you?" than when the words were paired with other types of questions. Furthermore, subjects with a creative schema showed better recall of creative-relevant words than did subjects without a creative schemata. (Source: Based on data from Katz, 1987.)*

Self-schemata and memory

"Focus on Research" insert on page 70 about some classic research about how we organize our impressions of other people on the basis of initial information.)

Role Schemata. We also have *role schemata,* or organized sets of expectations about how people in certain roles are supposed to act. Imagine the first time you go to hear a new rock band and the first time you go to a new dentist. You will have some definite expectations about how these people will act, even though you never met them before.

Event Schemata. Last, we have organized beliefs about the normal or typical course of events

in various familiar situations, called *event schemata* or *scripts* (e.g., Schank and Abelson, 1977). For example, imagine you observe the following exchange (Read, 1987): Anne walks in the front door and is greeted by her husband Dave.

"The doctor thinks the operation will be quite expensive," says Anne.

"Oh well," replies Dave, "there's always Uncle Henry." Dave then reaches for the telephone book.

If we ask you why Dave reached for the phone book, you would probably reply that Dave was going to phone Uncle Henry to ask for a loan for the operation. This seemingly simple inference actually requires a large number of inferences about people and the world (Read,

THE IMPORTANCE OF FIRST IMPRESSIONS: EARLY RESEARCH ON SOCIAL COGNITION

We often hear that it is important to make a good first impression, and perhaps it is no surprise that many people make great efforts to put their best foot forward on job interviews or in other initial encounters. But is it the case that initial impressions are so important in forming judgments of other people? In the 1940s, social psychologist Solomon Asch began research providing insight into how people form impressions of others. His efforts also represent some of the first research in the area of social cognition. Asch proposed that impressions of others are organized and integrated conceptions. If one already possesses some information about another person, new information will not simply be added to the previous information; rather the meaning of the new material will be influenced by the meaning of existing knowledge about the person. This proposal suggests that the initial information one has about someone strongly influences the interpretation of information you may receive later.

To evaluate this idea, Asch read to a group of subjects a list of traits that supposedly described an individual: intelligent, industrious, impulsive, critical, stubborn, and envious. The same list was read to another group of subjects, but in the reverse order. Note that the first list started with desirable characteristics and ended with less desirable ones. In the second list, the sequence was just the opposite. If people form impressions on the information given, then the impressions formed by the two groups should be the same. However, if initial information sets the tone or changes the meaning of

subsequent information, as Asch thought, then the impressions formed by the groups should be different.

Consistent with Asch's prediction, the impressions of the groups were strikingly different. Subjects who heard the positive information first had a much more favorable impression than the second group. The state of affairs when initial information in a sequence has a greater effect on the final impression than later information is called the **primacy effect**; it has been found in many subsequent studies. Asch's explanation for the primacy effect is that the meaning of later traits is changed by that of the earlier traits. This is referred to as the *assimilation of meaning hypothesis*. There is much evidence supporting this view. For example, the trait "proud" in a positive context is taken as meaning "confident," but in a negative context it is taken as "conceited" (Zanna and Hamilton, 1977).

Alternative approaches to explaining impression formation and the primacy effect have been advanced by others. Norman Anderson (1965) proposed that people hold implicit values for the positivity or negativity of person attributes. For example, "intelligent" has a more positive value than "stingy." People "compute" an average of the values of all the person attributes to form an overall impression. Note that if final impressions are the result of simply averaging the individual values placed on single traits, then primacy effects should not occur. But Anderson believes that some information, such as initial information, obtains greater weight and thus has a larger effect on the final im-

pression. Earlier traits get greater weight according to Anderson, not because the meaning of traits coming later in the series is changed by earlier traits, but because people pay more *attention* to the earlier information. Evidence for Anderson's contention comes from the fact that the primacy effect disappears if subjects are given instructions requiring them to pay attention to all of the words in the list (Hendrick and Costantini, 1970). Because Anderson proposes people average available information with each item weighted by its relative importance, his theory is called the *weighted averaging model* of impression formation.

It is possible that both Asch and Anderson are correct about the origins of the primacy effect. The meaning of later information may be interpreted in terms of what came earlier, *and* earlier information may receive more attention and weight in averaging all of the single bits of information one has. Independent of these particulars, Asch and Anderson helped to uncover an important phenomenon—the primacy effect. This effect may explain why it is sometimes hard to alter impressions of strangers, political candidates, and others once they are formed on the basis of initial information. Furthermore, Asch and Anderson were among the first social psychologists systematically to research how we think and process information about other people.

1987). Nonetheless, most of us have no difficulty knowing in advance what will happen when we take an exam, get a haircut, or go on a picnic. We don't need to be told specifically to bring a pen rather than a harmonica to an exam because our exam-taking script tells us that we will have to write and that the professor usually brings paper but rarely supplies the pen.

How Schemata Guide Information Processing

What do schemata do? What are they good for? To answer these questions, we will look at schema effects on three main cognitive processes: attention, encoding, and retrieval. **Attention** refers to what you notice. **Encoding** refers to what gets stored in memory. **Retrieval**—that is, retrieval from memory storage—refers to what actually gets remembered later on. A basic principle is that some information gets lost during each of these processes. You notice only a small part of the world that confronts you; you encode only a small part of what you notice; and you retrieve only part of what was previously stored in your memory. (This loss of information is depicted in Figure 3.11.) Another way to think of this loss of information is that each of these three processes requires *selection* among all the possible things that could be noticed, encoded, and retrieved. This selection is not random. Rather, the mind has ways of choosing what to notice and remember. This is where *schemata* enter the picture. Schemata are among the mind's main weapons for coping with information overload. But schemata do not operate simply as "cognitive filters." In addition, they play a more active role, changing or distorting incoming information (or at least, our understanding of it), filling in gaps in such input, and, in general, shaping our comprehension of the social world. Some of the major effects of schemata upon information processing are summarized below.

Attention. Attention comes before encoding and retrieval; obviously, you can't remember something you never noticed in the first place. Schemata guide attention by telling us what to

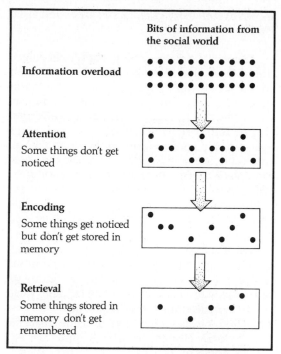

Figure 3.11 At each state of cognitive processing, some information is lost.

Information loss during cognitive processing

expect. Things that violate these expectations may stand out. There may be a hundred people at a wedding reception—far too many to pay attention to all of them. However, if one is wearing a tee shirt and jeans, you are more likely to notice that person, because your event schema for wedding receptions says that everyone will be fully and formally clothed.

On the other hand, another possible effect of schemata on attention is that the person will ignore whatever doesn't fit the schema. Recent work has focused on what makes people notice things or ignore things that don't fit their schema. The more dependent you are on someone, for example, the more you attend to the subtleties or particulars of that person's behavior (Neuberg and Fiske, 1987). For instance, if you are dependent on someone (perhaps your boss), you are more likely to notice he or she acting unusually than if the same sort of behavior were shown by a casual acquaintance (Erber and Fiske, 1984).

Encoding. Not everything that is noticed gets stored in memory. Attention does not lead to encoding in all cases. Instead, much information "goes in one ear and out the other." Schemata are a powerful influence over what gets encoded.

The role of schemata in selective encoding is shown in a recent experiment by Bodenhausen and Lichtenstein (1987). The schemata they used were *stereotypes,* which are schemata about social groups (see Chapter Five). Specifically, Bodenhausen and Lichtenstein used stereotypic preconceptions of Hispanics as more likely to be aggressive and engage in criminal acts.

One-half of the subjects in the experiment read information about a defendant in a criminal trial, with instructions to judge his guilt; the other half were instructed to rate his aggressiveness. Also, the ethnicity of the defendant was manipulated by assigning him a name that was either clearly Hispanic (Carlos Ramirez) or ethnically nondescript (Robert Johnson). All subjects read the same evidence concerning a criminal assault (the evidence was complex and ambiguous, containing favorable and unfavorable information), and then were asked to make judgments about his level of guilt or level of aggressiveness.

How did subjects evaluate the defendant? Bodenhausen and Lichtenstein predicted that stereotypes are more likely to be used to encode and use information when the judgments people have to make are complex. Since judging a person's guilt for a crime involves the consideration of several factors—detecting a motive, establishing there was an opportunity to commit it, and assessing conflicting sources—the authors expected that the ethnic label would exert a greater impact for those subjects who were instructed to evaluate the defendant's guilt. In contrast, because judgments of aggressiveness should be simpler to make, subjects would have less need to rely on a simplifying heuristic such as an ethnic stereotype.

As Figure 3.12 shows, the Hispanic defendant was viewed in more negative terms than an ethnically nondescript defendant when the subjects had the (complex) objective of making guilt

judgments. In contrast, ethnic labels had little influence on the judgments made by subjects who were asked to make a simpler type of judgment—how aggressive was the defendant? The reason for this difference appears to be that there was selective encoding of information according to the stereotype label when subjects had a complex judgmental task. Although this research suggests that people may be more susceptible to the biasing effects of stereotyping when confronted with difficult decisions, the research also has a more positive implication. It appears that not all kinds of social judgments are equally susceptible to encoding bias.

Retrieval. Finally, schemata affect what is retrieved from memory on a particular occasion. Out of all the information you have encoded in memory, your mind will select some and distort some in order to fit whatever schema is active at the moment. This selected, distorted retrieval has been demonstrated in several studies (Conway and Ross, 1984).

McFarland and Ross (1987) proposed that people should want to perceive that their impressions of people with whom they are close are relatively stable, even when these impressions have really changed. To study whether people exaggerate similarity between the past and present, subjects rated themselves and their dating partner on a series of trait dimensions. Two months later they were asked to rate their current impressions and recall their earlier ratings. Subjects whose impressions became more favorable over time recalled their earlier impressions as more positive than they had been. Similarly, when subjects' impressions became more unfavorable, they recalled their earlier evaluations as more negative than they had been. Thus, the schema about the other person selected information that was compatible with one's present impressions.

SELF-AWARENESS: The Effects of Looking Inward

Up to now, we have focused mainly on the processing of information from the social world around us. The external world is not the only

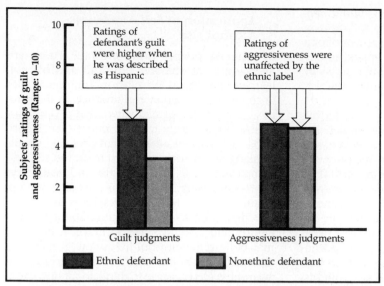

Figure 3.12 *Subjects are more likely to use a stereotypic label when faced with a complex judgmental situation such as deciding the defendant's guilt than when making a simpler judgment, such as how aggressive the defendant was. Subjects' guilt judgments were more extreme if the defendant was described as Hispanic than if no ethnic label were provided. In contrast, judgments of aggressiveness were unaffected by the ethnic label. These findings illustrate the impact of schemata on the encoding of social information. (Source: Based on data from Bodenhausen and Lichtenstein, 1987.)*

Evidence for the impact of schemata upon encoding

focus of our interest, however—sometimes our attention is directed inward, toward the self. Many psychologists have studied the causes and consequences of *self-focused attention,* also called self-attention or **self-awareness.**

One of the first systematic views of the process of self-awareness was offered by Duval and Wicklund (1972). These researchers suggested that attention can be directed either inward or outward, and that it sometimes oscillates back and forth between the self and the external world. According to Duval and Wicklund, then, self-awareness involves comparing oneself to one's ideals and goals. They further reasoned that, since we don't usually measure up to our ideals completely, self-awareness must usually be unpleasant. Later research on self-awareness, though, has abandoned the idea that self-awareness is typically unpleasant. When we succeed, when we stand up for our beliefs, or when

we do anything else that makes us feel good about ourselves, we tend to seek out self-awareness (Greenberg and Musham, 1981). And, obviously, many people enjoy having their pictures taken, appearing before an audience, or looking at themselves in a mirror—all events that increase self-awareness.

A more complex theory of self-awareness was proposed by Carver and Scheier (1981). They treat self-awareness as a *feedback loop,* similar to regulatory mechanisms in guided missiles and thermostats. Carver and Scheier suggest that self-awareness involves checking our current self against our goals and then altering our behavior (if necessary) to fit more closely with those goals. This is analogous to the way a thermostat "checks" the temperature in a room and turns on the heat or air conditioning.

Scheier and Carver (1983, 1987) also distinguish between two distinct types of self-awareness (or self-consciousness): *public self-consciousness* and *private self-consciousness.* The first of these refers to our awareness of ourselves as social objects—how we appear to others. The second (private self-consciousness) involves awareness of our own feelings, attitudes, and values.

Evidence for the feedback loop model has been provided by several different studies. For example, Gibbons (1978) first gave female subjects a questionnaire designed to measure sex guilt (guilt or anxiety over sexual matters). Two weeks later, he had them read and evaluate pornographic descriptions of sexual acts. Some of the women read the sexual passages while sitting in front of a mirror, a procedure that raises self-awareness. Their reactions to the pornographic materials were consistent with their personal standards: women with high sex guilt disliked the passages, whereas women with low sex guilt liked them. In contrast, among the women who read the sexual passages in the absence of a mirror, there was no relationship between personal standards and ratings of the pornography. Without self-awareness, subjects' reactions were not strongly determined by their inner attitudes or beliefs.

So far, we have discussed self-awareness as *attention* to the self, but attention is not the only cognitive process involved in self-awareness. Hull and Levy (1979) point out that self-awareness often pertains to *encoding,* not attention. They treat self-awareness as a matter of processing information about the self, rather than just noticing the self (Hull et al., 1988). Self-awareness can also be approached as a *personality trait* (Fenigstein, Scheier, and Buss, 1975). Some people are frequently self-conscious, think about their inner feelings and moods a lot (that is, private self-conscious). Others are focused and attentive to how they appear to others—their public image (that is, public self-consciousness). And still other people are relatively unconcerned except when circumstances force them to think about their private or public selves.

While self-awareness is interesting in its own right, it also has several practical applications. Among the most interesting of these are its implications for alcohol use and group behavior.

Application of Self-Awareness: Alcohol Use

Why do people drink alcohol? There are many different reasons, but Hull and his colleagues have identified a factor common to a lot of them. Alcohol apparently reduces self-awareness, even with a drink or two, and people turn to the bottle partly for that effect (see Figure 3.13). Remember that self-awareness entails thinking about how events bear on the self and comparing onself with goals and standards. When something bad happens—losing your job, failing an exam, breaking up with your lover—you may want to stop brooding about being a failure, and alcohol helps accomplish this. You may believe that alcohol helps you "forget your troubles," but in fact its effect is to reduce self-awareness so you cease to think about how these troubles reflect on your self. Conversely, when you want to cease matching behavior to standards of proper conduct—for example, to enjoy a wild party, unconstrained by normal inhibitions—alcohol helps accomplish this too, again by reducing self-awareness (Hull, 1981).

Various laboratory studies have supported Hull's theory. In one experiment, Hull and Young

THE LOCKHORNS

"I STARTED DRINKING TO FORGET SOMETHING OR OTHER."

Figure 3.13 *People may drink to avoid thinking about their problems. (Source: The Lockhorns, copyright, 1987. Reprinted with special permission of King Features Syndicate.)*

The use of alcohol to reduce self-awareness

(1983) reasoned that people who tend to have high self-awareness would want to drink more alcohol after failure, because it is painful to focus on oneself after failing. Male subjects were given an IQ test. The questions were difficult, so subjects could not be sure how well they were doing. Afterwards, half of them were told they had scored very high, while the rest were told they had done very poorly. Then the subjects went to another room, ostensibly to participate in a second experiment on taste perception of alcoholic beverages. The subjects had to rate a series of wines. Hull and Young were not interested in how the subjects rated the wines but rather in how much wine they drank while doing the rating task. The results (see Figure 3.14) depended on the personality trait of *self-consciousness,* which had been assessed earlier. People high in self-consciousness drank far more wine after supposedly failing than after succeeding at the IQ test. The reason, presumably, is that they wanted to escape from the self-focused thinking about the implications of their failure. People whose personality included a low level of self-consciousness, however, drank about the same amount of wine regardless of prior success or failure.

A field study made a similar point (Hull, Young, and Jouriles, 1986). High school students filled out a series of questionnaires about their recent consumption of alcoholic beverages (with strong assurances that any information would be held in strictest confidence). The students also answered questions about their academic average and a measure of self-consciousness. Hull and his colleagues then separately tabulated the association between grades and alcohol use for high and low self-conscious subjects. There was a stronger association between drinking and poor grades among the self-conscious subjects than the non-self-conscious subjects. The implication is that subjects who are self-conscious may use alcohol so as not to dwell on their academic failings.

Application of Self-Awareness: Group Composition and Matching to Standards

As we mentioned earlier, self-awareness is increased by looking at oneself in a mirror or being in front of an audience. Self-attention is also increased when one has minority status in a group. The more one feels outnumbered, the

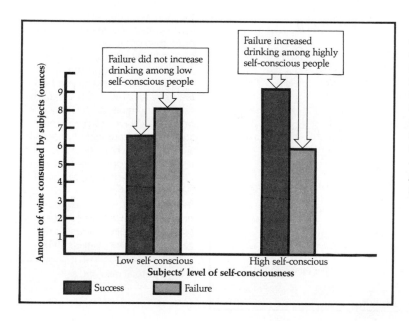

Figure 3.14 *Following a failure experience, subjects high in self-consciousness drank more wine. In contrast, subjects low in self-consciousness did not demonstrate similar effects. These findings suggest that at least some persons consume alcohol to reduce their self-awareness.* (Source: Based on data from Hull and Young, 1983.)

Alcohol as an escape from self-awareness

more self-attentive one tends to become. According to Mullen (1983), the increased self-attention prompted by being outnumbered increases the motivation to match to standards or ideals on the part of the minority group members. In contrast, members of the majority group should become less self-attentive as their number increases because each group member should stand out less as their group becomes larger. The implication is that a minority subgroup should be more concerned with meeting standards as its size decreases; majorities should become less concerned about standards as they become larger.

This approach can be stated formally as a ratio: degree of self-attention to one's standards is a function of the number of people in the other subgroup divided by the sum of the number of people in one's own group plus the number of people in the other group. This is referred to as the *other-total ratio* (see Figure 3.15). Based on this model, a number of predictions can be made. For example, violent behaviors by groups should be more intense as the size of the transgressing group increases because normal standards of behavior should become less salient. That is, in large groups, the members are characterized by **deindividuation**—a psychological state of reduced self-awareness or self-consciousness in which individuals feel less constrained by normal standards of behavior (Diener, 1980).

Consistent with this prediction, examination of archives from newspaper articles over a one-hundred-year period showed that the degree of atrocity of lynch mobs increased as the number of lynchers became more numerous relative to the number of victims. In another study, Mullen (1986b) examined the effects of the other-total ratio on stuttering. Mullen's hypothesis was that stutterers would become increasingly self-conscious as they were outnumbered by the size of their audience. Since they were not perfect

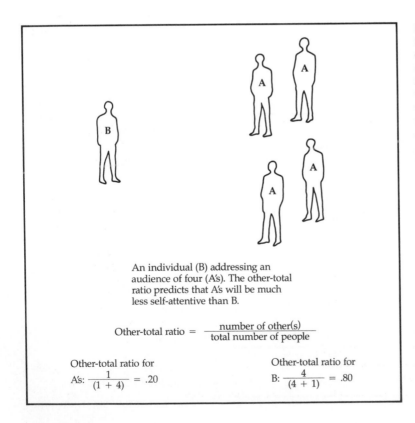

An individual (B) addressing an audience of four (A's). The other-total ratio predicts that A's will be much less self-attentive than B.

$$\text{Other-total ratio} = \frac{\text{number of other(s)}}{\text{total number of people}}$$

Other-total ratio for
A's: $\dfrac{1}{(1 + 4)} = .20$

Other-total ratio for
B: $\dfrac{4}{(4 + 1)} = .80$

Figure 3.15 Group size, specifically, the other-total ratio, influences the degree to which one is concerned or self-conscious about normal standards of behavior. The other-total ratio is the number of people in the other subgroup divided by the total number of people present in one's own group plus the number of people in the other group. When the ratio is low, the person should be relatively unself-attentive and hence less likely to comply with standards. Thus, for example, as the number of lynchers increases relative to the increase in the number of potential victims, the lynchers should become less concerned about the morality of their behavior and more brutal. Or, for example, when a lone individual must speak before a large group of strangers, the ratio should be high and the speaker highly self-conscious. (Source: Mullen, 1987.)

The other-total ratio and self-attention

speakers to begin with, self-attention should only make things worse by focusing on the disparity between their speech and standards regarding normal speakers. The degree to which individual stutterers had difficulties was evaluated in three different situations: speaking alone, before an audience of one, or before five to ten people. Consistent with the prediction, as the size of the audience grew (that is, the other-total ratio became larger for the stutterer), stuttering increased.

We can therefore see how the size of the subgroup that one finds oneself in may influence the degree to which people are self-attentive and concerned about standards of appropriate behavior.

SUMMARY

Social cognition is the study of how people interpret, analyze, remember, and use information about the social world. Because of information overload, it is necessary for the human mind to develop ways of sorting information and making judgments quickly and easily. These cognitive strategies include the use of *heuristics* and *schemata.* Heuristics apply decision rules that are quick, easy to use, and often correct, although they sometimes lead to errors. Schemata guide information processing by providing a model of what to expect. The person then notes, encodes, and remembers material in relation to his or her schema.

Use of **cognitive strategies** leads to some systematic fallacies, biases, and errors. For example, people tend to ignore base-rate information, to overestimate others' agreement with them, to draw false conclusions about expected patterns of events, and to cling to a schema or belief despite contradictory evidence—especially if new information is threatening to the self. Also, when events evoke an "only if" reaction (*counterfactual thinking*)—that it almost did not happen—sympathy for a victim is greater.

Motivational variables, moods, and emotions also influence mental processes. Good moods produce positive, optimistic judgments, and they increase memory for good things. The effects of

bad moods are less clear-cut, partly because some people try to overcome their bad moods by positive thinking and by good deeds.

Self-awareness is a state in which attention is focused inward on the self. This state is associated with the use and abuse of alcohol. People who find themselves in a large group may become less self-conscious and less concerned about normal standards of behavior.

GLOSSARY

action identification The process of labeling and interpreting one's own behaviors.

attention The first step in social cognition. It refers to the act of noticing something.

availability heuristic A strategy of making judgments based on how easily information comes to mind. Information we can remember quickly or easily is used as if it were equally important or frequent.

base-rate fallacy In making social judgments, people tend to ignore or underuse *base-rate information,* which is information about how prevalent or frequent something is in general.

cognitive strategies Techniques the mind uses to sort, analyze, and use information; "mental shortcuts."

confirmation bias The tendency to pay most attention to information that supports our preconceptions and beliefs. Information that contradicts our beliefs may be overlooked.

counterfactual thinking Refers to evaluations of events which evoke an "only if" response; that is, events for which we can easily conceive of an alternative to what actually happened. Stronger reactions to an event (such as an accident) are produced when the alternative outcome readily comes to mind.

deindividuation A psychological state of reduced self-awareness or self-consciousness in which individuals feel less constrained by normal standards of behavior. The probability of this state increases as the number of people in one's own group outnumbers the other group.

encoding The second step in social cognition: putting something into memory.

fallacies and biases Typical errors in human social judgment that are caused by systematic use of cognitive strategies.

false consensus effect The individual's tendency to believe there are more people who behave or think like them than do individuals behaving or thinking differently.

heuristics Basic principles or rules that allow us to make social judgments easily and rapidly (see *cognitive strategies*).

illusory correlation Because one expects a certain pattern or relationship, one tends to believe it is confirmed, even though the pattern or relationship is not objectively valid.

information overload The social world is very complex and has too many stimuli for the mind to handle. Hence the need for cognitive strategies or heuristics.

primacy effect Refers to the state of affairs when initial information in a sequence has a greater effect on the final impression than later information.

priming Planting ideas or categories in someone's mind, causing the person to use them to interpret subsequent events, due to increased availability.

representativeness heuristic Making judgments on the basis of resemblance to typical patterns or general types.

retrieval The third step in social cognition (after *attention* and *encoding*): remembering something that has been stored in memory.

schema An organized collection of one's beliefs and feelings about something. Types of schemata include self-schemata, person schemata, role schemata, and event schemata (scripts).

self-awareness A state in which one's attention is focused on oneself.

social cognition The study of how people interpret, analyze, remember, and use information about the social world.

theory perseverance The tendency to keep beliefs or conclusions even after the evidence for them has been shown to be false.

FOR MORE INFORMATION

FISKE, S. T., and TAYLOR, S. E. (1984). *Social cognition.* Reading, Mass.: Addison-Wesley.

A well-written, thorough review of recent research on social cognition, starting with attribution theory and covering the major cognitive processes.

KAHNEMAN, D., SLOVIC, P., and TVERSKY, A. (Eds.) *Judgment under uncertainty: Heuristics and biases.* Cambridge: Cambridge University Press.

A collection of articles and chapters that focus on heuristics, biases, and fallacies. This is the best source on mental shortcuts.

NISBETT, R. E., and ROSS, L. (1980). *Human inference: Strategies and shortcomings.* Englewood Cliffs, N.J.: Prentice-Hall.

A classic book that generated many of the ideas guiding subsequent research.

SULS, J., and GREENWALD, A. G. (1983). *Psychological perspectives on the self* (Vol. 2). Hillsdale, N.J.: Erlbaum.

One of a series of volumes presenting chapters on different aspects of the social psychology of self-knowledge by active researchers and theorists.

Chapter Four
Attitudes: Evaluating the Social World

FORMING ATTITUDES/Learning and Experience
Social Learning: Acquiring Attitudes from Others/Forming Attitudes by Direct Experience

PERSUASION/Changing Attitudes
Passive Persuasion/Two Routes to Persuasion

COGNITIVE DISSONANCE/Changing Your Own Attitudes
Dissonance: Its Basic Nature/Dissonance: Some Factors That Affect It

WHEN ATTITUDE CHANGE FAILS/Resistance to Persuasion
Reactance: Protecting Your Personal Freedom/Forewarning: Prior Knowledge of Persuasive Intent/Selective Avoidance

ATTITUDES AND BEHAVIOR/The Essential Link
Attitude Specificity/Attitude Strength, Vested Interest, Relevance, and Self-Awareness/Accessibility Model of Attitude-Behavior Consistency

Special Inserts
FOCUS ON RESEARCH/Classic Contributions
    Cash, Lying, and Dissonance
FOCUS ON RESEARCH/The Cutting Edge
    Individual Differences and Persuasion: "Different Messages for Different Folks"

"What baloney," Faye Johnson remarks as she and two of her friends—Marie Schlegel and Jean Thornton—join the crowd shuffling slowly out of the large auditorium. "You'd have to be either stupid or crazy to pay any attention to any of *his* ideas."

Faye is describing her reactions to one of the many presidential hopefuls now actively campaigning for their party's nomination, and it's easy to see that she's made up her mind: Senator Brazen is not her cup of tea. "Hey, speak for yourself," Jean replies. "I thought that a lot of what he said made sense. Sure, some of his ideas are a little far out. But maybe that's what we need—someone with vision. I'm so *tired* of all these little people with little plans. I think Brazen's just what the ticket needs."

"Ooooh!" Faye replies, clutching her head in disbelief. "Just what we need! Maybe we need to jump off the nearest cliff, too! You must be kidding; he's a jerk with a capital 'J.' If they nominate him, I'm staying home. It'll be like choosing between quicksand and a garbage dump."

"You know what I think?" Jean answers. "You have a closed mind. You didn't listen to a word he said. If you did, you'd come to your senses and realize that the problem with this country is too much government. Spend, spend, regulate, regulate. That's what's gotten us where we are today—the biggest debtors on earth. Go ahead, vote against him. But don't complain when they close down all our factories, too."

"Did they brainwash you or what?" Faye sputters. "I thought you had more sense than that. What we need right now is *more* action from those turkeys in Washington, not less. If they'd only get up off their rears and pass the right laws, we wouldn't be losing all our jobs to foreigners. That's the main reason why Brazen's a loser. He's confused. And so are you!"

Turning to the third member of the group for support, Jean says: "You've been so quiet, Marie. What did *you* think of him?"

Marie looks vaguely at her friends. "What do you mean? His ideas? Well, to tell the truth, I didn't pay much attention."

"What!" both of her friends shout simultaneously. "Why did we come here in the first place?"

"I don't know about you, but I just wanted to see him in person . . . And I wasn't disappointed. Mmm . . . those eyes . . . and that dimple in his chin . . . he gives me goosebumps . . . I'd love to see him as President; he's so . . . so . . . *cute* . . . Anyway, I guess that what I heard seemed fine to me . . . but I wasn't really thinking about it real hard."

"Marie, you're hopeless!" Faye remarks.

"Yeah, hopeless!" Jean agrees. "I guess that on election day you'll just vote for the best-looking one . . . What are you going to do in a few years when most of the candidates are women?"

And at this comment, the tension is broken as all three friends break into grins and chuckles.

Attitudes are a pervasive part of human life. Without **attitudes**, we wouldn't know how to react to events, we wouldn't be able to make decisions, and we wouldn't even have much to talk about (see Figure 4.1). It is no wonder that attitudes have been a major concern of social psychologists since the early days of the field. Over half a century ago, Gordon Allport (1935) wrote that attitude was social psychology's most important concept. Many social psychologists today would agree that this is still true (Greenwald, 1988).

Attitudes can be defined as *lasting, general evaluations of people* (including oneself), *objects, or issues* (e.g., Petty and Cacioppo, 1985). Saying that an attitude is *lasting* means that it tends to persist across time. A momentary feeling does not count as an attitude. Saying that an attitude is *general* means that it involves at least some degree of abstraction. To drop a book on your toe and find that particular experience to be unpleasant is not an attitude, because it applies to only one event. But if the experience makes you dislike books or clumsiness *in general,* that dislike is an attitude.

Of course, attitudes do not have to be general. They can be specific, as liking brown mustard with Swiss cheese, or being a fan of a particular movie or football star. At the other extreme, attitudes can be as general as being a political conservative, or believing that women are gener-

WORK IN AMERICA?
YOU AUTO BUY AMERICAN
Distributed By UAW LOCAL 160

Figure 4.1 Attitudes are a pervasive part of life.

Attitudes in everyday life

ally superior to men. As we shall see, the level of specificity turns out to be an important factor in determining how attitudes guide behavior. Another important dimension involves *active versus passive processes* for forming and changing attitudes. For example, U.S. senators' attitudes about American government are shaped by years of firsthand, direct, experience (active), whereas elementary school pupils' attitudes are shaped by TV, magazines, and what their parents tell them about the government (passive).

Most social psychologists accept the **ABC model of attitudes**, which suggests that an attitude has three components: affect, behavior, and cognition (e.g., Breckler, 1984). The *affective component* refers to positive or negative emotions—our gut-level feelings about something. The *behavior component* involves our intentions to act in certain ways, to engage in behav-

iors that are somehow relevant to our attitudes. Finally, the *cognitive component* refers to the thinking and interpreting that goes into forming or using an attitude. Each attitude, then, is made up of a cluster of feelings, likes and dislikes, behavioral intentions, thoughts, and ideas. Although the ABC model is a handy way in which to remember that an attitude involves three components, please do not forget that the three are closely interrelated.

Because social psychologists have studied attitudes closely for several decades, a great deal of information has been acquired about them. To present this information, we will use the following organizational scheme. First, we will examine how attitudes are *created*. We'll look at how children learn their attitudes, and later at how individuals form attitudes out of their personal experiences. Then, we'll consider how attitudes are *changed*. We will start with the passive forms of persuasion and proceed to the most active type of attitude change, in which people revise their opinions to justify their own behavior. Next, we'll consider how we resist persuasion. Finally, we'll consider evidence about how attitudes affect *behavior,* a complex issue with some rather surprising evidence.

FORMING ATTITUDES:
Learning and Experience

Heros and heroines may be born, but liberals, bigots, conservatives, and baseball fans are clearly made. Hardly any psychologist would suggest that babies enter the world with political preferences, racial hatreds, or religious views already fully formed. Rather, such attitudes are acquired over a long period of time. But how, precisely, are they gained? What processes account for their formation and development? Research has suggested several. We will look first at some learning processes in which the individual acquires attitudes in a rather passive fashion. Then we will consider direct experience in which the individual participates actively in the formation of his or her attitudes and indirect experience in which the individual is a more passive recipient. Please note: the terms "active" and "passive" are relative; people are almost never completely passive.

Social Learning:
Acquiring Attitudes from Others

Learning attitudes is a large part of **socialization,** the process by a which a wild, helpless creature (a newborn baby) is transformed into a responsible and capable member of human society. As we saw at the beginning of this chapter, adult human social life is practically unthinkable without attitudes. It is no mystery *where* children get their attitudes. They get them everywhere— from parents and later from teachers, from the media, from friends and acquaintances. *How* children learn attitudes is a little harder to answer, but psychologists have identified at least three main processes that play a role in this re-

gard: classical conditioning, instrumental conditioning, and modeling.

Classical conditioning involves learning by association. Imagine a child's first encounter with the word "wabble." The child doesn't know what wabble means, so she asks her mother about it. Mother frowns or acts upset while answering. The odds are that the mother's negative emotions will be noticed by the child, who will then develop negative associations to wabble. As the child grows up, that negative attitude toward wabble may continue. This is especially likely if the association is strengthened by similar parental reactions on other occasions. Now cross out "wabble" and substitute "work," "sex," a certain TV program, or "Democrats," and you can appreciate the potential power of parental attitudes in shaping children's attitudes by classical conditioning.

Instrumental conditioning refers to learning in which responses that yield positive outcomes or eliminate negative ones are acquired or strengthened. A father who is a Democrat may praise his son for claiming to be one too, and he may punish his son for expressing contrary views. Probably, most children identify themselves as Republicans or Democrats long before they understand the real historical and philosophical differences between these two parties. Essentially, children want to hold the "right" views, and parents are able to have the final say about what the right views are, at least before their youngsters reach adolescence. By rewarding and punishing their children, parents can play a significant role in shaping their attitudes on many issues.

Modeling refers to learning by observation. Even when parents are not trying to influence their child's attitudes directly, they may be setting examples the child will imitate. For example, little girls' career ambitions sometimes depend on their mothers' examples. If the mother is employed outside the home, the daughter is more likely to want her own career than if the mother is a full-time homemaker (see Hoffman, 1979).

Parents aren't the only ones to guide the passive form of attitudes, of course. Much learning of attitudes goes on in schools, churches, and

Figure 4.2 *Mass media such as television and movies present models that contribute to the formation of attitudes. (Source: © 1988; Reprinted courtesy of Bill Hoest and Parade Magazine.)*

Modeling: A key source of attitudes and behavior

"That's what you get for letting him watch The Three Stooges."

elsewhere. Television and other mass media also may shape attitudes and behaviors, particularly through modeling (see Figure 4.2).

Forming Attitudes by Direct Experience

So far we have considered how parents and others teach attitudes to children. People also form attitudes as a result of their own experience. They actively draw conclusions or make generalizations based on what has happened to them. Do not be surprised if you recognize material on social cognition that was covered in Chapter Three used in this section. Social cognition tells us how people come to such conclusions, so it contributes heavily to our understanding of how attitudes are formed.

Attitudes as Heuristics. Why do we have attitudes in the first place? What are they good for? One major answer is that attitudes help us to make decisions by reducing *information overload.* Saying that attitudes help reduce information overload is another way of saying that attitudes are *heuristics*—cognitive strategies for processing information quickly and easily (Fazio, Lenn, and Effrein, 1984). Attitudes help simplify human social life, which can be complicated and full of information. Even simple acts like stopping at the supermarket to pick up something for dinner would be enormously difficult if you tried to perform them without attitudes. You

would end up looking at everything in the store, considering various criteria such as price and nutritional value, and it would be very late by the time you got home. Attitudes such as preferences for certain foods make the job much simpler.

Attitudes Developed Through Direct Contact Versus Indirect Contact. There's an old saying that goes something like this: "You can't know what you'll like until you try it." What this statement suggests, of course, is that try as we may, we cannot always predict our reactions to various persons, situations, or objects. Only after we have had direct contact with them do our attitudes take shape. In fact, this suggestion seems to be correct. In many cases our attitudes are formed through direct contact with attitude objects—not simply "borrowed" from other persons through some form of modeling. For example, imagine that you ask a friend to describe some new dish he has just tried. His comments may provide you with some idea of its ingredients and how it is cooked. But they probably will *not* reveal directly whether you will like it yourself. Only actual tasting will answer this question and permit you to formulate a strong attitude.

Some of our attitudes are based on direct experience, while others are based on indirect experience, such as through the words or observations of others. Research has shown that the distinction between attitudes formed through direct experience versus those formed through indirect experience is an important one (Fazio and Zanna, 1981). For example, research shows that subjects who formed their attitude about an object through direct experience rather than watching someone else interact with the object are able to respond more quickly regarding their opinion (Fazio et al., 1982). Related research indicates that attitudes stemming from direct experience are also more clearly and confidently held (Fazio and Zanna, 1978) and are more resistant to change than indirect experience attitudes (Wu and Shaffer, 1987).

PERSUASION: Changing Attitudes

In the 1980s the business of changing attitudes is definitely a big one. If you have any doubts on this score, simply switch on your TV or radio or flip through the pages of any magazine. Almost at once, you will be flooded by attempts to alter your opinions. Commercials urge you to buy various products; political candidates plead for your vote; and public service organizations caution you against smoking, drinking, speeding, or overeating. In short, you will encounter attempts to change your attitudes at every turn (see Figure 4.3). Sometimes these attempts succeed; on other occasions they fail. For a long time now, social psychologists have studied the causes of successful versus unsuccessful persuasion. Let's take a look at what they've found.

Passive Persuasion

One major approach to studying persuasion was developed more than three decades ago by a group of social psychologists at Yale University. These researchers would measure someone's attitude, try to change it by various means, and then measure it again. By comparing different ways of attacking the attitude, they could see what worked best. Consider some of the following findings of this approach, which is still used to some extent in today's research:

1. Experts are more persuasive than non-experts (Hovland and Weiss, 1952). The same arguments carry more weight when delivered by someone who seems to have all the facts.

Figure 4.3 How many attempts at persuasion do you encounter each day? If your experience is like that of most persons, you would probably find it hard to keep count!

Attempts to change our attitudes: A common part of social life in the 1980s

2. We are more easily persuaded if we think the message is not deliberately intended to persuade or manipulate us (Walster and Festinger, 1962). Probably that's why you do not succumb to every television commercial you see: when you know or suspect others are trying to persuade you, you tend to be on your guard.

3. People with low self-esteem are persuaded more easily than people with high self-esteem (Janis, 1954).

4. Popular and attractive communicators are more effective than unpopular and unattractive ones (Kiesler and Kiesler, 1969). People are more easily swayed by someone they like than, say, by someone they don't know or someone they dislike, even if the same arguments are used (see Figure 4.4).

5. People are sometimes more susceptible to persuasion when they are distracted than when paying full attention, at least when the persuasive message is simple (Allyn and Festinger, 1961).

6. When persuasion is tough—that is, when the audience has attitudes contrary to what the speaker is trying to get them to believe—it is more effective to present both sides of the issue than just one side—that is, to strongly advocate one side but acknowledge that the other side does have a few good points. (Hovland, Lumsdaine, and Sheffield, 1949).

7. People who speak rapidly are more persuasive than people who speak slowly (Miller et al., 1976). This is contrary to the common view that people are distrustful of "fast-talking" salespeople and seducers. One reason, apparently, is that rapid speech conveys the impression that the person knows what he or she is talking about.

8. Persuasion can be enhanced by messages that arouse fear in the audience. This is particularly the case when the message provides specific recommendations about how a change in a person's attitudes and behavior will prevent the fear-provoking negative consequences de-

scribed in the message (Leventhal, Singer, and Jones, 1965). To persuade people to stop smoking, for example, it may be best to create high fear of dying from lung cancer, such as showing them what a smoker's lung looks like when it is operated on for cancer. However, it is best to provide them also with specific suggestions about how they might quit smoking.

This is quite a list! Table 4.1 summarizes it for you. Obviously, there are plenty of ways to try to persuade someone. Different advertisers use different principles in their ads. Hence, one commercial may use a medical doctor to plug its product, relying on the value of the expertise. Another may use a famous athlete or movie star, hoping to capitalize on popularity and attractiveness. Still others may try to distract the audience with humor or sexual suggestion, while yet others may try to arouse fear by warning that if you don't use their product you'll end up unloved, rejected, sick, or fired!

Not all the findings based on the early Yale research on persuasion have stood the test of time. Baumeister and Covington (1985), for example, challenged the conclusion that people with low self-esteem are more easily persuaded.

Figure 4.4 Attractive sources tend to be more persuasive than unattractive sources.

The attractive source: A commonly used technique by advertisers

Table 4.1 A summary of some of the major findings uncovered in research
on passive persuasion

Persuasion: Some key results

Factor	More Attitude Change (successful persuasion)	Less Attitude Change	Comment
Characteristics of the person who is trying to persuade someone	Expert Popular Attractive Speaks fast	Nonexpert Unpopular Unattractive Speaks slowly	Rapid speech suggests expertise
Characteristics of the persuasive message	Persuasive intent is not obvious Considers both sides of the issue Fear arousing Distraction	Obviously trying to persuade Presents only one side No fear Not distracted	When audience is initially opposed Distraction may determine whether persuasion occurs via central or peripheral routes
Characteristics of the person who is being persuaded	Low self-esteem	High self-esteem	High self-esteem persons may be persuaded, but don't want to admit it

They found that people with high self-esteem are just as persuaded as those with low self-esteem, but they don't want to admit it. Acknowledging that you have changed your attitude can often seem like an admission of gullibility, indecisiveness, or lack of personal conviction, so sometimes people may resist persuasion. And when persuasion does occur, people may deny it. Indeed, one classic study showed that when people do succumb to persuasion, they conveniently "forget" what their original opinion was (Bem and McConnell, 1970). Instead of saying, "Yes, you are right, I was wrong and now I have changed my mind," they say, in effect, "Yes, you're right—but I already believed that before I heard your argument"! The reader may recognize that this kind of distortion is similar to the memory reconstruction described in Chapter Three in which subjects overestimated the similarity between their past and present impressions of their dating partners (McFarland and Ross, 1986).

Two Routes to Persuasion

More recent research has replaced the Yale group's question, "What kinds of messages produce the most attitude change?" with the question, "What mental processes determine when someone is persuaded?" This approach was first promoted by several researchers who described it as **cognitive response analysis** (e.g., Greenwald, 1968; Petty, Ostrom, and Brock, 1981).

Cognitive response analysis emphasizes that what makes you change your mind is how and what you think about a persuasive message. People don't just passively absorb persuasive messages (such as speeches, arguments, and advertisements). Instead, they often actively think about them, and their thoughts lead either to attitude change or to resistance. While thinking, people often *elaborate* on the content of the persuasive message—in other words, they consider arguments and ideas that may not have been part of the original message.

The latest version of cognitive response analysis is a theory called the **elaboration likelihood model** (ELM) (Petty and Cacioppo, 1986). **Elaboration** involves scrutinizing the arguments in a persuasive message and thinking about them (which includes considering relevant arguments the message may have left out). According to this theory, there are two different kinds of persuasion processes, or rather there are two different "routes" to persuasion. The **central route** involves careful and thoughtful consideration of the issue and of arguments that are being used to persuade. The attitudes in question are at the center of the person's attention at the moment, so to speak (hence the name "central route"). In contrast, the **peripheral route** leads to attitude change without careful or deliberate thinking, such as persuading someone who is distracted. High elaboration puts you on the central route to attitude change; low elaboration refers to the peripheral route. When is the central rather than the peripheral route used? Petty and Cacioppo argue that persuasion via the peripheral route is more likely to occur when the subject is not able or motivated to think extensively about the persuasive message or there are salient peripheral cues that induce the person to accept the message's conclusion without giving it much scrutiny.

The ELM model provides an explanation for the impact of a wide variety of variables that influence persuasion. For example, researchers have found that people are more persuaded by information presented by multiple sources than by the same information presented by a single source (Harkins and Petty, 1987). (Think of advertisements in which a number of consumers extoll the virtues of a product.) The explanation for the "multiple source effect" appears to be that people do more central (elaborate) processing of the message because each time a new source appears, the person "gears up" to process the message. If the same source appears again, people put less effort in because this source has been heard already.

Unlike those situations in which people use central processing (ones in which specific arguments are important), persuasion in the peripheral route depends on subtle *persuasion cues.*

Chaiken (1987) put these effects in terms of social cognition in the **heuristic model of persuasion.** As you may recall from comments in Chapter Three, a heuristic is a mental shortcut. So if the mind can't think carefully about a message, it relies on shortcuts to evaluate the message. In the peripheral route, then, the mind relies on cues such as how long the message is, how physically attractive or how much expertise the persuader appears to have, and whether the message is bolstered by statistics or multiple reasons. The person does not really think about what the arguments really say—rather, he or she just operates on the basis of how many arguments there are or how likely it seems that the arguments are good. The heuristics in this case are general assumptions such as "the more arguments there are, the more likely the conclusion is correct," or "experts usually know what they are talking about, so they must be right," or "statistics don't lie" (Eagly and Chaiken, 1984).

The heuristic model helps to provide clarification about certain variables about which attitude researchers have long disagreed. Have you ever attended a political rally where a speaker was heckled? Was the speaker less persuasive as a result of the derisive comments of the audience? The question is whether overhearing the reaction of an audience has an effect on persuasion. For years, research provided conflicting findings (Landy, 1972; Sloan, Love, and Ostrom, 1974), but recently the heuristic model has provided some clarification. Axsom, Yates, and Chaiken (1987) reasoned that audience reaction should be important when subjects have little involvement in the issue because then simple heuristics are relied upon such as "if other people think the message is correct, then it probably is." Audience reaction provides such information. In contrast, if personal involvement is high, subjects should rely less on heuristics (or peripheral cues) such as the audience's response and more on the quality of the arguments made in the message.

To test this reasoning, subjects in a study by Axsom, Yates, and Chaiken (1987) were recruited to listen to a recording of what was supposedly a debate on public radio concerning whether probation should be used as an alternative to imprisonment. Some of the subjects were given instructions about the importance of the issue and their responses to it in order to create high involvement; others were told the study was "preliminary . . . and that they could just relax while the tape was playing" (low involvement condition). The quality of the arguments during the debate was also manipulated: some subjects heard six high-quality arguments, while others heard six weak arguments favoring probation. A third variable, audience response, was also manipulated by inserting either audience cheers and bursts of enthusiastic clapping (enthusiastic audience) or tentative claps and cries of derision

in the high- and low-quality versions of the debate. After listening to the tape, subjects indicated their opinions about using probation as an alternative to imprisonment.

Although this is a rather complex study, the results are clear-cut. As predicted, under high involvement, when central processing should be important, argument quality influenced opinions regardless of audience response. In contrast, under low involvement, when heuristics such as audience cues should be relied upon, the cheering or the jeering of the audience was more important than the level of argument (see Figure 4.5). Thus, we see that whether heckling affects a

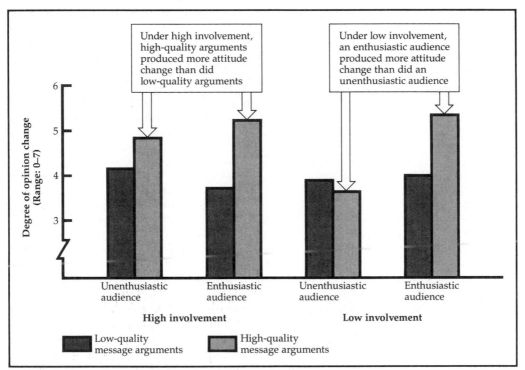

Figure 4.5 *Under high involvement, the quality of message arguments influenced opinions regardless of audience response. Under low involvement, audience response affected opinions regardless of message quality. These findings support the view that people use the central route and direct careful thought to the message arguments when the issue is an involving one. However, under noninvolvement, people rely on heuristics such as, "If other people think the message is correct, then it is probably valid." (Source: Based on data from Axsom, Yates, and Chaiken, 1987.)*

Audiences and persuasion: Central vs. peripheral routes

speaker's persuasiveness depends on whether the central or peripheral routes of persuasion are used.

In short, the elaboration likelihood model suggests that persuasion depends on how the mind reacts to the message. In the central route, the mind evaluates the quality of arguments used and often considers other possible arguments. Persuasion is most likely if the arguments are intrinsically strong and if the person is able to think about and appreciate them fully. On the peripheral route, however, the mind evaluates the message based on simple and superficial cues, without really thinking about the arguments. In this case, persuasion is most likely if the message seems to resemble a type that is usually correct—regardless of how strong its specific arguments really are.

COGNITIVE DISSONANCE: Changing Your Own Attitudes

Remember the last time you had a difficult decision to make, such as choosing between two different but appealing colleges? Perhaps one college offered a great climate, friendly students, and a relaxed and easygoing atmosphere, but the other had a better academic program in the field you wanted to study. You wavered between the two, and even after you made your choice you still felt some regrets about forsaking the advantages of the other place. If you are like most people, you probably wonder now and then whether you made the right decision, after all.

Remember the last time your actions deviated from your inner convictions? This, too, is a common experience. Perhaps you had resolved to diet, but you succumbed to temptation and ate a chocolate sundae, or cheesecake with whipped cream. Or perhaps your boss asked you whether you liked the new policy, and you said yes even though you really didn't. Or perhaps someone gave you an unattractive gift and you had to pretend you were glad and grateful for it.

What all these examples have in common is **cognitive dissonance**, or feelings of discomfort generated by conflicts among a person's beliefs or by inconsistencies between a person's actions and attitudes. You wanted a college with a re-

laxed atmosphere, but you chose the more academically rigorous one—so you have dissonance because your choice didn't mesh with your attitude about having a relaxed environment. Your choice did mesh with some of your other attitudes, such as the desirability of a good program: but it's often hard to satisfy all of one's attitudes. That's why dissonance is such a common experience. Each person has many attitudes, which often don't agree as to the best course of action. Similarly, you felt dissonance because eating cheesecake was inconsistent with your intention to diet, or because pretending you liked the gift was inconsistent with your belief in being honest. Dissonance is the struggle with personal inconsistencies, and social psychologists have given this struggle considerable attention (e.g., Festinger, 1957; Cooper and Fazio, 1984).

Dissonance: Its Basic Nature

Most researchers agree that cognitive dissonance can be viewed as a motivational state: individuals experiencing dissonance are motivated to reduce it. There are three main ways in which this can be accomplished (see Figure 4.6). The first is to *change your attitudes and/or behavior,* so as to make them more consistent. Imagine a 45-year-old man who has dissonance because every day he goes to work at a job he hates. To reduce dissonance, he can try to convince himself that he doesn't really hate his job (changing his attitude), or he could quit and search for a new job (changing his behavior).

The second way to reduce dissonance is to get *new information*—specifically, information that supports your attitude or your new behavior. The information reassures you that there is really no problem or inconsistency to worry about, so you don't have to change your attitude or behavior. People who smoke cigarettes or take drugs may feel dissonance because these habits can harm their health. Risking one's health is inconsistent with most people's attitude that they want to have a long, healthy life. These people may reduce their dissonance by looking for evidence that cigarettes or drugs are not dangerous—such as research studies that fail to prove health damage, or thinking of old grandpa

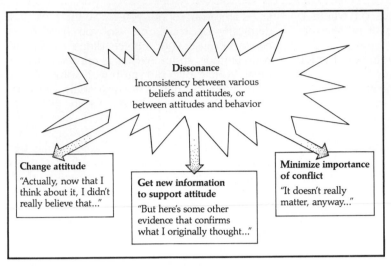

Figure 4.6 *Dissonance can be reduced in many different ways, but among the most important are: (1) changing one's attitudes or behavior, (2) acquiring new information that supports one's attitudes or behavior, and (3) minimizing the importance of the dissonance.*

Techniques for reducing dissonance

who lived to be 87 despite smoking a pack every day.

The third way to reduce dissonance is to *minimize the importance of the conflict,* so that it can safely be ignored. A young smoker may tell herself, for example, that it really doesn't matter if she takes a chance on getting lung cancer, because there is likely to be a nuclear war before she ever gets that old. Or she may decide that the risk is unimportant because a cure will probably be found by the time she's old enough to get the disease.

How much dissonance someone feels depends on the magnitude of inconsistency and on the importance of the issue. The three approaches to reducing dissonance, therefore, try to reduce either the inconsistency or the importance. Although all three modes of reducing dissonance are viable, social psychologists have been mainly concerned with dissonance as a way of changing attitudes. Much research has focused on getting a person to behave in a way that contradicts his or her beliefs, and then determining whether this **counterattitudinal behavior** led to attitude change as a means of reducing disso-

nance. (To learn about some of the early research on cognitive dissonance, read the "Focus on Research" insert.)

Dissonance: Some Factors That Affect It

What factors contribute to dissonance? Researchers have identified several. One is choice. If you hate oatmeal but someone holds a gun to your head and orders you to say you love oatmeal, will your attitude toward it become more favorable? It's unlikely. Being forced to do something is a lot like being paid a huge amount to do it—you have ample external justification, so you don't feel dissonance and you don't have to revise your opinion. Normally, dissonance only occurs when people feel that their inconsistent behavior was done by their own free choice.

The importance of choice was first demonstrated in a study by Linder, Cooper, and Jones (1967). They asked subjects to write a counterattitudinal essay arguing that controversial speakers should not be permitted on campus. Half their subjects were simply told that this was the

CASH, LYING, AND DISSONANCE

The theory of cognitive dissonance was proposed by Leon Festinger (1957), and several researchers raced to provide initial tests of its accuracy. One of the most famous was by Festinger and Carlsmith (1959) Their strategy was to create dissonance by putting subjects through an incredibly boring procedure and then getting them to tell others that it was a fascinating experience (see Figure 4.7).

Subjects signed up for a study called "Measures of Performance." When they arrived, the experimenter explained that he was studying how people perform routine tasks. The subject was then

shown a tray with 12 spools on it. He was instructed to take them off the tray one at a time. When they were all off, he was told to put them back on, again one at a time. And then he took them off again, over and over, for half an hour. Next, the subject was shown a large board with 48 square pegs. His task was to turn each peg one-quarter turn clockwise, and then do them all another quarter turn, and another, and so on for half an hour. By now the subject was probably very sorry he had signed up for this experiment, for a more boring and repetitive task could scarcely be imagined!

At this point the experimenter explained that there really was more to the experiment. Actually, said the experimenter, the purpose of the research was to motivate people to perform routine tasks. He said that some subjects had been told in advance by an assistant that the experiment would be exciting, interesting, and enjoyable, to see whether that motivated them to perform better.

Then came the crucial part of the study. The lab supervisor came in and informed the experimenter that the assistant had failed to show up, and he was supposed to be there now to tell the next sub-

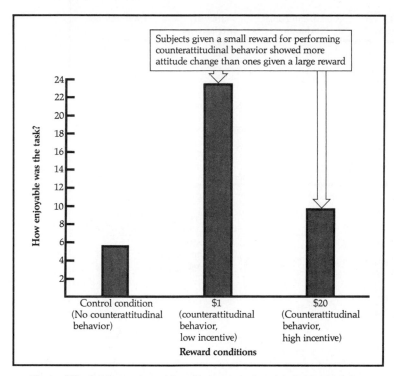

Figure 4.7 Subjects who told another person that they had enjoyed a boring task later reported liking it more when they engaged in this counterattitudinal behavior for a small reward ($1) than for a large one ($20). (Source: Based on data from Festinger and Carlsmith, 1959.)

Dissonance and counterattitudinal behavior

ject that the experiment was interesting. The experimenter asked the subject to fill in, offering a cash payment for doing so. All subjects consented, and each then went out to the waiting room where the subject told the person there (actually an accomplice pretending to be the next subject) that the study was exciting, intriguing, and a lot of fun. Later, in another setting, subjects were asked how much they had in fact enjoyed the experiment. Some had been given $20 for lying—for telling the accomplice the experiment was a lot of fun—while others had been paid only $1 for such counterattitudinal behavior. Who do you think changed their attitudes most?

Common sense seems to suggest that the bigger reward should produce the larger change. Surprisingly, though, the opposite actually occurred (see Figure 4.7). Subjects paid $1 ended up liking the task more than subjects paid $20.

Why? According to cognitive dissonance theory, people experience dissonance when they can't justify their actions by making them fit their attitudes. Nobody approves of lying, but subjects paid $20—a lot of money in those days—believed that their behavior was justified by the large reward. Consider the people who lied for $1, however. They couldn't tell themselves, "I said it was interesting because they paid me a lot of

money to do so." To reduce their dissonance, they had to change their attitudes. "I said it was interesting because I really found it kind of interesting" (see Figure 4.8).

This study set the pattern that many dissonance experiments have followed. The subject is paid to perform counterattitudinal behavior, and the subject's attitude is measured. Typically, the smaller payment produces greater attitude change. This early example shows dissonance reduction in action. People change their own attitudes in order to justify their behavior. When they say something for low pay, they convince themselves that they meant what they said.

Figure 4.8 When subjects receive small rewards (incentives) for engaging in counterattitudinal behavior, dissonance occurs, and attitude change follows. When they receive large rewards, however, dissonance is not aroused, and attitude change fails to take place.

The impact of counterattitudinal behavior: A closer look

task assigned them in the experiment. The other half were told that the decision to write the essay was entirely up to them, although the experimenter said he would appreciate their help. Everyone consented to write the essay. Initially, nearly all subjects were opposed to prohibiting controversial speakers. When attitudes were surveyed after writing the essays, the students who had simply been *told* to write the essay were still opposed. The students who had been told the decision was up to them, however, had changed their attitudes and become more favorable toward prohibiting such speakers on campus. Apparently, dissonance had only been aroused when the person had been reminded of having free choice and personal responsibility.

Several other factors also play a role in dissonance. First, the inconsistent behavior has to have some foreseeable, possibly bad consequences (e.g., Goethals, Cooper, and Naficy, 1979). You don't feel dissonance if your behavior doesn't cause any harm, or if its consequences were an accident and could not have been anticipated. Second, the inconsistent actions have to involve the self in some important way (Greenwald and Ronis, 1978; Schlenker, 1982). This can come about either because the behavior was performed by free choice, which creates inner feelings of personal responsibility for the behavior, or because the behavior is witnessed by others so that one's reputation is involved (Baumeister and Tice, 1984). In other words, the inconsistent behavior must be linked either to the private self-concept, through inner feelings of personal responsibility, or to the public self, through other people's knowledge of what you did—or else dissonance will not be created. Third, dissonance seems to depend on physiological, bodily arousal (e.g., Croyle and Cooper, 1983). Getting at least mildly upset seems to be part of dissonance (Elkin and Leippe, 1986). In one study, dissonance and attitude change were prevented by giving people tranquilizers before they performed the counterattitudinal behavior (Cooper, Zanna, and Taves, 1978).

So, many factors contribute to dissonance: personal choice, foreseeable consequences, the public or private self, and arousal. No doubt others will be found in the future. Dissonance has been one of the most intensively studied topics in social psychology. One reason for its popularity is that its active approach to changing attitudes (by getting people to change their own attitudes) has such a reliable, powerful effect.

WHEN ATTITUDE CHANGE FAILS: Resistance to Persuasion

We have just seen how dissonance may fail to result in attitude change if certain conditions are not present. But what determines whether we are susceptible to the persuasive messages presented in commercials, political speeches, and editorials? All of these are designed to alter our views in some manner. Given the frequency of such attempts, and the fact that they are often contradictory in nature, one point is clear: if we yielded to all of these appeals—or even to a small fraction of them—we would soon be in a pitiable state. Our attitudes would change from day to day, or even from hour to hour; and our behavior would probably show a strange pattern of shifts, reversals, and re-reversals! Obviously, this does not happen. Usually, our attitudes are quite stable and do not change from moment to moment. In fact, we generally show a great deal of stability in this respect. Thus, it is probably safe to conclude that far more attempts at persuasion fail than succeed. Why? What factors arm us with impressive resistance to even powerful efforts to change our views? As you can probably guess, many play a role. Among the most important, however, seem to be reactance, forewarning, and selective avoidance.

Reactance: Protecting Your Personal Freedom

Have you ever been in a situation where, because you felt that someone was trying to exert undue influence on you, you leaned over backwards to do the opposite of what he or she wanted? If so, you are already familiar with the operation of **reactance**. In social psychology this term refers to the unpleasant, negative reactions we experience whenever we feel that someone is trying to limit our personal freedom. Research findings suggest that when we perceive this to be the case, we often tend to shift in a direction directly *opposite* to that being recommended—an effect known as *negative attitude change* (e.g., Brehm, 1966; Rhodewalt and Davison, 1983). Indeed, so strong is the desire to resist undue influence that, in some cases, individuals shift away from a view being advocated, even if it is one they might normally accept.

Regardless of the basis for reactance and negative attitude change, the existence of these processes suggests that "hard-sell" attempts at persuasion will often fail. When individuals perceive such appeals as direct threats to their personal freedom (or their public image), they may be strongly motivated to resist. And such resistance, in turn, may result in total failure for many would-be persuaders.

Forewarning: Prior Knowledge of Persuasive Intent

On many occasions when we receive a persuasive message, we know full well that it is designed to change our views. Indeed, situations in which a communicator manages to catch us totally unprepared are probably quite rare. But does such advance knowledge, or **forewarning**, of persuasive intent help? In short, does it aid us in resisting later persuasion? A growing body of research evidence suggests that it may (e.g., Cialdini and Petty, 1979; Petty and Cacioppo, 1981).

When we know that a speech, taped message, or written appeal is designed to alter our views, we are often less likely to be affected by it than if we do not possess such knowledge. Moreover, this seems to be especially true with respect to attitudes and issues that we consider important (Petty and Cacioppo, 1979). The basis for these beneficial effects seems to lie in the impact of forewarning upon key cognitive processes. When we receive a persuasive message, especially one that is contrary to our current views, we often formulate counterarguments against it. (See Figure 4.9.) Knowing about the content of such a message in advance, then, provides us with extra time in which to prepare our defenses. Similarly, forewarning may also give us more time in which to recall relevant facts and information from memory—facts that may prove useful in refuting a persuasive message (Wood, 1982). For these and related reasons, to be forewarned is to be forearmed, at least in cases where we care enough about the topics in question to make active use of knowledge.

Selective Avoidance

Still another way persuasion attempts are resisted is by **selective avoidance**—the way people direct their attention away from information that challenges their attitudes. Understood in social

Figure 4.9 When we receive a persuasive message, especially one contrary to our views, we often form counterarguments against it. (Source: Drawing by Mort Gerberg; ©1987 the New Yorker Magazine, Inc.)

Resistance to persuasion

cognition terms (see Chapter Three), selective avoidance reflects one way in which attitudes (a type of schema) guide the selective attention and processing of information. For example, Sweeney and Gruber (1984) have found that people do not simply sit and absorb whatever the media (such as television) decide to present. Instead, viewers change channels or "tune out" when confronted with news coverage that seems biased against their opinions. When the news supports a viewer's attitude, however, the viewer pays considerable attention. This represents **selective exposure**—the deliberate seeking out of information that supports one's views. Through the selective attention of attitude-relevant information, the individual can help to maintain his or her current views and "nip in the bud" attempts to change them.

To conclude, because of the operation of reactance, forewarning, and selective avoidance, our resistance to persuasion is considerable. Of course, attitude change does occur in some cases; to deny this fact would be to suggest that advertising, propaganda, and persuasive messages always fail. But the opposite conclusion—that we are helpless pawns in the hands of powerful communicators—is equally false. Resisting persuasion is an ancient human art, and there is every reason to believe that it is just as effective today as it was in the past. Because of this fact, attitude change is often much easier to plan or imagine than it is to achieve (Hovland, 1959; Chaiken and Stangor, 1987).

ATTITUDES AND BEHAVIOR:
The Essential Link

Do attitudes shape behavior? Your first answer is likely to be, "Of course!" After all, you can recall many incidents in which your own actions were strongly determined by your opinions. Besides, social psychologists wouldn't have spent so much time and energy studying attitudes if they didn't predict behavior. Behavior is the bottom line in social psychology. Without behavior, attitudes become irrelevant whims.

But is there proof that attitudes shape behavior? Many studies have examined attitude-behavior relationships. Some years ago, Wicker

(1969) reviewed all these studies and arrived at a shocking conclusion: attitudes and behavior are at best very weakly related, and often there is no relationship between them. In study after study the correlation between attitude and behavior was found to be weak and negligible. Wicker even suggested that the concept of attitude should be abandoned as useless!

At this point, you are probably wondering why you should bother to finish this chapter, or perhaps, why we even included a chapter on attitudes in the first place. The answer is simple: new evidence indicates that attitudes *can* predict behavior effectively under some conditions. Wicker had challenged social psychology by showing that attitudes do not predict behavior well, but it now appears that sometimes they do. Let's look at what factors determine the strength of the essential link between attitudes and behaviors.

Attitude Specificity

Consider two of your attitudes. Suppose, for example, that you like pickles on your hamburger (a specific attitude) and that you oppose racial discrimination and prejudice (a general attitude). Which one will show a stronger, more consistent relationship with your actual behavior? Probably you don't always take every opportunity to work for racial equality—you don't always take part in every demonstration, you don't sign every petition that comes along, and you don't always seek out the companionship of people of other races. Sometimes you do those things, but sometimes you don't—which translates into a *weak* (inconsistent) relationship between your attitude and behavior. In contrast, if you like pickles, you may order them almost every time you have a hamburger. Thus, your behavior is highly consistent with your attitude. No doubt you would say that racial equality is more important than pickles on your hamburger, but the link between attitude and behavior is nonetheless stronger (more consistent) for pickles— that is, for the specific attitude than for the general attitude.

Most attitude researchers have studied general attitudes, such as ones about religion, political issues, or groups of people, because these seem the most important and interesting ones.

Ajzen and Fishbein (1977) suspected that the emphasis on general, global attitudes may have led to the weakness of the attitude-behavior link that Wicker described. They argued that it may be unreasonable to expect *general* attitudes to predict *specific* behaviors with high statistical reliability. For example, they suggested, a researcher might look at attitudes toward Christianity to see how these are linked to attending church on a particular Sunday. A weak relationship might be found, indicating that not all devout Christians attended church that day, and that some of the relatively indifferent Christians happened to show up. Ajzen and Fishbein noted that instead of looking at general attitudes about Christianity, the researchers should have focused on the narrow and specific attitude about attending that church on that day. The specific attitude would show a much higher correlation with actual church attendance than would the general or global attitude.

Ajzen and Fishbein reviewed considerable research on the attitude-behavior problem (sometimes called the "**A-B problem**"). Their conclusion strongly supported the advantages of attitude specificity for predicting behavior. Research studies that measured very specific attitudes showed high correlations with behavior. Research studies that measured global and general attitudes, however, found the weak or negligible correlations that Wicker had criticized. So the conclusion is this: to predict overt behavior from attitudes, it is usually more effective to look at specific, narrow, and precise attitudes rather than general or global ones.

Attitude Strength, Vested Interest, Relevance, and Self-Awareness

Obviously, strong attitudes predict behavior better than weak ones. That is no surprise. Several less obvious factors are related to attitude strength, however. One is direct experience, a topic discussed earlier in this chapter. Attitudes formed by direct personal experience tend to be stronger and tend to predict behavior better than attitudes formed through indirect experience (such as hearing how other people feel about the attitude object) (Fazio et al., 1982; Sherman et al., 1982).

A second factor is whether the person has a **vested interest** in the issue. A vested interest means that the events or issues in question will have a strong effect on the person's own life. Having a vested interest increases the relation between attitudes and behavior, as shown in an experiment by Sivacek and Crano (1982). They contacted students and pretended to solicit their help in campaigning against a proposed state law that would raise the drinking age from 18 to 20. Nearly all students were opposed to the law, regardless of their own age. But some of them had a vested interest—those young enough so that the law would interfere with their social lives if it passed. Students who were a little older had no vested interest, for even if the law passed they would already be over age 20 by the time it took effect. Who do you think agreed to campaign against the law? The younger students, of course. The older students were equally opposed to the law in principle but lacked any vested interest (see Figure 4.10). Their attitudes did not lead to the corresponding behavior.

A third factor determining the strength of the attitude-behavior link is whether the situation calling for a given behavior makes the attitude **relevant.** Our span of attention is limited; only so many things can be retrieved from memory and attended to at one time. Hence, even if we have a strong attitude about some issue or object, we may not act upon it unless the situation "calls up" our attention or makes our attitude appear relevant to the situation. Snyder and Kendzierski (1982) surveyed college students about their attitudes toward participating in psychological research. Then months later they read a notice asking them to devote more time as subjects for no extra credit. One-half of the subjects heard another student (actually an experimental accomplice) say, "whether you volunteer or not is really a question of how worthwhile you think experiments are." This comment was made to make the subjects' attitudes relevant to the behavior. Subjects in this condition were much more likely to show consistency between their attitude and volunteering for extra participation than were subjects who had not heard the relevance cue.

Still another way the A-B link can be strengthened is through self-awareness. As discussed in

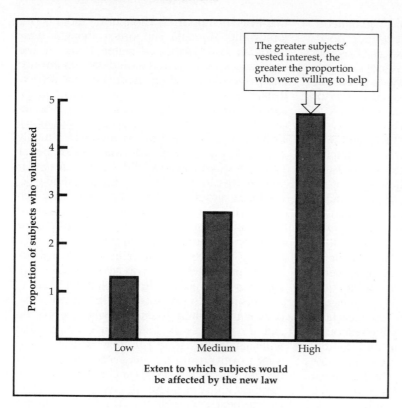

The greater subjects' vested interest, the greater the proportion who were willing to help

Figure 4.10 *Subjects who would be strongly affected by a new law were more willing to campaign against it than individuals who would be affected by it to a lesser degree. In short, the greater their vested interest in defeating the proposal, the stronger their tendency to translate their negative attitude toward it into overt action. (Source: Based on data from Sivacek and Crano, 1982.)*

Vested interest and attitude-behavior consistency

Chapter Three, self-awareness makes women's reactions to pornography more consistent with their general attitudes about sex (Gibbons, 1978). Other studies have likewise shown that heightened self-awareness increases consistency between attitudes and behavior (e.g., Pryor et al., 1977). There are two reasons why self-awareness increases such consistency. First, self-awareness increases people's access to their own attitudes, so they report their attitudes more accurately when self-aware than when not self-focused. Second, in a behavioral setting, self-awareness can "remind" the person of his or her attitude, enabling the attitude to guide behavior. Increasing someone's self-awareness is like saying to the person, "Before you act, stop for a moment and consider who you are and what you believe in. What course of action suits you best?" That makes subsequent behavior more likely to follow from the person's own inner attitudes and less likely to be determined mainly by external, situational factors.

Accessibility Model of Attitude-Behavior Consistency

Recall the importance of availability in social cognition that was discussed in Chapter Three. Attitude researchers have a similar concept, called **accessibility**, that ties together the evidence about attitudes and behavior discussed in the previous section (e.g., Fazio et al., 1986; Fazio, 1988). Attitude accessibility means bringing the attitude to mind. Strong attitudes come to mind more readily, so they exert more influence over behavior than do weak attitudes. Direct experience, vested interest, relevance, and self-awareness also make the attitude accessible; that is why, at least partly, those factors increase the attitude's effect on behavior.

If accessibility is high, even general attitudes can exert a strong influence on behavior. This occurs through a three-step process. First, something calls the general attitude to mind. Second, the general attitude influences how the person perceives the situation, "coloring" judgments and interpretations. The general attitude operates like a *schema* in creating expectations and guiding attention, encoding, and retrieval. Third, behavior is determined by these judgments and interpretations of the present situation (Fazio, Powell, and Herr, 1983). If the general attitude is not accessed, it won't affect behavior.

A three-part experiment by Fazio and Williams (1986) provides support for the importance of attitude accessibility. In the first phase, a sample of townspeople in the Midwest were interviewed about their attitudes toward Reagan and Mondale during the presidential campaign of 1984. The accessibility of their attitudes was measured by the amount of time (latency) they took to indicate their degree of agreement or disagreement with a set of attitude statements concerning the candidates. The reasoning (also confirmed in earlier experiments) is that the time it takes to report one's attitude reflects how accessible the attitude is; the faster the response, the more accessible or available the attitude. Two months later, the subjects received a letter inquiring about who they thought had been more impressive in the recent TV debates that had been held (that is, if the subjects had watched at least one of the debates). Finally, in the third phase, the subjects were telephoned one day after the presidential election and asked for whom they voted.

Looking first at the relationship between attitude, accessibility, and impressions of the candidates' debate performance, it is not surprising that Reagan supporters thought he did a better job, while Mondale supporters thought their candidate had performed better. However, the association between initial candidate preference and perceptions of their candidate's debate performance was stronger for subjects whose initial attitudes were highly accessible (that is, who indicated their initial opinions without hesitation). In other words, when the attitude was a highly accessible one, the opinion was a much better predictor of impressions of the debate. A similar pattern was found between initial attitude accessibility and actual voting behavior. Although those with initially favorable attitudes toward Mondale or Reagan were more likely to vote for their own candidate four months later, the relationship between initial opinion and actually voting for the candidate was stronger if the attitude was more accessible (see Figure 4.11).

This research suggests that the concept of accessibility may help to explain when people do and do not act on their attitudes. Fazio and Williams (1986) speculate that pollsters who want to obtain more precise estimates of how people vote may want to include not just the standard kinds of questions ("A good President for the next four years would be X?"), but also consider the accessibility of the respondent's attitudes. If their attitudes appear to be highly accessible, more faith might be placed in their views as an estimate of their future behavior.

(Before concluding this chapter, read the "Focus on Research" insert about the important role of individual differences in persuasion.)

Figure 4.11 In Fazio and Williams' (1986) study, subjects whose initial attitudes about Reagan and Mondale were highly accessible tended to perceive their candidate as winning the presidential debate. Subjects with highly accessible attitudes were also more likely to go out and vote for their candidate.

Attitude accessibility influences perceptions and behavior.

INDIVIDUAL DIFFERENCES AND PERSUASION: "DIFFERENT MESSAGES FOR DIFFERENT FOLKS"

We have made little mention in this chapter of the role of individual differences in attitude change because our focus has been on general processes. But is everyone equally susceptible to persuasion attempts? Actually, for a time, there was some skepticism that individual differences contributed much to our understanding of persuasion (Mischel, 1968). However, social psychologists have given renewed attention to how different types of individuals respond differently to persuasion attempts (Zaller, 1987; Zanna, Olson, and

Herman, in press). Let's consider one recent example of this work.

Some attitude theories propose that attitudes serve different needs or functions for different people (Katz, 1960; Smith, Bruner, and White, 1956). Let us consider two of these functions. *Value expressive* attitudes allow the individual to express his or her underlying values and dispositions. *Social adjustive* attitudes, in contrast, are formed on the basis of how well they allow individuals to fit into important social situations (Katz, 1960; Smith, Bruner, and White,

1956). The distinction between these two functions may have a common parallel with an important individual difference called **self-monitoring** (Snyder, 1974, Snyder, 1987). Those persons who are high in self-monitoring tend to regulate their behavior on the basis of the situation. They pay a great deal of attention to what is socially appropriate in a given interaction and behave accordingly. On the **Self-Monitoring Scale,** a test designed to measure this personality dimension, those who score high endorse items such as:

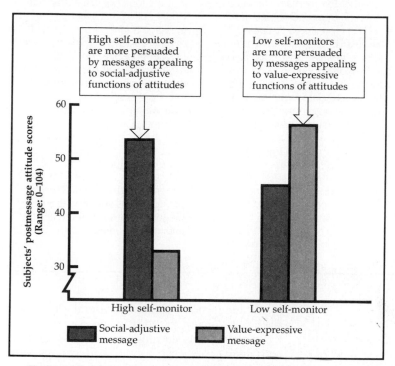

Figure 4.12 High self-monitors are more responsive to messages that appeal to the social-adjustive functions of attitudes. In contrast, low self-monitors are more persuaded by messages that emphasize the value-expressive functions of holding a particular opinion. The research shows that specific personality factors can influence the success of various types of persuasive messages. (Source: Based on data from DeBono, 1987.)

Self-monitoring, attitude function, and persuasion

- When I am uncertain how to act in social situations, I look to the behavior of others for cues.
- In different situations and with different people, I often act like very different persons.

In contrast, low self-monitors tend to regulate their behavior on the basis of internal factors. On the Self-Monitoring Scale, they agree with such statements as:

- My behavior is usually an expression of my true inner feelings, attitudes, and beliefs.
- I would not change my opinions (or the way I do things) to please someone else or to win their favor.

It should be no surprise, based on the above description, that high self-monitors (compared to lows) show less correspondence between private attitudes and public behavior (Zanna and Olson, 1982). More recently, DeBono (1987) recognized that attitudes may serve mainly a socially adjustive function for high self-monitors because of their desire to be socially appropriate. In contrast, the value-expressive function should be more important for low self-monitors, because for them attitudes should be opportunities to express their underlying values. If this is the case, DeBono predicted that high self-monitors should experience more attitude change after exposure to a message addressing the social-adjustive function. Low self-monitors, however, should experience more attitude change after listening to a message directed at the value-expressive function.

To test these predictions, DeBono recruited college student subjects who had scored either as high or low on the self-monitoring scale earlier in the term. All subjects were told there would be a mental health week in which students would be asked to participate in discussion groups. To familiarize them with the discussion issues, they would hear a tape by one of the leaders in the mental health field concerning whether the mentally ill should be institutionalized. One-half of the subjects received a "value-expressive message" in which the expert informed them that favoring institutionalization had been found, in much research, to be highly associated with being a responsible and loving person (important personal values). The other subjects heard a "social-adjustive message" in which they were simply told that a large majority of their peers favored such institutionalization. After listening to the tape, subjects were asked to indicate their attitudes about the issue.

The results shown in Figure 4.12 are precisely as DeBono had predicted. High self-monitoring individuals experienced more attitude change after being exposed to the social-adjustive message, whereas low self-monitors experienced more change after exposure to the value-expressive message. It is also worth noting that when asked to recall the lecture, subjects had better memory for the talk that most matched their functional orientation.

This work has several important implications. First, it shows that certain individual differences qualify or limit the impact of persuasive messages. Second, the research demonstrates that a better understanding of individuals' responses to persuasion requires that we look not just at the individual but also at whether the message addresses the function the attitude serves the individual (Snyder and DeBono, 1988).

Of course, self-monitoring is not the only important individual difference that affects how susceptible we are to persuasion attempts (Cacioppo et al., 1986). And the social-adjustive and value-expressive orientations do not exhaust the list of functions that attitudes can serve. The list of important individual differences and functions will probably get longer as attitude researchers continue their studies.

SUMMARY

We have numerous **attitudes**, and we use them constantly. Attitudes enable us to evaluate our experiences by guiding positive and negative reactions to things (and to people). Each attitude is made up of certain thoughts or labels (cognitive component), the good or bad feelings (affective component) associated with these thoughts, and behavioral patterns or at least intentions to behave in certain ways.

Attitudes can be created in several ways. Children learn many attitudes in the course of *socialization*. Such learning can occur when they are taught to associate good or bad feelings with certain actions or things, or it can occur simply when they are rewarded or punished for expressing certain views. Learning attitudes can also occur when children copy the example set by parents or other people. Adults form attitudes spontaneously based on their personal experiences.

Persuasion is the process of changing attitude. According to the *elaboration likelihood model,* there are two routes to persuasion. The *central* route involves careful thought about the issue and the arguments, so persuasion is most likely if there are strong, convincing arguments. The *peripheral* route, however, involves convincing someone in the absence of his or her full attention or careful thought to the arguments. Here, the strength of the arguments is less important than superficial cues, such as the credibility or the physical attractiveness of the message source.

Cognitive dissonance is an unpleasant feeling that results from conflict or inconsistency between one's thought and/or actions. People want to avoid cognitive dissonance, so they will often change their attitudes in order to justify their behavior. For example, people may change their attitudes in order to justify their behavior. When they say something for low pay, they convince themselves that they meant what they said.

Sometimes, of course, people resist persuasion. This occurs when they know in advance that someone will attack their beliefs, or when they feel someone is trying to take away their freedom to make up their mind. People also resist persuasion by **selective avoidance** of materials and information that presents views contrary to their own.

Surprising as it may seem, the connection between the attitudes and behavior is sometimes weak. Specific attitudes, strong attitudes, attitudes involving a vested interest, and attitudes reported under self-awareness seem to have the most direct influence on behavior. Recent research on individual differences shows that **self-monitoring** may be important in determining how people respond to persuasive messages.

GLOSSARY

A-B problem The research issue concerned with whether or how strongly attitudes are related to behavior.

ABC model of attitudes Each attitude is composed of affect, behavior, and cognition.

accessibility The ease with which an attitude is brought to mind.

attitudes Lasting, general evaluations of people, objects, or issues.

central route When persuasion occurs by means of careful and thoughtful consideration of the issue and arguments (opposite of peripheral route).

classical conditioning Learning by association.

cognitive dissonance The feeling of discomfort caused by conflicts or inconsistencies between a person's attitudes and/or behaviors.

cognitive response analysis Studying how people's thought processes mediate persuasion.

counterattitudinal behavior Actions that seem contrary to one's attitudes. Counterattitudinal behavior often causes cognitive dissonance.

elaboration Thinking about and analyzing the arguments relevant to the persuasive message.

elaboration likelihood model The theory that there are two routes to persuasion, the *central* route and the *peripheral* route, which are distinguished by the amount of cognitive *elaboration* they involve.

forewarning Advance knowledge that one is to be the target of the persuasion attempt. Forewarning often produces resistance to persuasion.

heuristic model of persuasion The theory that attitude change sometimes occurs when the person evaluates the persuasive message on the basis of superficial cues.

instrumental conditioning A form of learning in which responses that yield positive outcomes or eliminate negative ones are acquired or strengthened. (Also known as *operant conditioning.*)

modeling Learning by observation of someone else's behavior.

peripheral route When persuasion occurs without careful or deliberate thinking about the issue or the arguments (opposite of central route).

reactance Unpleasant, negative reactions to threats to one's freedom. Reactance often entails resisting external influence.

relevance Refers to whether the situation calling for a given behavior makes the attitude *relevant.* An attitude is more strongly related to behavior in situations that make the attitude *relevant.*

selective avoidance Directing one's attention away from information that challenges one's attitudes.

selective exposure Deliberately seeking out or attending to information that supports one's attitudes.

self-monitoring A personality dimension that ranges from the tendency to regulate one's behavior on the basis of the situation (high self-monitoring) to the tendency to regulate one's behavior on the basis of internal factors (low self-monitoring).

Self-Monitoring Scale The test devised by Snyder to measure individual differences in self-monitoring.

socialization The process of teaching a child the basic beliefs, values, and practices of society. This process makes the child a responsible and capable member of society.

vested interest Refers to instances in which events or issues will have a strong effect on one's life.

FOR MORE INFORMATION

FESTINGER, L., RIECKEN, H. H., and SCHACHTER, S. (1956). *When prophecy fails.* Minneapolis: University of Minnesota Press.

One of the earliest works to deal with issues of cognitive consistency and dissonance, this clas-sic book provides an absorbing case study. A small group predicted the end of the world on a precise date, but, of course, it never happened. Three social psychologists infiltrated the group to learn how it would deal with disconfirmation of its basic beliefs.

PETTY, R. E., and CACIOPPO, J. T. (1986). *Attitude change: Central and peripheral routes to persuasion.* New York: Springer-Verlag.

This book provides the most up-to-date account of this fascinating approach to persuasion research.

PRATKANIS, A., BRECKLER, S. J., and GREENWALD, A. G. (Eds.). (1988). *Attitude structure and function.* Hillsdale, N.J.: Erlbaum.

The chapters in this volume deal with a variety of current topics related to attitudes. You may find some of them to be difficult, because they are written primarily for an audience of experts, but reading them is a good way to become acquainted with the latest ideas of several leading researchers.

Chapter Five
Prejudice and Discrimination: When "Different" Is Definitely Not "Equal"

PREJUDICE AND DISCRIMINATION/What They Are and How They Differ
Prejudice: Group Membership and Rejection/Discrimination: Prejudice in Action

WHY PREJUDICE OCCURS/Some Contrasting Views
Direct Intergroup Conflict: Competition as a Source of Bias/"Us" Versus "Them": Social Categorization as a Basis for Prejudice/Early Experience: The Role of Social Learning/Cognitive Sources of Prejudice: Stereotypes, Illusory Correlation, and Illusion of Out-Group Homogeneity

COMBATING PREJUDICE/Some Plans of Action
Breaking the Chain of Bigotry: On Learning Not to Hate/Direct Intergroup Contact: The Potential Benefits of Acquaintance/Desegregation: The "Grand Social Experiment"

SEXISM IN THE 1980S/A Closer Look at One Form of Prejudice
Prejudice Toward Females: Its Nature and Origins/Discrimination Against Females: Subtle, But Sometimes Deadly/An Optimistic Conclusion: Sexism in the World of Work—Going, Going . . . ?

Special Inserts
FOCUS ON RESEARCH/Classic Contributions
    Tajfel and the Minimal Group Paradigm: Prejudice on the Flip of a Coin
ON THE APPLIED SIDE
    Prejudice and the AIDS Epidemic

Carl Phelps, foreman of the jury, looks pained. "OK, OK," he says to Beverly Johnson, "Take it easy. We'll never reach a verdict if we keep shouting at each other." "I don't care!" Beverly answers, pounding the table with her fist. "He's guilty and he's got to pay for it!"

"Oh shut up, already!" Hillary DeGuzzo tells her. "We're all sick and tired of listening to you. Weren't you awake during the trial? Didn't you see all that evidence go down the drain? What's wrong with you, anyway!"

"She's right," Hal Berkowitz adds. "Why are you being so difficult? All the rest of us agree: we *can't* convict him. We'd be sending an innocent person to jail. Come on, shape up!"

Now Carl interrupts again. "Please, *please!* This is getting us nowhere fast. Bev, tell us again why you think he's guilty."

"Like I said before, I could tell as soon as I saw his face. Those shifty eyes, that arrogant look. And the way he answered when that nice Mrs. Oliver was questioning him. He's guilty all right! Besides, didn't he admit that he was in a bar just two blocks away an hour before the holdup? What more do you need?"

"But just because he was nearby doesn't mean he pulled the holdup," Hillary replies. "Remember: not *one* of the witnesses was certain; they all had doubts about whether he was the man they saw. No, there's nothing that proves he did it."

"I don't care," Beverly answers. "He did it, and I'm not changing my mind."

For a moment there's a pause, and then Hal Berkowitz remarks: "You know, I think you're just out to get him because he's Puerto Rican. You don't care about the evidence; you're just prejudiced."

Beverly explodes. "Ha! A lot you know, you rotten bleeding heart liberal . . . *You* want to let him off just *because* he's Puerto Rican. But that's just what I'd expect from one of *you*; you're all alike. You see a dark skin and you turn to mush. Turn 'em all loose, put 'em in special programs; don't punish them for terrible crimes they do— oh no . . . give 'em all medals instead! Well, I've had it up to here with you miserable pinkos and your phony compassion! You're what's wrong with this country! Why, if I had my way . . ."

And then, suddenly realizing that she may have gone too far, she stops.

"OK," Carl says standing up. "I've heard enough. There's no point in continuing. The judge told us to consider the evidence, and in my mind, that's not what we're doing. I'm going to tell them that we're deadlocked. That means they'll have to go through the whole process all over again and Hernandez will have to stay in jail for six more months. But at least we'll get out of here and be able to go home!"

Consider the following list: blacks, Hispanics, Yankees, conservatives, Russians, Jews.

Do you have an "image" of persons belonging to each of these groups? For example, if you learned that someone you were about to meet was a member of one of these groups, would you have any expectations about the kind of person he or she is likely to be? If you are completely honest, your answer is probably "yes." Despite the age-old warning against jumping to conclusions, most of us do just that where other persons are concerned. Hopefully, we are not as extreme as Beverly in the story, but, to some degree, all of us form judgments about others, assume that they possess certain traits, and predict that they will act in certain ways simply because they belong to specific groups. Our tendency to jump to "social conclusions" about others in this manner plays a central role in the topics we will consider in this chapter: prejudice and discrimination.

As we're sure you already realize, these processes pose a serious and continuing threat to human welfare all over the globe. Indeed, it is virtually impossible to pick up a newspaper or tune in the evening news without learning of some new atrocities stemming from their impact (see Figure 5.1). For this reason alone, prejudice and discrimination have long been of major interest to our field. In their efforts to understand these unsettling processes, social psychologists have focused on many issues. Among the most important of these, though, have been the following: (1) what is the basic nature of prejudice and discrimination? (2) what factors account for their occurrence? and (3) what steps can be

Figure 5.1 Today, as in the past, prejudice and discrimination are major causes of human suffering.

Prejudice and discrimination: The costs are high

taken to reduce their impact? We will consider each of these questions below. In addition, we will also focus on one type of prejudice which seems especially pervasive and which has recently been the subject of a great deal of research interest: prejudice based on sex (sexism).

PREJUDICE AND DISCRIMINATION: What They Are and How They Differ

In everyday speech, many persons seem to use the term "prejudice" and "discrimination" interchangeably, as synonyms. Are they really the same? Most social psychologists feel that they are not. **Prejudice** refers to a special type of attitude—generally a negative one—toward the members of some distinct social group. In con-

trast, **discrimination** refers to negative actions directed toward those individuals. Since this is an important distinction, we will now expand on it in more detail.

Prejudice: Group Membership and Rejection

Let's begin with a more precise definition: *prejudice is an attitude (usually negative) toward members of some group based solely on their membership in that group.* In other words, when we state that a given person is prejudiced against the members of some social group, we generally mean that she or he tends to evaluate its members in some characteristic manner (again, usually negatively) merely because they belong to that group. Their individual traits or behaviors play little role; they are liked or disliked simply because they belong to a specific social group.

When prejudice is defined as a special type of attitude, two important implications follow. First, as noted in Chapter Four, attitudes often operate as *schemata*—cognitive frameworks for organizing, interpreting, and recalling information (Fiske and Taylor, 1984; Wyer and Srull, 1986). Thus, when people are prejudiced against the members of some group, they tend to notice, to encode accurately (i.e., store in memory), and later to remember certain kinds of information—for example, information consistent with their prejudice (e.g., Bodenhausen and Wyer, 1985).

Second, as an attitude, prejudice involves the three major components described in Chapter Four. That is, prejudice encompasses affective, cognitive, and behavioral aspects. The *affective component* refers to the negative feelings or emotions prejudiced persons experience when in the presence of members of specific groups, or merely when they think about them for some reason. The *cognitive component* involves beliefs and expectations about members of these groups, plus the ways in which information about them is processed. Finally, the *behavioral component* involves tendencies to act in negative ways toward groups who are the objects of prejudice, or intentions to do so. When these tendencies or intentions are translated into overt actions, they constitute *discrimination*—the next major topic we will consider.

Discrimination: Prejudice in Action

As noted in Chapter Four, attitudes are not always reflected in overt actions. Indeed, there is often a substantial gap between the views individuals hold and their actual behavior. In many cases, persons holding negative attitudes toward members of various groups find they cannot express these views directly. Laws, social pressure, and the fear of retaliation all serve to prevent them from openly engaging in negative actions against the targets of their dislike. On other occasions, however, such restraining forces are absent. Then, the negative beliefs, feelings, and be-

havior tendencies described above may find expression in overt actions. Such *discriminatory behaviors* can take many different forms. At relatively mild levels, they involve simple avoidance. At stronger levels, they can produce exclusion from jobs, education, or residential neighborhoods. And in extreme cases, discrimination may take the form of overt aggression against targets of prejudice. Regardless of their precise form, however, the ultimate outcome is always the same: members of the target group are harmed in some fashion.

Bigots, like other persons, prefer to "have their cake and eat it too." If possible, they prefer to harm the targets of their prejudice without any cost to themselves. How do they seek to accomplish this goal? One answer is through the use of several *subtle forms of discrimination*—ones that permit the users to conceal their underlying negative views. A number of these exist, but here we will focus on three that seem most common: (1) withholding aid from persons who need it, (2) various forms of tokenism, and (3) reverse discrimination.

Reluctance to Help Unless You Have to. The first of these tactics—withholding aid from members of disliked groups—is often used with considerable finesse. Contrary to what you might expect, prejudiced persons do not engage in blanket refusals to assist the objects of their bigotry. Rather, they act in this manner only when they feel they can get away with such actions—when there are other plausible explanations for their failure to help, aside from prejudice (Gaertner and Dovidio, 1977).

Bigoted individuals may provide help to the object of their prejudice when to do otherwise would reveal their true feelings and be socially inappropriate. This is illustrated in a recent experiment (Frey and Gaertner, 1987). White female undergraduate subjects were assigned to be "director," while two accomplices played the roles of "supervisor" and "worker" in a task involving anagrams. Following some practice, subjects received a note requesting help for the "worker." The worker was either black or white and needed help either because she had a very difficult task (external locus) or because she didn't try very hard (internal locus). For some subjects the note supposedly was sent by the supervisor (a third party), while for others the note was supposedly sent by the worker herself. Frey and Gaertner measured the amount of help (in terms of letters for the anagrams task) given to the target.

Figure 5.2 shows that the white students were less helpful to blacks than to whites only when recipients requested help for themselves and were responsible for their dependency owing to their lack of effort. When a third party asked that the help be given or the help was needed because of factors outside the worker's control, giving help was apparently seen as the socially appropriate thing to do. In fact, subjects probably feared they would appear bigoted if they refused help when it was socially appropriate to do so. These results suggest that racial discrimination should not appear in situations in which norms clearly defining appropriate behavior are present because the "wrongdoing" would be obvious. At least, this should be true among individuals with prejudiced attitudes who fear appearing bigoted.

Tokenism: Small Benefits, High Costs? A second form of subtle discrimination involves **tokenism**. The basic mechanism here is simple. Prejudiced individuals engage in trivial, positive

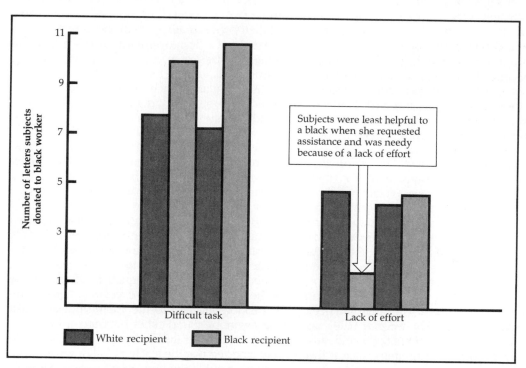

Number of letters subjects donated to black worker

Subjects were least helpful to a black when she requested assistance and was needy because of a lack of effort

Difficult task   Lack of effort

White recipient   Black recipient

Figure 5.2 Subjects were less helpful to blacks than to whites when recipients requested assistance themselves and were responsible for their dependency because of a lack of effort. Thus, only when the failure to help was justifiable were blacks denied more help than whites in the same situation. These results suggest that many whites fear appearing bigoted, so they will provide help unless they can find an excuse (the persons were undeserving). (Source: Based on data from Frey and Gaertner, 1987.)

Whites discriminate against blacks when they can get away with it!

actions toward the members of the groups they dislike (e.g., they hire or promote a single "show" black, Jew, or Hispanic). Then, they use these actions as a rationale for refusing other, more important actions (e.g., the adoption of truly fair hiring or promotion practices) or as a justification for later discrimination. "Don't bother me," they seem to say. "Haven't I done enough for those people already?" Evidence for the use of such tactics has been reported in several studies (e.g. Dutton and Lake, 1973; Rosenfield et al., 1982). In these experiments, white subjects who had performed a small favor for a black stranger were less willing to engage in more effortful forms of helping at a later time than those who had not performed such a favor.

Unfortunately, various forms of tokenism do more than deny groups who are the object of prejudice important forms of aid. Being the recipient of such grudging help—for example, being hired as a "token" black, woman, or Hispanic—can also play havoc with the self-esteem and careers of the persons involved. Evidence for such conclusions has been reported by Chacko (1982). He asked young women holding managerial jobs to rate the extent to which several different factors (their ability, experience, education, or sex) had played a role in their hiring. In addition, they completed questionnaires designed to measure their organizational commitment (favorable attitudes toward their companies) and their satisfaction with their jobs. When subjects who rated their ability as the most important factor in being hired were compared with those who rated their sex as most important, unsettling differences emerged. Those who felt they were mere "tokens" (that they had been hired mainly because they were female) reported significantly lower commitment and satisfaction. These and related findings suggest that the impact of tokenism is largely negative, even for those few individuals who seem to profit most from its existence.

Reverse Discrimination: Giving with One Hand, Taking Away with the Other. Reverse **discrimination** occurs in situations when persons holding at least residual prejudice toward the members of some social group actually lean

over backwards to treat these persons favorably—more favorably than would be the case if they did not belong to this group. Such effects have been observed in several investigations. For example, Chidester (1986) had subjects engage in a brief, "get acquainted" conversation with a stranger who was described as being either black or white. (The conversation took place through microphones and headphones.) When subjects later evaluated this person, they reported more favorable reactions toward strangers who were ostensibly black than ones who were supposedly white. (All participants were white; only subjects' beliefs about the race of their partner were varied; see Figure 5.3.) Unless one assumes that the white subjects actually held more favorable views of blacks than of members of their own race, these findings point to the occurrence of a "lean-over-backwards" or "demonstrate my lack of prejudice" approach among participants.

At first glance, such behavior may not seem to fit our definition of discrimination; after all, it yields positive rather than negative outcomes for its "victims." On one level, this is certainly true; individuals exposed to reverse discrimination do receive raises, promotions, and other benefits. At the same time, though, such favorable treatment may actually prove harmful, especially over the long haul.

Both the operation and potential negative impact of reverse discrimination are forcefully illustrated by a recent study conducted by Fajardo (1985). In this investigation, teachers were asked to grade essays designed, in advance, to be either poor, moderate, or excellent in quality. Information attached to the essays indicated that they were prepared either by white or black students. If reverse discrimination exists, it would be expected that the teachers (all of whom were white) would rate the essays more favorably when they were supposedly prepared by black than by white students. (The essays themselves were identical in both cases; only the supposed race of the authors was varied.) Results indicated that this is precisely what happened. Moreover, the tendency of white teachers to favor black students was strongest under conditions where the essays were of moderate rather than excellent or

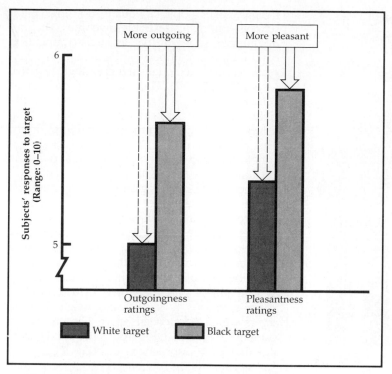

Figure 5.3 *White subjects who believed they were conversing with a black perceived he was more outgoing and pleasant than if they believed they were talking to a white. Unless one assumes that these white subjects actually held more favorable attitudes about blacks than their own race, the results demonstrate the occurrence of a "lean-over-backwards" approach among participants. (Source: Chidester, 1986.)*

"Leaning over backwards" so as not to appear prejudiced

poor quality. In short, it was when the students in question appeared to be of average ability that reverse discrimination was most likely to occur.

As you can readily see, while such practices may help minority students in the short run, they can set the stage for later problems. For example, they may lead some students, at least, to develop inflated opinions of their own abilities and unrealistic expectations about the likelihood of future success. Similarly, reverse discrimination may prevent minority students from seeking the help they may sometimes need early in their academic careers. As a result, they may later face an especially difficult task in compensating for their disadvantaged backgrounds. Needless to

say, when reverse discrimination produces such effects, it can be as harmful as other, more obvious forms of discrimination.

WHY PREJUDICE OCCURS:
Some Contrasting Views

That prejudice exists is an all too obvious fact. Indeed, it seems to have been present in all societies throughout recorded history (see Figure 5.4). This fact raises an important question: how do such attitudes originate? Why, in short, do so many persons hold negative views about people belonging to specific social groups—especially

Figure 5.4 Prejudice seems to have been part of human society throughout recorded history.

Prejudice: An ever-present danger

ones different from their own? The answer seems to involve a number of different factors, but the following seem most important: (1) direct intergroup conflict, (2) social categorization, (3) early learning experiences, and (4) several aspects of social cognition.

Direct Intergroup Conflict: Competition as a Source of Bias

Unfortunately, the things that most people value—good jobs, money, status—are in short supply: there's never quite enough to go around or keep everyone happy. This basic fact serves as the foundation for one influential explanation of prejudice—**realistic conflict theory**. According to this view, prejudice stems from competition between various social groups over valued commodities. In short, prejudice develops out of the

struggle over jobs, adequate housing, good schools, and many desirable outcomes. The theory further suggests that as such competition continues, the members of the groups involved come to view each other in increasingly negative ways (White, 1977). They label one another as "enemies," view their own group as totally in the right, and draw the boundaries between themselves and their opponents ever more firmly. The result, of course, is that what begins as simple competition soon develops into full-scale prejudice, with all that this implies.

Sherif and his colleagues (1961) were the first to examine the effects of intergroup competition on prejudice in a field experiment. This ambitious study involved sending 11-year-old boys to a special summer camp where, free from many external influences, the nature of conflict could be carefully observed. When the boys first arrived at the camp, they were divided into two separate groups at random and assigned to different cabins located far apart. For one week, campers in each of these groups lived and played together. Not surprisingly, the boys developed strong attachments to their groups. Indeed, they soon named themselves the *Rattlers* and the *Eagles,* and made up separate flags. At this point there was no animosity between the groups because they had no contact. Then Sherif held a series of tournaments (tug of war, races, etc.) involving the Rattlers and Eagles in which only the winning team could win prizes, and once obtained, the prizes were shared only among group members. Sherif reasoned that the competition would produce tensions and animosity between the two groups. Sure enough, as the boys competed, tension rose with insults, name-calling, and teasing. The day after the competition, the Rattlers burned the other group's flag, which provoked retaliation by the Eagles in terms of overturning the others' beds, taking personal property, etc. Each group also considered their opponents to be "bums" and "cowards," while perceiving their own group as superior. In two short weeks, by instituting competition for valued goods, Sherif had produced all of the key components of strong prejudice.

In the final phase of the study, Sherif attempted to reduce these negative reactions (we will discuss what he and others have done to reduce prejudice in a subsequent section). Obviously, this study has many limitations: it took place over a short time, the camp setting was special, and the subjects were quite homogeneous in background—they did not belong to different social groups. Despite these limitations, the role of intergroup conflict and competition in prejudice is suggested in other settings. For example, Blake and Mouton (1979) studied corporate executives in a management training program who worked in competing small groups. The groups soon entered into intense conflicts and came to view each other in highly negative ways.

"Us" Versus "Them": Social Categorization as a Basis for Prejudice

A second perspective on the origins of prejudice begins with a basic fact: often, individuals divide the social world around them into two distinct categories—"us" and "them." In short, they view other persons either as belonging to their own group (usually termed the **in-group**) or to some other category (an **out-group**). If this process of **social categorization** stopped there, it would have little bearing on prejudice. Unfortunately, though, it does not. Sharply contrasting feelings and beliefs are usually attached to members of the in-group and members of various out-groups. While persons in the former ("us") category are viewed in favorable terms, those in the latter ("them") are often seen in a negative light (Wills, 1981; Crocker et al., 1987). They are assumed to possess undesirable traits and are strongly disliked (e.g., Hemstone and Jaspers, 1982). To read more about our tendencies to divide the social world into contrasting groups see the "Focus on Research" insert on page 112.

Early Experience: The Role of Social Learning

You will probably find a third explanation for the occurrence of prejudice far from surprising. It suggests that such reactions are *learned,* and that they develop in much the same manner, and

through the same processes, as other attitudes (refer to our discussion in Chapter Four). Thus, this **social learning view** holds that children acquire negative attitudes toward specific social groups because they are exposed to such views on the part of others (e.g., their parents, friends), or because they are specifically rewarded for adopting them (e.g., with praise for expressing the "right" views).

While parents, teachers, and friends seem to play a key role in this process, the mass media, too, are important. For example, until quite recently members of racial and ethnic minorities appeared infrequently in movies or on television. And when they did appear, they were usually shown in low status or comic roles. Given repeated exposure to such materials, it is far from surprising that many children soon came to believe that members of such groups must be inferior. After all, why else would they always be shown in such contexts?

Fortunately, the situation has changed greatly in recent years in the United States and elsewhere. Members of racial and ethnic minorities now appear more frequently than in the past and are often presented in a favorable manner (see Figure 5.6). Whether these shifts will contribute to reduced racial and ethnic prejudice, however, remains uncertain. Given the tremendous impact of television and other mass media on both attitudes and behavior (Bandura, 1986; Liebert and Sprafkin, 1988), such benefits seem plausible. However, only time—and systematic research—will reveal whether they do in fact materialize.

Cognitive Sources of Prejudice: Stereotypes, Illusory Correlation, and Illusion of Out-Group Homogeneity

A final source of prejudice is, in some ways, the most unsettling we will consider. It involves the basic ways in which we think about other persons—in short, the key process of *social cognition.* Unfortunately, growing evidence points to the conclusion that several basic aspects of this process may contribute to the development and maintenance of prejudice. Among the most im-

TAJFEL AND THE MINIMAL GROUP PARADIGM: PREJUDICE ON THE FLIP OF A COIN

Realistic conflict theory suggests that competition for resources creates divisiveness between groups. However, the late Henri Tajfel proposed that people demonstrate a tendency to distinguish between "us" and "them" on the basis of even inconsequential, trivial distinctions. Furthermore, on the basis of these differences we tend to treat members of the "in-group" favorably and members of the "out-group" unfavorably.

Tajfel (1970) had teenagers individually express their preferences about paintings by the modern artists Paul Klee and Wassily Kandinsky (see Figure 5.5). Then they were told they would be placed in a group of other boys who shared their preferences (the Klee group or the Kandinsky group). Next, before meeting the others, they were given the opportunity to divide some monetary rewards between their group and the other group. Even in this situation, called the "minimal group paradigm" (because the shared preference is or should be an inconsequential one and the group has never met), subjects divided the resources unequally: they favored their group at the expense of the other.

This result has been repeated with even more trivial group categorizations (Brewer and Silver, 1978). For example, the same in-group bias occurs if subjects are divided into groups based on their being "overestimators" of the number of dots on a slide or "underestimators," or even if the groups are arbitrarily formed on a *flip of a coin* in front of the subject. It seems that the tendency to perceive an "us" and a "them" is an all-pervasive phenomenon (Turner, 1987). Results from the minimal group paradigm suggest that in some settings prejudice may stem from our tendency to perceive others as belonging either to our own or some other group.

Figure 5.5 Subjects who preferred the paintings of modern artist Paul Klee (left) over those of Wassily Kandinsky gave a larger monetary reward to subjects with the same preference. In-group favoritism has also been shown by people in experimentally formed groups based on the flip of a coin.

In-group favoritism in the minimal group paradigm

Figure 5.6   *Members of various racial and ethnic minorities appear more frequently on TV and in the movies and are represented in a more favorable manner than in the past. These changes may contribute to reduced racial and ethnic prejudice.*

The mass media are presenting more favorable views of racial and ethnic minorities.

portant of these are stereotypes, illusory correlation, and the illusion of out-group homogeneity.

Stereotypes: Negative Schemata for Social Groups. We have already examined the nature of stereotypes in Chapter Three, where we noted that they can be viewed as a special type of *schema*—a kind of cognitive framework for interpreting and processing social information. Specifically, **stereotypes** consist of information and beliefs about specific groups, much of it negative in nature. Like other schemata, stereotypes strongly affect the ways in which we deal with (i.e., process) incoming information. For example, information relevant to a particular stereotype is processed more quickly than information not related to that stereotype (Dovidio, Evans, and Tyler, 1986). Similarly, stereotypes lead the persons holding them to pay attention to specific types of information—usually input that is consistent with the stereotypes. Or, if inconsistent information does become the subject of attention, strongly entrenched stereotypes may induce the individuals involved to engage in efforts to refute it, perhaps by recalling facts that *are* consistent with their schemata (O'Sullivan

and Durso, 1984). Third, stereotypes also determine what we remember; usually, again, we remember information that is consistent with them (Miller, 1986).

Now consider how these effects apply to prejudice. Once an individual has acquired a stereotype (a negative schema) for some social group, he or she tends to notice information that fits readily into this cognitive framework and to remember "facts" that are consistent with it. Thus, the stereotype is, to a large degree, self-confirming: even exceptions to it make it stronger, for they simply induce the person in question to bring supporting information to mind (as we discussed in Chapter Three).

Evidence for the operation of such negative schemata has been reported in several recent studies. For example, Dovidio, Evans, and Tyler (1986) presented subjects with the words "white" and "black," and then asked them to decide whether various traits stereotypically attributed to these groups (presented one at a time) could ever be true of each of these racial groups. The subjects—all of whom were white—were faster in deciding whether positive traits described whites, and faster in deciding whether negative traits described blacks (see Figure 5.7). Thus, their cognitive representations of these two groups appeared to differ sharply.

A more disturbing illustration of the operation of racial stereotypes has recently been reported by Kirkland, Greenberg, and Pyszczynski (1987). These researchers had subjects read a trial transcript and asked for evaluations of the attorney and defendant. In all conditions, the defendant was always white, but in some conditions the defense attorney was either black or white. While reading the trial case, an accomplice posing as a subject also reading the case made a derogatory comment in which the defense attorney was referred to either as a "shyster" (nonethnic label) or a "n--r" (a racist remark). As shown in Figure 5.8, the derogatory

ethnic label led to derogation of the defense attorney. Furthermore, the white defendant received a more negative evaluation and a harsher verdict when defended by a black who was the target of a derogatory ethnic label. The researchers reasoned that the racial slur activated negative racial schemata (stereotypes) among subjects, and so lowered the evaluations of the defense attorney. It is also of interest that the (white) defendant was negatively evaluated, apparently as a result of being associated with the target of the ethnic slur.

Illusory Correlation: Perceiving Relationships That Aren't There. Unfortunately, negative schemata are not the only cognitive source of prejudice and discrimination. Another involves

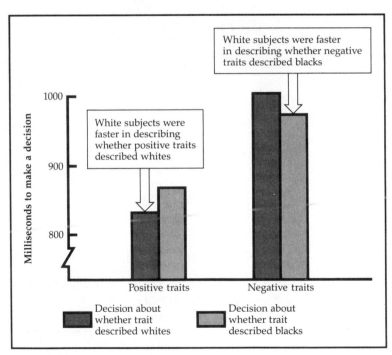

Figure 5.7. *White subjects were faster in deciding whether positive traits described whites, and faster in deciding whether negative traits described blacks. These results provide evidence that stereotypes (schemata) facilitate the processing of information. Moreover, the cognitive schemas about blacks and whites differ sharply. (Source: Based on data from Dovidio, Evans, and Tyler, 1986.)*

Some effects of schemata about social groups

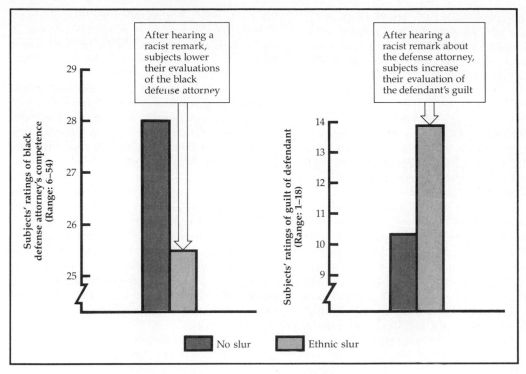

Figure 5.8 *When white subjects heard an accomplice make an ethnic slur about a black defense lawyer, they lowered their evaluations of this person. They also suggested a harsher verdict and made a lower evaluation of the white person he was defending. (Source: Based on data from Kirkland, Greenberg, and Pyszczynski, 1987.)*

Racial slurs activate negative racial schemata.

illusory correlation—a topic we have already considered in Chapter Three (Hamilton, Dugan, and Troilier, 1985; Troilier and Hamilton, 1986). As you may recall, illusory correlation refers to our tendency to perceive associations (correlations) between variables that do not, in fact, exist. It seems to stem primarily from the co-occurrence of distinctive stimuli or events. For example, consider the following facts. Violent crimes are fairly rare events, even in the United States, which has a higher rate of such events than other developed nations. For this reason, violent crimes are quite distinctive. Similarly, being a member of a minority group is also a distinctive event; there are, after all, many more members of the majority. Because these two events are relatively unusual, their co-occurrence is highly distinctive. Thus, a report of a violent crime committed by a person of Cuban descent will draw the attention of majority readers. Such heightened attention, in turn, assures that the event is entered strongly into memory. As a result, it will be readily recalled on later occasions—more readily than other, less distinctive events (e.g., the report of a violent crime by a white person). Because of this process, an illusory correlation may develop: individuals may come to perceive that ethnic identity is closely linked to violent crime. Moreover, and here is the important point, they may reach this conclusion even if the rate of violent crime is equal in both the minority and majority groups. In short, illusory correlations, which seem to develop because of our basic tendency to pay most attention to unusual or distinctive events, can sometimes play a role in the development of stereotypes and prejudice (Spears, van der Pligt, and Eiser, 1985; Sanbonmatsu, Sherman, and Hamilton, 1987).

The Illusion of Out-Group Homogeneity. A third cognitive factor worthy of our attention involves what has sometimes been termed the **illusion of out-group homogeneity**. Briefly, this refers to our tendency to perceive the members of out-groups as much more similar or homogeneous than members of our own in-group (Linville, 1982; see Figure 5.9). At first glance, it is tempting to assume this tendency stems from a simple fact: we have more contact with members of our own group, and so develop richer and more differentiated cognitive representations of them. However, research findings suggest that this is not the only factor involved. The illusion of greater homogeneity among persons belonging to groups other than our own seems to exist even in cases when we have a great deal of contact with them. For example, males perceive women as more homogeneous in their attitudes and behavior than men, while females perceive men as being more homogeneous than women, despite the fact that the two groups are in continuous, intimate contact with each other (Park and

Rothbart, 1982). Apparently, then, our tendency to perceive the members of groups other than our own as all "very much alike" reflects a very basic type of bias in the way we think about others (Mullen and Hu, 1987).

Before concluding this section, we should mention that there may be situations in which we see our own group (the *in-group*) as more homogeneous than the *out-group*. Specifically, if we are members of a minority group, this may pose a threat to self-esteem. One way to counteract this threat is to accentuate or magnify the degree of groupness or similarity among other minority group members—the "we" feeling (Simon and Brown, 1987). This does not mean that the out-group homogeneity effect disappears, but only that minorities may also perceive an even stronger homogeneity among members of their own group. This may explain the existence of very strong ties among minority group members even long after they have been "accepted" by the majority.

Together, stereotypes, illusory correlations, and perceptions of out-group homogeneity go a long way toward explaining the occurrence—and persistence—of prejudice. Such attitudes, it would appear, rest on basic aspects of social cognition, as well as intergroup conflict, early social learning, and the desire to enhance one's self-esteem. The practical message contained in such findings seems clear: in order to be successful,

Figure 5.9 There is a tendency to perceive members of out-groups as much more similar or homogeneous than members of our own group. (Source: Reprinted with special permission of King Features Syndicate.)

The illusion of out-group homogeneity

techniques designed to combat prejudice and reduce its negative impact must take careful account of its cognitive as well as its social foundations.

COMBATING PREJUDICE: Some Plans of Action

Prejudice, wherever it occurs, poses serious problems. In its least harmful forms, it can be viewed as a thorn in the side of society—or one producing unnecessary annoyance, friction, and irritation. At worst, it is an open wound—one through which a given culture or nation can be drained of its vitality, precious human resources, and social conscience. Reducing prejudice and combating its negative effects, therefore, are important tasks. But how can they be accomplished? Fortunately, several strategies for reaching these goals exist. While none, by itself, can totally eliminate prejudice or discrimination, together they seem capable of making substantial "dents" in these persistent problems. Three of these tactics will now be described.

Breaking the Chain of Bigotry: On Learning Not to Hate

At several points in this book, we have noted that parents play a key role in shaping their children's attitudes. Included among the many views that they transmit in this respect are various forms of prejudice. Given this central fact, one useful technique for combating prejudice and discrimination is obvious: somehow, discourage parents from providing their offspring with training in ethnic or racial bigotry. As we're sure you realize, this is a difficult task. Psychologists cannot intervene directly in parent-child relations; doing so would be unethical, if not simply illegal. What they *can* do, however, is call parents' attention to their own crucial role in maintaining the chain of bigotry. While some die-hard fanatics may actually wish to turn their children into hate-filled copies of themselves, most parents genuinely wish to provide their children with a more positive view of the social world. Thus, campaigns designed to enhance parents' aware-

ness of this process, and to discourage them from demonstrating prejudice in their own behavior, may yield positive results.

Direct Intergroup Contact: The Potential Benefits of Acquaintance

Answer honestly: how frequently do you have contact with people outside your own racial, ethnic, or religious group? For example, if you are white, how often do you interact with blacks? If you are Christian, how often do you interact with individuals who are Jews? Unless you are different from most persons, or live in an environment that actively encourages such cross-group contacts, your reply is probably, "Not very often." Even in the late 1980s most people have most of their social contacts with persons belonging to their in-group (Ickes, 1984).

This basic fact raises an intriguing question: can prejudice be reduced by somehow increasing the degree of contact between different groups? The idea that it can is known as the **contact hypothesis**, and there are several good reasons for predicting that such a strategy might prove effective (Stephan, 1985). First, as individuals belonging to different social groups become better acquainted, they may come to realize that they are more similar than they initially believed. As we will see in Chapter Six, growing recognition of such similarity, in turn, may generate increased mutual attraction, Second, while stereotypes *are* resistant to change, they can be altered when sufficient information inconsistent with them is encountered. Thus, as persons from different groups get to know one another better, these negative schemata may begin to crumble, or at least to change. Third, increased contact may help counter the illusion of out-group homogeneity described above. For these and other reasons, it seems possible that direct intergroup contact may be effective in combating prejudice. Is it? The answer, unfortunately, is somewhat mixed. Such contact does seem capable of producing beneficial effects, but only when it occurs under highly specific conditions (Cook, 1985).

First, the groups interacting must be roughly equal in social, economic, or task-related status.

If, instead, they differ sharply in such respects, communication between them may be difficult, and prejudice may actually increase. Although this is an important factor, by itself, contact on equal terms is not sufficient to reduce prejudice. This was demonstrated by Sherif and his colleagues in their study with the summer campers described above. After animosities had formed between the Rattlers and the Eagles, Sherif tried to reduce negative reactions by increasing contact. The groups took their meals at the same mess hall, watched movies together, had a July 4 celebration together, etc., but the animosity remained. But Sherif found that if conditions were arranged so the groups worked together to reach *superordinate goals*—ones they both desired—this helped to reduce intergroup friction. For example, the researchers forced the Eagles and Rattlers to cooperate and work together to restore their mutual water supply (which had been "sabotaged" by the researchers). This example illustrates the importance of a second factor: the contact situation must involve cooperation and interdependence, so that the groups work toward shared goals. Third, contact between the groups must be informal, so that they get to know each other on a one-to-one basis. Fourth, contact must occur in a setting where existing norms favor group equality and increased association between persons belonging to each category. Fifth, the groups must interact in ways that permit disconfirmation of negative, stereotyped beliefs about each other. And, finally, the persons involved must view one another as typical of their respective groups; only if they do will they generalize their pleasant contacts to other persons or situations, and demonstrate more positive reactions toward the out-group (Wilder, 1984).

When contact between initially hostile groups occurs under the conditions just described, prejudice between them does seem to decrease (Cook, 1985; Riordan, 1978). For example, in a series of studies, Aronson and his colleagues have employed increased contact under cooperative conditions as a means of reducing racial prejudice among children (e.g., Aronson, Bridgeman, and Geffner, 1978). The basic procedure they used—the jigsaw method—was simple.

Groups of six students worked together on a specific lesson. Each member of the group was required to master a single portion and present it to the others. Successful group performance could be attained only if each person performed adequately. Thus, all members had to cooperate in order to attain a shared group goal. The results achieved with this simple procedure were impressive. Following exposure to the jigsaw method (and the cooperative intergroup contact it involved), students showed reduced racial stereotyping and increased liking for members of the other race (see Figure 5.10). Additional encouraging results have also been reported by others (e.g., Cook, 1984a). It appears that friendly, cooperative contact may be an effective tool for combating cross-group hostility and prejudice.

Desegregation: The "Grand Social Experiment"

In the United States, the contact hypothesis has been put to actual use in the context of *school desegregation*. In the 1950s, the U.S. Supreme Court declared that segregated schools (blacks and whites attending separate schools) were illegal. In the subsequent years, the schools were desegregated. Many social observers believed that desegregation was a moral necessity and predicted that the increased contact between black and white children would reduce prejudice. Others resented the forced busing that was in some cases used to achieve desegregation and believed that forced contact might only intensify rather than reduce racial prejudice.

The results of this vast undertaking are something of a mixed bag. For one thing, educational achievement among both blacks and whites has *not* improved in the decades since school desegregation began (e.g., Gerard, 1983; Miller and Brewer, 1984). Whether this is due to the disruption associated with efforts to attain fully integrated schools is unclear. On the other hand, there do appear to have been reductions in stereotyping and prejudice, although not all the results are uniformly positive (Cook, 1984a, 1984b; Miller and Brewer, 1984).

These mixed results should not be surprising in light of the other conditions needed for direct

Figure 5.10 *Intergroup contact can reduce racial prejudice and discrimination if, among other things, the groups interacting are equal in status, the situation involves cooperation and interdependence, and the interaction occurs in a setting where norms favor group equality (see text for other important factors).*

Intergroup contact: Sometimes, it works.

contact to reduce prejudice (described earlier). For example, government and school authorities have overlooked the need to assure that students who are in intergroup contact are of equal status. On the contrary, the typical pattern has been one in which minority children from disadvantaged backgrounds are suddenly placed in schools where the white students enjoy higher socioeconomic status. Similarly, the norms surrounding such schools have often been opposed to facilitating intergroup contact; indeed, integration has frequently taken place within a context of angry demonstrations and protests. Given such conditions, it is hardly surprising that school desegregation has often failed to yield the benefits predicted by its advocates. There is still hope, however, if key factors determining the impact

of intergroup contact are taken carefully into account. (For some comments about another form of prejudice which our society will have to cope with see the "On the Applied Side" insert on page 120.)

SEXISM IN THE 1980s: A Closer Look at One Form of Prejudice

Females constitute a clear majority of the world's population. Yet they have often been treated much like a minority in many cultures. They have often been excluded from economic and political power. They have been the subject of pronounced negative stereotyping, and they have had to confront overt discrimination in many spheres of life (e.g., exclusion from certain jobs, kinds of training, social organizations). Fortunately, the situation appears to be changing in many nations. Overt discriminatory practices are decreasing, and there has been at least some shift toward more egalitarian sex-role attitudes on the part of both men and women (Helmreich, Spence, and Gibson, 1982). Despite such changes, though, prejudice based on gender, or **sexism**, persists in many settings (e.g., Crosby, 1982; Steinberg and Shapiro, 1982). Because this type of prejudice affects more individuals than any other kind, and because it produces negative outcomes for men and women, it is a serious problem, fully deserving of our attention.

Prejudice Toward Females: Its Nature and Origins

As we noted earlier, females have often been the object of widespread stereotyping. To an extent, this is also true of males; they, too, are perceived as being "all alike"—possessing certain traits. Usually, though, stereotypes concerning females are more negative in content than those for males (see Figure 5.12). For example, in several cultures males are assumed to possess such traits as assertiveness, ambition, self-confidence, decisiveness, and dominance. In contrast, the corresponding stereotype for females includes such characteristics as submissiveness, concern with others, dependence, emotionality, and passivity (Williams and Best, 1982).

PREJUDICE AND THE AIDS EPIDEMIC

The United States (and the entire world) is facing a health threat that is apparently increasing prejudice and discrimination toward some groups about whom there were already widespread negative feelings. The growing incidence of and publicity about AIDS (acquired immune deficiency syndrome) has resulted in widespread public concern and fear. One result has been a backlash of prejudice and discrimination against those identified as being at greatest risk for this disease—homosexuals, intravenous drug users, and certain ethnic groups (e.g., Haitians). Evidence of a backlash comes from several quarters: gay rights legislation that was pending in several state legislatures has been tabled, the Gallup poll indicates that attitudes toward homosexuals have become more negative since the outbreak of the disease (Morganthau, 1983), and Haitian immigrants report greater discrimination in housing and employment (Greco, 1983). Furthermore, children born of AIDS-infected mothers have been forced out of their schools because of the fear that they will spread the disease, despite the fact that there is good evidence it cannot be transmitted by casual contact. It has even been suggested that high-risk groups be quarantined!

Prejudice toward groups at high risk can only make things worse. For example, highly prejudiced persons may assume that by avoiding gays they are immune from the disease (see Figure 5.11). But this ignores the fact that AIDS can also be acquired from sexual contact with heterosexuals who carry the virus. Further, there is evidence that people with negative attitudes toward homosexuals are the least knowledgeable about AIDS and how it is transmitted. Without accurate knowledge and adequate precautions, anyone is a potential victim of the disease. Perhaps even more serious is that fact that nurses and health care workers with strongly negative attitudes about homosexuals tend to be less knowledgeable about the disease than others who work with AIDS patients (Bielass, 1987). Such prejudice might create serious barriers to the quality of the patients' medical care (O'Donnell et al., 1987).

The above comments suggest that while medical researchers search for a cure for AIDS, social scientists should study the social and psychological effects of the disease. How can health education programs be created to provide appropriate information to the public—especially those persons most prejudiced and resistant to thinking about the problem? Can the techniques for reducing prejudice described earlier in this chapter be applied to prejudice about groups at high risk for AIDS?

Figure 5.11 Prejudice toward homosexuals may lead heterosexuals to avoid information about AIDS and erroneously to believe they don't need to take precautions.

Prejudice: An obstacle to health prevention

Figure 5.12 *Though there have been changes in negative stereotypes about females in recent years, prejudice and stereotyping still exist. (Source: Reprinted with special permission of King Features Syndicate, Inc., 1987.)*

Negative stereotyping of women persists.

That such stereotypes exist is no longer open to question: their presence is supported by a large body of research evidence (e.g., Deaux and Lewis, 1984; Berndt and Heller, 1986). Two important questions relating to them, however, are these: (1) to what extent are they accurate? and (2) why do they persist?

Stereotypes About Women and Men: Myth or Reality? To what extent do men and women actually differ, either in their behavior or their traits? This is a complex question that can be addressed on several different levels. Thus, no simple or clear-cut answer yet exists. Existing evidence, however, seems to point to the following general conclusion: where differences between the sexes are concerned, "common sense" probably overstates the case. Males and females do seem to differ in several respects (e.g., Parsons, Adler, and Meece, 1984), but the number and size of such differences are less than prevailing stereotypes suggest (Martin, 1987).

For example, in a series of related studies, Rice and his colleagues (e.g., Rice, Instone, and Adams, 1984) have compared the behavior of male and female cadets at West Point (the United States Military Academy). Results indicated that few, if any, differences could be observed. Similarly, in other investigations (e.g., Steinberg and Shapiro, 1982) male and female managers have been compared in terms of a large number of personality dimensions. In general, results offer little support for the view that they differ in important ways.

Together, such findings suggest that stereotypes concerning differences between the sexes are only partly true at best (Eagly, 1987). While the behavior of males and females does differ in some respects, these differences are smaller, both in degree and number, than has often been assumed. In sum, there appears to be more myth than reality in such cultural stereotypes.

Gender Stereotypes: Why Do They Persist? If, as we have seen, stereotypes about the supposed traits of males and females are largely inaccurate, why do so many people continue to believe in them? Again, this is a complex question with no simple answers. However, research conducted recently by Eagly and her associates (e.g., Eagly and Steffen, 1984, 1986) points to an interesting possibility: perhaps these stereotypes have their foundations in the fact that males and females often occupy somewhat different roles in society. Even today, after several decades of rapid social change, a larger proportion of males are employed in full-time jobs outside the home. It may be that individuals who fill such positions, *regardless of their sex,* are perceived as possessing the traits often ascribed to males (e.g., assertiveness, self-assurance, decisiveness). Correspondingly, a larger proportion of females than males are homemakers, with no employment outside this context. Persons filling this role may be perceived as possessing the traits often attributed to females (e.g., selflessness, concern with others). In short, gender stereotypes may persist because men and women are not equally distributed across these contrasting social roles. To examine this notion, Eagly asked subjects to evaluate males and females who are employed full-time outside the home or work as homemakers. Because an increasing number of adults in the United States are employed part-time (20 percent according to the U.S. Department of Labor, 1984), Eagly also examined perceptions of male and female part-time employees.

In several studies, Eagly and Steffen (1986) asked male and female students to rate imaginary persons described as being employed full-time outside the home, part-time, or as a home-

maker, and as being either a man or a woman. The traits on which subjects rated these persons were ones included in traditional stereotypes for both sexes. (In a fourth condition, no information about occupation was given, but each individual was still identified as being either a man or woman.) Results offered strong support for the view that stereotypes persist because males and females occupy different roles in society. As shown in Figure 5.13, homemakers were rated as being more feminine (in their traits) than persons employed full-time outside the home, *regardless of whether they were men or women.* Similarly, full-time employed persons were rated as being more masculine (in their traits) than homemakers, again regardless of whether they happened to be men or women. Thus, it was the

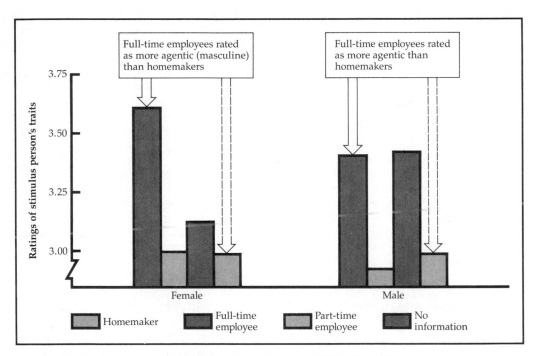

Figure 5.13 *Individuals holding full-time jobs were rated as more masculine in their traits than individuals who were described as being homemakers. Further, this was true whether they were men or women. However, women described as part-time employees were rated as no more masculine than full-time homemakers. Part-time male employees were seen as lower in masculinity than full-time employees. (Source: Eagly and Steffen, 1986.)*

Social roles and full-time and part-time employment: A basis for gender stereotypes

role individuals played, not their actual sex, that determined how they were perceived. The results also indicate that full-time and part-time employees are perceived differently. Even though female part-time employees' efforts are divided between domestic duties and earning money, they were perceived as being similar to homemakers. Male part-time employees were rated as low in masculine traits probably because they were perceived as being unable or unwilling to fulfill their traditional obligation of full-time employment.

As we're sure you can readily appreciate, these findings are quite optimistic in some of their implications. They suggest that as women enter new fields as full-time employees and take on new roles, traditional stereotypes about them may fade. They will come to be perceived (and evaluated) mainly in terms of the roles they fill, rather than on the basis of their sex. On the other hand, the results for perceptions of part-time employees are not as optimistic. A woman who adds to her homemaker role the extra burden of part-time employment is not seen as having more of the self-assertiveness and concern with mastery that are stereotypically associated with full-time employees. A man who is only employed part-time is seen as either incapable of or shirking his duties. Thus, there still appears to be some distance to go until gender stereotypes fade completely.

Discrimination Against Females: Subtle, But Sometimes Deadly

Although the Equal Rights Amendment failed to gain passage in the United States, other legislation and court rulings have gone a long way toward eliminating overt discrimination on the basis of sex. It is no longer feasible for businesses, schools, or other organizations to reject applicants for jobs or admission simply because they are female (or male). Yet, despite this fact, women continue to occupy a disadvantaged position in society, at least in some respects. For example, they still tend to be concentrated in relatively low-paying and low-status jobs. As Steinberg and Shapiro (1982, p. 306) have noted: "Women populate corporations but rarely run them." Why is this the case? The answer seems to

involve a number of subtle but often damaging forces that operate against success and achievement by females in many settings. Some of these are considered below.

Subjective Task Value and Career Choice. In recent years only 6 percent of the bachelor's degrees in engineering and 18 percent of those in computer science were awarded to women, despite the fact that females make up approximately 50 percent of college enrollment. Clearly, such differences are not due to overt discrimination: few colleges or universities currently tolerate barriers designed to prevent persons of either sex from choosing specific majors. What, then, accounts for this state of affairs? Findings reported by Parsons (Parsons, Adler, and Meece, 1984) indicate that it may stem from differences in the *subjective value* attached by males and females to different fields of study.

When these researchers questioned a large group of junior high school students, they found that females rated English as more important than math, while males rated the two subjects as equally important. Similarly, females expressed stronger interest in taking English courses than did males. Since jobs in high-paying fields (e.g., engineering, information science) require considerable background in mathematics, and since top executives are often drawn from such areas, these findings point to one potential reason why women often hold second-class status in the world of work: they select career routes that lead to less rewarding jobs. The question of *why* they choose such paths is very complex, and probably involves contrasting socialization practices for males and females (e.g., little boys are encouraged to work with tools and numbers, while little girls are not), as well as persisting stereotypes about the relative abilities of the two sexes (e.g., many people assume that males possess superior quantitative skills and that females possess superior verbal ones).

Women and Computing: There's Even Bias in the Software. As noted above, relatively few women go into high-level quantitative or information science (computing) careers. Why are computers less alluring to women? Huff and Cooper (1987) speculated that the stereotypes

Figure 5.14 Computer software tends to be created with males rather than females in mind. This may contribute to the fact that fewer women than men seek careers in engineering and computer science.

Sexism and software

about the two genders (described earlier) even "creep" into the way people design software for children when they first have contact with computers. These researchers asked forty-three educators with programming experience to design a software program to teach junior high students to use commas correctly (see Figure 5.14). Some were asked to design a program for girls, others to design a program for boys, and others to design for students. Upon their completion, the various programs were rated on a variety of dimensions by the designers and three independent raters. The ratings showed that software designed for girls emphasized features for "learning" or academic uses. In contrast, programs for both boys *and* students tended to have more competitive, action-oriented game features. It appears, then, that programmers who write software for "students" tend to have boys in mind as the predominant users and to create the software with regard to what they think boys will find appealing. This is especially interesting in light of the fact that the majority of the programmers were females! Educational software may be designed to appeal to boys, without consideration for the effect of girls' motivation to

use them or on girls' educational profit from them. This kind of bias could contribute to women being less likely to use computers and to find them less interesting or pleasurable to interact with.

Differences in Expectations of Males and Females. Expectations often have a self-fulfilling impact. If females have lower expectations concerning rewards or outcomes than males, they may behave in ways that cause their beliefs to be confirmed (Deaux and Major, 1987). Major and Konar (1984) asked male and female business majors to estimate their future starting and peak salaries and those of other persons in their fields. Females consistently expected their own and others' starting and peak salaries to be considerably lower (by several thousand dollars) than did males. These different expectations can make a difference in light of subsequent research showing that the higher the starting salaries individuals requested, the more money they were actually paid (Major, Vanderslice, and McFarlin, 1985). Of course, women may hold lower expectations than males because they perceive the reality—that females usually *do* receive less pay than men for the same work. Needless to say, as sex discrimination in the world of work is eliminated, these barriers to success should be overcome.

An Optimistic Conclusion: Sexism in the World of Work— Going, Going . . . ?

Though sexism has a long history, there are signs that things have and will continue to improve. As many persons of both sexes have come to understand the basic unfairness of many existing practices, considerable change has taken place. Perhaps nowhere is this shift more visible than in the world of work. For example, while less than 5 percent of first-line managers were females two decades ago, more than 30 percent are females at present. That such shifts have been accompanied by corresponding reductions in prejudice toward women is suggested by a growing number of studies reporting little, if any, evidence for sexism in several areas, including ones where such bias was formerly noted. For example, contrary to earler findings (e.g., Bartol and Butterfield, 1976), a recent investigation by Izraeli and Izraeli (1985) found no tendency for their male or female managers to evaluate female leaders less favorably than male leaders. Similarly, in a study involving evaluations of more than six hundred male and female store managers by their male and female supervisors, Peters and his colleagues (Peters et al., 1984) found no indication of discrimination against females. Indeed, both male and female supervisors assigned *higher* performance ratings to female managers than to male managers.

When these and other findings are combined, a picture of major change—and a shift toward reduced sex discrimination in many employment settings—emerges. This is not to suggest that the battle for equality is over, and that the victory is already at hand—far from it. Women still face serious barriers and problems in work settings (e.g., they still continue to be the victims of sexual harassment to a much greater degree than males; Gutek, 1985). We do believe, though, that the campaign is going well, and that further progress is likely to occur in the years ahead.

SUMMARY

Prejudice involves the tendency to evaluate others negatively simply because they belong to a specific social group. **Discrimination** refers to specific harmful actions directed toward persons or groups that are the targets of prejudice. Discrimination is sometimes overt, but frequently it takes subtle forms. Among the most damaging of these are reluctance to offer aid to members of disliked groups, *tokenism,* and *reverse discrimination.*

Several explanations for the existence of prejudice have been offered. *Realistic conflict theory* suggests that it derives primarily from competition between various groups for possession of valued resources (e.g., jobs, status). *Social categorization*—our tendency to divide the social world into two distinct groups ("us" and "them")—also plays a role. Prejudice may also stem from *early social learning experiences,* in which children are exposed to prejudiced attitudes on the part of others, or are actively rewarded for holding them. Finally, prejudice seems to derive, at least in part, from basic aspects of *social cognition.* These include the operation of *stereotypes, illusory correlation,* and the *illusion of group homogeneity.*

Several tactics appear to be effective in reducing prejudice. Changes in child-rearing practices and in the way members of various groups are depicted in the mass media may be useful. *Increased contact* between persons belonging to different groups can succeed, but only when such contacts occur under favorable conditions (e.g., equal status, in the context of norms supporting cross-group ties).

Sexism, prejudice based on sex, has received a great deal of attention from social psychologists in recent years. Stereotypes concerning the supposed traits of the two sexes appear to be misleading; males and females do not differ to the extent these stereotypes suggest. Such views persist, however, because males and females occupy different roles in society (e.g., a greater proportion of males are employed outside the home). While overt discrimination against females has decreased, some factors contribute to its persistence. These include differences in the subjective value attached by males and females to different fields of study. Such differences, in turn, may stem from contrasting socialization practices for boys and girls.

GLOSSARY

contact hypothesis The suggestion that increased contact between members of various social groups will be effective in reducing prejudice between them. Such effects seem to occur only when contact takes place under specific, positive conditions.

discrimination Negative behaviors directed toward members of social groups who are the object of prejudice.

illusion of out-group homogeneity The tendency to assume that members of various out-groups are more similar to one another than are members of one's own in-group.

illusory correlation The perception of an association (correlation) between two variables when in fact no such relationship exists. This form of cognitive bias appears to be based primarily on the co-occurrence of highly distinctive events.

in-group The social group to which an individual perceives herself or himself as belonging.

out-group A group other than the one to which individuals feel they belong.

prejudice Negative attitudes toward members of specific social groups.

realistic conflict theory The view that prejudice often stems from direct competition between various social groups over valued outcomes (e.g., jobs, status).

reverse discrimination The tendency to evaluate or treat members of out-groups (especially racial or ethnic minorities) more favorably than members of one's own in-group.

sexism Prejudice based on gender.

social categorization Our basic tendency to divide the social world into two separate categories: "us" and "them."

social learning view (of prejudice) The view that prejudice is acquired through basic mechanisms of learning (modeling, instrumental conditioning).

stereotypes Beliefs and expectations (generally negative) about the members of specific social groups. Stereotypes can be viewed as negative schemata relating to such groups.

tokenism Instances in which individuals perform trivial positive actions for members of groups toward whom they are prejudiced, and then use such behavior as an excuse for avoiding more meaningful beneficial actions toward them.

FOR MORE INFORMATION

DOVIDIO, J. F., and GAERTNER, S. L. (Eds.). (1986). *Prejudice, discrimination, and racism.* San Diego: Academic Press.

This book reviews research suggesting that racial prejudice has not shown a significant decrease, but has adopted more subtle forms.

GUTEK, B. A. (1985). *Sex and the workplace.* San Francisco: Jossey-Bass.

A thoughtful analysis of sexual harassment and related issues in work settings. Individual chapters examine the causes of sexual harassment, the attitudes of men and women toward such behavior, and techniques for coping with this important problem.

MILLER, N., and BREWER, M. B. (1984). *Groups in conflict: The psychology of desegregation.* New York: Academic Press.

This book focuses primarily on the *contact hypothesis*—the view that increased contact between groups can reduce the level of prejudice between them. Separate chapters describe attempts to investigate this hypothesis in a wide range of situations. Suggestions for enhancing the outcomes of desegregation are also considered.

STEPHAN, W. G. (1985). Intergroup relations. In G. Lindzey and E. Aronson (Eds.). *Handbook of social psychology* (Vol. 2). New York: Random House.

A thorough review of current knowledge about intergroup relations by a well-known researcher in the area. Many processes that play a role in the development of prejudice, as well as several techniques for combating such reactions, are examined. This is an excellent place to begin if you'd like to know more about prejudice and related topics.

Chapter Six
Interpersonal Attraction: Friendship, Love, and Relationships

Upon receiving a college scholarship, Laura felt proud of her accomplishments and very excited at the prospect of living away from home in a world that was new to her. She also looked forward to making new friends. After she arrived at the campus on a hot August afternoon, unloaded all of her belongings from her parents' car, packed them into her dormitory room, and said good-bye to her family, her excitement was replaced by a jumble of not very pleasant feelings. She realized that she didn't know even one person on the entire campus. She suddenly felt very lonely.

The arrival of her new roommate was not much help. When they met, it was dislike at first sight. Pam was obviously on campus to have a good time, and she reminded Laura of one of the Popples, saying "Let's party!" and then giggling.

The first few weeks of school, involving orientation, registration, and classes, passed by without making life any easier for Laura. She went through her scheduled activities feeling like someone from another planet. Everyone else seemed to know one another, and they talked and joked about people and events that she knew nothing about. Others were constantly making plans for the evening or the following weekend, and Laura had no plans at all.

After a week or two, she began to pick up a few familiar faces—students she passed in the hallway, some who sat near her in class, and so forth—but their interactions did not go much beyond saying "Hi." Laura was as lonely as ever, and the comings and going of Pam and her gang only made it worse.

Early in October everything changed. One evening, Laura was in the room alone, studying, when she became aware of the clanging fire alarm down the hallway. "Not another firedrill . . . I don't have time for this nonsense." She was tempted to ignore it and hope that no one caught her. Then, there was the sound of students coming out of their rooms, shouting. She decided that she had better go out, too, and was surprised to find a good deal of smoke in the hall. By then, the sound of the fire truck sirens could be heard, and Laura rushed to join the crowd of students hurrying toward the nearby exit.

On the lawn outside, students were gathering in small groups, talking, and pointing to the windows on the third floor where smoke was coming out. Laura spotted one of the students whose face she recognized and walked up to her, "What's going on? How bad is it?" They talked excitedly, exchanging what little information they had and observing the progress of the firemen.

After about an hour, the small fire was extinguished, and the residents slowly went inside. Laura's new acquaintance, whose name was Nancy, asked her to come to her room to have a cup of cocoa. "I'd love to," she said, "cocoa is my secret sin."

A lack of acquaintances, friends, and close companions is painful for most people, as suggested by Laura's early experience in coming to college. In finding and choosing friends, falling in love, and establishing and trying to maintain close relationships, we each respond to specific factors that have been of interest to social psychology since its earliest beginnings. The general question has been, "What are the determinants of interpersonal evaluations?" That is, why does a given individual like one person, dislike another, and feel indifferent about a third? We tend to react to others on the basis of such attitudes. **Attraction** is based on the direction and strength of interpersonal evaluations. These evaluations range from hate to love. When you hate someone, it may make you angry just to see or hear the person's name (emotional reaction), and you are likely to avoid that person and even think about harming the individual in some manner (behavior). In the case of mild liking for someone, you probably have generally positive feelings toward the person and may enjoy talking to this individual, but may make no special contacts. When one is in "love," by contrast, the person may mean everything to you, and you may desire to be with the person constantly. Social psychologists are interested in those variables and processes that lead to different degrees of attraction toward others.

In addition to identifying the determinants of attraction, social psychologists have become increasingly interested in how relationships develop and change (Duck, 1985; Duck and Gilmore, 1981; Hatfield and Walster, 1981; Clark and Reis, 1988). For example, it is important to know how friendships grow out of acquaintanceships and how people fall in love (see Figure 6.1). It is also crucial to know why some close relationships are maintained over long periods of time, while others are unsuccessful. We will touch on each of these major issues in the following pages. In this chapter we will first examine the process by which strangers become acquaintances on the basis of such variables as proximity, emotions, and the need to affiliate. Then, we look at what determines why some acquaintances become friends in response to such factors as physical attractiveness, similarity, and reciprocal judgments of one another. In the final section of the chapter, we take a close look at

what it means to fall in love and the difficulties of maintaining an ongoing relationship. Two special topics will also be covered: the pains and pleasures of being close and discussion of recent societal trends in the relationship between happiness and marriage.

EVALUATING STRANGERS: Physical Proximity, Emotional States, and the Need to Affiliate

Over 5 billion people inhabit our planet, and each of us is likely to come into extended contact with only a very small proportion of these people during a lifetime, perhaps several thousand. Of these thousands of potential friends, enemies, and lovers, we tend to limit those we know at any given time to a handful of individuals. On what basis do we select whom to know and to ignore, and whom to like and to dislike? To some extent we react to specific aspects of others, but we are also influenced by factors having nothing to do with the other person. The stage is set for acquaintanceships to form if two people are brought in contact through physical proximity or **propinquity**, if each is experiencing positive rather than negative **emotions**, and if each has strong **affiliative needs**.

The Role of Propinquity: Physical Contact, Familiarity, Acceptance

Acquaintanceship most often begins as the result of a series of accidental contacts. Strangers are assigned adjoining seats in a classroom, rent apartments across the hall from one another, or walk down the same sidewalk on the way to catch a bus or to buy groceries. Propinquity in such instances leads to a gradual increase in familiarity. We feel more comfortable with a familiar face and are more likely to exchange greetings. Even infants respond more positively to a stranger after several exposures to that individual (Levitt, 1980).

Figure 6.1 Social psychologists are concerned with the factors that determine why we like some people, dislike others, and feel indifferent about still others.

Interpersonal attraction: Attitudes toward others

Propinquity: The Role of the Physical Environment. Research has established that any aspect of the environment that increases propinquity, or physical proximity, of two individuals on a regular basis increases the probability that they will gradually get to know and to like one another. Evidence for the effects of propinquity comes from many sources (Festinger, Schachter, and Back, 1950). For example, in universities, students often become acquainted on the basis of classroom seating assignments or dormitory location, regardless of whether they have similar academic majors, religious backgrounds, or hobbies (Caplow and Forman, 1950). Students sitting side by side in a classroom are also very likely to become acquainted as the school term progresses. When seats are assigned alphabetically by the instructor, friendships are most likely to form between those whose last names begin with the same letter or nearby letter of the alphabet (Segal, 1974). Such physical details may well help to determine some of your friendships, some of your romantic relationships, and maybe even your future spouse.

These environmental effects are by no means confined to a college campus. In a housing project for the elderly in a large city, the residents were most likely to become friends if they were given rooms on the same floor (Nahemow and Lawton, 1975)—precisely the same pattern that holds true in college dormitories (Evans and Wilson, 1949). A similar trend is found in non-university apartment complexes; also, the closer two people live, the more likely they are to become "best friends" rather than simply "good friends" (Ebbesen, Kjos, and Konecni, 1976).

Why? Repeated Exposure Is the Key. Classroom or apartment locations lead to liking because certain physical arrangements lead strangers to experience **repeated exposure**. That is, because of spatial arrangements, some individuals are more likely to see one another time after time as part of their regular daily routines. Zajonc and his colleagues have consistently shown that repeated exposure to a given stimulus usually leads to increasingly favorable attitudes toward that stimulus (Zajonc, 1968; Moreland and Zajonc, 1982).

In one experiment (Saegert, Swap, and Zajonc, 1973), college students were told they were participating in an experiment having to do with the sense of taste. They were to enter a series of booths, two at a time, to sample and rate various flavored liquids. The real purpose of the experiment was to test the repeated exposure effect by arranging for different numbers of interactions to occur among subjects. The schedule was carefully arranged so that a given subject was in a booth with another subject either zero times, once, twice, five, or ten times. When the series of taste tests was completed, the students filled out a questionnaire which included an indication of attraction toward others in the experiment. As can be seen in Figure 6.2, the more contacts an individual had had with someone else during the brief experiment, the more he or she was liked.

The repeated exposure effect even occurs under conditions when the individual is unaware of the fact that he or she is more familiar with some stimuli than others (see discussion in Chapter Three of the occurrence of emotions without conscious cognition). For example, in one recent experiment (Bornstein, Leone, and Galley, 1987), subjects interacted with two confederates in a discussion of a neutral topic. Before interacting with the confederates, the subjects were exposed to a photograph of one of the confederates for a period so brief they were unaware of the exposure (accomplished with a device called a *tachistoscope*). Though the subject could not recall being exposed to the confederate previously, he or she interacted more positively with that confederate and made more positive ratings of the confederate after the discussion than to the confederate to whom they had not been previously exposed. Apparently, then, our reactions to various stimuli can be affected by prior exposures to them, even if we are quite unaware of such experiences.

Despite the importance of propinquity and repeated exposure, these factors do not *always* have a positive effect. Studies show that repeated exposure to a rewarding or neutral stranger leads to increased attraction, while repeated exposure to a punishing stranger leads to *decreased* attraction (Swap, 1977). We would expect that close propinquity and repeated exposure to an unpleasant individual would lead to more and more intense feelings of dislike.

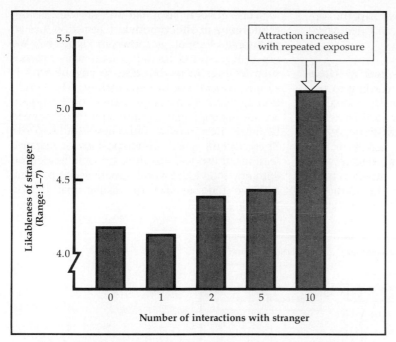

Attraction increased
with repeated exposure

Figure 6.2 *In an experiment testing the effects of mere exposure on attraction, subjects had a series of brief interactions with strangers that ranged from no contact at all to ten meetings. The results showed that the more frequently they interacted, the more positively the other person was rated. (Source: Based on data from Saegert, Swap, and Zajonc, 1973.)*

Repeated exposure increases attraction.

Feelings: Conditioned Emotional Responses

Most of us are aware that positive and negative events in our daily lives can have an immediate and intense effect on our general mood (Stone and Neale, 1984). A growing body of research indicates that mood, in turn, affects many aspects of behavior, including interpersonal attraction.

Sources of Emotion. Experiments have consistently indicated that events eliciting positive feelings increase interpersonal attraction, while negative feelings decrease attraction. For example, reactions to strangers are more negative in hot, uncomfortably humid rooms than in comfortable settings (Griffitt, 1970). Similarly,

one's attraction to a stranger is reduced after being exposed to a sad rather than a happy film (Gouaux, 1971). In a similar way, listening to enjoyable music increases attraction, while unpleasant music has a negative effect (May and Hamilton, 1980). Also, depressed people make us feel uncomfortable, and we like them less than people who are in a good mood (Winer et al., 1981).

Even good versus bad news on radio and television can affect interpersonal behavior. To test this prediction, Veitch and Griffitt (1976) arranged for subjects to hear a news broadcast just before the study supposedly started. The "radio" was actually a cassette recording containing a series of either good or bad news stories. The good news caused a positive emotional reaction, and subjects exposed to it expressed greater liking toward a stranger. Bad news had the opposite effect—negative feelings and decreased attraction.

Why Our Emotional Responses to Other People Can Be Conditioned. According to one theory developed to explain interpersonal attraction, all our likes and dislikes are based on emotional responses (Clore and Byrne, 1974). This means that when anyone makes us feel good, we respond with liking; we dislike whoever makes us feel bad. Any variable (such as repeated exposure) that leads to greater attraction does so because positive feelings are aroused.

This general formulation, known as the **reinforcement-affect model** of attraction, has an additional element, as shown in Figure 6.3. We not only respond to the person who *arouses* such feelings in us, but also to anyone who is simply *associated* with such feelings. This conditioning of emotional responses to those who are around us explains why attraction is influenced by music, heat, movies, radio news, and so forth. These factors arouse either positive or negative feelings; these feelings then become associated with any individual who happens to be present; and we tend to like or dislike that person accordingly.

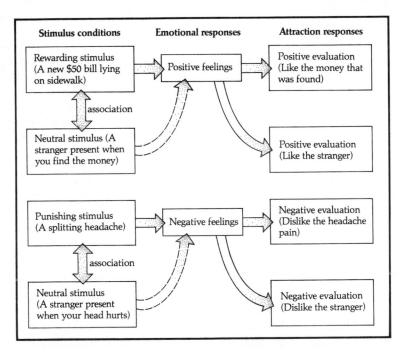

Figure 6.3 According to the *reinforcement-affect model* of attraction, our likes and dislikes are based on the feelings aroused by rewarding and punishing events. Rewards elicit positive feelings and are liked; punishments elicit negative feelings and are disliked. In addition, conditioning can occur. When a stranger (or any other neutral stimulus) is present when feelings are aroused, that person is associated with the reward or punishment. As a result, feelings are *conditioned* to the stranger. Thus, a person to whom we might have responded in a neutral way is now evaluated either positively or negatively.

Feelings and conditioned feelings: The reinforcement-affect model of attraction

Need for Affiliation: People Differ in Their Desire to Have Friends

We spend much of our time interacting with other people. Such activities as making new friends, spending time with friends, and being able to share personal feelings are rated as *very important* by most Americans who are surveyed (Research and Forecasts, 1981). It has been proposed that having friends is intrinsically positive. It is also true that people differ in their **need for affiliation**. That is, some people prefer to be alone much of the time, while others behave in a very sociable fashion. Presumably, such personality differences help to determine whether propinquity and positive emotions actually lead two strangers to interact.

Need for Affiliation as a Trait. Beginning with the pioneer work of Murray (1938), several measures of the *need for affiliation* have been constructed. Research with these tests has revealed, for example, that males high in affiliation need are relatively self-confident and tend to talk more to attractive females than do males whose affiliation need is low (Crouse and Mehrabian, 1977). In a college classroom, students whose need-for-affiliation score is high tend to make more friends during a semester than do students whose scores are low (Greendlinger and Byrne, 1985).

There is evidence that after a relationship forms, students high in need for affiliation are increasingly satisfied as the relationship progresses over the first several months (Eidelson, 1980). Those with low affiliative needs tend to feel less affiliative over time, especially if they have a high need for independence. You can see that two individuals with different need patterns might be puzzled by one another as their friendship grows. One person might be pleased by the tightening bonds of a close relationship, while the other person becomes unhappy, feeling tied down.

The general need to affiliate has been further refined recently by Hill (1987). He proposes that there are four basic motives that may underlie a disposition to be affiliative. One motive is *social comparison*—the need to affiliate or have social contact in order to reduce uncertainty in ambiguous circumstances. Another motive is for *positive stimulation*—affiliation for interesting lively contact with others. *Emotional support* is affiliation sought to obtain attention and positive regard from others when in a negative state. *Attention* is affiliation in the interest of increasing self-worth and importance by receiving praise and attention from others. Hill also proposes that people differ in the degree to which each of these motives is important. To evaluate differences across people, Hill developed the Interpersonal Orientation Scale (see Table 6.1). Research suggests that people differ in ways other than in their general interest in being with others; that is, some people are more motivated to affiliate to receive attention, others for emotional support, and so on (Hill, 1987). Or, as Hill (1987) subtitled his paper, "People Who Need People . . . But in Different Ways."

Need for Affiliation as a Response to Arousing Situations. You are sitting in your social psychology class when suddenly you hear screaming through the window, followed by a great deal of shouting. What do you do? Does such a potentially frightening situation have an effect on interpersonal behavior? In a series of now-classic experiments, Schachter (1959) was able to show that fear increases one's desire to affiliate with others. When experimental subjects were led to believe they would receive painful electric shocks, they preferred waiting with other subjects rather than by themselves. When no painful shock was involved in the experiment, subjects preferred waiting alone or had no preference.

The explanation for the effect of fear on affiliation seems to be that frightened individuals seek out others—even total strangers—to talk about what is happening, to compare perceptions, and to decide what, if anything, to do. The ability to engage in this kind of *social comparison* process may reduce one's uncertainty and reduce anxiety (Suls and Fletcher, 1983; Rofe, 1984). The way in which fear increases interpersonal contact was shown in an experiment in which college students were waiting for what

Table 6.1 Four dimensions of affiliation motivation measured by the Interpersonal Orientation Scale plus representative test items for each dimension. (Source: Based on Hill, 1987.)

The varieties of affiliative need		
Social comparison	When I am not certain about how well I am doing at something, I usually like to be around others so I can compare myself to them.	I find that I often have the desire to be around other people who are experiencing the same thing I am when I am unsure of what is going on.
Positive stimulation	Just being around others and finding out about them is one of the most interesting things I can think of doing.	I think it would be satisfying if I could have very close friendships with quite a few people.
Emotional support	If I feel unhappy or kind of depressed, I usually try to find other people to make me feel better.	One of my greatest sources of comfort when things get rough is being with other people.
Attention	I often have a strong need to be around people who are impressed with what I am like and what I do.	I like to be around people when I can be the center of attention.

they had been told was an electric shock experiment. Compared to controls who were not expecting to be shocked, the experimental subjects actually did interact more and spent more time discussing the upcoming experiment (Morris et al., 1976).

WHY ACQUAINTANCES BECOME FRIENDS: Attractiveness, Similarity, and Reciprocity

Once two individuals are brought together by such variables as propinquity, if their feelings are generally positive, and if each has sufficiently strong affiliative needs, they may be expected to begin interacting. At this point in the process, however, some additional variables become important. Whether friendship (or even an ongoing acquaintanceship) develops now depends on the *physical attractiveness* of each member of the potential pair, their *similarity* on a variety of characteristics, and the extent to which they demonstrate *reciprocity* with respect to positive evaluations of one another. We will take a look at the research that has dealt with each of these factors.

Physical Attractiveness: Judging Others on the Basis of Appearance

First impressions rest in large part on appearances. When we encounter others for the first time, we notice such things as gender, race, height, weight, clothing, facial features, hair color, and so forth. We tend to have various beliefs and prejudices about such factors on the basis of our past experiences and on the basis of stereotypes we have developed. Whatever the basis of these reactions and whatever their validity, we nevertheless are strongly affected by them.

One of the most powerful and most studied of such factors is **physical attractiveness**. This aspect of others turns out to be a primary determinant of whether a person seeks to form a relationship (see Figure 6.4).

The Effects of Attractiveness. When males and females interact, the attractiveness of the other person affects the behavior of both sexes (Folkes, 1982; Hatfield and Sprecher, 1986). In a commercial video-dating service, attractive males and females are most likely to be chosen as dates, though females also respond to high-

Figure 6.4 *Physical attractiveness has a strong effect on the assumptions we make about others and on the degree of attraction we feel toward them. However unreasonable this may be, we attribute more positive and desirable qualities to those who are attractive than to those who are not.*

Physical attractiveness: A major determinant of attraction

status males (Green, Buchanan, and Heuer, 1984).

There is a general assumption that attractive people also possess a number of other positive qualities. Both males and females indicate that attractive individuals are also poised, interesting, sociable, independent, exciting, and sexually warm (Brigham, 1980). Physically attractive males are judged to be more masculine and attractive females to be more feminine than those who are less attractive (Gillen, 1981). There is a "downside" to being attractive, however; attractive females are also seen as more vain, materialistic, and more likely to have extramarital affairs than other women (Cash and Duncan, 1984). Also, while being attractive is an asset for male political candidates, attractiveness has no consistent effects for attractive female candidates (Sigelman et al., 1986). It may be that attractiveness in women signals femininity, which for some people is not considered appropriate for political office.

Being with attractive people seems to "rub off"; the friends of an attractive same-sex peer are rated more positively than the friends of someone who is unattractive (Kernis and Wheeler, 1981). This effect even holds when subjects rate sets of photos of unassociated individuals (Geiselman, Haight, and Kimata, 1984).

Beliefs about physically attractive and unattractive individuals are generally thought to be based on cultural biases. Dion and Dion (1987) recently suggested that physical attractiveness stereotyping may reflect a person's **belief in a just world** (Lerner, 1980). This belief refers to the notion that "people get what they deserve and also deserve what they get." Dion and Dion theorized that those who subscribe to the "just world" notion may be especially prone to perceive physically attractive people as possessing socially desirable traits and fortunate outcomes. In essence, the "reward of beauty" is seen as being deserved and deserving of good outcomes. To test this hypothesis, Dion and Dion

(1987) had adults fill out a scale designed to measure their belief in a just world (containing such as items as "People who get lucky breaks have usually earned their good fortune") and judge the personalities and life outcomes of an attractive or an unattractive stimulus person. Although there was a general trend for all subjects to perceive attractive people as possessing more desirable traits and life outcomes, believers in a just world showed this tendency to a greater degree.

Some behavioral and personality differences are related to appearance (Erwin and Calev, 1984), perhaps in part because of the way others react to attractive and unattractive individuals (Adams, 1977). Attractive males and females interact well with the opposite sex and have more dates (Reis, Nezlek, and Wheeler, 1980). Attractive people also expect to succeed in social situations (Abbott and Sebestian, 1981), and they apparently *do* succeed. In a large sample of several thousand adults, Umberson and Hughes (1984) found that attractiveness is positively related to educational attainment, income, occupational prestige, and psychological well-being.

It might seem logical to expect that attractive individuals would be higher in self-esteem than unattractive ones, but the relationship between these two characteristics is actually very weak and not entirely consistent across studies (Maruyama and Miller, 1981). One explanation is that attractive people receive so much praise they tend to question or discount it: "People only pay attention to the way I look, not to what I do or say." Unattractive individuals, on the other hand, would assume that any praise they receive is genuine and deserved. Major, Carrington, and Carnevale (1984) tested these general propositions by arranging for attractive and unattractive undergraduates to write a brief essay that was evaluated by another student. The evaluator was supposedly able to observe them as they wrote or was unable to observe them. Actually, all subjects received a positive evaluation from an opposite-sex observer. As shown in Figure 6.5, attractive subjects were more likely to attribute praise to the quality of their work if they were not seen by the evaluator, while unattractive subjects felt the praise was deserved if they *had*

been observed. The authors point out that in real life most social interactions take place with others who *are* aware of how we look. Less attractive people receive less praise, but they give a lot of weight to the praise they do receive; in contrast, more attractive individuals receive more praise but discount it. For that reason, attractiveness and self-esteem are not strongly related.

What Do We Mean by "Physically Attractive"? Though we have no problem deciding who is attractive and unattractive, it is difficult to pin down the variables responsible for such judgments (see Figure 6.6). Probably a number of physical and behavioral factors are involved. Cunningham (1986) made precise measurements of the facial features in an international sample of photographs of 50 females from college yearbooks and from the yearbook section of a Miss Universe beauty pageant program. He also had a group of male undergraduates rate all of the faces for attractiveness. Cunningham found that childlike features such as large eyes, small nose, small chin, and widely spaced eyes were associated with attractiveness. Males were also attracted to females with mature features such as prominent cheekbones, narrow cheeks, high eyebrows, large pupils, and a large smile. Interestingly, though black and oriental beauty contestants possess ethnically distinct features (greater distance between their eyes and wider nostrils), they also displayed most of the facial features associated with attractiveness in Caucasians. Cunningham notes that facial features may be universally attractive, though one cannot rule out the possibility that ethnic contestants were chosen as their nations' representative because they approximate Western standards of beauty. In any event, within a culture there appear to be certain facial features that most people agree are attractive.

Research on other bodily features shows that females respond more positively to males with Robert Redford physiques—thin legs, thin waist, broad shoulders, and small buttocks (Beck, Ward-Hull, and McLear, 1976; Horvath, 1979; Lavrakas, 1975). Though a tall male may seem to be an ideal romantic partner (Gillis and Avis,

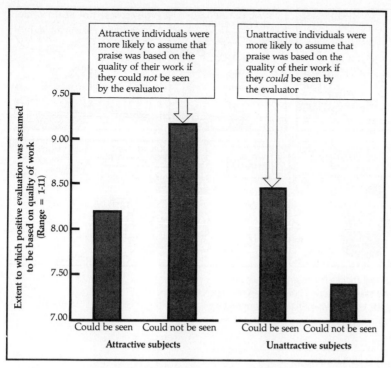

Figure 6.5 *Those who are physically attractive tend to discount praise from those who can see them, because they tend to assume that it is probably based on their looks. In contrast, those who are unattractive are more impressed by positive evaluations from those who can see them than from those who cannot, because they assume that those who saw them based their evaluations on how well they did—in spite of their looks. These opposite tendencies may explain the lack of relationship between attractiveness and self-esteem. Attractive individuals receive more praise than unattractive ones, but unattractive individuals place more weight on such praise than attractive ones. The end result is equivalent levels of self-esteem. (Source: Based on data from Major, Carrington, and Carnevale, 1984.)*

Interpreting praise: Attractive and unattractive persons react differently to praise.

1980), female college students actually prefer males of medium height (Graziano, Brothen, and Berscheid, 1978).

Males (despite what they see in magazine centerfolds) are attracted to females with medium-sized breasts (Kleinke and Staneski, 1980) and medium-sized legs and buttocks (Wiggins, Wiggins, and Conger, 1968). For both sexes, obesity is perceived as unattractive (Harris, Harris, and Bochner, 1982), but espe-cially so when the overweight individual is a fe-male (Franzoi and Herzog, 1987). There is also evidence that a relatively unattractive body dras-tically reduces the overall attractiveness of a fe-male who has a highly attractive face. However, the effect does not work in the opposite direc-tion; that is, presence of an unattractive face does not drastically lower the overall attractiveness of a female with a very attractive body (Alicke, Smith, and Klotz, 1986).

Figure 6.6 People seem to agree about facial characteristics that are physically attractive at least within the same society. There are also findings suggesting that certain features may be *universally* perceived as attractive, though more research is needed. (Source: Reprinted by permission: Tribune Media Services.)

Are some physical features universally attractive? Possibly.

Some aspects of external behavior play a role in addition to physical appearance. Smiling is generally attractive to both males and females, while sad expressions evoke judgments of unattractiveness (Lau, 1982; Mueser et al., 1984). Also, studies show that dominant behavior (independence, more active nonverbal gestures) on the part of males enhanced their perceived attractiveness. Dominance neither enhanced nor decreased the attractiveness of females (Sadalla, Kenrick, and Vershure, 1987).

There may also be some situational determinants of perceived attractiveness. For example, males who had just been watching the glamorous "Charlie's Angels" on television rated a female stranger as less attractive than males who had not been watching that show (Kenrick and Gutierres, 1980).

Similarity of Attractiveness: The Matching Hypothesis. People may *prefer* the best looking of all possible friends and marriage partners, but not everyone can obtain such a partner. Males tend to be afraid of being rejected by extremely

attractive females; they need some extraneous excuse even to approach them (Bernstein et al., 1983). Because people differ in physical attractiveness, who is actually chosen as a friend, lover, or spouse? There is a tendency to select partners similar to oneself in physical attractiveness—the **matching hypothesis** (Berscheid et al., 1971; see Figure 6.7). This matching tendency influences casual dates, engagements, and marriages (Murstein, 1972). Married couples, regardless of age or length of marriage, are similar in attractiveness (Price and Vandenberg, 1979). The importance of matching is shown by the fact that mismatched couples are more likely to break up than couples similar in attractiveness (White, 1980b).

It should be mentioned that matching among couples may not represent their actively seeking out of people of their own attractiveness level. Kalick and Hamilton (1986; 1988) point out that everyone may want a highly attractive partner, but as highly attractive individuals select each other, there will be fewer of them available, thereby leaving less attractive individuals to pair

Figure 6.7 *In general, there is a tendency to select partners similar to oneself in physical attractiveness. But there are exceptions!*

The odd couple

off. However, regardless of whether people match because the less attractive consciously lower their sights or because there is a limited supply of highly attractive people, the result is the same; people tend to form friendships, date, and marry others similar to themselves in attractiveness.

Similarity: Liking Those Who Are Like Ourselves

When two people first meet, they are more inclined to ask one another questions than is true in established relationships (Kent et al., 1981). One reason is that we want to know one another's likes and dislikes. As has been suggested since the days of Aristotle, we tend to accept those who agree with us and reject those who differ. Most people are quite aware of this social norm (Jellison and Oliver, 1983). Thus, it has long been assumed that **attitude similarity**

leads to attraction. In a more general sense, we respond positively to those who most closely resemble ourselves (see Figure 6.8).

Attitude Similarity and Attraction. Beyond formal and informal observations of the effect of similarity on attraction, a great many experiments have established the way in which this relationship operates. In typical laboratory investigations, attitude similarity toward a stranger is manipulated to determine the effect on attraction (for example, Schachter, 1951; Smith, 1957). The effect is a powerful and very consistent one, so it is possible to predict with reasonable accuracy how much one person will like another on the basis of the *proportion* of attitudinal topics on which they agree (Byrne and Nelson, 1965).

These laboratory studies were verified in field studies involving such situations as computer dating (Byrne, Ervin, and Lamberth, 1970) and sharing a fallout shelter with same-sex strangers (Griffitt, May, and Veitch, 1974). For socially anxious subjects, these effects are eliminated, possibly because the subjects are too upset to pay attention to the characteristics of others (Heimberg, Acerra, and Holstein, 1985). The attraction generated by the discovery of similar attitudes leads to behavioral effects, such as being more likely to return to a laboratory to work with an agreeing stranger than with a disagreeing stranger (Gormly and Gormly, 1981).

As mentioned in Chapter 3, we also *assume* that people agree with us (Ross, Green, and House, 1977; Mullen et al., 1985). This is especially strong with respect to those we like. If a person feels attraction toward someone on the basis of nonattitudinal characteristics, such as physical attractiveness (Marks and Miller, 1982; Marks, Miller, and Maruyama, 1981) or general charisma (Granberg and King, 1980), that other individual is perceived as attitudinally similar. It seems that positive responses to the superficial characteristics of others lead us to the often mistaken belief that we have the same attitudes and values. It is not difficult to find unhappy examples of this tendency when someone chooses the wrong mate or votes for a likable political candidate whose positions on various issues are later found not to match one's own.

CBarsotti   "Sir, would you mind changing places with me?"

Figure 6.8 There is consistent evidence that we like others who are similar to us. (Source: Drawing by C. Barsotti; © 1986 The New Yorker Magazine, Inc.)

Similarity leads to attraction.

Why Do We Like Similar Others? Most theorists agree that attitude similarity is positive because it confirms one's judgments about the world. There is a *social comparison* process in which we find out whether some other person "validates" what we have already concluded about politics or religion or whatever by agreeing with us (Festinger, 1954; Suls and Miller, 1977; Goethals, 1986a). If someone believes what you believe, he or she provides "evidence" that you are correct. This affirmation of your good judgment is a positive affective experience, and you like the individual responsible for making you feel that way. Disagreement has just the opposite effect; it suggests you are wrong, elicits negative emotions, and causes you to dislike the person who generated such uncomfortable feelings.

Another approach to explaining the similarity effect is provided by **balance theory**. Newcomb (1961) and others have suggested that human beings have a natural inclination to organize their likes and dislikes in a symmetrical fashion that results in **balance** (Cacioppo and Petty, 1981; Insko, Sedlak, and Lipsitz, 1982; Rodrigues and Newcomb, 1980). There is balance when two people like one another and agree about whatever they are discussing. When two people like one another and disagree, there is **imbalance**, and this unpleasant state motivates each individual to do something (such as changing attitudes about the topic) in order to restore balance. When two people do not like one another, there is **nonbalance**, and either agreement or disagreement results in indifference.

We have emphasized the attractive value of attitudinal similarity; however, in the initial stages of relationship development, we may be more sensitive to people's dissimilarities. That is, initially we may exclude others from further consideration as friends, dates, or lovers on the basis of their dissimilarity (Rosenbaum, 1986). Later, we respond to the reduced field of eligibles and rely increasingly on positive factors such as similar attitudes to select the final candidates for interpersonal closeness (Byrne, Clore, and Smeaton, 1986).

Keep in mind that we do not *always* reject those with dissimilar views. Though we wish to validate our views, we have other needs as well. Interactions with a dissimilar stranger can provide new information (Gormly, 1979; Kruglanski and Mayseless, 1987), reduce one's confusion (Russ, Gold, and Stone, 1980), and make a person feel special and unique instead of being just like everyone else (Snyder and Fromkin, 1980). Dissimilarity can be threatening, and people assume that those who disagree with them will dislike them (Gonzales et al., 1983). This threat can be eliminated if we know in advance that the dissimilar other is not going to reject us and that he or she is open to discussing alternative points of view (Broome, 1983; Sunnafrank and Miller, 1981).

Similarity of Other Characteristics. Even though most social psychologists are in agreement that attitudinal similarity leads to attraction, effects of personality and behavioral similarity are the subject of some controversy. Put in its simplest form, do birds of a feather flock together or do opposites attract? Convincing arguments can be—and have been made—for both suggestions.

In the first place, some personality characteristics are liked by almost everyone, *regardless* of degree of similarity. For example, relatively dominant individuals are preferred to relatively submissive ones by both dominant and submissive others (Palmer and Byrne, 1970). In a similar way, competitive individuals are liked by both men and women (Riskind and Wilson, 1982), and strangers who are willing to disclose information about themselves are preferred to those who are unwilling to reveal much (McAllister and Bregman, 1983).

For many characteristics, though, we tend to choose friends who are similar to ourselves. For example, heterosexual males are fairly negative toward homosexual ones, regardless of how much their attitudes on other topics are in agreement (Aguero, Bloch, and Byrne, 1984; Krulewitz and Nash, 1980), presumably because sexual preference is judged as a matter of overriding importance. After age 7 or 8, there is an increasing tendency for children to seek companions close to their own age (Ellis, Rogoff, and Cramer, 1981; Rubin, 1980). Among high school best friends, there is greater than chance similarity in age, sex, religion, and race (Kandel, 1978). On various personality characteristics—such as androgeny (having both masculine and feminine characteristics) versus traditional sex roles, degree of masculinity and femininity, sensation-seeking, and cognitive style—similarity is preferable to dissimilarity (Antil, 1983; Lesnick-Oberstein and Cohen, 1984; Pursell and Banikiotes, 1978). The personality similarity effect is generally weaker than the attitude similarity effect, however. It also seems true that personality similarity increases when people interact (Blankenship et al., 1984). On those personality dimensions on which friends are actually no more similar than random strangers, they *believe* themselves to be similar (Feinberg, Miller, and Ross, 1981).

We also like those who behave as we do. With college students paired in a series of games, partners with similar game behavior liked one another (Knight, 1980). Those who are similar in disclosing—or not disclosing—intimate information about themselves tend to be attracted (Daher and Banikiotes, 1976). Elementary school children prefer peers who perform about as well as they do in academics, sports, music, and the like (Tesser, Campbell, and Smith, 1984). We even like those who imitate our behavior and make the same choices and decisions we do (Roberts et al., 1981; Thelen et al., 1981). Among high school students, friends tend to be similar with respect to engaging in deviant behavior such as drug use (Kandel, Single, and Kessler, 1976), and for females at least, similar with respect to smoking, drinking, and premarital sex (Rodgers, Billy, and Udry, 1984). College roommates who differ in being morning-active versus evening-active evaluate one another more negatively than students who are similar in this respect (Watts, 1982). Finally, there is a tendency for us to form relationships with persons who have similar preferences for activities (Werner and Parmelee, 1979; Jamieson, Lydon, and Zanna, 1987).

The greatest amount of controversy about the effect of personality variables involves *needs*. It has been proposed that **need compatibility** (having similar needs) is a positive factor in a relationship. It has also been proposed that **need complementarity** (having opposite needs) leads to liking because both individuals find it rewarding. For example, someone who is motivated to talk a lot should like a good listener, and vice versa. As reasonable as the complementarity idea seems, research generally supports the importance of similarity. In one study, Meyer and Pepper (1977) found that husbands and wives who were similar in their needs tended to have better adjusted marriages than spouses with dissimilar needs. Need compatibility seems to be important in an ongoing relationship. (Of course, it is hard to imagine that any two people can be similar on all things. Refer to the "Focus on Research" insert which describes factors that determine whether we feel pleasure or pain when a close friend or relative performs better or worse than ourselves.)

THE PAIN AND PLEASURE OF BEING CLOSE

We apparently prefer others who have similar attitudes and similar interests. What happens, however, when people close to us perform better in some domain, whether it be a hobby, a sport, or on the job? Tesser and his colleagues (Tesser and Campbell, 1983; Tesser, 1986) propose that being close to an-

other person can be painful if your friend outperforms you. But sometimes people take pleasure in the fact that a relative or friend has been successful in some area. This phenomenon has been dubbed **"basking in reflected glory"** (Cialdini et al., 1976).

According to Tesser, one's feel-

ings in such circumstances depend on whether the performance domain is important for one's own self-definition and the closeness of the relationship. If someone outperforms you in an area that is important to you, the closer the other (for example, a friend or relative), the greater the threat to your self-

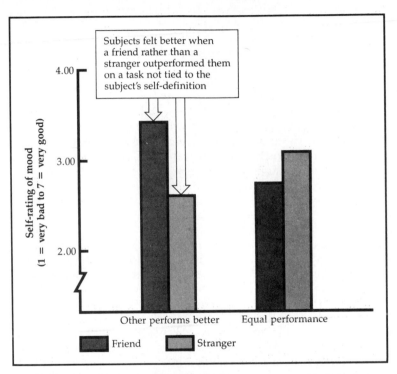

Figure 6.9   The results of one experiment indicate that subjects had very positive feelings when their friend outperformed them on a task that was not relevant to their own self-definition. This is evidence for a phenomenon called "basking in reflected glory." One can take pleasure by being associated with someone who is very successful as long as the task is not strongly tied to one's own self-definition. In contrast, subjects were not as positive when the friend (and especially when a stranger) performed at their same level. Other research indicates that subjects have very negative reactions when a friend outperforms them on tasks that are important to them. Hence, people either feel pleasure or pain, depending on how close others perform relative to them and whether the performance domain is one that is strongly tied to one's self. (Source: Based on data from Tesser, Millar, and Moore, 1988.)

The pleasure and pain of being close

esteem, and the worse you may feel. In contrast, when someone outperforms you on a task that means little for your self-definition, the closer the other, the better you will feel because you can bask in his or her reflected glory.

Tesser has found support for his model in several experiments. In one recent study, Tesser, Millar, and Moore (1988) tested the notion that a friend's better performance on a task of low self-relevance will be associated with more positive reactions than when both the subject and the other perform at the same level. Subjects were asked to bring a close friend with them for an experiment. After being ushered into separate rooms, the individuals indicated the importance of a variety of topics according to their knowledge and interest. The topic they rated lowest was the topic about which the subject and either their friend or a stranger were subsequently quizzed (a domain of low importance to the subject's self-definition). Subsequently, the subject received (bogus) feedback that either the friend or the stranger performed about the same or much better than he or she had done. At the end of the study, subjects made ratings indicating their positive or negative feelings.

As indicated in Figure 6.9, a close other's better performance was associated with more positive affect than when the close other performed comparably to the subject. This result represents a case of "basking in reflected glory." In contrast, better performance by a stranger produced more negative affect, suggesting that when one cannot gain from an association with the other, poorer performance engenders unpleasant feelings. Still other research demonstrates that friends produce even more negative feelings than strangers when friends outperform oneself in domains that are important to one's self-definition.

We see that comparisons with people close to us can be a source of pain or pleasure. Perhaps it is not surprising that parents encourage their offspring to pursue different interests and careers from one another to avoid invidious comparisons. And perhaps this explains why many married couples prefer to develop separate careers.

Reciprocal Evaluations: I Like You If You Like Me

One of the most influential factors affecting your attraction toward a given person is that individual's evaluation of you (Byrne, 1971; see Figure 6.10). For example, when a female interacts positively with a male by maintaining eye contact, leaning toward him, and engaging in conversation, he is attracted to her even if he and she are dissimilar in attitudes (Gold, Ryckman, and Mosley, 1984). Friendships are strengthened by verbal and nonverbal signs of mutual respect, consideration, interest, wanting to be together, wanting to communicate, affection, and liking (Hays, 1984). Almost everyone likes a positive response from others and dislikes any indication of negative feelings. Even if a positive evaluation is believed to be inaccurate (Swann et al., 1987) or consists of flattery from someone who has something to gain, we are pleased to receive it (Drachman, deCarufel, and Insko, 1978). With negative evaluations, we tend not to like the person who voices them, even when other people are the targets (Amabile, 1983).

Even simply believing that others like you can help to create attraction. Curtis and Miller (1986) divided a group of college students into pairs for a "get to know one another" session. Before the discussion began, the subjects were individually told that, based on examining a survey they filled out earlier, their discussion partner liked them; others were told their partner disliked them. All of this information was bogus. Then the researchers unobtrusively observed the ten-minute discussion. As shown in Figure 6.11, subjects who expected to be liked made more eye contact, spoke in a warmer tone, and were more self-disclosing than those who expected to be disliked. Furthermore, these behaviors led to reciprocal behaviors or more liking for one another at the conclusion of the experiment if the subjects had been initially led to believe the other liked them. It appears that the belief that someone likes you produces behavior that can help to make it so. This represents a kind of **self-fulfilling prophecy** (Darley and Fazio, 1980; Ickes et al., 1982). The results also point out the importance of even the simplest forms of reciprocity for interpersonal attraction.

Figure 6.10 People like others who like them. That is, reciprocity in evaluations induces interpersonal attraction. Actually, most people also like themselves so this cartoon presents a peculiar (and imbalanced) situation, which is why it is humorous. (Source: Drawing by Ed Arno; © 1987 The New Yorker Magazine, Inc.)

Reciprocity induces interpersonal attraction

"I don't like <u>my</u>self, and Peter doesn't like <u>him</u>self, but we do like each other."

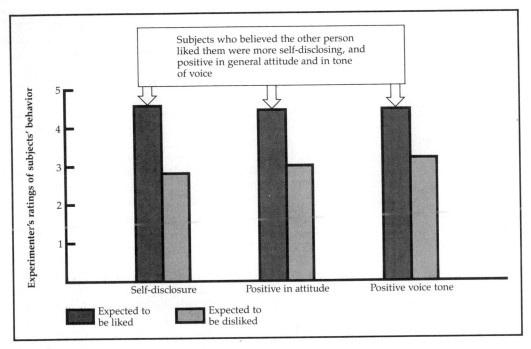

Figure 6.11 Subjects who believed they were liked self-disclosed more, disagreed less, and had a more positive tone of voice than did subjects who believed they were disliked by the other person. These behaviors led to reciprocal behaviors on the part of the other. As a result, believing one was liked actually made the belief come true. Hence, not only does actual reciprocity produce attraction, but the belief someone likes you can help to produce mutual attraction. (Source: Curtis and Miller, 1986.)

Believing another likes you makes it happen!

IT'S SO EASY TO FALL IN LOVE AND SO DIFFICULT TO MAINTAIN A RELATIONSHIP

Whenever two people perceive one another as potential sexual partners, a relationship can move beyond acquaintanceship and friendship. There is the possibility of **love**. Only in the last two decades have social psychologists made attempts to study this emotional state. We will describe what is now known about what it means for one person to "fall in love" with another.

Passionate Love Versus Companionate Love

In the course of interacting with members of the opposite sex, there comes a time when we are likely to ask ourselves whether or not we are in love with a particular person. Because there are at least two quite different kinds of romantic love, the answer may depend on exactly what we mean by the term.

Passionate Love: I've Got a Feeling I'm Falling. The majority of recent theoretical and research interest has centered on **passionate love**. This refers to an intense, sometimes overwhelming emotional state in which a person thinks about a lover constantly, wants to spend as much time as possible with that individual, and is often quite unrealistic in his or her judgments about that person (Murstein, 1980). Contacts with other friends become less frequent, and attention is focused on one, all-important individual (Milardo, Johnson, and Huston, 1983). One measure of passionate love (Hatfield, 1983) includes items that indicate the intensity of feelings involved. Examples are: "Since I've been with _____, my emotions have been on a roller coaster." "Sometimes I can't control my thoughts; they are obsessively on _____." Our language (for example, "falling in love" or "head over heels in love") suggests some sort of accidental process, much like slipping on a banana peel (Solomon, 1981). That may be an accurate description.

A widely held current theory of passionate love indicates that three major conditions are necessary (Hatfield and Walster, 1981). First of all, one must be raised in a culture that believes in the concept and teaches it to young people in fiction as well as in real life. The idea of love arose in Europe in the Middle Ages, and it was thought to be a pure and holy emotion unrelated to sexual desire. It was not until the end of the seventeenth century in England that it became generally accepted that an ideal marriage was based on love (Stone, 1981). In present-day India, romantic love is just now replacing arranged marriages among the middle class. Popular Indian movies have begun to depict couples who fall in love and defy their parents to get married (Kaufman, 1980). In Western nations, most adolescents raised on stories and songs about love are well prepared to undergo such an experience in their own lives (Dion and Dion, 1975). It has even been found that the more a person thinks about love, the more likely he or she is to fall in love (Tesser and Paulhus, 1976).

The second condition for passionate love to occur is the presence of an appropriate love object. For most people, that means a physically attractive member of the opposite sex, about the same age, with the male taller than the female, and neither deeply involved in another relationship. If one believes strongly that it is possible to experience "love at first sight," that can happen, too. Approximately 50 percent of the adults in one study reported having this happen to them at least once (Averill and Boothroyd, 1977).

The third condition is probably crucial to intense infatuation. Any emotional arousal can be *interpreted* as love (see Figure 6.12). It has been found that the way we label emotional excitement can depend on external cues. In Chapter 8 we will describe how one kind of emotional arousal can transfer to another. Various types of arousal have been found to influence romantic feelings, attraction, and sexual interest in experiments focusing on fear (Dutton and Aron, 1974), on erotic excitement (Istvan, Griffitt, and Weidner, 1983), and on embarrassment (Przybyla, Murnen, and Byrne, 1985). Even anger at parents' attempts to break up an affair leads to increased feelings of love (Driscoll, Davis, and Lipetz, 1972).

Though the mislabeling hypothesis has been the most widely studied explanation for the arousal-love phenomenon, it has also been sug-

For Better or For Worse®   by Lynn Johnston

Figure 6.12 According to the mislabeling hypothesis proposed by Hatfield (1983), any emotional or physical arousal may be interpreted as love given a cultural background in which the person has learned about love and expects it to happen and the presence of someone who is appropriate as a love object. (Source: For Better or for Worse. Copyright 1987 Universal Press Syndicate. Reprinted with permission. All rights reserved.)

Mislabeling arousal as love

gested that the reinforcement-affect model (discussed earlier) explains these various findings. It is proposed that the presence of an opposite-sex stranger is simply reinforcing—any subsequent attraction is thus based on the positive feelings elicited by the reinforcement (Kenrick, Cialdini, and Lindner, 1979; Kenrick and Johnson, 1979). In one experiment, when subjects expected to receive an electric shock, the presence of a confederate was found to reduce their fear and to increase attraction toward a confederate (Riordan and Tedeschi, 1983). Whatever the ultimate explanation of the role of emotional arousal, it is clear that such arousal affects how one responds to potential love objects.

Companionate Love: A Close, Caring Friendship. Despite the somewhat flimsy and often unrealistic basis of a passionate love affair, it is possible for a relationship to begin in that fashion and yet mature into **companionate love**. This term refers to a deep and lasting friendship that involves the factors discussed earlier in the chapter such as positive emotions, similarity, and reciprocal liking and respect. In addition, love involves *caring* about the other person (Steck et al., 1982). There are not many songs or movies

about companionate love, but this seems to be the kind of emotional attachment that makes a relationship possible. In a mature, lasting relationship, two individuals must learn to enjoy one another as close *friends.* Each comes to place great value on the other, and both individuals are concerned about the other's welfare (Rubin, 1974). (To learn about some recent trends regarding the relationship between marriage and happiness, see the "Applied Side" insert.)

The "Triangular Model of Love: A General Model. Of course, love, comes in many packages (Hendrick and Hendrick, 1986). Besides romantic love, there is love for one's parents, one's siblings, and one's children. Recently, Sternberg (1986) has proposed a "triangular" model to conceptualize the similarities and differences among the different kinds of love. He proposes there are three major components of love: (1) **intimacy**, which refers to the closeness or bondedness between two people; (2) **passion**, which refers to the physical drives or arousal associated with the relationship; and (3) the **decision/commitment** component, which refers to the cognitive elements involved in decision-making about the existence and commitment to

MARRIAGE AND HAPPINESS OVER THREE DECADES:
HAS MARRIAGE BECOME LESS FUN?

For most of us, marriage is probably considered to be the most significant loving relationship we will have. But it is also widely known that in the United States the incidence of divorce is very high. A marriage is approximately as likely to end in divorce as to last through the couple's lifetime. But we may assume that marriages that last are happy ones. After all, the couple is supposed to settle down and "live happily ever after." Social scientists have found that indeed married people tend to be happier than unmarried people. For example, surveys inquiring about happiness reported that in general married people in the 1950s, 1960s and early 1970s were much happier than people who were never married, or who were divorced, separated, or widowed. In the last fifteen years, however, the association between marriage and happiness has become weaker among both men and women. Married people still report more happiness, but not to the degree that they did in the past (Glenn and Weaver, 1988).

These results are based on a large representative national sample of persons in the United States. A significant question is whether this trend is a result of unmarried people becoming happier, married people becoming less

happy, or some combination of the two. Careful analysis shows that never-married individuals, particularly men, report greater happiness than did their counterparts fifteen years ago. In contrast, married women show decreases in happiness compared with their past counterparts.

Interpretation of these trends is difficult because it is impossible to identify cause and effect relationships definitively from survey data. But we can speculate about why marriage has become less of a source of happiness. One reason that unmarried people may be happier is that the life-styles of married and unmarried people have become more similar. For example, our society has become more accepting of sex outside of marriage (Reed and Weinberg, 1984; Glenn and Weaver, 1979). (We should point out that this trend may be reversing itself since the advent of the AIDS epidemic; Gerrard, 1987). This means that sexual gratification need not depend as much on marriage. Also, unmarried women have greater access to better-paying, higher-level employment than women in the past who may have relied on their husband for financial security. The decline in happiness in married women could reflect the strain of balancing career, home, and

child-rearing as an increasing proportion of marriages now involve both spouses working full-time. Furthermore, we know that while husbands are sharing more domestic tasks than ever before, women still have the major domestic responsibilities. Perhaps the busier schedules of both partners are making marriage less satisfying than it once was. Actually, there is some reason to doubt this explanation because other studies show that married women with multiple responsibilities are happier and more satisfied than women who remain homemakers (Verbrugge, 1983).

Regardless of the explanation for the decreasing happiness associated with being married, it appears to be a reliable trend and has some people wondering whether marriage is becoming a declining institution. In light of the fact that an increasing proportion of people are getting married, it would seem not. In any event, while marriage does not apparently provide as much happiness as it once did, married people still have the edge. Given the high rate of marital dissolution and the apparent decline in the satisfaction it provides, however, there is even more reason to give careful thought to the choice of a mate and the decision to marry.

the relationship. Each of these components can be viewed as forming the vertices of a triangle (see Figure 6.13, top panel). The importance of each of the three components differs as a function of a variety of factors. For example, passion (as noted earlier) tends to play a larger role in short-term involvements, while intimacy and commitment tend to be more important for long-term relationships.

Whether the relationship is between a parent, sibling, lover, or child, intimacy seems to be a core component. In contrast, passion is limited to certain kinds of loving relationships, whereas the decision/commitment component can be highly variable across different types of loving relationships. Relationships differ in the degree to which the three components are balanced. Thus, the triangle at the top represents a bal-

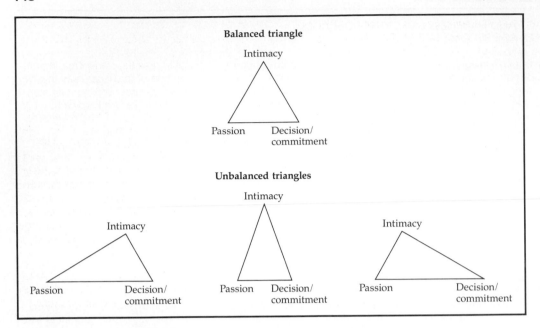

Figure 6.13 According to Sternberg's "triangular" model, love has three basic components: intimacy, passion, and decision/commitment. The equilateral triangle at the top represents a balanced love in which all three components are equally matched. The triangle in the bottom left represents a relationship in which the passion component plays a larger role than intimacy or commitment. Some predominantly sexual relationships are characterized in this way. The triangle in the bottom middle represents a relationship in which intimacy plays a large role compared with passion and decision. In this case, two lovers may be very close friends, but the physical aspects and commitment to the future are more marginal. The triangle on the right represents a relationship in which decision/commitment predominates over intimacy and passion. This is a highly committed relationship in which intimacy and physical attraction have waned or were never there initially. (Source: Based on suggestions by Sternberg, 1986.)

The three faces of love

anced love in which all three components are roughly equally matched. The triangle in the bottom left part of Figure 6.13 shows a relationship in which passion is emphasized over the other components—that is, physical attraction plays a very large part. Figure 6.13 also illustrates other examples of relationships in which one of the three components is emphasized over the others. Sternberg's approach helps us to understand why there are different kinds of loving relationships and how each represents a different combination of the three basic factors.

Early Attachments: Their Effect on Later Loving Relationships. Do early relationships influence the kinds of relationships we form later in life? Some social psychologists think so. Hazen and Shaver (1987) have proposed that adult romantic relationships may be strongly influenced by the kinds of attachments people form with their parents during childhood. To study this intriguing notion, the researchers polled readers of a newspaper and college students about their most important romance and also about their childhood relationships with their parents. The responses revealed three types of individuals. The first group consists of *"securely attached"* people. Securely attached people believe it is easy to get close to others, and they report few problems with mutual dependence in current relationships. These persons tended to have good relationships (their romances lasted the longest of the three groups and ended in divorce least often) and also reported that as children they perceived their parents as loving and warm. A second group, the *"avoidant"* persons, feel uneasy and untrusting when people grow close. These people tended to rate their parents as rejecting and had relationships with emotional highs and lows. The third group are characterized as *"anxious/ambivalent"* people who want a level of closeness their partners seem unwilling to give; they also worry a lot about their lovers leaving them. Their relationships with their parents were mixed—they reported that they were loving in some cases and cold and rejecting in others.

The implication of these results is that patterns of relationship or attachment during childhood may be repeated in adulthood. Of course, some people work out the problems of their early childhood, so history need not necessarily repeat itself. The viability of this approach remains to be determined by further research, but it has the unique possibility of understanding love from both a social and developmental perspective.

When Relationships Fail

Levinger (1980) describes relationships as passing through five possible stages: initial attraction, building a relationship, continuation, deterioration, and ending. Table 6.2 summarizes some of the factors operating at each stage. Much of the social psychological research on attraction over the past several decades has dealt with the first two stages. Currently, there is increased interest in pinpointing the factors that influence the remaining three stages. Most of this research deals with heterosexual relationships, but studies of homosexual couples suggest that identical variables are involved when one has a same-sex partner (Schullo and Alperson, 1984).

Attempting to Continue a Relationship: Jealousy and Other Pitfalls. One of the more common problems in a relationship is **jealousy**. When an individual perceives a rival for the affections of the one he or she loves, this can be a powerful source of negative emotion (Salovey and Rodin, 1986) and causes two kinds of suffering. An individual may lose the rewards the relationship offered, and there is also a lowering of self-esteem (Mathes, Adams, and Davies, 1985; White, 1981). The response is a consuming flood of unpleasant thoughts, feelings, and behaviors that we label as jealousy (Pines and Aronson, 1983). The rival may be real or imaginary, and the romantic attraction between the rival and one's partner may take place in the present, in the past, or even as a potential event in the future. Those who are most prone to become jealous tend to feel inadequate, dependent, and excessively concerned about sexual exclusivity (White, 1981).

Some people (about one in three college females and one in five males) deliberately attempt to make their partners jealous by their actions such as flirting or talking about former lovers (White, 1980a). Obviously, those who try to induce jealousy are playing a dangerous game that can lead to deterioration of the relationship.

An important aspect of any relationship is the extent to which each partner feels *equitably treated.* Equity exists, for example, when couples believe they are approximately equal in attractiveness, sociability, and intelligence. It is also important for partners to feel equally loved, equally desired sexually, and equally committed to the relationships. Equity also invokes such aspects of life as relative earnings, contributions to housework, and being easy to live with. Research has shown the importance of equity in the satisfaction of dating couples and in marital happiness and stability (Utne et al., 1984; Fletcher et al., 1987).

The Deterioration and Ending of a Relationship. Same-sex friendships often fade away simply because of physical separation, as when one individual moves to another area (Rose, 1984). Relationships involving love are more difficult and more painful to dissolve. In gen-

Table 6.2 Levinger (1980) proposes that relationships are divided into five stages, from initial attraction to a point at which they may end. At each stage are positive and negative factors that cause the relationship to develop and maintain itself or to move toward dissolution.

The five stages of a relationship

Stage of Relationship	Positive Factors	Negative Factors
Initial Attraction	Propinquity and repeated exposure	Absence of propinquity and repeated exposure
	Positive emotions	Negative emotions
	High affiliative need and friendship motivation	Low affiliative need and friendship motivation
Building a Relationship	Equivalent physical attractiveness	Nonequivalent physical attractiveness
	Similarity of attitudes and other characteristics	Dissimilarity of attitudes and other characteristics
	Reciprocal positive evaluations	Reciprocal negative evaluations
Continuation	Seeking ways to maintain interest and variety	Falling into a rut and becoming bored
	Providing evidence of positive evaluation	Providing evidence of negative evaluation
	Absence of jealousy	Jealousy
	Perceived equity	Perceived inequity
	High level of mutual satisfaction	Low level of mutual satisfaction
Deterioration	Much time and effort invested in relationship	Little time and effort invested in relationship
	Work at improvement of relationship	Decide to end relationship
	Wait for improvement to occur	Wait for deterioration to continue
Ending	Existing relationship offers some rewards	A new life appears to be the only acceptable solution
	No alternative partners available	Alternative partners available
	Expect relationship to succeed	Expect relationship to fail
	Commitment to a continuing relationship	Lack of commitment to a continuing relationship

eral, romantic relationships characterized by increases over time in rewards, commitment, and decreases in the quality of possible alternative relationships are less susceptible to dissolution (Simpson, 1987). Deterioration begins when one or both of the partners come to view conditions as less desirable than was previously the case.

The response to perceived deterioration can be either active or passive (Rusbult and Zembrodt, 1983). Actively, individuals can decide to end the relationship ("exit" behaviors) or to work at improvement ("voice" behaviors). Pas-

sively, one can wait for improvement to occur ("loyalty" behaviors) or for deterioration to continue ("neglect"). Voice and loyalty behaviors are judged to be constructive, while exit and neglect are destructive to the relationship (see Figure 6.14). Destructive behavior is considered the crucial element in causing distress in a relationship (Rusbult, Johnson, and Morrow, 1986).

Whether a breakup is long and painful or relatively rapid is found to depend on the amount of attraction the two individuals feel (Lee, 1984). Thus, a very loving relationship that

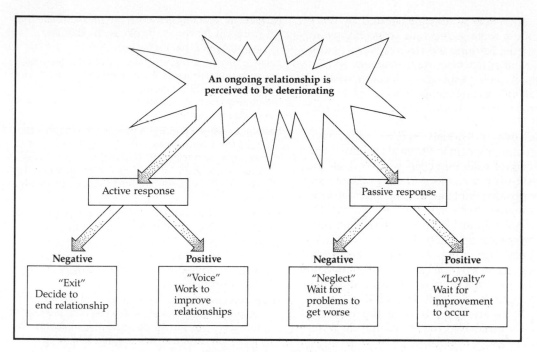

Figure 6.14 Once an individual perceives that a relationship is beginning to fail, he or she can respond either *actively* or *passively*. Within each of these possibilities, the person can make positive or negative assumptions about where the relationship is headed. On the positive side, it is possible to work actively in an attempt to improve the relationship or to wait passively for improvement to occur. Negatively, the person can actively end the relationship or passively wait for matters to get worse. (Based on suggestions of Rusbult and Zembrodt, 1983.)

Reacting to a bad relationship

fails leads to more unpleasantness, fear, and loneliness than one with weaker emotional bonds.

In any event, deterioration is likely to end in a breakup unless three factors are present. The relationship has to provide a high level of satisfaction; both partners must have already invested a great deal of time and effort; and alternative partners should not be readily available (Rusbult, 1980; 1983; Rusbult, Musante, and Solomon, 1982; Simpson, 1987). Sometimes individuals expect a relationship to fail because they have observed the failure of other couples. Other times, a new life appears to be the only acceptable solution. This body of research leads us to conclude

that love may strike an individual suddenly and effortlessly. Maintaining a relationship, in contrast, requires hard work over a long-term period by two committed individuals.

SUMMARY

Attraction is the evaluation of another person along a dimension ranging from love to hate. Acquaintanceship with a stranger often begins when two people are brought together by such environmental factors as seating arrangements in a classroom; **propinquity** leads to repeated exposure which leads to a positive emotional response. Attraction is strongly affected by emotions. One's feelings become *conditioned* to other people, forming the basis of liking or disliking. Initial contact between strangers is most probable if their respective affiliation motives are sufficiently strong, either in terms of dispositional traits or motivation elicited by external factors.

Once two individuals interact, other variables become important. **Physical attractiveness** plays a central role, especially when a romantic relationship is a possibility. There is also a consistently positive effect for various types of *similarity,* ranging from attitudes to personality characteristics. In an ongoing relationship, reciprocity becomes vital, in that each person wants and expects the other to express a positive evaluation in words and deeds from time to time. When friends outperform us in areas that are important to our self-definition, it can be painful. In contrast, we **bask in the reflected glory** of our friends' success when they do better in areas irrelevant to our self.

The ultimate attraction response is love. Most familiar is **passionate love**, an intense emotional state that occurs when one is raised in a culture that stresses love, when an appropriate love object is present. **Companionate love** is a more stable and more lasting basis for a relationship, in that it involves a deep and caring friendship.

Relationships often come to an end, and the reasons include jealousy, feelings of inequity, lack of commitment, changes in one or both partners, and the presence of more desirable alternatives. The closer two individuals have been, the more painful and more prolonged the breakup is likely to be. Maintaining a good relationship is a full-time job—one that requires more effort than falling in love in the first place.

GLOSSARY

affiliative need The motive to seek interpersonal relationships and to form friendships.

attitude similarity The degree to which two individuals share the same attitudes.

attraction The degree to which we like other individuals.

balance In Newcomb's theory, the pleasant state that exists when two people like each other and agree about some topic.

balance theory A cognitive theory of interpersonal attraction. Attraction is assumed to be based on the relationships among cognitions about another person and about various objects or topics of communication.

basking in reflected glory A positive feeling that results from being associated with someone (for example, as a friend or relative) who is successful in some area. This appears to occur when the skill or ability is not one that you are personally invested in.

belief in a just world The belief that people get what they deserve and also deserve what they get.

companionate love Love that rests on a firm base of friendship, common interests, mutual respect, and concern for the other person's happiness and welfare.

decision/commitment A component of the *triangular model of love* which refers to the cognitive elements involved in decision-making about the existence and commitment to the relationship.

emotion A physiological state of arousal associated with specific cognitive labels and appropriate behavior.

imbalance In Newcomb's theory, the unpleasant state that exists when two people like one another but disagree about some topic. Each is motivated to change some aspect of the interaction in order to achieve balance or nonbalance.

intimacy A component of the *triangular model of love* which refers to the closeness or bondedness between two people.

jealousy The thoughts, feelings, and actions that are instigated by a real or imagined rival. Such a rival is a threat to the relationship and to one's self-esteem.

love An emotional state involving attraction, sexual desire, and concern about the other person. It represents the most positive level of attraction.

matching hypothesis The proposal that individuals with approximately equal social assets (such as physical attractiveness) will select one another as friends, lovers, spouses, and so on.

need compatibility The proposal that, for at least some sets of needs, similarity should have a positive influence on attraction. For example, a highly sexed person would be expected to get along well with a highly sexed spouse, whereas an individual with low sex needs would prefer a spouse whose needs are equally low.

need complementarity The proposal that, for at least some sets of needs, dissimilarity should have a positive influence on attraction. For example, a person with a need to dominate would be expected to get along well with a spouse who had a need to submit to domination.

need for affiliation The motive to seek interpersonal relationships and to form friendships.

nonbalance In Newcomb's theory, the indifferent state that exists when two people dislike one another and don't care whether they agree or disagree on various topics.

passion A component of the *triangular model of love* which refers to the physical drives or arousal associated with the interpersonal relationship.

passionate love An intense and often unrealistic emotional response to another person. It is interpreted by the individuals involved as "love."

physical attractiveness The combination of facial features, bodily shape, and grooming that is accepted in a given culture as being that which is most pleasing.

propinquity Physical proximity. As propinquity between two individuals increases, the probability of their interacting increases. Repeated interaction tends to lead to familiarity and acquaintanceship.

reinforcement-affect model A theory that all evaluations are based on positive and negative emotions. These evaluations are directed at the stimulus object responsible for the emotion *and* at any other previously neutral stimulus that happens to be associated with the emotional arousal.

repeated exposure The theory that repeated exposure with any neutral or positive stimulus results in an increasingly positive evaluation.

self-fulfilling prophecy Refers to a phenomenon whereby a perceiver's expectations about another person may elicit behavior from him or her that confirms the expectancy.

FOR MORE INFORMATION

BERSCHEID, E. (1985). Interpersonal attraction. In G. Lindzey and E. Aronson (Eds.), *Handbook of social psychology* (Vol. 2). New York: Random House.

This chapter is an up-to-date overview of the empirical research and theoretical formulations related to the subject of interpersonal attraction. Professor Berscheid has done extensive work in this field, and she brings an expert's knowledge to bear in summarizing this very large body of knowledge.

DUCK, S., and PERLMAN, D. (Eds.). (1986). *Understanding personal relationships: An interdisciplinary approach.* London: Sage.

This collection of chapters is designed to integrate the work on personal relationships from the fields of social psychology, sociology, clinical psychology, and family studies. This is an optimistic report on the progress being made in a rapidly growing field of social psychological interest.

HATFIELD, E., and SPRECHER, G. (1986). *Mirror, mirror. . . . The importance of looks in everyday life.* Albany, N.Y.: SUNY Press.

A well-written, interesting summary of research on the effects of physical attractiveness in interpersonal relationships.

STERNBERG, R., and BARNES, M. (Eds.). (1988). *The nature of love.* New Haven: Yale University Press.

This collection of chapters presents the most recent thinking on the nature of love by noted experts.

Chapter Seven
Social Influence: Changing Others' Behavior

OBEDIENCE/Social Influence by Demand
Destructive Obedience: Why Does It Occur?/Destructive Obedience: Resisting Its Effects

CONFORMITY/How Groups Exert Influence
Asch's Conformity Experiments/Factors Affecting Conformity: Group Size, Social Support, and Sex/The Bases of Conformity: Why We Often Choose to "Go Along"/Does the Majority Prevail? Not Always

COMPLIANCE/To Ask—Sometimes—Is to Receive
Ingratiation: Liking as a Key to Influence/Multiple Requests: Two Steps to Compliance

Special Inserts

FOCUS ON RESEARCH/Classic Contributions
   Destructive Obedience: Harm by Demand

FOCUS ON RESEARCH/The Cutting Edge
   Increasing Compliance with the "That's-Not-All" Technique

"Come on, Jess. Nobody will ever know. Let me use it, please."

"I don't know . . ." Jessica Halliday answers hesitantly. "I promised my Dad I wouldn't let anyone else drive it . . . If he ever found out I'd be in real trouble."

"But how could he find out?" her friend Patti Burke answers. "He's five hundred miles away. Besides, I'll be real careful, I promise. But I've just *got* to see Stephen this weekend; it's been way too long. And there's no other way to get there."

"You could take a bus," Jessica murmurs in a weak voice.

"Stop kidding; you know . . . what's bothering you? Lots of other people lend their cars to their friends. Just last week Dede McCullough lent hers to Carole, and it's practically brand new. Don't be such a worrier; be loose like everyone else."

"I want to help, honest," Jessica answers, "but I gave my Dad my word, and I hate to go back on it. He'd be so disappointed."

At this comment, Patti changes tactics. "Look, you're such a sharp person. And we've been friends for ages. Have I ever let you down? You can trust me, really."

"It's not that. *You* can be careful and still have trouble. There's so many nuts on the road these days. And I know how you get when you're around Stephen—you just stop thinking."

"Yeah, I know," Patti says with a sigh, "he does have that effect on me. But that's why I want to see him so much. Please, you've just got to help me." And now she shifts strategies once again.

"Look, I'll tell you what. I won't stay until Sunday night; I'll drive back early in the afternoon. That way I won't be on the road at night. OK?"

"Well, that's a step in the right direction," Jessica replies. "If you go down early on Friday you won't have to do any night driving at all . . ."

"I will, I will. So it's all settled, OK?" But Jessica still hesitates, so Patti, sensing success, continues: "Oh please, please, Jess! You're so sweet and considerate . . . you don't want to see me suffer . . . Help me out just this once

and I'll pay you back, cross my heart. Just name it; I'll do anything!"

"Anything?" Jessica asks, a new note of interest in her voice.

"Well, practically anything," Patti answers.

At one time or other, almost everyone has had the following daydream: somehow, we gain a special skill or power that permits us to exert total control over others. Through this power, we can get them to do, think, feel anything we wish. This is a tantalizing fantasy, and for good reason. After all, if we possessed this ability, we could satisfy most of our desires instantly, and with very little effort. Unfortunately, of course, no magic formula for gaining such control exists. The people around us have minds of their own, and are willing to do our bidding only sometimes, and to a limited degree. Thus, the fantasy of exercising complete control over them must remain just that—an enticing but unattainable daydream.

While total control over others is beyond our grasp, we can use many tactics, such as the ones employed by Patti in the story, at least to move in this direction. In short, we can employ many procedures to exert **social influence** over others—to change their behavior, attitudes, or feelings in ways we desire (Cowan, Drinkard, and MacGavin, 1984; see Figure 7.1). Among the most important, common, and effective forms of social influence are obedience, conformity, and compliance.

Obedience occurs in situations in which persons change their behavior in response to direct commands from others. Usually, the individuals who issue such orders have some means of enforcing submission to them: they hold *power* over those on the receiving end. Surprisingly, though, direct orders can frequently be effective in altering others' behavior even when the persons who employ them actually possess little or no authority over the recipients.

Conformity occurs when individuals change their behavior in order to adhere to existing *social norms*—widely accepted rules indicating how people should behave in certain situations or under specific circumstances (Mosco-

Figure 7.1 There are many different tactics for exerting influence over others. This cartoon depicts a tactic that would be considered inappropriate by nearly everyone. (Reprinted with special permission of King Features Syndicate, Inc.)

Social influence in action

vici, 1985). Thus, it represents a crucial means through which groups, or even entire societies, mold the actions of their members. A clear example of conformity is provided by the fact that most persons speak in a whisper when in libraries or hospitals, even if they usually prefer to converse in louder tones. They do so because both formal and informal rules indicate that this is the "correct" (appropriate) way to behave. As we will soon see, pressures toward conformity exist in many settings, and often exert profound effects on social behavior.

In contrast, **compliance** represents a more direct or personal form of social influence. It takes place in situations in which individuals alter their behavior in response to direct requests from others. Many techniques for enhancing compliance—for increasing the probability that target persons will say "yes"—exist, and when used with skill, these can prove very effective indeed.

The remainder of this chapter focuses on the three major types of social influence described above. For each, we will consider why they seem to work—what makes them effective in changing others' behavior—as well as some of the factors that influence their success in this regard. In addition, we will touch on the use of these forms of social influence in practical settings—how they are often applied by persons who hope to profit (either financially or socially) from getting others to say "yes."

OBEDIENCE: Social Influence by Demand

What is the most direct technique one person can use to change the behavior of another? In one sense, at least, the answer is straightforward: simply ordering the target to do something. This approach is less common than either conformity or compliance, but it is far from rare (see Figure 7.2). Business executives often issue orders to their subordinates. Military officers shout commands that they expect to be followed at once. And parents, coaches, and umpires, to name just a few, seek to influence others in this manner.

Figure 7.2 Fawn Hall, secretary to Lt. Col. Oliver North, followed his orders to destroy papers describing clandestine and illegal actions carried out by North and his associates with respect to Iran and the Nicaraguan Contras. Hall's destruction of important records led her to be questioned before the special Congressional Investigative Committee on the Iran-Contra scandal in 1987.

Obedience to authority: A real-life example

Obedience to the commands of such sources of authority is far from surprising; they usually possess some means of enforcing their directives. More surprising, though, is the fact that even persons lacking in such power can sometimes induce high levels of submission from others. Perhaps the clearest evidence for the occurrence of such effects has been reported by Stanley Milgram in a series of famous and controversial experiments. For a summary of his influential work, see the "Focus on Research" insert.

Destructive Obedience: Why Does It Occur?

The results obtained by Milgram are disturbing. The parallels between the behavior of subjects in these studies and atrocities against civilians during time of war or civil uprising are too clear to require additional comment. But why, precisely, do such effects occur? Why were subjects in these experiments—and many persons in tragic life situations outside the laboratory—so willing to yield to the commands of various authority figures? Several factors appear to play a role.

First, in many situations, the persons in authority relieve those who obey of the responsibility for their own actions. "I was only carrying out orders" is the defense many offer after obeying harsh and cruel directives. In life situations, this transfer of responsibility may be implicit; in research on obedience, however, it was quite explicit. In Milgram's experiments, subjects were told, at the start, that the experimenter (the authority figure), not they, would be responsible for the victim's well-being. Little wonder, then, that they tended to obey.

Second, persons in authority often possess visible badges or signs of their status and power. These consist of special uniforms, insignia, titles, and related factors. Faced with such obvious reminders of who's in charge, most people find it difficult to resist. In one study dealing with such effects (Bushman, 1984), pedestrians stopped on the street were ordered by an accomplice dressed as a firefighter to give a dime to another individual for a parking meter. Nearly 80 percent of the subjects complied with the request as compared to 40 percent when asked by an

DESTRUCTIVE OBEDIENCE: HARM BY DEMAND

Milgram (1963; 1974) wished to learn whether individuals would follow commands from an experimenter to inflict considerable pain and suffering on another person—a totally innocent stranger. To see if people would do this, he informed subjects they were participating in a study of the effects of punishment on learning. Their task was that of delivering electric shocks to another person (actually an accomplice) each time he made an error in a simple learning task. These shocks were to be delivered by means of thirty switches on the equipment shown in Figure 7.3. Subjects were told to move to the next higher switch each time the learner made an error. Since the first switch supposedly delivered a shock of 15

volts, it was clear that if the learner made many errors, he would soon be receiving powerful jolts. Indeed, according to the labels on the equipment, the final shock would consist of 450 volts! In reality, of course, the accomplice (the learner) never received any shocks during the experiment. The only real shock ever used was a mild demonstration pulse from one button given to subjects to convince them the equipment was real (see Figure 7.3).

During the session, the learner (following prearranged instructions) made many errors. Thus, subjects soon found themselves facing a dilemma. Should they continue punishing this person with what seemed to be increasingly painful shocks? Or should

they refuse to go on? The experimenter pressured them to choose the former path, for whenever they hesitated or protested, he made one of a series of graded remarks. These began with "Please go on," escalated to "It is absolutely essential that you continue," and finally shifted to "You have no other choice, you *must* go on."

Since subjects were all volunteers and were paid in advance for their participation, you might predict that they would be quite resistant to these orders. Yet, in reality, fully *65 percent showed total obedience.* They proceeded through the entire shock series to the final 450-volt level (see Figure 7.4). In contrast, subjects in a control group who were not exposed to such commands generally used

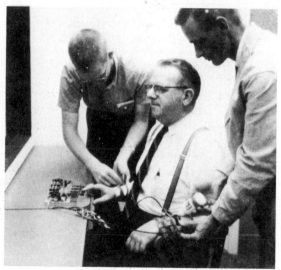

Figure 7.3   The photo on the left shows Stanley Milgram and the apparatus he used in his famous experiments on obedience. The photo on the right shows the experimenter (wearing a lab coat) and a subject attaching electrodes to the learner's (accomplice's) wrists. (Source: From the film "Obedience," distributed by the New York University Film Library. Copyright 1965 by Stanley Milgram. Reprinted by permission of the copyright holder.)

Studying destructive obedience: The Milgram technique

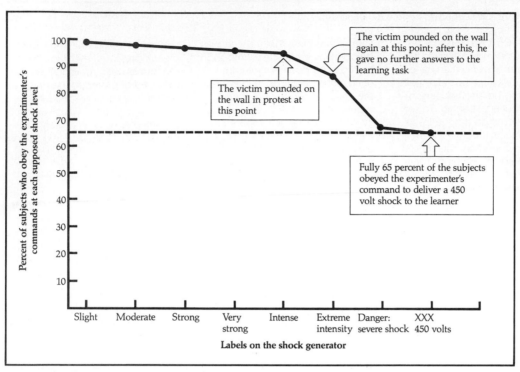

The victim pounded on the wall again at this point; after this, he gave no further answers to the learning task

The victim pounded on the wall in protest at this point

Fully 65 percent of the subjects obeyed the experimenter's command to deliver a 450 volt shock to the learner

Percent of subjects who obey the experimenter's commands at each supposed shock level

Labels on the shock generator: Slight, Moderate, Strong, Very strong, Intense, Extreme intensity, Danger: severe shock, XXX 450 volts

Figure 7.4 A surprisingly high proportion of the subjects in Milgram's research obeyed the experimenter's commands to deliver electric shocks of increasing strength to an innocent victim. Indeed, fully 65 percent demonstrated total obedience in this regard. (Source: Based on data from Milgram, 1963.)

Obedience in action: An unsettling demonstration

only very mild shocks during the session. Of course, many persons subjected to the experimenter's commands often protested and asked that the session be ended. When ordered to proceed, however, a majority yielded to social pressure and continued to obey. Indeed, as you can see from Figure 7.4, they continued to do so even when the victim pounded on the wall as if in protest against the painful treatment he was receiving.

In further experiments Milgram (1965, 1974) found that similar results could be obtained even under conditions that might be expected to reduce such obedience. For example, when the study was moved from its original location on the campus of Yale University to a rundown office building in a nearby city, subjects' level of obedience was virtually unchanged. Similarly, a large proportion continued to obey even when the accomplice complained about the pain and begged to be released. Most surprising of all, many (about 30 percent) continued to obey even when this required that they grasp the victim's hand and force it down upon the shock plate! That these unsettling results were not due to special conditions present in Milgram's laboratory is indicated by the fact that similar findings were soon reported in several different countries (e.g., Jordan, West Germany, Australia) and with children as well as adults (e.g., Kilham and Mann, 1974; Shanab and Yahya, 1977). Thus, they seemed to be alarmingly general in scope.

accomplice dressed in a business suit. In sum, the possession of an outward badge of authority—even though it was totally irrelevant to the present situation—strongly affected the subjects' behavior.

A third reason for obedience in many situations in which the targets of such influence might resist involves its gradual nature. Often, commands are relatively small and innocuous at first. Only later do they increase in scope and come to require those who receive them to behave in dangerous and objectionable ways. For example, police or military personnel may at first be ordered to question, arrest, or threaten potential victims. Gradually, demands are increased to the point where they are commanded to beat, torture, or even kill unarmed civilians. In a similar manner, subjects in laboratory research on obedience were first required to deliver only mild and harmless shocks to the victim. Only as this person continued to make repeated errors did the intensity of these "punishments" rise to harmful levels.

Related to the above, of course, is the question of when subordinates should disobey. Where should they draw the line, so to speak? Unfortunately, since commands escalate in a gradual manner, there is no clear-cut point at which disobedience rather than obedience becomes more appropriate.

In sum, many different factors contribute to the high levels of obedience witnessed in laboratory studies and in a wide range of real-life contexts. Together, these factors merge into a powerful force—one that most persons find difficult to resist. Unfortunately, the consequences of this compelling form of social influence can be highly dangerous for countless innocent, defenseless victims.

Destructive Obedience: Resisting Its Effects

Now that we have considered some of the factors responsible for our strong tendency to obey persons in authority, we can turn to a related—and crucial—question: how can this type of influence be resisted? Fortunately, several strategies seem effective in this regard.

First, individuals exposed to commands from authority figures can be reminded that they—not the authority person—are responsible for any harm produced. Under these conditions, we may expect sharp reductions in the tendency to obey, and the results of several studies suggest that this is actually the case (e.g., Hamilton, 1978; Kilham and Mann, 1974). When subjects in these investigations were informed that *they* would be responsible for the victim's safety, they showed much lower levels of obedience than when they were not provided with such information.

Second, the tendency to obey can be reduced by providing individuals with a sign that beyond some point, unquestioning submission to destructive commands is inappropriate. Evidence for such effects is provided by the results of several studies in which subjects have been exposed to *disobedient models*—other persons who refuse to obey an authority's commands. Individuals exposed to such clear signs that obedience is inappropriate found it much easier to disobey, too (Milgram, 1965; Powers and Geen, 1972).

Third, individuals may also find it easier to resist influence from sources of authority if they question the expertise and motives of such persons (Cialdini, 1988). Are they really in a better position to judge what is appropriate and what is inappropriate? What motives lie behind their commands—selfish gain or socially beneficial goals? By asking such questions, persons who might otherwise obey without hesitation may find support for independence rather than submission.

Finally, we might add that simply knowing about the power of authority figures to command blind obedience may be helpful in itself. Some research findings (e.g., Sherman, 1980) suggest that when individuals read about the findings of social psychological research, they become sensitized to the phenomena studied and to the effects described. They may then change their behavior to take account of this knowledge. With respect to obedience, there is some hope that knowing about this process may enhance individuals' ability to resist.

In sum, the power of authority figures to command obedience is certainly great. But it is definitely not irresistible. Under appropriate conditions it can be countered and reduced. We should hasten to add that in many cases, resisting such influence is not essential: the persons exercising authority do so appropriately, and for acceptable reasons. When we have grounds for suspecting that their commands are unjustified, stem from objectionable motives, and will produce harmful effects, however, our course of action is clear. In such cases, it is our *obligation,* as well as our right, to resist.

CONFORMITY: How Groups Exert Influence

Have you ever found yourself in a situation in which you felt you stuck out like the proverbial sore thumb? If so, you have already had first-hand experience with pressures toward *conformity.* In such situations, you probably felt a strong desire to "get back in line"—to fit in with the other people around you. Such pressures toward conformity seem to stem from the fact that in many situations there are both spoken and unspoken rules indicating how we should or ought to behave. Known as *social norms,* these rules can be quite precise and explicit. For example, governments often function through constitutions and written codes of law. Athletic contests are usually regulated by written rules. And signs along highways, in airports, and countless other public places often describe expected behavior in great detail.

In contrast, other norms are unspoken and implicit (e.g., Zuckerman, Miserandino, and Bernieri, 1983). For example, most of us obey such unwritten rules as "Don't stare at strangers on the street or in elevators," and "Don't come to parties or other social gatherings exactly on time." And we are often strongly influenced by current and rapidly changing standards of dress, speech, and personal style. Regardless of whether social norms are explicit or implicit, however, most are obeyed by most persons much of the time. For example, few people visit restaurants without leaving some sort of tip. Few drivers park in places for handicapped motorists. And virtually everyone, regardless of political beliefs, stands when the national anthem is played at sporting events and other public gatherings. At first glance, this strong tendency toward conformity—toward going along with society's expectations about how we should behave in various situations—may strike you as objectionable. After all, it does prevent us from "doing our own thing" on many occasions. Actually, though, there is a strong and eminently rational basis for the existence of so much conformity: without it, we would quickly find ourselves in the midst of social chaos! For example, imagine what would happen outside movie theaters, at voting booths, and at supermarket checkout counters if people did not follow the simple rule, "Form a line and wait your turn" (see Figure 7.5). Similarly, consider the danger to both drivers and pedestrians if there were no clear and widely followed traffic regulations. Often, then, conformity serves a very useful function. But please note: this does not imply that it is *always* helpful. At times, norms governing individual behavior appear to have no obvious purpose—they simply exist. Why, to mention one instance, must both men and women often wear clothing that is ill-suited to prevailing weather (e.g., ties, jackets, and vests in summer, and skirts and sheer nylon hosiery in winter)? It is in cases such as these, where norms governing behavior persist without offering any obvious practical benefits, that some persons, at least, find them objectionable.

While the existence of strong pressures toward conformity was recognized both within social psychology and outside it for many decades, it was not until the 1950s that this important process was subjected to systematic study. At this time, a series of ingenious studies by Solomon Asch (1951) paved the way for later research on conformity. We'll turn to these ground-breaking experiments before describing more recent investigations.

Asch's Conformity Experiments

Imagine that you find yourself in the following situation: you are having a discussion with some people at a party about the most recent political candidates. Before you have a chance to state your preference, you learn the others hold

Figure 7.5 There would be social chaos if people did not obey the simple rule, "Form a line and wait your turn." Conformity to this rule is clearly of social benefit. Of course, all norms governing individual behavior are not necessarily helpful or logical.

"Form a line and wait your turn". One common social norm

sharply contrasting views. Do you remain independent and state your opinion accurately, or do you yield to social pressure and go along with the group?

Asch created a laboratory parallel of this kind of social dilemma. Subjects were asked to respond to a series of simple perceptual problems such as the one in Figure 7.6. On each problem, they indicated which of the three comparison lines matched a standard line in length. Several other persons were also present during the session (usually six to eight), but, unknown to the actual subject, they were all accomplices of

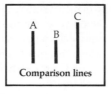

Figure 7.6 One of the perceptual problems used by Asch in his classic research on conformity. Subjects' task was to indicate which of the three comparison lines (A, B, or C) matched the standard line in length.

Asch's line-judging task: An example

the experimenter (see Figure 7.7). On various prearranged occasions (twelve out of eighteen problems) those persons offered answers that were clearly false (e.g., they unanimously stated that line C matched the standard line in Figure 7.6). On such trials, subjects faced a dilemma: should they go along with the group, or stick to their guns and provide what they felt were correct answers? You may be surprised to learn that in fact, participants in Asch's research showed strong tendencies to conform. Indeed, 76 percent of those tested went along with the group's false answers at least once. In contrast, only 5 percent of the subjects in a control group, who responded to the same perceptual problems but in the absence of any falsely answering accomplices, made such errors. It is also important to note, though, that most subjects resisted conformity most of the time: almost 24 percent never conformed, and many others yielded on only a few critical trials (trials on which the accomplices gave wrong answers). Yet, a large majority did conform to the accomplices' false answers at least a part of the time. These results, and those obtained in many later studies (Tanford and Penrod, 1984), point to an unsettling conclusion: many persons find it less upsetting to publicly

Figure 7.7   Asch is conducting his subjects through the line-judging task. Unbeknownst to the real subject (No. 6 from the left), the other individuals are confederates of Asch who on a prearranged schedule give an incorrect response. The dilemma for the subject is whether to conform to the others or to state his mind. Seventy-six percent of the subjects went along with the group's false answers at least once. (Source: Vandivert and *Scientific American,* 1955.)

The Asch dilemma

contradict the evidence of their own senses than to disagree openly with the unanimous judgments of other persons—even those of total strangers.

In subsequent research, Asch (1957) repeated the above procedures with one important change: instead of stating their answers out loud, subjects wrote them down on a piece of paper. As you might suspect, conformity dropped sharply under these conditions. This finding points to the importance of distinguishing between *public compliance*—doing or saying what others around us say or do—and *private acceptance*—actually coming to think or feel as they do. Often it appears, we overtly adhere to social norms or yield to group pressure without changing our private views or interpretations of the social world (Maas and Clark, 1984).

Factors Affecting Conformity: Group Size, Social Support, and Sex

Asch's research demonstrated the existence of powerful pressures toward conformity. However, even a moment's reflection indicates that conformity does not occur to the same degree in all settings or among all groups of persons. This fact, in turn, raises an intriguing question: what factors determine the extent to which individuals yield to conformity pressure? Several decades of research on this issue have generated a long list of variables that play a role in this regard. Among the most important of these appear to be (1) group *size,* (2) absence or presence of *social support,* and (3) sex of the persons exposed to social pressure.

Conformity and Group Size: Why, with Respect to Social Influence, "More" Is Not Always "Better." One factor that exerts important effects on our tendency to conform is the size of the influencing group. At first glance, you might guess that the greater the number of persons around us who act in some manner or who state some opinion, the greater the tendency to do the same. In fact, though, the relationship between group size and conformity is more complex. Studies designed to investigate this issue have often reported that conformity does increase with rising group size, but only up to a point. And surprisingly, this point seems to occur quite rapidly. Conformity pressure, and the tendency to yield to it, seems to rise quickly up to about three or four group members (influence sources). Beyond this level, further increments in group size produce less and less additional effect (e.g., Gerard, Wilhelmy, and Connelley, 1968). One reason for this relationship may be that as group size rises beyond three or four members, individuals exposed to social pressure may begin to suspect *collusion*. That is, they may conclude that group members are not expressing individual views or behaving in accordance with individual preferences. Rather, they are working together to exert influence (Wilder, 1977).

A recently proposed formal model of social influence (the **social influence model** or **SIM model**) by Tanford and Penrod (1984) helps to clarify some issues regarding the effects of the size of a group and social influence. These investigators suggest that the function relating group size to conformity or social influence is S-shaped in form (see Figure 7.8). At first, each person added to the group (each additional source of influence) produces a larger increment in conformity pressure than the one before. Soon, however, this function levels off, so that each additional person adds *less* to the total amount of

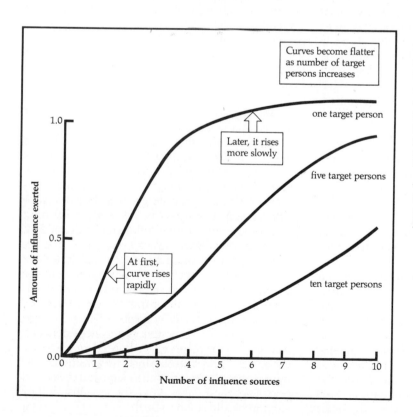

Curves become flatter as number of target persons increases

Later, it rises more slowly

one target person

1.0

five target persons

At first, curve rises rapidly

ten target persons

0.5

Amount of influence exerted

0.0

0   1   2   3   4   5   6   7   8   9   10

Number of influence sources

Figure 7.8 *The SIM model predicts that first, influence rises rapidly as group size increases. Soon, however, this function levels off, so that additional group members add less and less effect. The model also predicts that the curve relating group size to social influence becomes flatter as the number of targets rises. (Source: Based on suggestions by Tanford and Penrod, 1984.)*

Group size, number of target persons, and social influence: The SIM model

social influence than did the preceding ones. Actually, there is some dispute about whether the first person has the greatest impact and each additional influence source has a decreasing influence (Latané, 1981; Campbell, Tesser, and Fairey, 1986) or whether the second and third source has greater impact than the first (Tanford and Penrod, 1984). This point remains to be resolved in future work. Perhaps the critical point is that adding influence sources has a diminishing effect and rather quickly.

The SIM model also suggests that as the number of targets of social influence increases, the function relating to group size becomes flatter in shape (see Figure 7.8). This makes a great deal of sense. After all, even as a group increases in size, its impact on several different members will be less than its impact on a single holdout. This aspect of Tanford and Penrod's model is also related to the topic we discuss next—social support.

The Effects of Support from Others: Does Having an Ally Help? In Asch's research (and in many later studies of conformity), subjects were exposed to social pressure from a unanimous group. All of the other persons present seemed to hold different views from their own. What would happen, though, if persons facing such pressure discovered that they had an *ally*—someone who shared their views, or at least failed to endorse the same position as the majority? Under such conditions, perhaps, conformity might be reduced. That this is actually so is indicated by the results of several different experiments (e.g., Allen and Levine, 1971; Morris and Miller, 1975). In these investigations, subjects provided with an ally or partner showed much less conformity than subjects not supplied with social support.

Perhaps the impressive effectiveness of such support in reducing conformity is best suggested by two additional facts. First, conformity is reduced even when the partner or ally is someone not competent in the present situation. For example, in one study involving visual judgments, conformity was reduced even by a partner who wore thick glasses and who could not see the relevant stimuli (Allen and Levine, 1971). Second, it is not even crucial that the ally share

the subject's views. Conformity is reduced even if this person merely differs from the other group members—breaks their united front, so to speak.

These and other findings suggest that almost any form of social support can be helpful from the point of view of resisting social pressure. Certain types of support are more effective than others, however. For example, it appears that support received early—before pressures toward conformity have grown—is more helpful than support received later, after such pressures are in place (Morris, Miller, and Spangenberg, 1977). That is, subjects conform less if they find social support before most of the majority have expressed their position. Apparently, learning that someone else shares their views can help strengthen individuals' confidence in their own judgments and so enhances ability to resist group pressure as it develops. This fact may have an important implication for real-life settings. If you ever find yourself in a situation in which pressures toward conformity are rising, and you feel they should be resisted, try to speak out as quickly as possible. The sooner you do, the greater the chances of rallying others to your side and resisting the powerful impact of the majority.

Sex Differences in Conformity: A Matter of Status? Many early experiments on conformity yielded a result that, from the perspective of the late 1980s, is somewhat unsettling: females seemed to be much more conforming than males (e.g., Crutchfield, 1955). This finding was consistent with then-prevailing views about the supposed characteristics of the two sexes (e.g., men are "tough" and women more yielding). Indeed, for more than two decades the view that females are more susceptible to social influence than males went unchallenged. Beginning in the 1970s, however, it was subjected to renewed examination. The result of this "second wave" of research was directly contrary to those of the first: no large or consistent differences between the sexes with respect to the tendency to conform were uncovered. Since these studies are more sophisticated in both design and execution (e.g., Eagly and Carli, 1981), the conclusion they support would seem to be the correct one. But it is interesting to ask *why* the earlier experiments often found greater conformity on the part of females. The answer seems to lie in the type of materials employed in such research.

Briefly, in some investigations, the tasks or items presented to subjects tended to be more familiar to males than to females. Since individuals are usually more willing to yield to social influence from others when they are uncertain about how to behave than when they are more confident, it is hardly surprising that females demonstrated higher levels of conformity: after all, the dice were loaded against them. That this factor was indeed responsible for the sex differences obtained in early research is indicated by the findings of an experiment carried out by Sistrunk and McDavid (1971). These researchers found that when females were less familiar with the items used than males, they did in fact show greater yielding to group pressure. However, when the tables were turned, so that the items used were less familiar to males, it was *they* who showed greater conformity. Clearly, then, in yielding to social pressure, differences related to conformity or familiarity should *not* be attributed to basic and important differences between the two sexes.

In sum, it now seems clear that there are no important differences between males and females in terms of the tendency to conform. Yet, as you probably realize, the view that the sexes *do* differ in this respect continues to persist. Many persons still seem to believe that females are easier to "push around" or influence than males. Why is this the case? One possibility involves widespread beliefs about *status* and its relationship to both influencability and sex. Consider the following points. First, many persons believe (and with some justification) that individuals low in status are somewhat easier to influence than are individuals high in status (e.g., Kipnis, 1984). Second, many also believe that, on the average, females have lower status than males, both in society generally and in a wide range of work settings. Together, these beliefs lead to the assumption that females are often more conforming than males. Indeed, there is evidence that men and women assume female employees have lower status in work situations and are more yielding than male employees.

However, if specific information about a person's status is provided (via job titles), this overrides assumptions about the sexes. Thus, a high-status female is seen to have more influence over a low-status male (Eagley and Wood, 1982). It is also worth noting that a recent follow-up study in which status information was not provided did not even find that males were perceived as more influential and females as more yielding (Steffen and Eagley, 1985). This may partly be a function of increasing numbers of women moving into high-level jobs so the perception that women occupy only the lower rungs on the corporate or occupational ladder may be fading (Peters et al., 1984). To the extent such changes continue, they may ultimately help to eliminate the widespread but false belief that females are more susceptible to social influence than males.

The Bases of Conformity: Why We Often Choose to "Go Along"

As we have just seen, many factors determine whether, and to what extent, conformity will occur. Yet, despite such variations, one fact is clear: such behavior is very common. Why is this so? Why do we usually choose to "go along" with the expectations of others, the rules established by society, or the norms of various groups to which we belong? There are no simple answers to this question, as many factors contribute to our strong tendency to conform. The most important of these, however, seem to involve two basic needs possessed by all human beings: the desire to be liked and the desire to be right (Insko, 1985).

The Desire to Be Liked: Normative Social Influence. How can we induce other persons to like us? This is one of the eternal puzzles of social life. As we saw in Chapter Six, many strategies can prove effective in this regard. One of the most successful, though, is that of being as similar to others as possible. From our earliest days we learn that agreeing with the persons around us, and behaving much as they do, causes them to like us. Indeed, parents, teachers, friends, and others often heap praise and approval on us for demonstrating such similarity. One important reason we conform, therefore, is simple: we have learned that doing so can yield the love and acceptance we so strongly desire. Conformity stemming from this source is known as **normative social influence**, since it involves altering our behavior to meet the expectations of others. And as you probably know from your own experience, it is extremely common.

The Desire to Be Right: Informational Social Influence. If you want to determine the dimensions of a room, you measure them directly. Similarly, if you need to know the population of a particular city, you can look it up in an atlas. But how can you establish the "accuracy" of various political views or decide what kind of clothes are most stylish and attractive? Here, there are no simple physical tests or handy reference sources to consult. Yet, you probably have just as strong a desire to be "right" about such matters as you do about questions relating to the physical world. The solution to this dilemma is obvious: in order to answer such questions, at least to obtain information about them, we turn to other people. We use *their* opinions and *their* actions as guides for our own (Festinger, 1954; Suls and Miller, 1977; Olson, Herman, and Zanna, 1986; Goethals and Darley, 1987). This second important source of conformity is known as **informational social influence**, and is also a basic part of everyday life. In countless situations we choose to act and think like others because doing so assures us that we are "right"—or at least on the right track.

The first experimental demonstration of informational social influence was made by Muzafer Sherif (1935). He took advantage of a perceptual illusion. When a person is placed in a completely dark room and is exposed to a single, stationary point of light, he or she cannot determine precisely where the light is located in space. There are no cues to size or distance. The typical subject in such a situation perceives the light is moving about, even though it is actually not moving at all. This illusion is called the **autokinetic phenomenon.**

Sherif (1935) used this illusion to observe the creation of a social norm and of the effects of informational social influence. Previous research

had shown that an individual who is exposed to the light on a series of trials will gradually settle on a particular range within which it is seen as moving. Also, different subjects develop specific ranges. Sherif found that when several individuals are placed in this setting, and each person is asked to report about what the light is doing, the group establishes its own range, and each individual tends to report that the light moves within that range. Thus, subjects modified their own estimates because of the information conveyed by the other subjects' estimates. The most stunning evidence of informational social influence, however, is that when the same individuals later are in the experimental room alone, they continue to respond to the norm established by the group. Thus, faced with the ambiguous situation provided by the autokinetic phenomenon, each person's perceptions are influenced by what others say they perceive.

Together, these two factors—our strong desire to be liked (normative social influence) and our strong desire to be right (informational social influence)—go a long way toward assuring that conformity, not independence, tends to be our *modus operandi* (our standard manner of behaving). Indeed, given their powerful impact, it is hardly surprising that we choose to fit in with the crowd in most situations, much of the time.

Does the Majority Prevail? Not Always

Though social pressure commonly "wins out," motives other than the desire to be liked or to be correct may prompt people to resist social pressure and certain situations may even make a minority more persuasive than a majority. Below we consider one such motive and then go on to describe some intriguing research concerning when minorities can "win over" a majority.

The Need for Individuation. In addition to wanting to be liked and to be correct, people also wish to feel unique (Snyder and Fromkin, 1980). This tendency may prompt a person to resist social pressure to conform. Maslach, Stapp, and Santee (1985) developed a scale to measure people's general **need for individuation**—that is, their willingness to engage in behaviors that publicly differentiate them from others. A representative item from the scale is "Speak up about your ideas even though you are uncertain of whether you are correct."

Studies show that subjects with a high need for individuation are more likely to disagree with the opinions of other group members (Maslach, Santee, and Wade, 1987). Interestingly, subjects high in the need for individuation are more likely to dissent in a unanimous group than in a group where one other person has already dissented (Santee and Maslach, 1982). It may seem contradictory that the individuators are less conforming when there is already a dissenter (recall the ally effects described earlier). However, it makes sense if we recognize that the subject can only look distinctive if no one else is dissenting.

In addition to the need for individuation, people may also refuse to "give in" to majority pressure if they have a high need for control (Burger and Cooper, 1979). Indeed, studies demonstrate that people who hold a strong desire to be in control over events in their lives are less susceptible to group norms in Asch-type situations (Burger, 1987).

Minority Influence: Why the Majority Doesn't Always Rule. We have seen that individuals can—and do—resist group pressure (Latané and Wolf, 1981; Wolf, 1985). But resistance is one thing; can a lone individual or a minority "overturn" the prevailing majority view? It has happened. History is filled with events in which small but determined minorities have turned the tables on even overwhelming majorities and have *exerted* rather than yielded to social influence. For example, such giants of the scientific world as Galileo, Pasteur, and Freud faced large and virtually unanimous majorities who rejected their theories and views. Yet, over time, they won growing numbers of colleagues to their side, until ultimately their views prevailed. Similarly, in recent decades, initially small but resolute groups of reformers (e.g., environmentalists, persons seeking the elimination of racial and sexual prejudice) have often suc-

ceeded in altering even deeply entrenched attitudes and values. Such events suggest that minorities are not always powerless in the face of large and unified majorities. On the contrary, they can sometimes overcome the odds, and make *their* views prevail.

Direct evidence for the occurrence of **minority influence** has been obtained in many different experiments (Maas and Clark, 1984; Moscovici, 1985). For example, in one well-conducted study, Bray, Johnson, and Chilstrom (1982) arranged for groups of six persons—four subjects and two accomplices—to discuss a series of problems of considerable interest to them (e.g., a plan to charge students for athletic tickets which had previously been free). During discussion of each problem, the accomplices adopted a dissenting position, opposite to the one held by the four subjects. Later, after the discussions, subjects indicated their views on each issue. Results offered clear support for the occurrence of minority influence; subjects exposed to the dissenting views of the two accomplices did shift in the directions recommended by these persons, relative to subjects in a control condition who were never exposed to minority influence. These findings, and similar results reported in other studies (e.g., Moscovici and Faucheux, 1972), indicate that minorities can indeed affect the views of even larger majorities. Additional research, however, suggests that such effects are more likely to occur under some conditions than others (see Figure 7.9).

First, in order for a minority to be effective in influencing a majority, it is important that its members be consistent. If, instead, they "waffle" or oscillate back and forth between their own view and that of the majority, their impact will be lessened. Second, in order for a minority to affect a larger majority, such persons must avoid appearing rigid and dogmatic (Mugny, 1975). A minority that merely repeats the same position over and over again will often be less effective than one that demonstrates a degree of flexibility in its stance. Third, the general social context in which a minority operates is important. If a minority argues for a position that is consistent with current social trends (e.g., conservative views at a time of growing conservatism), its

"That's it? <u>That's</u> the minority report?"

Figure 7.9 Minorities can make their opinions prevail, but more is required than is depicted in this cartoon. (Source: Drawing by Dana Fradon; © 1987 The New Yorker Magazine, Inc.)

Ineffective tactics in "winning over" the majority

chances of influencing a majority are greater than if it argues for a position that is "out of phase" with such trends. Finally, it appears that *single minorities*—minorities that differ from the majority only with respect to their beliefs or attitudes—are more effective in exerting influence than *double minorities*—minorities that differ both in their attitudes and in their group membership. For example, in the United States members of a black radical group holding extreme political views would constitute a double minority; members of a white radical group holding similar views would represent a single minority.

In sum, it appears that under appropriate conditions committed, consistent minorities can indeed change the views of even larger majorities. This fact, in turn, raises an important question: why is this the case? One possible answer is provided by key aspects of attribution theory (Maas and Clark, 1984). As you may recall from our discussion of this topic in Chapter Two, we

tend to view others' behavior as stemming from internal causes under conditions where (1) consensus is low (other people don't act in the same way they do), (2) consistency is high (the persons in question act in the same manner across time), and (3) distinctiveness is low (these persons act in the same manner in other situations). Clearly, these conditions apply very well to the actions of highly committed minorities. Such persons adopt an unpopular stand, maintain it consistently, and act in accordance with it in many different situations. The result: their actions are viewed as stemming from deep conviction and commitment. Little wonder, then, that their views are often taken seriously, and are at least considered with care by the majorities around them. (See Figure 7.10 for a summary of these suggestions.)

Even given these conditions, minorities may not have an observable effect. That is, the majority may still rule. A review of relevant studies indicates that majorities tend to influence people

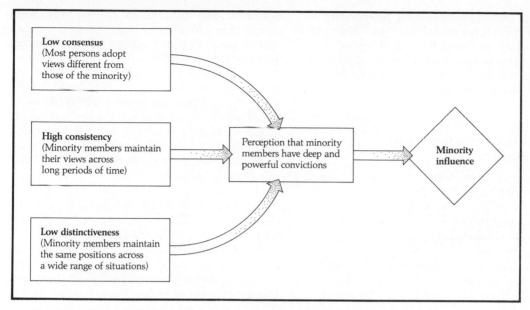

Figure 7.10 *Because minorities demonstrate low consensus, high consistency, and low distinctiveness, they are often perceived as possessing very strong convictions. This may account, at least in part, for their ability to exert influence upon larger majorities.*

The impact of minorities: One possible explanation

at the *public* level. People pay attention to what the majority is saying and publicly comply with the majority position. However, minorities may produce *private* or latent influence or genuine change in underlying views (Moscovici and Lage, 1976; Maas and Clark, 1984). Minorities may also have another effect, even if they do not sway the majority to their side publicly or privately. Nemeth (1986) has demonstrated that a persistent minority tends to foster greater thought about the issue under consideration ("How can they be so wrong and yet be so sure of themselves?"). This process is akin to central processing, which was discussed in Chapter Four. As a result, the majority is stimulated to consider the alternatives, which increases the potential for detecting novel solutions or decisions that even the minority may not have advanced. Hence, even when a persistent minority fails to shift the majority to its position, it may serve a useful function by stimulating thought. "Long live the loyal opposition!"

COMPLIANCE: To Ask— Sometimes—Is to Receive

Requests from others are a basic part of social life. As in the story in the beginning of this chapter, friends ask for favors. Salespersons try to induce us to purchase their products. Lovers, spouses, and roommates ask us to change various aspects of our behavior. And politicians request our votes or financial support. The list is practically endless. Attempts to gain compliance through direct requests are one of the most common, if not *the* most common forms of social influence.

At first glance, this approach to changing others' behavior seems quite straightforward. And in its most basic form, it is: persons seeking compliance simply express their basic wishes and hope they'll be granted. Often, though, attempts to gain compliance are much more subtle. Instead of presenting their petitions "cold," they begin with preliminary steps or maneuvers designed to enhance the likelihood that targets of their requests will say "yes." Many different tactics are used for this purpose, and you have probably encountered most in your daily life. Among the most successful, though, are ones based on ingratiation and multiple requests.

Ingratiation: Liking as a Key to Influence

Earlier we noted that most people have a strong desire to be liked by others. While this motive probably stems from several different sources, one of the most important is that we realize that if others like us, they are more willing to do things for us—to say "yes" to our requests. Recognition of this basic fact lies behind a common technique for gaining compliance: **ingratiation**. What this involves, in essence, is a strategy in which we first try to get others to like us, and then, after this has been accomplished, expose them to various requests (Jones, 1964). Several different procedures for enhancing our appeal to others in this fashion exist (Cialdini, 1988).

First, we can seek to accomplish this goal by improving our physical appearance; in general attractive persons are liked more than unattractive ones (Berscheid, 1985). Second, we can attempt to convince them that we are similar to them in some respect. This can involve demonstrating that we hold the same attitudes, that we have similar interests, or even that we possess the same traits (Byrne, 1971). Third, we can use a set of tactics best described by the phrase *other-enhancement* (Wortman and Linsenmeier, 1977). These all center on the goal of communicating a high degree of personal regard to the individuals we later wish to influence—convincing them that we like and care about *them*. Other-enhancement can involve complimenting such persons, hanging on their every word, or transmitting subtle nonverbal cues suggestive of positive feelings about them (Godfrey, Jones, and Lord, 1986). Fourth, we can engage in *impression management*—that is, efforts to "put our best foot forward" and convince others that we possess many desirable traits. Finally, we can sometimes gain others' liking merely by associating

ourselves with positive events or even with people they already like. For example, we can "name drop," thus indicating that we are linked to important successful people. This is similar to the "basking in reflected glory" effect discussed in Chapter Six. Or we may try to distance ourselves from others with whom we could be associated who have failed in some way ("cutting off reflected failure"; Snyder, Lassegard, and Ford, 1986). Thus, people enhance their public image by emphasizing their association with successful others and distancing themselves from unsuccessful others.

Through various tactics, then, we can increase others' liking for us, and so their willingness to say "yes" to later requests. Of course, all of these procedures can be overdone (see Figure 7.11). If they are, the target persons may realize that we are simply trying to "butter them up," and the chances of later compliance may be reduced rather than increased. When ingratiation is used with skill, though, it can indeed serve as an effective entering wedge for gaining compliance from others.

Multiple Requests: Two Steps to Compliance

Often, when individuals seek compliance with their wishes, they employ a kind of two-step procedure designed to increase their chances of success. The rationale behind this multiple-request strategy is simple: an initial request can serve as a kind of setup for a second request— the one the influencer wanted all along. Several different techniques are used in this manner, but among the most common are the foot-in-the-door, the door-in-the-face (also known as the rejection-then-retreat tactic), and low balling.

The Foot-in-the-Door: Small Request First, Large Request Second. Door-to-door salespersons often start their pitch by asking potential customers to accept a free sample or even a brochure describing their products. Confidence artists frequently begin by asking potential "marks" to do something that seems totally safe and innocuous (e.g., help them find an address, hold a receipt or safe deposit key for them). Only after these small requests are granted do they

"Bernie's problem is his technique draws attention to itself."

Figure 7.11   Ingratiation and other tactics used to induce compliance can be overdone. If so, the target persons may realize they are being manipulated, and the chances of compliance may be reduced rather than increased. (Source: Drawing by Weber; © 1987 The New Yorker Magazine, Inc.)

Compliance tactics can be overdone and produce the reverse of what was intended.

move on to requests that can cost their victims their entire life savings. Friends, co-workers, and lovers, too, often start with small requests they know we won't refuse, and only gradually increase the scope of their demands. In all such instances, the strategy is the same: somehow induce another person to comply with a small initial request and thereby increase the chances that he or she will agree to a much larger one. Is this technique, called the **foot-in-the-door technique**, really successful? The findings of many different studies suggest that it is (Beaman et al., 1983).

In perhaps the most famous study concerned with the topic (Freedman and Fraser, 1966), a number of homemakers were phoned by a male experimenter who identified himself as a member of a consumers' group. During this initial contact, he asked subjects to answer a few simple questions about the kind of soap they used at home. Several days later, the same individual called again and made a larger request: could he send a crew of six persons to the subject's home to conduct a thorough inventory of all the products he or she had on hand. It was explained that this survey would take about two hours, and that the crew would require freedom to search in all closets, cabinets, and drawers. This was truly a huge request! In contrast, subjects in a one-contact control group were called only once, and were presented with the large, second request "cold." Results were dramatic: while only 22.2 percent of those in the one-contact condition agreed, 52.8 percent of those in the two-contact "foot in the door" group complied. While results have not been as dramatic in later studies (Beaman et al., 1983), existing evidence suggests that the foot-in-the-door tactic *is* effective in producing enhanced compliance in a wide range of settings and in response to a wide range of requests—everything from signing a petition (Baron, 1973) to contributing to a charity (Pliner et al., 1974; Schwarzwald, Bizman, and Raz, 1983) or placing a giant sign on one's front lawn (Freedman and Fraser, 1966). But how precisely does it operate?

First, it may be the case that once individuals agree to a small, initial request, they experience subtle shifts in self-perceptions. That is, they may come to see themselves as the kind of person who does that sort of thing—one who offers help to people who request it (Bem, 1972). Thus, when contacted again and presented with a much larger request, they agree in order to be consistent with their changed (and enhanced) self-image (Snyder and Cunningham, 1975). Indirect support for this view is provided by the fact that the technique is stronger under conditions in which external reasons for complying with the initial request are absent than under conditions in which such reasons are present (e.g., DeJong and Musilli, 1982). Presumably, if external reasons for complying exist, individuals will attribute their helpfulness to these factors and will fail to experience shifts in self-perception. When such external justifications are absent, in contrast, they may attribute their initial compliance to internal causes, and so experience shifts in self-perception. The importance of self-perceptions for the effectiveness of the foot-in-the-door tactic is also congruent with the fact that children are not responsive to this procedure until 7 years of age, which is the period when children first understand and feel the need to behave consistently with self-labels (Eisenberg et al., 1987).

Second, it is possible that after agreeing to a small request, individuals come to hold a more positive view of helping situations generally. They now perceive such situations as less threatening or potentially unpleasant than would otherwise be the case. As a result, they are more willing to comply with later—and larger—requests (Rittle, 1981).

At present, it is not possible to make a clear choice between these two interpretations. Indeed, such a choice may be unnecessary, for both shifts in self-perception and changes in overall reactions to helping situations may contribute to the success of the foot-in-the-door tactic.

The Door-in-the-Face: Large Request First, Small Request Second. A strategy that is the opposite of the foot-in-the-door can also be effective in inducing compliance. Here, persons seeking compliance start by asking for a very big favor—one the target is almost certain to refuse. Then, when refusal occurs, they shift to a smaller request—the favor they really wanted all along. This approach, known as the **door-in-the-face** or the **rejection-then-retreat technique**, has been studied in several experiments and also appears to be effective.

In a well-known study on this tactic, Cialdini and his colleagues (Cialdini et al., 1975) stopped college students on the street and presented a huge request: would they serve as unpaid counselors for juvenile delinquents two hours a week for the next two years? As you might guess, none agreed to this proposal. When the experimenters then scaled down their request to a much smaller one—would they take a group of delinquents on a two-hour trip to the zoo—fully 50 percent agreed. In contrast, less than 17 percent agreed to this smaller request when it was presented alone rather than after the giant request. It should be pointed out that effective use of this technique requires considerable skill. If the initial set of demands is so extreme as to seem unreasonable, then the process may "backfire" and produce *less* compliance than merely presenting the requests they really want "cold" (Schwarzwald, Raz, and Zvibel, 1979).

The use of this technique can also be observed in many real-life situations. For example, the door-in-the-face tactic is often used in politics, where groups or persons seeking funds for their own pet projects begin with requests for budgets far in excess of what they actually need. Then, when these are rejected by their opponents, they reduce their demands substantially but still obtain adequate funding. Again we can ask, "Why does this two-step approach to gaining compliance succeed?" Two explanations have been proposed.

The first relates to the notion of *reciprocal concessions.* When individuals who start with a very large request back down to smaller ones, this may be viewed by the persons they hope to influence as important concessions on their part. The targets of this strategy may then feel obligated to make a matching concession themselves. After all, the requester has retreated in order to meet them halfway: how can they now refuse to do likewise? The result: they may become more willing to comply with the second, smaller request.

Another possibility involves concern over *self-presentation*—presenting ourselves in a favorable light to others. If we refuse a large and unreasonable request from another person, this is justifiable, and our "image" probably won't suffer. If we then also refuse a much smaller request from the same source, though, we may appear unreasonable. Thus, we may often yield to the rejection-then-retreat tactic because we are afraid that failing to do so will cause us to look bad in the eyes of others (Pendleton and Batson, 1979).

Comparing the Foot-in-the-Door and the Door-in-the Face: The Role of Source Legitimacy. One interesting question is whether these techniques work for everyone. Thus far, most research studies have involved appeals or requests for good causes made by experimenters posing (or actually serving) as representatives of civic and environmental organizations. Recently, Patch (1986) tested the notion that the legitimacy of the source of the request is more important for the success of the door-in-the-face than the foot-in-the-door. The reasoning is that effectiveness of the door-in-the-face is derived from a sense of obligation to the source of the request. As a result, if the source is not highly legitimate, the door-in-the-face is less likely to be effective than if the source is high in legitimacy. In contrast, the foot-in-the-door is based on pressure for the target to be self-consistent; thus, the legitimacy of the source is less critical.

Patch (1986) made telephone calls employing either the foot-in-the-door (small request), door-in-the-face (large request), or no prior request. Then all subjects were asked to comply with a request of moderate size involving their answering questions about their television habits. Half of the subjects received the request from a high legitimacy source (Parents for Good Television Programming), while others received a request from a low legitimacy source (Multi-media Programming Associates, a consulting group for commercial television interests). As Figure 7.12 shows, the legitimacy of the requester had little effect on the success of the foot-in-the-door. In contrast, an influencer with low legitimacy had much less success with the door-in-the-face than one with high legitimacy. Thus, it appears that the legitimacy of the source of the request is more critical for the success of the door-in-the-face tactic. Apparently, this results from the fact that one feels greater obligation toward a legitimate source, and the door-in-the-face capitalizes on a feeling of obligation.

Low-Balling: Changing the Rules in Midstream—And Getting Away with It. If you ever shop for a new car and are unlucky enough to fall into the hands of a dishonest dealer, you may encounter the following chain of events. First, the salesperson with whom you are dealing will make an extremely attractive offer; he or she will offer to sell the car you want at a price much lower than that quoted by the competition. In fact, the deal may be so good that you agree to accept it at once. As soon as you do, however, some complication will arise. For example, she or he may return from the manager's office with the sad news that this person has refused to approve the deal as it stands. Then, in a key, final step, the salesperson will offer you another arrangement, less attractive than the one you eagerly accepted.

Common sense suggests that under these conditions, you should refuse to be "had" and should take your business elsewhere. But, surprisingly, this is not what usually happens. On the contrary, even though the deal now offered is less favorable than the initial one, many customers groan, sigh, and actually accept it. In short, they stick to their decision to make the purchase, even though the conditions that led them to make this choice no longer prevail. This technique of gaining compliance is known as **low-balling** or "throwing the low ball," and is all too common. Further, it can be used in gaining

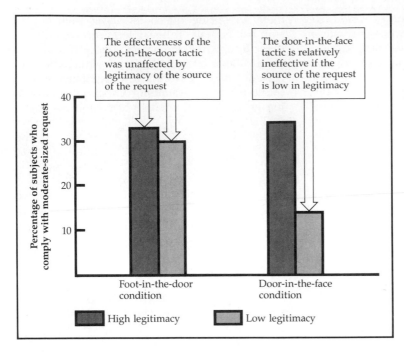

The effectiveness of the foot-in-the-door tactic was unaffected by legitimacy of the source of the request

The door-in-the-face tactic is relatively ineffective if the source of the request is low in legitimacy

Foot-in-the-door condition

Door-in-the-face condition

Percentage of subjects who comply with moderate-sized request

High legitimacy   Low legitimacy

Figure 7.12 *These results show that the effectiveness of the foot-in-the-door technique is not affected by the legitimacy of the source of the request. In contrast, the success of the door-in-the-face technique is affected by this factor—subjects showed a higher rate of compliance to a moderate-sized request from a source of high legitimacy than a request from a source of low legitimacy. The difference probably lies in the fact that the door-in-the-face tactic is derived from a sense of obligation to the requester. If the requester is not particularly legitimate, then the sense of obligation on the part of the subject should be less. (Source: Based on data reported by Patch, 1986.)*

Legitimacy of the source and the impact of multiple requests

compliance in many different settings. In essence, it operates as follows. First, a target person is induced to make a commitment to performing some behavior the would-be influencer wants him or her to perform. Then, the situation is changed so that some of the reasons behind the target person's decision (some of the inducements or rewards offered by the influencer) are removed. The low ball succeeds if the target person sticks to his or her initial commitment despite these changes.

Systematic evidence for the success of the low-ball technique has been obtained in several intriguing studies (Cialdini et al., 1978; Pallak, Cook, and Sullivan, 1980). In one (Burger and Petty, 1981), subjects were first told that they could earn extra credit by serving in an experiment. A few minutes later, they were informed either by the same person or by another individual that this credit could not be awarded. Yet, at this time, they were still asked to donate their time. Only when the request came from the same person did the low-ball effect occur. That is, only here did subjects agree to donate their time, even though they would earn no credit for it. When, instead, the second request was pre-

sented by a different person, subjects generally refused to help and showed the same low level of compliance as that demonstrated by subjects in a control group who had never been promised any extra credit.

These results suggest that the success of the low-ball tactic may stem in part from felt obligations toward the initial requester, just as the door-in-the-face also seems to result, at least in part because of a feeling of obligation to the requester. The low-ball effect may also occur because once people become committed to a particular course of action they are reluctant to change this commitment, even if the factors that led to its adoption are later altered. This may stem from the fact that once a commitment has been made, individuals quickly begin thinking up additional reasons that support it. (This is similar to the research on theory perseverance described in Chapter Three.) Whatever the exact processes that underlie the low-ball tactic, the practical implication is clear: always be wary of deals that sound too good to be true; they may be setups for what follows. (For a description of still another compliance tactic, see the "Focus on Research" insert.)

INCREASING COMPLIANCE WITH THE "THAT'S-NOT-ALL" TECHNIQUE

All of us have probably been the targets of sales campaigns and salespersons who use a technique that we can label the "that's-not-all" approach. The salesperson presents a product and price but does not allow the buyer to respond immediately. Instead, after a few seconds of mulling over the price, the potential customer is told "that's not all." There's an ad-

ditional small product that goes along with the larger item or that "just for you" or "today only" the price is lower than originally mentioned. Of course, the seller had planned to sell the items together or at the lower price all along. Is this technique more effective than simply presenting the eventual deal to the customer in the beginning?

To find out, Burger (1986) conducted a series of experiments on the effectiveness of the "that's-not-all" (TNA) technique. In one study a bake sale was set on a college campus. Cupcakes were displayed on the table, but no prices were listed. Potential customers who inquired about the price in the TNA condition were told the price by the seller, who waited a few sec-

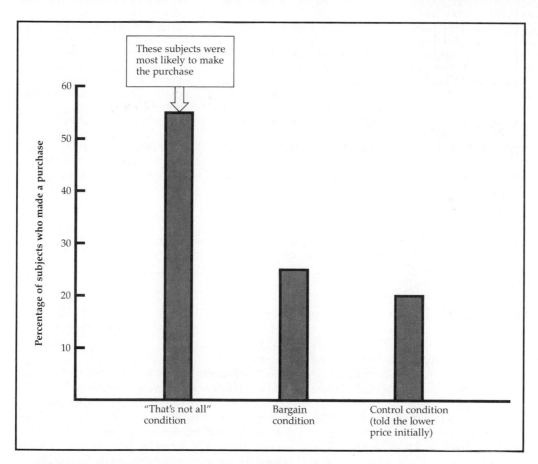

Figure 7.13   Subjects who were told the initial price of a product and then, before they could respond, were given a lower price (the "that's-not-all" tactic) were more likely to make the purchase than subjects who were told the lower price initially or subjects who were told the product was a "bargain." (Source: Based on data reported by Burger, 1986.)

The "that's-not-all" tactic

onds and then before the customer could respond, pulled out a bag of two cookies and announced the price also included the cookies. In contrast, control subjects were shown the cookies as soon as they asked about the price of the cupcakes. Results showed that the TNA technique is effective: 73 percent of the experimental subjects bought the package, while only 40 percent of the control subjects complied.

In another version of the TNA technique, subjects in the experimental condition were first told the price of the cupcake was $1.25. Then, before they could respond, the experimenter said he was planning to close down soon, so he was willing to sell the cupcake for only $1.00. Subjects in the control condition were told only that the price was $1.00. There was also a third "bargain" condition in which the experimenter, when asked the price, said, "These are only a dollar now. We were selling them for $1.25 earlier." This condition was added to see if it is merely the product being seen as a bargain that is responsible for the TNA's effectiveness. If this is the case then both the TNA and the "bargain" condition should be equally effective.

As shown in Figure 7.13, more than half of the subjects purchased a cupcake if they were first told the price was $1.25 and then, before having a chance to respond, were given a lower price. Control subjects who were given the lower price to begin with and subjects told that the cupcakes had originally been more expensive (and, therefore, are now a bargain) were less likely to purchase them. It appears that either adding something to the package or lowering the price is more effective than giving people the offer initially. Furthermore, the TNA technique does not work simply because something is perceived as a bargain: both the TNA subjects and the bargain subjects believed they were being offered a $1.25 product at $1.00, yet only the TNA technique increased compliance above the control condition.

Why, then, is this technique effective? One thing that may be operating is the **norm of reciproc-** ity" (Gouldner, 1960; Regan, 1971). This social rule states that we should treat others as they have treated us. In this case, since the seller has offered to come down in price or sweeten the deal with an additional product, the reciprocity norm suggests that the customer should feel an increased obligation to purchase the product and thereby reciprocate the seller's negotiating action. Consistent with this view, other experiments show that the TNA only works if the subject perceives the seller's negotiation as a personal gesture and not something he or she was forced to do by someone else.

The norm of reciprocity does not exhaust the possible explanations for the "that's-not-all" technique. Future research will, no doubt, focus on other reasons for its effectiveness. In any case, now that you know about this compliance technique, as well as the ones described earlier, we hope you are better "equipped" to resist techniques designed to trick you into saying "yes" when it would be more in your interest to say "no."

SUMMARY

Social influence involves efforts by one or more persons to alter the attitudes or behavior of one or more others. It takes many different forms, but among the most important are *obedience, conformity,* and *compliance.*

Obedience, the most direct form of social influence, occurs when one person orders one or more others to behave in some manner. Most individuals seem to have a strong tendency to obey the commands of those in authority, even when such persons actually have little power to enforce their directives. Fortunately, these tendencies toward obedience can be reduced in several ways—for example, reminding the persons involved that they will be held responsible for their own actions, or inducing them to question the expertise or the motives of authority figures.

Conformity occurs when individuals change their attitudes or behavior in order to be consistent with *social norms* or the expectations of others. Conformity rises with the number of persons exerting influence, but only up to a point. Conformity is reduced by the presence of *social support*—one or more others who share the target person's views or simply deviate from the majority. Contrary to early findings, recent studies suggest that there are no significant differences between males and females in the tendency to conform.

Compliance occurs when individuals alter their behavior in response to direct requests from others. Many techniques exist that are designed to increase compliance—the likelihood that others will say yes. These include *ingratiation* and several procedures based on *multiple requests* (e.g., the *foot-in-the-door,* the *door-in-the-face, low-balling,* and the *"that's-not-all"* techniques). In the foot-in-the door tactic, a person who agrees with a small initial request is more likely to subsequently agree to do something larger. The door-in-the-face is based on the strategy of beginning with a large request, and then, when it is refused, retreating to a smaller request. In low-balling, individuals are induced to agree to some request. And then the advantages of doing so are reduced. Despite these changes, many persons stick to their commitment and comply.

GLOSSARY

autokinetic phenomenon The apparent movement of a single light in a dark room.

compliance A form of social influence in which individuals change their behavior in response to direct requests from others.

conformity A type of social influence in which individuals change their attitudes or behavior in order to adhere to the expectations of others or norms of groups to which they belong.

door-in-the-face technique A procedure for gaining compliance based on the strategy of beginning with a small request and then, when this is refused, retreating to a smaller request (the one actually desired all along).

foot-in-the-door technique A procedure for gaining compliance based on the strategy of beginning with a small request and then, when it is granted, escalating to a larger one.

informational social influence Social influence based on our desire to be correct (i.e., to possess accurate perceptions of the social world). This often requires that we use others' actions and attitudes as guides for our own.

ingratiation A technique for gaining compliance based on the strategy of first inducing target persons to like us, and only then making various requests.

low-ball technique A form of social influence in which target persons are first convinced, through favorable conditions or other inducements, to perform some action desired by the would-be influencer. Then, these conditions are changed so as to be less beneficial. If the low-ball works, target persons will maintain their initial commitment, even in the face of these alterations.

minority influence Influence exerted by members of a minority over a majority.

multiple requests Techniques for gaining compliance based on the use of more than one request. The foot-in-the-door and the door-in-the-face provide examples of this basic strategy.

need for individuation Refers to the motivation to wish to feel unique or distinctive.

normative social influence Social influence based on our desire to be liked by other persons.

norm of reciprocity The social norm indicating that we should return favors and other benefits provided by other persons. Because of this norm, we often feel obligated to reciprocate favors or gifts we never requested, and did not want.

obedience A form of social influence in which one person orders one or more others to perform some action.

rejection-then-retreat technique See door-in-the-face technique.

social influence Effects on the part of one or more persons to alter the behavior or attitudes of one or more others.

social influence model on SIM model A general model of social influence designed to account for the impact of group size, number of targets, and several other factors upon the acceptance of influence in a wide range of settings.

FOR MORE INFORMATION

CIALDINI. R. B. (1988). *Influence: Science and practice* (2nd ed.). New York: Random House.

A witty and insightful account of the major techniques human beings use to influence the persons around them. The book draws both on the findings of careful research and on informal observations made by the author in a wide range of practical settings (e.g., sales, public relations, fund-raising agencies, and the like). Without a doubt, this is the most readable and informative account of current knowledge about influence now available.

FORSYTH, D. R. (1983). *An introduction to group dynamics*. Monterey, Calif.: Brooks/Cole.

A solid overview of the complex but fascinating processes that take place within groups. The sections on obedience, conformity, and other forms of social influence are clearly written and expand upon the coverage of these topics provided by the present chapter.

MILGRAM, S. (1974). *Obedience to authority*. New York: Harper & Row.

More than twelve years after it was written, this book is still the definitive work on obedience viewed as a social psychological process. The untimely demise of its author only adds to its value as a lasting contribution of our field to the comprehension of an important and all-too-common phenomenon.

MOSCOVICI, S. (1985). Social influence and conformity. In G. Lindzey and E. Aronson (Eds.), *Handbook of social psychology* (Vol. 2). New York: Random House.

This chapter gives special attention to the subject of social influence from the perspective of minorities.

Chapter Eight

Hurting and Helping: The Nature and Causes of Aggression and Prosocial Behavior

"Did you hear about Fredi?" Marsha Fitzgerald asks her husband Mark in an excited voice as she enters the front door.

"No, what?" Mark answers with a grin. "Come on, don't tease; let me have it."

"Well, it's nothing to laugh about, that's for sure. Last Tuesday Fredi broke a bottle over Dave's head. And it was a big one, too."

"What! No kidding! How did that happen?"

"The way I hear it, she came home in a real state. It had been one of those days—you know, nothing went right. Then, just a few blocks from home, she was almost run off the road by some stupid drunk. She says she was still shaking when she walked in the door."

"OK, OK, get to the point. Why did she haul off and belt him? You don't hear about that kind of thing every week."

"I'm coming to that. You know that things haven't been too good between them lately . . . Always fighting about something or other. Lately, it's been over Dave's brother. He's been lending him money without telling Fredi; that's why they're always in such a bind."

"She hit him because of that?"

"Well, not exactly. They were eating dinner, and you know how Dave gets. He started criticizing in that whining voice of his . . . One thing after another. 'Why didn't you do this; why did you do that.' All the time Fredi's getting angrier and angrier."

"Well, why the heck didn't she speak up? That's one of her problems; you never know when she's getting mad. She holds it all inside—and then blows up!"

"I guess that's what happened Tuesday; but she says that she did give Dave warning. He kept right on, though, oblivious as usual."

"That's some pair, all right. She hides her feelings and he couldn't tell if someone were about to explode."

"Right. Anyway, he let it slip about his brother, and she just saw red. Reached for the nearest thing she could get her hands on and let him have it."

"So it was a lot of things, really," Mark comments. "The situation kind of led up to it from the minute she walked in the door. Anyway, how's Dave doing?"

"Not so hot," Marsha replies. "He passed out, and I gather there was a lot of blood. He's in the hospital now, and still hasn't come out of it completely. Looks like he may have some permanent damage."

"Whew!" Mark utters with a whistle. "Talk about problems; as if there aren't enough bad things happening without people beating on each other, too." Then, reaching for his wife and encircling her in his arms, he adds: "I'm glad that we get along better . . . I'd rather kiss than fight anytime."

"Oh yeah?" Marsha answers, pushing him away. "Then why do you keep on throwing your clothes on the floor when you come in? I think you do it just to annoy me. I've told you once, I've told you a hundred times . . ."

Even brief inspection of any newspaper or magazine reveals the fact that human social behavior is extraordinarily varied. One page may feature a story of domestic violence, like the above example, and another page may report of harm or cruelty inflicted upon others. Yet one page may contain a report about someone who took considerable risks to help rescue a stranger who was in danger (see Figure 8.1). Social psychologists have focused a great deal of attention on both topics—the factors that influence whether we *hurt* others and the factors that influence whether we *help* others. In this chapter, we will summarize some of the key facts that have been uncovered about both subjects. The study of **aggression**—the intentional infliction of some type of harm upon others—will be discussed first. Then, in the second half of the chapter, we will discuss **prosocial behavior**—helping acts that have no obvious benefits for the person who carried them out and may involve risk or some degree of sacrifice.

AGGRESSION: Social Psychological Perspectives

We will begin by examining several different *theoretical perspectives* on aggression—contrasting views about the origins and nature of such

Figure 8.1 *Aggression and prosocial behavior: Two very important social phenomena*

Hurting and helping

behavior. Next, we will consider major *situational* causes of aggression—conditions in the social world around us that seem to stimulate or evoke such behavior. Finally, we will examine various techniques for the prevention and control of human aggression. A number of these exist and, fortunately, several appear to be effective when used with skill and care.

Theoretical Perspectives on Aggression: In Search of the Roots of Violence

What makes human beings turn, with brutality unmatched by even the fiercest of predators, against their fellow human beings? While many contrasting explanations for the paradox of human violence have been offered, most seem to fall into three basic categories. These suggest that aggression stems primarily from

(1) innate urges or tendencies, (2) externally elicited drives to harm or injure others, or (3) existing social conditions coupled with previous learning experience.

Aggression as Innate Behavior. The oldest and probably best known explanation for human aggression, **instinct theory**, suggests that human beings are somehow "programmed" for such behavior. The most famous early supporter of this view was Sigmund Freud, who held that aggression stems mainly from a powerful *death instinct* possessed by all human beings. According to Freud, this instinct is aimed at self-destruction but is soon redirected outward, toward others. Freud believed that the hostile impulses the death instinct generates increase over time and, if not released periodically, will soon reach high levels capable of producing dangerous acts of violence.

A related view of aggression has been proposed by Konrad Lorenz, a Nobel prize-winning scientist. According to Lorenz (1966; 1974), aggression springs mainly from an inherited *fighting instinct* that humans share with many other species. Presumably, this instinct developed during the course of evolution because it yielded many benefits. For example, fighting serves to disperse populations over a wide area, thus ensuring maximum use of available natural resources. And since it is often closely related to mating, fighting also helps strengthen the genetic makeup of a species by assuring that only the strongest and most vigorous individuals manage to reproduce.

The theories proposed by Freud, Lorenz, and many others differ in important ways. However, all are similar in one basic respect: they are pessimistic about the possibility of preventing or controlling human aggression. After all, if aggression stems from built-in urges or tendencies, it can probably never be eliminated. At best, it can be channeled or controlled, so as to inflict the least possible harm. Since it is part of our essential human nature, though, we can never escape it entirely.

Aggression as an Elicited Drive or Reaction to Aversive Events. The idea that aggression is a built-in part of human nature is very popular even today. Indeed, if you asked your friends to express their own views on this issue, many would probably indicate support for this position. In contrast, most social psychologists reject the instinct approach. The main reason behind this rejection can be simply stated: to a surprising degree, instinct theories of aggression are *circular* in nature. They begin by noting that aggression is a common form of human behavior. On the basis of this observation, they reason that such behavior must stem from universal, built-in urges or tendencies. Finally, they use the high incidence of overt aggression as support for the presence of these instincts or impulses. As you can see this is questionable logic! For this reason, and also because they object to the pessimism implied by instinct theories, many social psychologists have tended to favor an alternative view based on the suggestion that aggression stems mainly from an externally elicited *drive* to harm or injure others. This approach is reflected in several different **drive theories of aggression** (e.g., Berkowitz, 1978; Feshbach, 1984). Such theories suggest that various external conditions (e.g., frustration, loss of face) serve to arouse a strong motive to engage in harm-producing behaviors. Such an aggressive drive, in turn, then leads to the performance of overt assaults against others (see Figure 8.2). By far the most famous of these theories is the well-known **frustration-aggression hypothesis**. According to this view (which we will examine in detail later), frustration—the blocking of ongoing goal-directed behavior—leads to the arousal of a drive whose primary goal is that of harming some person or object (usually, but not always, the source of the frustration). This drive, in turn, leads to attacks against various targets, especially the source of the frustration.

A related theory—the **cognitive neoassociationist view** (Berkowitz, 1984)—suggests that exposure to aversive events (ones we prefer to

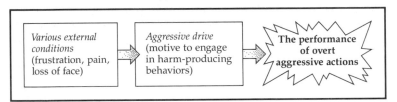

Figure 8.2 According to drive theories of aggression, various external conditions (frustration, physical pain, loss of face) elicit a drive to engage in harm-producing behaviors. Such *aggressive drive*, in turn, leads to the performance of overt acts against others.

Drive theories of aggression

avoid) generates unpleasant feelings. These unpleasant feelings activate tendencies toward both aggression and flight (efforts to escape the situation). Which of these actions occur depends in part on higher levels of thought. Thus, according to the cognitive neoassociationist perspective, frustration is not the only cause of aggression, since any event that generates unpleasant feelings can prompt aggressive behavior. Consistent with this approach, individuals exposed to painful cold are more likely to deliver punishment to others, even when the others had nothing to do with experiencing the cold (Berkowitz and Embree, 1987). Similarly, oppressively hot temperatures increase or "prime" (see Chapter Three) aggressive thoughts (Rule, Taylor, and Dobbs, 1987). Perhaps, then, it is not surprising that violent crimes are more prevalent during hotter times of the year and in hotter years (Anderson, 1987; Kenrick and McFarlane, 1986).

The cognitive neoassociationist model also proposes that if the individual realizes that aggressive behavior is inappropriate, he or she may actively restrain such tendencies. But we should point out that given the speed with which annoyed or irritated persons "lash out" against others, there may often not be enough time for such rational processes to come into operation.

In any case, because the frustration-aggression and the cognitive neoassociationist theories suggest that *external* conditions (that produce frustration or negative affect) rather than *innate* tendencies are crucial, these theories of aggression seem somewhat more optimistic about the possibility of preventing such behavior than do instinct theories. But since being frustrated or experiencing unpleasant feelings are all too common in everyday life, these theories, too, seem to leave us facing continuous—and largely unavoidable—sources of aggressive impulses.

Aggression as Learned Social Behavior. In recent years another theoretical perspective on human aggression—the **social learning view**—has gained increasing acceptance. Supporters of this view (Bandura, 1973; Baron, 1977; Berkowitz, 1984) emphasize the fact that aggression, dangerous and unsettling as it is, should be viewed primarily as a learned form of social behavior. In contrast to those who support the cen-

tral assumption of instinct theories, they argue that human beings are *not* born with a large array of aggressive responses at their disposal; rather, they must learn these in much the same way that they learn other complex forms of behavior. Going further, supporters of this modern view suggest that if we are fully to understand the nature of aggression, we must possess information about three basic issues: (1) the manner in which such behavior is acquired, (2) the rewards and punishments that affect its current performance, and (3) the social and environmental factors that influence its occurrence in a given context. In contrast to other theories we have considered, then, the social learning view does *not* attribute aggression to one or a small number of factors. Rather, it suggests that the roots of such behavior are highly varied in scope and involve a complex interplay among these factors (see Figure 8.3).

While the social learning view is more complex than some of the other perspectives on aggression we have considered, it offers important advantages. First, it is more sophisticated, and therefore almost certainly more accurate, than earlier approaches. Second, it is much more optimistic about the possibility of preventing or controlling human aggression. After all, if such behavior is primarily learned, it should be open to direct modification and change. Because of these advantages, the social learning view is now the most widely accepted theoretical perspective on aggression in the field.

Social and Situational Determinants of Aggression: External Causes of Violence

Contrary to popular belief, aggression does *not* usually take place in a social or situational vacuum. Most often, aggression springs from specific social or situational factors that pave the way for its occurrence and lead aggressors to choose specific victims. We will consider several of these factors here. Before doing so, however, we should consider another question about which you may already have begun to wonder: How can human aggression—especially physical aggression—be studied in a systematic manner without any danger to the persons involved?

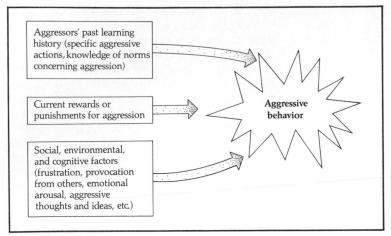

Figure 8.3 According to the *social learning view*, aggression stems from many different factors involving (1) the aggressor's past learning history; (2) current rewards or punishment for aggression; (3) a host of social, environmental, and cognitive factors that either elicit or inhibit its performance.

Aggression: The social learning view

Studying Human Aggression in the Laboratory. The most common technique is one devised by Arnold Buss (1961). In this procedure, two subjects (one is really an accomplice of the experimenter) arrive at the laboratory and are told that one is to act as teacher and the other as learner. In order to instruct the learner, the teacher is told he or she must administer nondangerous, but potentially painful, electric shocks to the learner whenever this person makes a mistake. The shocks are to be delivered via an apparatus with buttons indicating several levels of shock intensity (see Figure 8.4). This apparatus has come to be known in social psychology as the **aggression machine**. As you can probably guess, the real subject is always chosen to serve as the teacher, and the accomplice as the learner. The strength of the shocks that subjects choose to administer provides a measure of aggression. (The length of time the subjects depress the button—duration of their assault on the victim—also sometimes serves as a measure of aggression.) To convince subjects that the apparatus really works, mild sample shocks are administered to them from several of the buttons.

Of course, the subject is led to believe that the learner (accomplice) is receiving the shocks he or she is administering as the teacher. In actuality, the accomplice receives no shocks. Thus, it is possible to measure the willingness of one person to harm another in the absence of any real danger to participants. In some modifications of this procedure, the aggression machine supposedly delivers loud aversive noise rather than shock.

This basic procedure is used to study people's aggressive behavior as a function of various social and situational factors. For example, the subject might be angered by the accomplice in some way prior to the "learning task." Subsequently, the researcher could determine the degree to which the subject's anger results in aggressive behavior toward the accomplice.

Questions have been raised about the degree to which this procedure provides a valid measure of aggression. Though there is not complete agreement, evidence suggests it is valid, at least to a degree. For example, people with a prior history of violent behavior tend to inflict higher levels of shock or noise upon victims

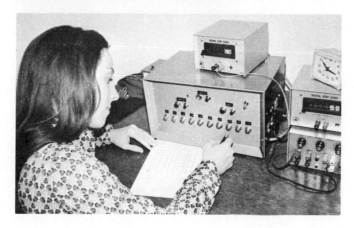

Figure 8.4 An *aggression machine* (top) similar to the one used by Buss. Subjects are informed that they can deliver electric shocks (or some other type of aversive stimuli) to another person by pushing the buttons on this equipment (bottom). Two measures of aggression are often obtained: the strength and the duration of the painful stimuli participants choose to deliver to their supposed victim. (Note: this person is an accomplice who never actually receives such stimuli.)

One technique for measuring physical aggression in the laboratory

than do people without such a history (e.g., Gully and Dengerink, 1983; Wolfe and Baron, 1971). Also, it is not *crucial* that laboratory situations closely resemble those outside the laboratory (Berkowitz and Donnerstein, 1982). Rather, what is crucial is that subjects believe that they can harm the supposed victim in some manner. Evidence shows that research participants employing the Buss procedure or similar methods generally accept this idea, so research using this method can be viewed as valid. Finally, findings obtained with the Buss procedure have been replicated with other, more realistic measures of aggression (e.g., verbal aggression, cutting in line in front of others, horn honking, ratings of overt aggressive actions). Thus, research on aggression does seem to employ a technique that permits us to measure hurting without actual harm to the participants.

Frustration: Thwarting as a Potential Cause of Aggression. Many people assume that the most important single cause of aggression is frustration. That is, the most potent means of in-

ducing humans to aggress is thwarting their goals—somehow preventing them from getting what they want. Acceptance of this view stems mainly from the well-known frustration-aggression hypothesis that we mentioned earlier. In its original form, this hypothesis made the following sweeping assertions: (1) frustration *always* leads to some form of aggression, and (2) aggression *always* stems from frustration (Dollard et al., 1939). Bold statements like these are always appealing; they are intellectually stimulating, if nothing else. But are they really accurate? The answer is almost certainly "no." Both portions of the frustration-aggression hypothesis seem to be far too sweeping in scope.

First, it is now clear that frustrated individuals do *not* always respond with aggressive thoughts, words, or deeds. Rather they show a variety of reactions, ranging from resignation and despair on the one hand, to attempts to overcome the source of their frustration on the other.

Second, it is apparent that all aggression does *not* result from frustration. People aggress for many different reasons and in response to many different factors. For example, boxers hit and sometimes injure their opponents because it is their role to do so, or because they wish to win some valued prize, not because they are frustrated. Similarly, people wishing to get ahead in their careers sometimes use complex political maneuvers to eliminate rivals (by derailing *their* careers), in the total absence of frustration from such persons. In these and many other cases, aggression stems from factors other than frustration.

In view of these considerations, most social psychologists believe that frustration is simply one of a host of different factors that can potentially lead to aggression (e.g., Berkowitz, 1978). Further, there is growing agreement that whether frustrations will, indeed, produce such effects depends largely on two conditions: its intensity and its perceived legitimacy. Only when frustration is strong, and only when it is viewed as arbitrary or illegitimate, does it tend to increase the likelihood of aggression. In contrast, when it is weak, or perceived as deserved and legitimate, it appears to have little impact on subsequent aggression (e.g., Kulik and Brown, 1979; Worchel, 1974).

Direct Provocation: When Aggression Breeds Aggression. While frustation must be quite intense before it can elicit overt aggression, another factor—*direct verbal or physical provocation*—seems capable of producing such effects

even when quite mild (see Figure 8.5). Informal observation suggests that individuals often react very strongly to mild taunts, glancing blows, or other actions by others that they perceive as some sort of attack. Moreover, when they do, they may begin a process of escalation in which stronger and stronger provocations are quickly exchanged, with dangerous consequences for both sides (Goldstein, Davis, and Herman, 1975).

Direct evidence for the strong impact of physical provocation on aggression has been obtained in many laboratory studies (e.g., Dengerink, Schnedler, and Covey, 1978; Ohbuchi and Ogura, 1984). In these experiments, individuals exposed to rising provocation from a stranger (usually in the form of ever-stronger electric shocks or verbal provocation) have been found to respond to their attacker in kind. As provocation rises in intensity, so does the retaliation. Thus, most people seem to follow a general rule of *reciprocity* where aggression is concerned. Instead of "turning the other cheek" in response to provocation from others, they attempt to balance the scales and to return treatment as harsh (if not slightly harsher) as they have received themselves (Geen, 1968).

Several factors play a key role in determining whether, and to what extent, individuals choose to respond in kind to attacks from others, or to overlook such treatment. Among the most important of these is the perceived intentionality of such provocation.

Figure 8.5 As this cartoon suggests, aggression breeds aggression. (Source: Reprinted with special permission of King Features Syndicate, Inc.)

People tend to act aggressively toward others who provoke them

PERCEIVED INTENTIONALITY AND REACTIONS TO PROVOCATION: ACCIDENT OR INTENTION Our response to apparent provocations from others is strongly mediated by our perceptions concerning the *intentionality* of these actions. If these appear to be intentional—purposely enacted—we respond with anger and efforts to return such treatment. If, instead, they seem to be unintentional—the result of accident or factors beyond others' control—we are much less likely to lose our tempers and behave aggressively. In short, our *attributions* concerning the causes behind provocative actions by others play a key role in determining just how we respond to such treatment.

Evidence for the importance of attributions in determining our response to provocation is provided by several experiments (e.g., Ferguson and Rule, 1983; Kramer and Stephens, 1983; Dodge, Murphy, and Buchsbaum, 1984). For example, in one intriguing study on this topic, Johnson and Rule (1986) exposed male subjects to strong provocation from an accomplice, and then measured both their physiological reac-

tions to such treatment and their later retaliation against this person. Half the subjects learned, prior to being provoked, that the accomplice was very upset over an unfairly low grade on a chemistry quiz; the remaining half received this information only after being angered. Results indicated that this information about *mitigating circumstances* had strong effects on subjects' reactions. Those who received it before they were provoked actually showed lower emotional upset (as measured by changes in heart rate) and lower retaliation against the accomplice (as indexed by the strength of bursts of noise they chose to deliver to him) than subjects who received such information only after being provoked (see Figure 8.6). Clearly, then, subjects' interpretations of the *causes* behind the accomplice's attacks played an important role in determining their reactions to such treatment.

These findings indicate that our reactions to provocation from others depend strongly on our understanding of the intentions behind their actions. Only when we view their annoying words or deeds as intentional do we respond in kind,

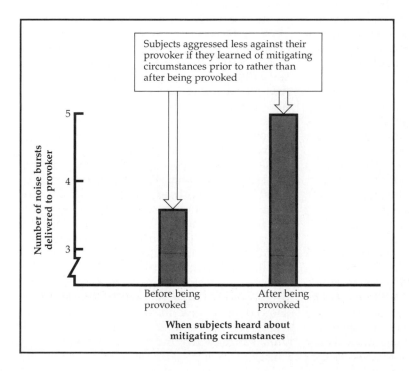

Figure 8.6 Subjects aggressed less against their provoker if they learned of mitigating circumstances for his behavior before they were provoked rather than after they were provoked. These subjects' interpretations of the causes behind the accomplice's attack played a significant role in determining their reactions. (Source: Based on data from Johnson and Rule, 1986.)

Effects of mitigating circumstances on responses to provocation according to the age-old principle of "an eye for an eye, and a tooth for a tooth." In fact, though, some persons are prone to attribute hostile intent to others when it is inappropriate—the so-called *hostile attributional bias*—and as a result rely on physical force in response to imagined or unintentional provocations on the part of others (Dodge and Coie, 1987). Fortunately, research shows that this bias is held by only a minority of persons (Dodge and Coie, 1987).

Exposure to Media Violence: The Effects of Witnessing Aggression. If there is one issue relating to human aggression that has gripped public attention in recent years, it is this: does continued exposure to filmed or televised violence cause an increase in similar behavior among its viewers? Obviously, this is an important question, with serious societal implications. It is not surprising, then, that it has been the subject of hundreds of research projects. The findings of these studies have been far from consistent; given the complexity of the issue they have addressed this is not surprising (Freedman, 1984; Friedrich-Cofer and Huston, 1986; Freedman, 1986). However, taken together, they point to one conclusion: exposure to media violence may, in fact, be one factor contributing to the high level of violence in American society and elsewhere. Several different lines of research, conducted in very different ways, are consistent with this interpretation.

One of the first studies to examine the effects of televised aggressive models on the behavior of children was conducted by Albert Bandura and his colleagues (Bandura, Ross, and Ross, 1961). They were interested in whether youngsters learn to imitate adults who act in an aggressive manner. Nursery school children were randomly assigned to two conditions. In the *aggressive model* condition, the children watched a short film in which an adult model aggressed against an inflated toy clown (e.g., she sat on the clown and punched it repeatedly in the nose). In the *nonaggressive model* condition, the children watched a film, but in this case the same model behaved in a quiet nonaggressive manner. Later, the children in both conditions were allowed to play freely in a room containing many toys,

including several used by the model. Careful observation of their behavior in this setting revealed that those who had seen the model behave in an aggressive manner were much more likely to attack the plastic toy (known as a Bobo doll) than those who had not witnessed such behavior (see Figure 8.7). These findings suggest that even very young children can acquire new ways of aggressing against others through exposure to filmed or televised violence.

Some critics have argued that attacking a plastic doll is not the same as aggressing against another human being (Tedeschi, Smith, and Brown, 1974). However, this criticism was countered by the results of subsequent laboratory studies in which subjects who viewed actual television programs or films were given the opportunity to attack (supposedly) a real victim rather than an inflated toy (Liebert and Baron, 1972). Once again, the results were the same: participants in such studies (both children and adults) who witnessed media violence later demonstrated higher levels of aggression than participants who were not exposed to such materials (Geen, 1978; Liebert and Sprafkin, 1988; Josephson, 1987).

In addition to the results of the Bandura and other short-term laboratory studies, there is evidence for the aggression-enhancing impact of media violence from a second group of studies using different methodology. In these *long-term field investigations,* different groups of subjects were exposed to contrasting amounts of media violence, and their overt levels of aggression in natural situations were then observed (e.g., Leyens et al., 1975; Parke et al., 1977). For example, in a study conducted by Leyens and his associates (Leyens et al., 1975), two groups of boys attending a private school in Belgium were exposed to contrasting sets of films. One group saw five violent movies, one each day, while the other group saw five nonviolent films presented in the same manner. When the boys' behavior was then observed as they went about their daily activities, an impact of media violence was obtained: those exposed to the violent movies showed an increase in several forms of aggression. That such results are not limited to children is suggested by the findings of several other

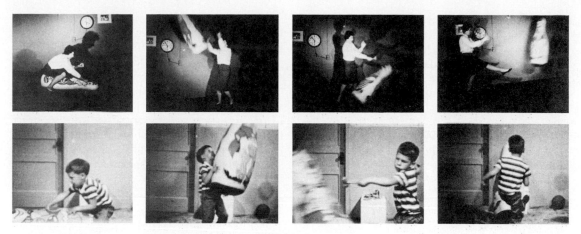

Figure 8.7 *Children who watched a film of an adult model act aggressively toward a plastic clown doll (shown in the upper panel) were more likely subsequently to do the same thing than were children who watched an adult model play quietly with the doll. These results and those of other studies demonstrate that adults and children can learn and perform aggressive behaviors as a result of watching filmed or televised aggressive models. (Source: A. Bandura, D. Ross, and S. A. Ross, "Imitation of Film-mediated Aggressive Models,"* Journal of Abnormal and Social Psychology, *1961,* 66, *3–11. Copyright 1961 by the American Psychological Association. Reprinted by permission of the author.)*

Aggressive models: What you see, you may do!

studies (e.g., Loye, Gorney, and Steele, 1977). In what is perhaps the most surprising of these studies, Phillips (1983) found that the number of homicides in the United States rose significantly several days after the television broadcast of championship heavyweight boxing matches. While it is difficult to interpet these results in a definitive manner, they do point to the possibility that exposure to highly publicized portrayals of aggression can have far-reaching social effects.

Finally, additional evidence for the impact of media violence is provided by several long-term correlational studies relating the amount of media violence watched by individuals as children to their rated level of aggression several years or even decades later (e.g., Eron, 1982; Huesmann, 1982; Eron, 1987). Information regarding the amount of violence watched is based on subjects' reports about the shows they watched plus

violence ratings of these programs. Information about their actual levels of aggression has been acquired from ratings of their behavior in elementary school by classmates and teachers. In addition, Eron (1987) has collected data about the incidence and seriousness of criminal acts committed by these subjects by age 30 (taken from state records). The results of these investigations indicate that the more media violence individuals watch as children, the higher their rated level of aggression later in life. Further, the strength of this relationship is cumulative; the more shows of this type the individuals watch over the years, the more likely they are to behave in an aggressive manner. Thus, the association between the amount of aggressive television viewing and aggression increases over the years. Particularly dramatic are recent data showing an association between the frequency of viewing television violence at age 8 and the seriousness of criminal acts by age 30 (see Figure 8.8). At this point, we should insert a word of caution: while some studies demonstrate the kind of increase just described, not all studies do (Feshbach and Singer, 1971). Clearly, then, such results should be viewed as suggestive rather than conclusive (Freedman, 1984; Friedrich-Cofer and Huston, 1986).

THE IMPACT OF MEDIA VIOLENCE: WHY DOES IT OCCUR?   *Why* precisely, do such media effects occur? How does exposure to aggressive actions

in films and television programs stimulate similar actions on the part of audience members? Four processes seem to be involved.

First, exposure to media violence seems to weaken the *inhibitions* of viewers against engaging in similar behavior. After watching many persons—including heroes and heroines—perform aggressive actions, some viewers seem to feel less restrained about performing such actions themselves. "After all," they seem to reason, "if *they* can do this, so can I."

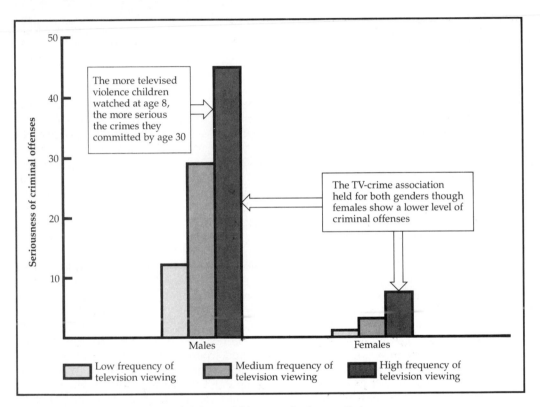

The more televised violence children watched at age 8, the more serious the crimes they committed by age 30

The TV-crime association held for both genders though females show a lower level of criminal offenses

Low frequency of television viewing

Medium frequency of television viewing

High frequency of television viewing

Figure 8.8 *The more televised violence children watched at age 8, the more serious the crimes they committed by age 30. Certainly, the specific programs the subjects watched as youngsters did not continue to influence their behavior for the next two decades. Rather, it is more likely that the attitudes and norms encouraged by continued exposure to those and similar programs are responsible for the harmful effects. You will also notice that the effects occurred among both males and females, although the latter show a lower level of criminal offenses. This is consistent with other data showing that females commit fewer and less serious criminal acts. (Source: Based on data from Eron, 1987.)*

Television violence and crime: Twenty-two years later

Second, exposure to media violence may arm viewers with new techniques for attacking and harming others not previously at their disposal. And once these are acquired, it is only one further step to putting them into use when appropriate conditions arise (e.g., in the face of strong provocation from others).

Third, watching others engage in aggressive actions can exert strong effects on viewers' cognitions (Berkowitz, 1984). For example, such materials can exert the type of *priming effect* discussed in Chapter Three; it can cause some audience members to have additional aggressive ideas and thoughts. Thus, following exposure to media violence, individuals may be more likely to perceive others in a negative or hostile light. Similarly, such persons may raise their estimates of the frequency of aggression in the social world around them, seeing it as more common and so more acceptable (e.g., Carver et al., 1983).

Finally, continued exposure to media violence may reduce emotional sensitivity to violence and its harmful consequences. In short, after watching countless murders, assaults, and fights, some viewers may become *desensitized* to such materials and fail to fully comprehend the damage such actions can produce (Geen, 1981; Thomas, 1982). As you can see, such shifts may make it easier for individuals to engage in aggression themselves.

Heightened Arousal and Aggression: The "Energization" of Violence. It is a well-established principle of psychology that heightened arousal intensifies ongoing behavior. When individuals are physiologically aroused, the vigor of their current responses—whatever these are—tends to increase. Do such effects occur with respect to aggression? Research evidence suggests that they do. Arousal stemming from such diverse sources as participation in competitive games (Christy, Gelfand, and Hartmann, 1971), vigorous exercise (Zillmann, 1983a), and even some types of music (Rogers and Ketcher, 1979) has been found to facilitate aggression in different experiments. One explanation for such effects is provided by the theory of **excitation transfer** (Zillmann, 1983a).

Briefly, this theory calls attention to the fact that physiological arousal dissipates slowly over time. As a result, some portion of such arousal may persist as individuals move from one situation to another. For example, a woman who is aroused by a near miss in traffic may continue to be slightly aroused even many minutes later, as she interacts with a friend or acquaintance. Such residual excitement can then serve to intensify later emotional experiences—even ones totally unrelated to the initial cause of arousal. Thus, if the woman's friend now makes a cutting remark, she may react more strongly to this provocation than would be the case if such residual, carry-over arousal were not present.

Excitation transfer theory calls attention to the fact that such effects are most likely to occur when the persons involved are unaware of their residual arousal, or when they attribute it to events occurring in the present situation. Thus, the character in our example would be more likely to react strongly to provocation from her friend if she were unaware of the arousal persisting from her near accident, and if she now attributed all of her emotional reactions to her friend's nasty remark. If instead, she realized that part of her arousal stemmed from the upsetting traffic mishap, she would probably be less likely to respond angrily to her friend's provocation.

The results of many studies offer support for predictions derived from excitation transfer theory (Zillmann, Katcher, and Milavsky, 1972; Zillman, 1983a,b; Ramirez, Bryant, and Zillmann, 1983). For example, Beezley and her colleagues (Beezley et al., 1987) found that while large doses of amphetamine (a stimulant) increase physiological arousal, they do not significantly increase aggression, presumably because individuals attribute their arousal to this drug rather than to provocation or other factors relating to aggression. Thus, as Zillmann contends, heightened arousal does not necessarily—or automatically—facilitate assaults against others. Rather, such effects occur only under specific, limited conditions.

Violent Pornography and Antisocial Behavior: A Social Dilemma. Recently, there has been much discussion among social scientists and policymakers about a social issue that concerns both the effects of arousal and media presentations of aggression: the effects of sexual materials (films and magazines) on aggression particularly directed at women. This concern stems partly from an apparent increase in a particular kind of sexual material—**violent pornography,** or sexually explicit materials, including scenes of rape, sadomasochism, and related acts of violence (much of it directed against women). This kind of material was given special attention by a commission formed by Attorney General Edwin Meese in 1985 and another panel convened by Surgeon General Everett Koop in 1986. Several different kinds of evidence point to potentially harmful effects of violent pornography. Such materials can apparently (1) increase the willingness of males to aggress against females (Malamuth and Briere, 1986); (2) increase the acceptance of false beliefs about rape (e.g., the myth that many women really want to be ravaged; Malamuth, 1984); (3) stimulate aggressive sexual fantasies (Malamuth, 1981); and generate high levels of sexual arousal, at least among individuals who find the use of force in sexual relations to be arousing (Malamuth, Check, and Briere, 1986).

Examination of such evidence partly inspired the Meese Commission to call for more strict enforcement of obscenity laws and to suggest additional measures to ban or restrict obscene materials. But some social psychologists take issue with parts of the commission's conclusions. Though the Meese Commission recognized the negative effects of violent pornography, it also considered other kinds of sexually explicit materials (display of nudity, nonaggressive sexual acts) as dangerous. Some social psychologists such as Linz, Donnerstein, and Penrod (1987) think the commission may have "missed the boat" in this regard. In brief, these critics argue that the real concern should be with media materials that are *violent,* because it is violent images rather than sexual ones that are most responsible for people's attitudes about women and rape.

This point is illustrated by the results of an experiment by Donnerstein, Berkowitz, and Linz (1987). In this study, male subjects were angered by a female accomplice and were then shown (1) an aggressive, pornographic film, (2) an X-rated film with explicit sex but no aggression or sexual coercion, or (3) a film containing scenes of ag-

gression against women but without sexual content. After viewing the films, the men were given the opportunity to aggress against a female accomplice. As shown in Figure 8.9, men who viewed the violent pornography showed the highest aggression. Men who watched the sexually explicit film that contained no violence produced the least aggression. The aggression-only film, which was devoid of explicit sex, produced an intermediate amount of aggression. These results, which replicate earlier findings (Baron and Bell, 1977; Baron, 1979; Malamuth and Check, 1981), suggest that violent pornography does indeed have strong negative effects. But perhaps the most important fact is that non-aggressive sexual materials produce *less* subsequent aggression than nonsexual aggressive materials. Thus, it appears to be the violent rather than the sexual images that present a greater risk of harm.

These findings take on importance in light of other research showing that R-rated films tend to portray more graphic aggression than X-rated sexual features (Palys, 1986). Since R-rated "slasher" films are not considered obscene and are readily available, they may actually pose a greater potential threat to our society than violent pornography, which by its nature is seen by a smaller audience (Smeaton and Byrne, 1987). We are, by the way, not suggesting that any materials be banned. Efforts to regulate purely violent materials or even violent pornography could be used as an "entering wedge" for suppressing other messages falling within everyone's First Amendment rights of free expression. Whether there is sufficient evidence to call for control of such materials remains largely a matter of personal judgment. As Linz et al. (1987) argue:

> Rather than call for stricter laws, we call for a more informed public. Based on the historical record . . . , we doubt that either pornography or violence is going to disappear from the mass media. Our own inclination has been to explore the possibility of developing educational programs that enable viewers to make wiser choices about the media to which they expose themselves. [p. 952]

(Refer to the "On the Applied Side" insert on page 196 for a discussion of another pressing issue regarding violence.)

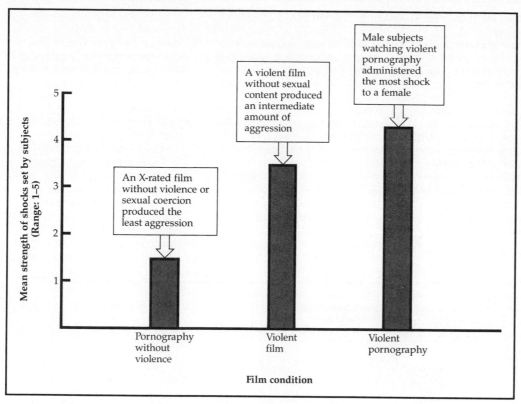

Figure 8.9 Male subjects provoked by a female accomplice administered high levels of shock when they had previously watched an aggressive pornography film. In contrast, subjects exposed to an X-rated film without aggressive or sexual coercion produced the least aggression. A violent film without explicit sexual content generated an intermediate effect on subsequent aggression. Taken along with other considerations, these results have two implications: (1) by combining explicit sexual and violent images, violent pornography may predispose people to high levels of aggression; (2) purely violent, rather than purely sexual content, may pose a greater risk for society in general because R-rated violence without sex is much more available to the general public than sexually explicit materials. (Source: Based on data from Donnerstein, Berkowitz, and Linz, 1987.)

Effects of violent and nonviolent pornography on aggression

The Prevention and Control of Human Aggression

Can aggression be prevented? Or are we doomed to repeat an endless cycle of violence and cruelty until, perhaps, it brings about our own demise as a species? While some are pessimistic on this score, we believe that effective, workable techniques for reducing human ag-

gression already exist and can be put to practical use (Baron, 1983). We will summarize several of these techniques.

Punishment: An Effective Deterrent to Aggression? Throughout history, most societies have used **punishment** as a primary means of deterring human violence. Thus, they have established harsh punishments for such crimes as

ON THE APPLIED SIDE

AGGRESSION IN CLOSE RELATIONSHIPS: THE INTIMATE ENEMY

Given the love and affection existing between the members of most families, common sense suggests that violence should be rare among such persons. However, a large-scale survey conducted by Straus, Gelles, and Steinmetz (1980) suggests that, in this case, common sense is wrong—dangerously wrong. After studying over two thousand families chosen to be representative of the total population of the United States, these investigators reached the following sad conclusion: **family violence** is quite common. A few statistics tell the story.

First, consider aggression between husbands and wives. Asked if they had directed any of eight violent acts toward their spouse during the past year, fully 16 percent of the participants in the survey answered "yes." Further, this number rose to fully 28 percent when the entire marriage (not just the preceding year) was considered. As you can see from Figure 8.10, the acts in question were not trivial ones; sizable proportions of married couples reported having slapped, kicked, or thrown something at one another. Interestingly, there appeared to be little differ-

ence between men and women: both sexes reported carrying out assaults against their spouse with approximately equal frequency (Mason and Blankenship, 1987). As you might guess, though, they reported using certain violent acts with contrasting frequency (e.g., wives reported being more likely to throw things, or to hit their spouse with various objects; husbands reported being more likely to push or slap their partner). These data are not isolated. For example, Briere (1987) found that nearly 80 percent of male college students said there was at least

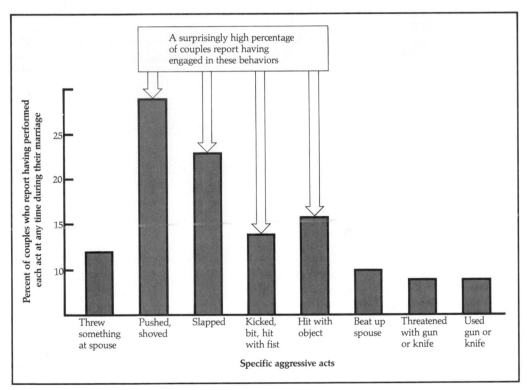

Figure 8.10 Many married couples report having engaged in acts of violence against their spouse at some point during their marriage. (Source: Based on data from Straus, Gelles, and Steinmetz, 1980.)

Husband-wife violence: More common than you might expect

some likelihood that they would hit their wife in a variety of situations. Responses varied somewhat with the hypothetical situation. For example, the male subjects thought they were more likely to resort to battering if they learned their wife had an extramarital affair than if she made fun of him at a party. Nonetheless, almost 40 percent thought there was some likelihood they would use force, even in the latter situation. Together, these data lend support to the view that for many persons, a marriage license is perceived as a "hitting license."

Perhaps even more disturbing, though, is the fact that parents often turn their rage upon their children. Data gathered by Straus, Gelles, and Steinmetz (1980) indicate almost three-quarters of parents report having used some form of physical aggression on their offspring at some point during their childhood. And again, these assaults are not uniformly mild in nature. Seventy-one percent mention using slaps or spankings, while 20 percent admit to striking their children with an object. It is estimated that approximately 2.3 million youngsters have been beaten by their parents at one time or another, and that perhaps one million have been threatened with a knife or gun! The highly publicized murder of an infant child by her father (*Newsweek,* 1987) has recently focused national attention on such child abuse.

In sum, existing evidence provides another and more chilling meaning to the phrase, "You always hurt the one you love." But why is violence so common in families? Many different factors have been suggested. Existing evidence indicates that persons who witnessed physical aggression between their parents are more likely to become violent husbands or wives than ones never exposed to such assaults. Individuals who were physically abused as children are more likely to abuse their own youngsters than ones not disciplined in this manner (Straus, Gelles, and Steinmetz, 1980). Second, families experiencing high levels of stress, such as economic problems or the death of a close friend or relative, are more likely to erupt in violent behavior than families fortunate enough to avoid such conditions (Mason and Blankenship, 1987). Third, families in which power is shared between husbands and wives, and in which decisions are reached democratically (through discussion among members) are much *less* likely to experience serious forms of violence than ones in which most power is concentrated in the hands of either the husband or wife, and in which this power-holder makes most of the decisions. Apparently, sharing and participation promote the resolution of the conflicts that are unavoidable when people live together, and so serve as buffers against the development of violent modes of behavior.

We see that violence in close relationships stems from a host of different factors. Fortunately, many—if not all—of these seem open to at least a degree of modification. Thus, the repetitive cycle of such aggression *can* be broken. However, this can only be accomplished through active, concrete steps. Simply assuming that people who love one another will rarely become involved in violent encounters is a serious error, and one that can place large numbers of persons at unnecessary risk.

murder, rape, and assault. Are such tactics actually effective? In one sense, of course, they are. If persons convicted of violent crimes are imprisoned or executed, they will obviously be unable to repeat these actions in the future. But what about the issue of *deterrence:* will punishment prevent such persons from repeating their aggressive actions, and will it discourage others from engaging in the same forms of behavior? Here, the pendulum of scientific opinion has swung back and forth across the decades. At present, though, there seem to be firm grounds for concluding that if used in an appropriate manner, punishment *can* be effective as a deterrent to future violence.

First, growing evidence suggests that punishment can exert a powerful and lasting effect upon behavior if it is administered under certain conditions (Bower and Hilgard, 1981). These include (1) *immediate delivery*—punishment must follow objectionable behavior as soon as possible; (2) *severity*—it must be of sufficient magnitude to be aversive to the recipient; and (3) *high probability* —it must follow undesirable behavior on almost every occasion when it occurs. Second, it is a well-established fact that individuals are often strongly affected by observing the outcomes of others. If they witness other persons being rewarded for some activity, their tendency to engage in it themselves is increased.

In contrast, if they observe others being punished for some behavior, they may refrain from similar actions (e.g., Bandura, 1977). Thus, there is a scientific basis for asserting that if potential aggressors witness the punishments received by former perpetrators, they may be reluctant to engage in similar actions themselves.

Unfortunately, of course, the conditions just described rarely prevail when punishment is used to deter human aggression. In many societies, the delivery of punishment for aggressive acts does *not* take place in accordance with the three principles listed above. The interval between the performance of a violent crime and punishment for it is often very long. The magnitude of punishment delivered varies greatly, being harsh in some localities and lenient in others. And the probability of being apprehended and punished for a given act of violence is very slight indeed.

In view of these facts, it is hardly surprising that punishment has been viewed, by many, as quite ineffective in deterring violent crime. Similarly, most persons have little opportunity to witness the punishments administered to those convicted of violent crimes. Thus, there is little chance for such treatment to influence the future behavior of potential aggressors. In sum, the fact that punishment does not currently seem to be effective in deterring human violence by no means implies that punishment itself is ineffective. Rather, it appears that this procedure is simply being used in ways that virtually guarantee its failure. Thus, the research of social psychologists helps to provide systematic information about how and under what conditions punishment can serve as a deterrent to aggression. Of course, whether such conditions can be and whether they should be changed (given different groups' attitudes about capital punishment, for example) are issues to be resolved by all of us in our role as citizens.

Catharsis: Does Getting It Out of Your System Really Help? Imagine that one day your boss criticizes you harshly for something that was not your fault. After she leaves, you are so angry that you slam your fist down on your desk over and over again. (Or you fantasize or dream about getting even, as in the cartoon in Figure 8.11.) Will this behavior make you feel better? And will it reduce your desire to "get even" with your boss in some manner? According to the **catharsis hypothesis**, it might. This view suggests that when angry individuals "blow off steam" through vigorous but nonharmful actions, they will experience (1) reductions in their level of arousal and (2) lowered tendencies to engage in overt actions of aggression. Both of these suggestions have received widespread acceptance for many years. Surprisingly, though, neither is strongly supported by existing research evidence (Feshbach, 1984).

First, with respect to the view that the emotional tension stemming from frustration or provocation can be reduced through participation in nonaggressive activities, results have been mixed. Performing physically exhausting activities does seem to reduce such arousal in some cases (Zillmann, 1979). However, such effects are temporary, and the best means of attaining them appears to be that of attacking the source of one's anger (Hokanson, Burgess, and Cohen, 1963). Obviously, this is not an effective tactic for reducing harmful aggression!

Turning to the suggestion that the performance of "safe" aggressive actions reduces the likelihood of more harmful forms of aggression, the picture becomes even more discouraging. Research on this topic indicates that overt aggression is *not* reduced by (1) watching scenes of filmed or televised violence (Geen, 1978), (2) attacking inanimate objects (Mallick and McCandless, 1966), or (3) aggressing verbally against others. Indeed, there is some evidence that aggression may actually be increased by each of these conditions.

Contrary to popular belief, then, catharsis does not appear to be a general or highly effective means for reducing overt aggression. While participating in exhausting, nonaggressive activities may produce temporary reductions in emotional arousal, and so in the tendency to aggress, such arousal may quickly be regenerated when individuals encounter or simply think about the persons who previously angered them. Thus, the potential benefits of catharsis have probably been overemphasized in the past.

Figure 8.11 This cartoon suggests that when angry, people can "blow off steam" through vigorous, nonharmful actions. However, research evidence does not support the value of catharsis in reducing overt aggression. (Source: Reprinted with special permission of King Features Syndicate, 1987.)

Catharsis: Ineffective in reducing harmful aggression

Other Techniques for Reducing Aggression: Nonaggressive Models and Incompatible Responses. While punishment and catharsis have probably received the most attention as potential tactics for controlling human aggression, additional procedures have been suggested—and carefully investigated—in recent years (Baron, 1983). One such technique involves *exposure to nonaggressive models.* If exposure to aggressive actions by others in films or in TV can increase aggression in viewers, it seems only reasonable to expect that parallel—but opposite—effects may result from exposure to persons who demonstrate or urge restraint in the face of provocation—*nonaggressive models.* That this is so is suggested by the findings of several experiments (e.g., Baron, 1972; Donnerstein and Donnerstein, 1976). In these studies, persons who were

strongly provoked but exposed to the actions of nonaggressive models later demonstrated lower levels of aggression than persons not exposed to such models. Such findings suggest that it may be useful to plant nonaggressive models in tense and threatening situations; their presence may well serve to tip the balance away from violence.

Another technique for reducing aggression rests upon the following basic principle: it is impossible to engage in two **incompatible responses** or experience two incompatible emotional states at the same time. Applying this idea to aggression, it seems possible that such behavior can be reduced through the induction, among potential aggressors, of feelings or responses incompatible with aggression or the emotion of anger. That this is indeed the case is indicated by a growing body of research evidence. When angry individuals are induced to experience emotional states incompatible with anger or overt aggression, such as *empathy, humor, or mild sexual arousal,* they do show reduced levels of aggression (Baron, 1983; Baron, 1984; Ramirez, Bryant, and Zillmann, 1983). This finding suggests that getting angry individuals "off the aggressive track," so to speak, may often be an effective means for preventing overt violence. Now that we have discussed what social psychologists have learned about aggression, we turn to the social psychology study of an equally intriguing and important phenomenon—altruistic or prosocial behavior. We ask such questions as why and when do some people help others for no obvious gain?

THE DYNAMICS OF PROSOCIAL BEHAVIOR

Suppose you are standing in a checkout counter at a supermarket and you observe a woman reach into a display rack, grab some expensive item, and quickly put it into her pocket (see Figure 8.12). Do you behave in the "right" way and report the theft, knowing that such action will require an expenditure of energy and the risk of retaliation? This would be an instance of **prosocial behavior**. Such behaviors, as mentioned earlier, have no obvious benefits (such as material reward or social approval) for the person who carries them out and may involve some degree of sacrifice. As will be discussed later, prosocial acts may have nonobvious benefits for the person performing them—for example, feeling good about oneself. Generally, those in a given culture are well aware of the "right" thing to do, though what is actually done may not conform to this ethical standard. In the sections below, we will first examine what happens when an individual is suddenly confronted with the possibility of *helping a stranger in distress.* Then we will turn to the kind of problem faced by someone in the checkout line who observed a crime being committed. The decision to be made is whether to take steps that involve *deterring a wrongdoer.* In addition, we will discuss the way in which particular *motivations* play a role in altruistic behavior.

Figure 8.12 The man in the photograph has observed someone shoplifting. Does he report the theft, which will require effort and the risk of retaliation? Or does he decide *not* to do anything about what he just saw? Social psychologists have been concerned with factors that determine whether people perform such prosocial acts as deterring a wrongdoer or helping a stranger in distress.

Would you do the "right" thing in this situation?

Facing an Emergency: To Help or Not to Help a Stranger in Distress

The following letter is based on an actual one written to a student newspaper describing an incident that occurred on a college campus:

> One Saturday night, as my friends and I were leaving the Student Union, we came across a student lying on a bench. At first glance, it seemed as if he were unconscious, but when we began to shake him and talk to him, he responded incoherently. It was cold, and he was not wearing a jacket. He was unable to move himself or open his eyes. We quickly called an ambulance, and he was taken to the medical center for emergency treatment.

> The reason we are writing is to point out that we observed several people passing by the immobile student, not bothering to see if he was hurt or in need of assistance—some drunken student. The problem is that he was alone and obviously in need of help. No one stopped. He could have been seriously ill, but it did not seem to matter to the Saturday night crowd.

> Those apathetic students who did not think twice about helping the man should be ashamed. Their behavior reinforced my beliefs about the severe lack of compassion and concern on this campus.

You have probably read of similar incidents in which bystanders failed to come to the aid of someone in need. In contrast, there are also quite different accounts of bystanders not only providing help to strangers in distress, but even risking their lives to do so. It is tempting to explain such events in terms of compassion versus indifference, but social psychological research indicates that quite different variables are of primary importance. Perhaps the most influential and most thoroughly studied factor that affects prosocial responding is whether the potential helper is alone or in the company of others. The fact that a lone bystander is more likely to help (and provide help more quickly) than a bystander who is part of a group is known as the **bystander effect**.

The Bystander Effect: The Greater the Number of Potential Helpers the Less Help. Actual incidents in which groups of people stood idly by, failing to help a stranger in distress, led Darley and Latané (1968) to hypothesize that a helping behavior becomes less likely as group size increases. This proposal was first tested in an experiment in which each subject was led to believe there was only one other person carrying on a discussion through an intercom system, or two other subjects, or five others. Actually, there was only the real subject and the appropriate number of voices on tape recordings. After the discussion began, the stranger on one of the recordings gasped and seemed to be undergoing a seizure. How did the subjects respond? As predicted, the more fellow bystanders who appeared to be present, the less likely the subject was to try to provide help. Even when help *was* offered, the presence of others led to a delay. Those who were alone responded in less than a minute. When there were supposedly five bystanders, the subjects hesitated for three minutes before responding. This same general inhibiting effect of fellow bystanders has since been found repeatedly in laboratory experiments and in field settings (Latané and Darley, 1970). It should be noted that the bystander effect occurs in situations in which there is a degree of ambiguity as to what is going on and what should be done. In the cognitive model to be described next, you can see why ambiguity is important. If the problem and solution were very clear, the presence of bystanders would be irrelevant.

The presence of others clearly interferes with prosocial behavior, but *why* does this occur? Such situations can be conceptualized as confronting individuals with a series of decision steps, at each of which he or she must make choices that lead either to no help or to the next step in the series (as shown in Figure 8.13). At each stage of the process, specific variables operate to facilitate or to interfere with prosocial behavior. Two such variables have been studied extensively: diffused responsibility and fear of ridicule.

WHOSE "JOB" IS IT? ASSUMING RESPONSIBILITY   At least one person has to assume responsibility in order for helping behavior to occur. When a number of bystanders are present, each is potentially able to help. As a result, there is a **diffusion of responsibility**. When there is a recognized leader in the group to organize what is

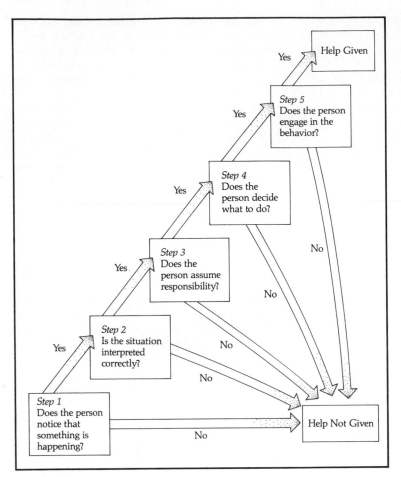

Figure 8.13 In the cognitive model of prosocial behavior formulated by Latané and Darley, the individual who is confronted by any emergency situation must go through a series of decision-making steps. At each point in the series, one decision leads to nonaltruistic behavior; the opposite decision takes the person one step closer to a helpful act. The person in need receives aid only if there is a "yes" decision at each of the five steps. (Source: Adapted from Byrne and Kelley, 1981.)

A cognitive model of prosocial behavior

to be done, a group can easily be galvanized into action (Firestone, Lichtman, and Colamosca, 1975). Even without a leader, the actions of just one helpful individual tend to serve as a model for other bystanders, who follow his or her example (Morgan, 1978).

One of the reasons people may fail to help a stranger is that they simply do not know what to do or how to do it. That is one reason that the presence of a leader or other model is of crucial importance. It would also be logical to expect that when an individual has learned how to handle a particular problem, this new-found competence should result in an increase in prosocial responding. In a study of reactions to a stranger who seemed to be bleeding badly, indi-

viduals who had Red Cross first-aid and emergency training were more likely to provide efficient help than those who were untrained, as shown in Figure 8.14 (Shotland and Heinold, 1985). Thus, the competence provided by the training made it possible for the subjects to assume responsibility.

AVOIDING POTENTIAL RIDICULE   Groups also inhibit prosocial acts because individuals are held back by their **fear of social blunders**. To respond to an emergency, a person must stop whatever he or she is doing in order to engage in some unusual, unexpected, out-of-the-ordinary behavior. Lone bystanders do just that, and without much hesitation. When several bystanders are present, the tendency is to wait for more information rather than to just make a mistake and appear foolish. What if you misunderstand the situation? What if it was all a joke? Generally, people decide that it is better to "keep their cool" in order to avoid the possibility of being laughed at. Such social caution results in a lower probability of help being provided and delays in helping.

In part, bystanders who are strangers to one another inhibit helpfulness because each individual hesitates to communicate with the others about the nature of the problem and what should be done. When bystanders are acquainted, there is much less inhibition of prosocial behavior than in a group of strangers (Latané and Rodin, 1969; Rutkowski, Gruder, and Romer, 1983). Even among strangers, there is less inhibition if there is an opportunity to see one another in the future and to be able to explain potentially foolish actions (Gottlieb and Carver, 1980). It can be concluded that the bystander effect is strongest when those involved are anonymous strangers who never expect to meet again.

Calculating Gains and Losses: The Rewards and Punishments of Helping. Though an individual's prosocial behavior may have no obvious benefits for him or her, many theorists assume that altruistic behavior occurs because it is,

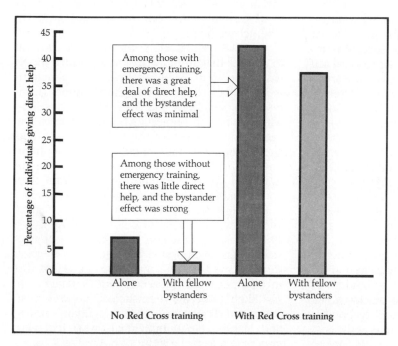

Figure 8.14 *The assumption of responsibility for helping in an emergency is much more probable if an individual has the expertise to help. When students were confronted with an "accident" that appeared to involve arterial bleeding, direct help was provided more often by those who had taken a Red Cross course dealing with first-aid and emergency care than by those who had not taken the course. Individuals who knew what to do (apply pressure to stop bleeding) were very likely to provide help, regardless of the presence or absence of fellow bystanders. (Source: Based on data from Shotland and Heinold, 1985.)*

Training in emergency behavior leads to the assumption of responsibility

in fact, rewarding. Generally, prosocial acts make you feel good about yourself. Interestingly enough, the more unpleasant or anxiety-provoking the prosocial act, the more rewarding it is to do, because a high level of drive is reduced by the behavior (Piliavin, Callero, and Evans, 1982). Why should helping others be a positive experience? One explanation is that altruism is a built-in response tendency that has survival value for the species (Cunningham, 1981). Cooperative behavior among related members of a species increases the odds of survival for the individual and for others who share common genes (Axelrod and Hamilton, 1981). Such reasoning leads to the conclusion that altruism is an integral part of human nature (Hoffman, 1981).

Even without a biological basis, it can be argued that prosocial behavior often leads to rewards and hence can be learned as easily as any other behavior. In some instances, prosocial acts result in punishment, so individuals can learn to *avoid* helping others (see Figure 8.15). Research to test this **reinforcement theory of prosocial behavior** has shown that altruistic acts are strongly affected by whether previous acts of helping were rewarded or punished (McGovern, Ditzian, and Taylor, 1975; Moss and Page, 1972).

The functions of rewards become more complex when we consider them in the context of thoughts the bystander may have. Human beings respond not only to simple external pleasures and pains but also to a set of beliefs, values, and expectancies about the consequences of behavior (Darley and Batson, 1973). Piliavin and her colleagues (1981) suggest that the bystander who encounters an emergency must quickly weigh the positive and negative aspects of responding by using a kind of **bystander calculus**. If the costs (punishments) of providing help are greater than the benefits (rewards) of such behaviors, the bystander is likely to pass the responsibility on to others, escape from the unpleasant situation, or misperceive what is going on (Kerber, 1984). In one test of this theoretical model, Batson and associates (1978) manipulated the costs of helping. A subject walking between buildings to an experiment was either hurrying to meet a deadline or had plenty of time; in ad-

dition, the subject had been told that participation in the experiment either was vital or was not very important. On the way, each individual passed a stranger slumped down in a doorway. The higher the costs for stopping to help, the less likely an individual was to do so. Thus, the least helpful passersby were those with a deadline to meet who believed that their participation in the meeting was essential.

Emotions, Attributions, and Altruism. Not surprisingly, a person's prior emotional state influences whether he or she will behave altruistically. In the next sections, we discuss the effects of positive and negative mood on helping. We also consider the way in which the attributions we make about *why* a person is in need can influence our mood, and, in turn, whether we help.

POSITIVE EMOTIONAL STATE   It seems logical to assume that an individual in a positive mood would be more likely to behave in a helpful manner than one in a negative mood (Cunningham, Steinberg, and Grev, 1980). Consistent with this notion, subjects who are made to feel positive in a variety of ways (for example, succeeding at a task, finding money in a telephone coin return slot, or thinking of happy events in the past) are subsequently more helpful than control subjects not given a pleasant experience (Isen, Horn, and Rosenhan, 1973; Isen, Clarke, and Schwartz, 1976; O'Malley and Andrews, 1983). Despite these consistent results, other research has complicated the picture somewhat (Shaffer and Graziano, 1983). Prosocial acts that involve potential embarrassment or danger are *less* likely to occur when subjects are in a positive mood (Forest et al., 1980; Rosenhan, Salovey, and Hargis, 1981). Individuals who feel very good seem to feel a sense of power. As a consequence, they feel free to refuse to provide help to a stranger.

NEGATIVE EMOTIONAL STATE   Negative feelings have an even less straightforward relationship to altruism. In some cases negative feelings inhibit prosocial acts, facilitate such behavior, or have no effect at all (Barden et al., 1981; Shelton and Rogers, 1981). The crucial factor seems to be whether the negative mood causes the person to

Figure 8.15 According to the reinforcement theory of prosocial behavior, people learn to be altruistic if prosocial behavior leads to rewards and not to punishments. Based on Dagwood's experience in this cartoon, we might expect that Dagwood will not be helpful to others for sometime afterward. (Source: Reprinted with special permission of King Features Syndicate, Inc.)

Prosocial behavior: Role of rewards and punishments

focus on his or her needs and self-concerns; self-focus causes the individual to neglect others who may require help, unless the request for help is made highly salient (Mayer et al., 1985). When negative feelings are focused on the person who needs aid, thus arousing empathy, helpfulness increases (Carlson and Miller, 1987; Thompson and Hoffman, 1980). In addition, when a person feels *personally responsible* for his or her negative mood, there is greater willingness to help others (Rogers et al., 1982).

ATTRIBUTIONS AND ALTRUISM   One additional factor is involved in the relationship between emotions and helping. A potential helper must decide *why* another person is in need of assistance. Weiner (1980) suggests that we engage in a causal analysis that influences emotions and subsequent altruistic actions. The sequence is shown in Figure 8.16. We observe a person in need, make an attribution as to the cause of the problem, experience a positive or negative emotional reaction, and then provide help or fail to do so. If someone seems to be in trouble because of internal, controllable causes, such as taking drugs, we are likely to respond with dis-

gust and walk away from the situation without bothering to do anything about it. In contrast, when the difficulty is caused by events beyond the victim's control, such as a mugging, we feel sympathetic and try to help (Meyer and Mulherin, 1980).

Empathy: A Characteristic Influencing Altruism. One important individual characteristic which affects whether a person offers assistance is **dispositional empathy**. This refers to the tendency to respond to the world from the perspective of others (Eisenberg and Miller, 1987). When you are simply aware of another person's problem, you may feel *sympathy;* when you attempt to understand that person's subjective experience, *empathy* occurs (Wispe, 1986). In general, when we observe someone suffering, we feel either personal distress and self-concern or empathy for the victim. However, only the feeling of empathy leads to an altruistic response (Batson, Fultz, and Schoenrade, 1987; Batson et al., 1983). It is interesting that those high in empathy are helpful even if no one, including the victim, knows about their actions (Fultz et al., 1986). The

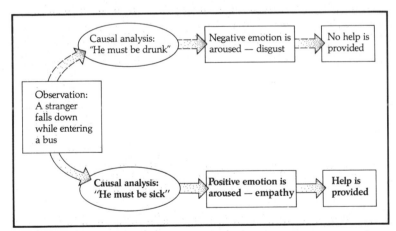

Figure 8.16   Weiner (1980) proposed that the observation of a person in need of help leads us to attempt to figure out the cause of the problem. If the cause seems to be internal and under the victim's control, we respond with negative feelings and decide not to be helpful. If the cause seems to be external and not under the person's control, our response is positive, and prosocial acts are much more likely to occur.

A causal analysis of attributions, emotions, and likelihood of helping

motivation clearly seems to be internal. Nevertheless, it can be argued that even the most altruistic behavior is based on selfish motives (Cialdini et al., 1987). That is, a person may simply be helpful because he or she wants to avoid sadness.

Empathic tendencies can be increased by telling subjects to try to imagine how the victim is feeling. Helping behavior increases when such instructions are given (Toi and Batson, 1982). Empathy and helping are also increased by information that indicates similarities between the victim and the observer (Batson et al., 1981), and this similarity effect even holds true for helping other nations by means of foreign aid (Taormina and Messick, 1983).

Intervening to Stop a Transgressor: A Difficult Prosocial Act

Helping a stranger in distress requires time, effort, and the decision to assume responsibility. Intervening to stop an ongoing act of crime or violence involves, in addition, the decision to cause harm to the wrongdoer and to risk the danger of possible retaliation. As you can imagine, the costs of this type of prosocial behavior are potentially quite high.

The Inhibiting Effect of Fellow Bystanders. Just as in other emergency situations involving a stranger in need, witnesses to a crime have been found to be inhibited by the presence of additional bystanders. In one of the first investigations of this phenomenon, male undergraduates who were waiting to be interviewed witnessed an accomplice steal $40 from a receptionist's desk (Latané and Darley, 1970). The subject was the only person to witness the crime or was one of two bystanders. Most of the students did nothing to stop the theft and failed to report the incident to anyone. Nevertheless, more individuals reported the crime when they were alone than when there were two witnesses. In this and other studies of wrongdoing, the bystander effect is generally found. One complicating factor, however, is the ambiguity in such situations. When the victim makes it clear that a theft or

other wrongdoing has occurred, witnesses are more likely to act (DeJong, Marber, and Shaver, 1980).

In studying responses to actual situations of danger, Huston and colleagues (1981) attempted to find out what personal factors differentiate those who intervened from those who did not. Individuals who had intervened in muggings, armed robberies, or bank holdups were interviewed and compared with a matched group of people who had failed to intervene in crimes. The major difference between the two groups was that those who intervened were found to be more competent to deal with such situations. As shown in Figure 8.17, those who did something in response to a violent crime were much more likely than noninterveners to have been trained to deal with emergencies. Those who intervened were also taller and heavier and more likely to describe themselves as strong, aggressive, emotional, and principled. Altogether, response to violence seems more probable if the individual is physically able to handle the wrongdoer, emotionally predisposed to action, and has had the appropriate training.

Responding to Shoplifters. Earlier we described a shoplifting scene. In real life, the average person simply ignores such incidents, despite the fact that this particular crime costs us about $10 billion annually and is on the increase (Klentz and Beaman, 1981).

Field experiments have shown that the majority of shoppers will inform the management about a theft if a fellow shopper (an accomplice of the experimenter) simply reminds them that shoplifters should be reported (Bickman and Rosenbaum, 1977). In contrast, posters or mass media messages are not very effective. Such impersonal reminders influence *attitudes* about shoplifting and about reporting of thieves, but actual behavior doesn't change (Bickman and Green, 1977).

A program was developed by Klentz and Beaman (1981) to inform people about shoplifting and its costs. The most effective method to increase the number of individuals who intervene in shoplifting situations was the presentation of a lecture about how and why to re-

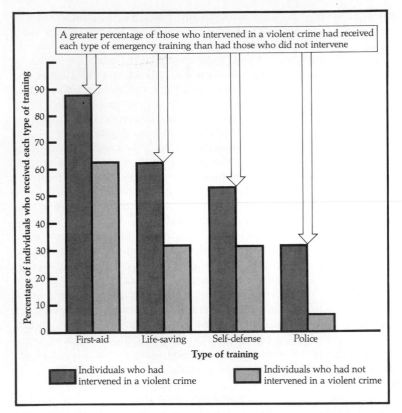

Figure 8.17 *When individuals who had intervened in actual instances of violent crime were compared with others who had failed to intervene, one major difference was the extent to which they had had emergency training. In addition, those who intervened were found to be taller and heavier than noninterveners. In part, intervention behavior seems to be most likely among those who are physically able to deal with the problem and who have been trained to do so. (Source: Based on data from Huston et al., 1981.)*

Stopping violent crime: Role of training

port this crime *and* the reasons that bystanders are usually inhibited about taking action. An interesting question is whether those who simply read about intervention and nonintervention in books—such as this one—will behave differently in the future!

Responsibility and Commitment. In this chapter, we have described how people are most likely to be helpful to others if they feel *responsible* for providing aid. For example, indi-

viduals are more likely to feel responsible if they are the sole observer, if they have been trained in dealing with emergencies, and if they are reminded of the right thing to do. It is also possible to manipulate the feeling of responsibility in a direct fashion. Moriarty (1975) proposed that a **prior commitment** to be responsible should increase the probability of intervention behavior. In a field experiment, an experimental accomplice selected individuals who were sitting alone as subjects on a crowded beach. He placed his own blanket near that of the subject and turned his portable radio on. A few minutes later, he spoke to the subject and either asked for a match or (to create commitment) said, "Excuse me, I'm going to the boardwalk for a few minutes. Would you watch my things?" All of the subjects agreed to do so, thus committing themselves in advance as responsible bystanders. The accomplice then walked away, and a second accomplice came along, picked up the radio, and hurriedly walked away. How did the subjects respond to this blatant theft of a stranger's radio? Of those subjects who had only been asked for a match, only 20 percent did anything about the stolen property. Among those who had been asked to be responsible, almost all (95 percent) took action. They ran after the thief, shouted at him, and even grabbed him to get back the radio. When people agree beforehand to take responsibility, they seem to do so with a vengeance.

The powerful effects of prior commitment have been shown under a variety of circumstances, such as watching a stranger's suitcase in an automat (Moriatry, 1975) and a fellow student's belongings in a library (Shaffer, Rogel, and Hendrick, 1975). With a slight nudge toward assuming responsibility, most people seem to respond to wrongdoing by taking appropriate action. Thus, we see, just as in the case of aggression, there are situational characteristics and techniques that can increase the chances that people will help. As social psychologists continue their efforts to understand aggression and prosocial behavior, we are likely to see additional approaches to reducing "hurting," and increasing helping.

SUMMARY

This chapter described the causes, nature and control of two very different forms of social behavior: **Aggression**—the intentional infliction of harm or injury upon others—and **prosocial behavior**—acts that have no obvious benefits for the individual engaging in them, but benefit others.

Though aggressive behavior has often been attributed to instincts or other innate tendencies, most social psychologists view it as a learned form of behavior, affected by many social, environmental, and cognitive factors.

Among the social and situational causes of aggression are frustration, direct provocation from others (especially when it appears to be intended), and exposure to media violence. Aggression can also be enhanced by residual (carryover) arousal from prior sources. Recently, people have become concerned about the contribution of violent pornography, which combines sexually explicit material with aggressive acts, and violence in *close relationships.*

Several techniques for the control of human aggression exist. These include *punishment, catharsis,* and *exposure to nonaggressive models.* In addition, aggression can often be reduced through the induction of responses or emotional states *incompatible* with such behavior (e.g., empathy, humor, mild sexual arousal).

The study of prosocial behavior shows that when emergencies arise that involve a stranger in need of help, aid is less likely to be provided (or to be provided less quickly) as the number of bystanders increases: the **bystander effect.** Among the explanations for this effect are **diffusion of responsibility** and **fear of social blunders.** Altruistic behavior also varies as a function of reward and punishment. In complex situations, individuals seem to weigh the potential costs and benefits of helping versus failing to help. Positive versus negative feelings affect altruism, but cognitive factors play an important intervening role. The degree to which a person experiences dispositional **empathy** also influences whether or not he or she behaves altruistically.

When someone observes another person engaging in wrongdoing, intervention becomes less likely as the number of bystanders increases. Help is most likely to be provided by those who are competent to deal with the wrongdoer physically and/or to provide aid to the victim. Shoplifting is more often reported when individuals are reminded of the right thing to do or informed about the way in which responding is ordinarily inhibited. When a person makes a **prior commitment** to be responsible, the likelihood of taking action against a wrongdoer is greatly increased.

GLOSSARY

aggression Behavior directed toward the goal of harming or injuring another living being who is motivated to avoid such treatment.

aggression machine Apparatus used to measure physical aggression under safe laboratory conditions.

bystander calculus The process that is hypothesized to occur when a bystander to an emergency calculates the perceived costs and benefits of providing help compared to the perceived costs and benefits of not helping.

bystander effect The fact that effective responses to an emergency are less likely to occur (and more likely to be delayed) as the number of bystanders increases.

catharsis hypothesis The suggestion that providing angry persons with an opportunity to behave in vigorous but nonharmful ways will reduce both (1) their level of emotional arousal, and (2) their tendency to aggress against others.

cognitive neoassociationist view An explanation for the occurrence of human aggression suggesting that aversive events generate negative affect. Such affect, in turn, activates tendencies toward both aggression and flight. Which of these actions then follows depends, in part, on higher levels of cognitive processing.

diffusion of responsibility The proposition that when there are multiple bystanders when an emergency occurs, the responsibility for taking the action is shared among all the members of the group. As a result, each individual feels less responsible than if he or she were alone.

dispositional empathy A personality characteristic that centers on the tendency to take the perspective of those who are unhappy, afraid, or otherwise in emotional difficulty. Individuals with this trait experience empathic emotional arousal when confronted by someone in need of help. The tendency to feel as the other person must feel leads to altruistic behavior. Situational variables can also increase empathy and, thus increase helping behavior.

drive theories of aggression Theories that view aggression as stemming from particular external conditions serving to arouse the motive to harm or injure others. The most famous of these is the frustration-aggression hypothesis.

excitation transfer A theory that explains the impact of heightened arousal upon aggression. According to this view, arousal occurring in one situation can persist and intensify emotional reactions occurring in later situations.

family violence Aggression between husbands and wives, parents and children, or siblings.

fear of social blunders The dread of acting inappropriately or of making a foolish mistake witnessed by others. The desire to avoid ridicule inhibits effective responses to an emergency by members of a group.

frustration-aggression hypothesis A view suggesting that frustration (the blocking of ongoing goal-directed behavior) is a very powerful elicitor of aggression.

incompatible responses Responses or emotional states incompatible with anger and acts of overt aggression.

instinct theory The view that aggression stems primarily from innate urges and tendencies.

prior commitment An individual's agreement in advance to assume responsibility if trouble occurs. An example is committing oneself to protect the property of another person against theft.

prosocial behavior Acts that have no obvious benefits for the person who carries them out and may involve risk or some degree of sacrifice. They benefit other people and are based on ethical standards.

punishment Procedures in which aversive consequences are delivered to individuals each time they perform certain actions. Under appropriate circumstances, punishment can be an effective deterrent to human aggression.

reinforcement theory of prosocial behavior The theoretical model that emphasizes the importance of rewards and punishments. Altruism is assumed to vary as a function of its intrinsic reinforcement value, the occurrence of exterr.al rewards and punishments, and the individual's expectations of future rewards and punishments as consequences of a given behavior.

social learning view of aggression A modern perspective that views aggression as a learned form of social behavior.

violent pornography Highly explicit erotic materials in which one or more of the persons shown engage in acts of violence against one or more others. Often, the victims are females.

FOR MORE INFORMATION

BARON, R. A. (1977). *Human aggression.* New York: Plenum.

An overview of major research findings concerning human aggression. Separate chapters examine the social, environmental, and personal determinants of such behavior. Techniques for preventing or controlling aggression are also discussed.

DONNERSTEIN, E., LINZ, D., and PENROD, S. (1987). *The question of pornography: Research findings and policy implications.* New York: Free Press.

An excellent survey of the growing body of research on the effects of pornography on aggression. The authors also discuss the implications of this research for social policy.

EISENBERG, N. (1985). *Altruistic emotion, cognition, and behavior.* Hillsdale, N.J.: Erlbaum.

Two of the crucial factors determining altruism—emotions and cognitions—are the central focus of this book. The specific topics include sympathy, conceptions of altruism, and moral decision-making.

GEEN, R. G., and DONNERSTEIN, E. (Eds.). (1983). *Aggression: Theoretical and empirical reviews.* New York: Academic Press.

A collection of chapters dealing with different aspects of aggression. Each was prepared by an expert on such behavior, so all are thorough and informative.

LEIBERT, R. M., and SPRAFKIN, J. N. (1988). *The early window: Effects of television on children and youth* (3d ed.). New York: Pergamon.

A clearly written review of research concerned with the behavioral impact of television. The effects of TV viewing on aggression and several other forms of behavior are discussed in an easy-to-follow style.

PILIAVIN, J. A., DOVIDIO, J. F., GAERTNER, S. L., and CLARK, R. D., III. (1981). *Emergency intervention.* New York: Academic Press.

This volume covers psychological research and theory dealing with the way bystanders become involved in crises and emergencies of others. The emphasis is on the responsive bystander and the variables that affect his or her behavior.

Chapter Nine
Groups and Individual Behavior: The Consequences of Belonging

"Look, all we've got to do is swing one more person," Ceci Estrada comments. "That'll be enough."

"Why? That still won't give us a majority," Dick Riley protests. "When push comes to shove, we may still lose out."

"Haven't you learned *anything* about committees?" Ceci replies. "You don't need a majority to win. All you've got to do is show momentum. If it looks as though you're picking up strength, a lot of people will jump on board. They just don't want to risk being left out in the cold."

"Yeah, I know about the 'sheep-wanting-into-the-fold' effect," Dick answers. "But when you're pushing a plan as risky as ours, it may not work. Opening a whole new operation. Whew! No wonder Jack LaFrance and his people are nervous."

"Oh, the heck with them!" Ceci says with a toss of her head. "They're just a bunch of scared old chickens. We'll never grow if we don't get into some new markets. What do they want to do, stand pat for the rest of their lives?"

"I guess so," Dick answers. "But you can't really blame them. And besides, you know how it is . . . when you get a bunch of people together, they seem to want to stick to the middle, do what's safe."

"That's never been *my* experience," Ceci responds. "I've always found that committees are more likely to go off the deep end than anyone . . . Don't you remember the Permatex disaster? *That* was a committee decision, and look what it cost us."

"Yeah . . ." Dick agrees. "You're right, no doubt about it . . . but anyway, who are we going to get to switch? Phil Cohen's too big these days . . . he's so full of himself since his promotion he hardly listens. And Bob, Nancy, and Tanya all take their cues from him."

"Right. So let's concentrate on Chuck. He's been feeling shaky since they chose Anne to negotiate the Portland deal—he wanted that one so bad he could taste it. I think he'll come right over once it looks like we can swing it. I just *know* he wants to be on the winning side for a change."

"OK, we'll work on him," Dick agrees, nodding his head. "Let's let him know we've singled him out, and are paying attention to what he says . . . Make sure he knows that he's either for us or against us; no more fence-sitting allowed. Once he knows we're watching him real close, he'll probably see the light."

"Yeah, and when he does, we've got it made," Ceci says with a grin. "The rest will fall into our laps like a bunch of ripe bananas!"

When we are part of a **group**—when we work together with other persons to reach common goals—our behavior is often quite different from what it is under other circumstances. This is the result of what social psychologists call **group influence** (McGrath, 1984). You are probably already familiar with this phenomenon yourself. For example, you realize that your actions may be quite different when you are in the presence of other persons (especially ones with whom you have an ongoing relationship) than when you are alone. One question raised by the story that introduced this chapter is whether people in groups tend to make conservative decisions or whether groups tend to "go off the deep end." This is an issue we will consider in this chapter.

Also, no doubt, you have noticed that when you joined various groups (e.g., neighborhood play groups, fraternities or sororities, unions, churches), you were expected to behave and think in certain ways—ones endorsed by these groups. Groups, in short, often exert powerful effects on their members. In the opening story, Ceci and Dick were planning to make a special effort to "get" Chuck's swing vote for an important decision. They assumed that once their co-workers perceived their position was picking up strength, then everyone would jump on board. Since most individuals join many different groups during their life, such effects play an important role in many contexts and involve a wide range of behavior (see Figure 9.1). It is on this topic, therefore, that we focus in the present chapter. Specifically, our discussion of group influence—the consequences of belonging—will proceed as follows.

First, we will consider the simplest kind of group effect: changes in the performance of various tasks stemming from the presence of others

Figure 9.1 Individuals are members of many different groups during their lives. As a result, group influence has important effects on a wide range of behaviors in many different contexts.

Groups: Important during all phases of life

(these are referred to as **social facilitation** effects), and the question of whether groups or individuals are more efficient in completing various tasks. Second, we will consider **decision-making** in groups, examining the processes through which group decisions are made, their nature, and several forces that tend to distort or bias their outcomes. Finally, because groups often exert their strongest influence on their members through the actions of leaders, we will conclude with a discussion of the important process of **leadership**.

GROUPS AND TASK PERFORMANCE: The Benefits—and Costs—of Working with Others

According to a famous poem, "No man is an island; No man stands alone" (read "person" for "man," of course!). While these words may not apply equally to all spheres of life, they certainly seem accurate where work is concerned. Human beings rarely perform their jobs or carry out other important tasks entirely on their own. More frequently, they work with others, or at least in their presence. A key question concerning groups, therefore, is this: what impact, if any, do they exert on task performance? In order to answer this question, it is necessary for us to consider two separate but related issues: (1) what are the effects of the mere presence of others on individual performance (in other words, do individuals perform differently in front of an audience or with other people working on the same task than when alone)? and (2) how efficient are groups, relative to individuals, in performing various tasks?

Social Facilitation: Performance in the Presence of Others

Imagine that as part of your job, you must make a speech in front of a large audience. You have several weeks to prepare, so you write the speech and then practice it at home in the evening and on weekends. Time passes, and the mo-

ment of truth arrives. You are introduced and begin your speech. How will you do? Will you stumble over the words and perform more poorly in front of a live audience than when you were alone? Or will the presence of these people actually spur you on to greater heights of eloquence? Early research concerned with the issue yielded confusing results (Triplett, 1898). Sometimes performance was *improved* by the presence of an audience. In other situations, though, the opposite was true. How could this puzzle be solved? One intriguing answer was offered by Zajonc (1965) in what has come to be known as the **drive theory of social facilitation**.

The Drive Theory of Social Facilitation: Other Persons as a Source of Arousal. Before describing Zajonc's theory, we should make one point clear. The term *social facilitation,* as used in social psychology, refers to *any* effects of performance stemming from the presence of others. Thus, it includes decrements as well as improvements in task performance. Another point is that the others can either be passive spectators (an *audience*) or *co-actors*—persons working on the same task (for example, students taking a test in a classroom).

The basic idea behind Zajonc's theory can be simply stated: the presence of others produces increments in our level of motivation or arousal. As you can readily see, this suggestion agrees with informal experience. Often the presence of other persons—especially in the form of an audience—*does* cause us to experience signs of heightened arousal (e.g., feelings of tension or excitement). But how do such increments in arousal then affect our performance? According to Zajonc, the answer involves two basic facts.

First, it is a well-established fact in psychology that increments in arousal enhance the performance of *dominant responses*—the ones an individual is most likely to perform in a given situation. (An example: your tendency to smile at others when they smile at you.) Thus, when arousal increases, our tendency to perform strong, dominant responses increases, too. Second, such dominant responses can be either correct or incorrect for any task we are currently performing.

When these two facts are combined with the suggestion that the presence of others is arousing, two predictions follow: (1) the presence of others will facilitate performance when an individual's dominant responses are correct ones; (2) the presence of others will actually impair performance when a person's dominant responses in the situation are incorrect (see Figure 9.2). Stated in slightly different terms, the presence of others will facilitate the performance of strong, well-learned responses, but may interfere with the performance of new and as yet unmastered forms of behavior.

Early studies designed to test these predictions generally yielded positive results (e.g., Matlin and Zajonc, 1968; Zajonc and Sales, 1966). That is, individuals were in fact more likely to emit dominant responses when in the presence of others than when alone, and performance on various tasks was then either enhanced or impaired, depending on whether these responses represented correct responses or errors (Geen and Gange, 1977). Further, additional findings

offered support for the view that the presence of others is indeed arousing; subjects showed higher levels of physiological arousal when in the presence of others than when they were alone (e.g., Martens, 1969).

Additional research, however, soon raised an important question: does social facilitation stem from the mere physical presence of others, as Zajonc's theory suggests? Or do other factors (e.g., concern over their possible evaluations) also play a role? Support for the latter possibility was provided by the findings of several intriguing studies. For example, Cottrell and his colleagues (1986) had subjects perform a task involving the emission of previously learned responses under one of three conditions: while each was (1) alone in the room, (2) in the presence of two other persons who wore blindfolds, and (3) in the presence of two other persons who expressed interest in watching the subject's behavior and who actually did so. Results indicated that social facilitation (an increase in the subject's tendency to emit dominant responses)

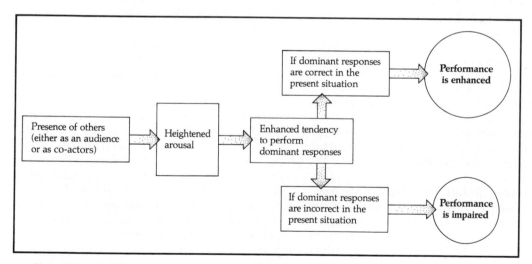

Figure 9.2 According to the *drive theory* of social facilitation, the presence of others increases our level of motivation or arousal. This increased arousal, in turn, enhances the performance of dominant responses (our strongest responses in a given situation). If these are correct, performance is enhanced. If they are incorrect, performance is reduced.

The drive theory of social facilitation: A summary

occurred only under the last condition—when members of the audience could observe and evaluate the subject's performance.

These and related findings (e.g., Bond, 1982; Bray and Sugarman, 1980) led some researchers to propose that social facilitation actually derives either from **evaluation apprehension**—concern over being judged by others—or related concerns over *self-presentation*—looking good in front of others (Carver and Scheier, 1981). Thus, it may be these factors—not the mere physical presence of others—that are crucial in determining the impact of an audience or co-actors on task performance.

At first glance, such suggestions seem quite reasonable. After all, most of us *are* concerned with the impressions we make on others and care about their evaluation of us. Further, such concerns might indeed be motivating or arousing in many situations. However, we must note that other evidence points to the conclusion that social facilitation effects can sometimes occur even in situations in which these factors do not seem to play a role (e.g., Markus, 1978; Schmitt et al., 1986). For example, many animals appear to be affected in the same manner as human beings by the presence of an audience or co-actors (e.g., Rajecki, Kidd, and Ivins, 1976). Indeed, even roaches show an increased tendency to perform dominant responses when in the presence of an audience of other roaches (Zajonc, Heingartner, and Herman, 1969)! Since it makes little sense to assume that animals or insects share our concerns about "looking good" to each other, it appears that social facilitation can occur quite apart from the impact of such factors.

A Potential Resolution: The Distraction-Conflict Model. The findings described above seem to leave us facing a dilemma. Does social facilitation stem from physical presence, evaluation apprehension, concerns over self-presentation, or other factors? At present, no conclusive answer exists. One possibility—supported by some recent findings—is that all (or at least several) of these variables play a role (Sanders, 1984b). Another is provided by the **distraction-conflict theory**, developed jointly by Sanders, Baron, and Moore (e.g., R. S. Baron, 1986; Sanders, 1983; Sanders, Baron, and Moore, 1978).

Like the other explanations of social facilitation we have already considered, this theory assumes that the impact of audiences and co-actors on task performance stems from heightened arousal. In contrast to earlier views, however, it suggests that such arousal stems from conflict between two tendencies on the part of organisms performing various tasks: (1) the tendency to pay attention to the task at hand, and (2) the tendency to direct attention to an audience or co-actors. The conflict produced by these competing tendencies leads to increments in motivation or arousal. These, in turn, enhance the tendency to perform dominant responses, and either increase or decrease performance, depending on whether such responses are correct or constitute errors (see Figure 9.3).

Growing evidence offers support for this theory. For example, various sources of distraction (even nonsocial ones such as flashing lights) do seem to produce increments in arousal, as the theory suggests (Sanders, 1983). Second, audiences seem to produce social facilitation effects (e.g., increased vigor in performing simple responses) only when directing attention to the audience conflicts in some way with task demands (Groff, Baron, and Moore, 1983). When paying attention to audience members does not conflict with task performance, social facilitation fails to occur. Third, individuals report experiencing greater degrees of distraction when they perform various tasks in front of an audience than when they perform such tasks alone (Baron, Moore, and Sanders, 1978). Fourth, when people have little reason to pay attention to others present on the scene (e.g., these persons are performing a different task), social facilitation fails to take place. When, in contrast, they have strong reasons for directing attention to others (e.g., these persons are performing the same task as themselves), social facilitation effects appear (Gastorf, Suls, and Sanders, 1980; Sanders, 1983).

We should hasten to add that not all findings have been consistent with predictions derived from distraction-conflict theory (e.g., Berger et al., 1982). However, most existing evidence provides support for its usefulness. In addition, distraction-conflict theory offers one important advantage not provided by any of the competing

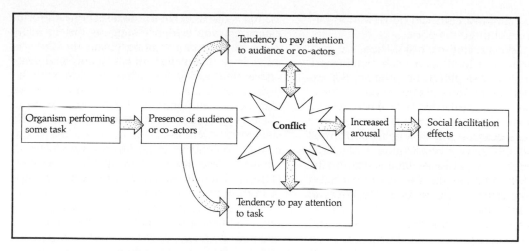

Figure 9.3 The *distraction-conflict theory* of social facilitation suggests that the presence of others induces competing tendencies to (1) pay attention to these persons, and (2) pay attention to the task being performed. The conflict generated by these competing tendencies results in heightened arousal, which then produces social facilitation.

The distraction-conflict theory of social facilitation

views. Since animals as well as people can experience the type of conflict shown in Figure 9.3, it explains why social facilitation occurs in many different species—even the lowly roach! To conclude, while the theory proposed by Sanders, Baron, and Moore may not offer a final answer to the persistent puzzle of social facilitation, it seems quite promising in this respect. In any case, it has added substantially to our understanding of what many social psychologists consider to be the simplest type of group effect.

Groups and Task Performance

Earlier we noted that most work is performed in group settings; individuals rarely perform their jobs (or other important tasks) entirely alone. The reason behind this reliance on groups is obvious: there is a strong and general belief that people working together can accomplish more than people working alone. By coordinating their efforts, groups of persons *can* often attain goals that none of them could hope to reach alone. But does this necessarily imply that groups are always, or even usually, more productive than individuals? The answer, it turns

out, is fairly complex. Working in groups does indeed offer advantages. For example, it allows individuals to pool their knowledge and skills. Similarly, it allows for an efficient division of labor, so that specific persons perform those tasks for which they are best equipped. On the other hand, though, group settings exact certain costs. When group members like one another, they may spend a lot of time engaging in pleasant—but nonproductive—social interaction. Further, pressures to adhere to existing norms and "do things the way we've always done them" may interfere with the development of new and better procedures for completing essential tasks. In short, group settings offer a mixed bag of potential pluses and minuses where performance is concerned. Perhaps the most important single factor determining whether groups or individuals are most efficient, however, involves the type of task being performed. Thus, it is to this topic that we turn next.

Type of Task and Group Performance. A useful framework for understanding the different types of tasks performed by groups has been proposed by Steiner (1972; 1976). According to this approach, most tasks can be viewed as falling into one of three categories.

First, there are **additive tasks**. These are ones in which the contributions of each member are combined into a single group product. For example, when several persons combine their strength to lift a heavy load, or when several carry petitions door-to-door to get the required number of signatures, the task being performed is additive. Obviously, coordination is crucial in such efforts; it would make little sense for the people trying to lift the load to exert their effort at different times, or for different canvasers to visit the same potential signers. Only if such coordination exists will there be anything to "add" in determining the group's final output.

Second, there are **conjunctive tasks**. Here, the group's final product is determined by its "weakest link"—by the poorest performing member. A clear example of this type of task is provided by the efforts of a group of acrobats who build a "human pyramid" as part of their act. Obviously, the height to which this pyramid can rise is determined by the strength of the weakest member of the team. At the point where this person cannot support additional weight, the whole structure will collapse.

Third, there are **disjunctive tasks**. Here, too, the group's product (and hence its success) is determined by a single member. However in this case, it is the best or most competent person who sets the limit. For example, consider a group of scientists faced with a complex problem relating to their research. The group can adopt only one solution or approach at a time, so its success will reflect the quality of the best idea or solution proposed by any of its members. (A word of caution: as we will see below, the best possible solution or course of action is not always recognized as such. If it is not, group performance will be below this level.)

Now to return to our basic question: how do groups and individuals compare with respect to each of these types of tasks? A general answer is as follows: On additive tasks, groups usually outperform individuals, *provided* that (1) the type of coordination mentioned above exists, and (2) a phenomenon known as **social loafing**, in which individual members decide to take it easy and let others do the work, does not develop (social

loafing is discussed in the next section). Unfortunately, existing evidence suggests that in many cases, coordination among group members is difficult to attain. Individuals seem to distract one another and get in each other's way, with the overall result that groups actually produce *less* than equivalent numbers of individuals working alone (e.g., Wood, Polek, and Aiken, 1985). The situation is even less favorable to groups in the case of conjunctive tasks, where overall performance is determined by the weakest member. Here, individuals usually tend to surpass groups in both output and quality. Finally, with respect to disjunctive tasks, groups tend to have an edge, provided they possess at least some competent, talented members, *and* provided such persons are successful in getting their ideas or solutions accepted (Laughlin, 1980). A summary of these proposals is offered in Figure 9.4; please review it carefully before reading further.

Social Loafing: "Passing the Buck" When Part of a Group

Have you ever watched a group of workers struggle to move a heavy piece of equipment or a large piece of furniture? If so, consider the following question: do you think all of the persons involved were exerting their full effort? Latané and his colleagues (Latané, Williams, and Harkins, 1979) say it is likely that they were not. They base this answer on the notion that when people work in groups, it is easier to pass their responsibilities on to others. As a result, group members tend not to put in as much effort as they could (notice the similarity to the concept of *diffusion of responsibility* in prosocial behavior discussed in Chapter Eight). This phenomenon, known as social loafing, has been found in numerous studies. For example, in one such study, groups of students were asked to clap or cheer as loudly as they could at specific times, supposedly so the experimenter could determine how much noise people make in social settings. Subjects engaged in clapping and cheering, either alone or in groups of two, four, or six persons. The findings were clear: the strength of the sounds made by each person decreased sharply as group size rose. Indeed, participants

Additive tasks

		GROUP PERFORMANCE
Contributions of all members combined into final group product	Group performance exceeds individual performance	⇕
		Individual performance

Disjunctive tasks

		GROUP PERFORMANCE
Group performance determined by most competent member	Group performance exceeds individual performance	⇕
		Individual performance

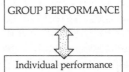

Conjunctive tasks

		INDIVIDUAL PERFORMANCE
Group performance determined by least competent member	Individual performance exceeds group performance	⇕
		Group performance

Figure 9.4 Groups often surpass individuals in the performance of *additive* tasks. The same pattern exists for *disjunctive* tasks, provided that groups possess at least some competent members. Individuals often surpass groups in the performance of *conjunctive* tasks, however.

Task performance: Do groups or individuals have the edge?

produced less than half as much noise when members of groups of six than when working alone.

Other research shows the social loafing effect for tasks involving physical effort, such as rope pulling (Ingham et al., 1974), pumping air (Kerr and Brunn, 1981), and cognitive effort such as evaluating essays (Petty et al., 1980). Such results are discouraging in that they suggest that many persons "goof off" when working with others. Since groups perform many key functions in society, this tendency could have serious practical implications. What accounts for social loafing and what can be done to prevent it?

Some intriguing answers are offered by Harkins (1987), who suggests that people reduce their efforts in the loafing experiments because when working together, particular outputs are pooled or combined. As a result, individual efforts are "lost in the crowd," and participants can receive neither credit nor blame for their performance. Harkins proposes that when people cannot "hide" in the group, the tendency to sit back and let others do the work disappears. Presumably, then, if the supervisor (teacher, boss, or whoever happens to be evaluating the effort) can identify an individual's specific contribution, then a maximizing of effort by all parties should be seen. Indeed, research studies have shown that when individual efforts can be monitored, participants work as hard in groups as when alone (Williams, Harkins, and Latané, 1981).

Recently, Szymanski and Harkins (1987) have proposed that social loafing may also occur because the individual cannot evaluate the contribution he or she is making. Under such conditions, it may make little sense to maximize one's efforts. If this notion is correct, then social loafing should be reduced when individuals believe that there will be an opportunity to receive feedback to evaluate their individual contributions (such as knowing how well others performed). In fact, Szymanski and Harkins propose that knowing that someone (the individual himself or another person) can evaluate one's individual contribution may be sufficient to reduce social loafing.

To test these notions, subjects were asked to work on a task in which they generated as many uses they could think of for various objects.

One-half of the subjects were given instructions suggesting that the experimenter would count how many uses each person had generated (*experimenter evaluation*); half were told that the experimenter would *not* be able to evaluate individual performances (no experimenter evaluation). Within each condition, half were told that after they finished they would be provided with the average number of uses generated by subjects in a previous experiment (*self-evaluation*). (Presumably, learning how others had performed would permit the subject to evaluate how well he or she had performed.) The remaining subjects were informed that they would *not* be provided with such information (*no self-evaluation*).

As shown in Figure 9.5, subjects who believed that the experimenter would be unable to identify their individual contributions produced fewer uses than subjects who believed their contributions could be identified—the social loafing effect. Also consistent with Szymanski and Harkins' predictions, social loafing was reduced when subjects believed that they would receive information allowing them to evaluate their *own* performance.

These and related findings (Zaccaro, 1984; Mullen and Baumeister, 1987) suggest that social loafing is not an unavoidable "side effect" of performance in group settings. If people believe that their individual contributions can be monitored by others *or* that they themselves will be able to evaluate their performance, then people may indeed maximize their efforts. It should be acknowledged, however, that large groups make it more difficult to readily identify each participant's individual efforts. Thus, given that much of the work in modern societies is carried out by committees, work groups, and teams, social loafing is always an ever-present danger because of the tendency to pass or "diffuse" responsibilities on to others.

DECISION-MAKING BY GROUPS: How It Takes Place, the Outcomes It Yields, and the Pitfalls It Faces

Groups are called on to perform a wide range of tasks—everything from conducting delicate surgical operations to harvesting the nation's crops.

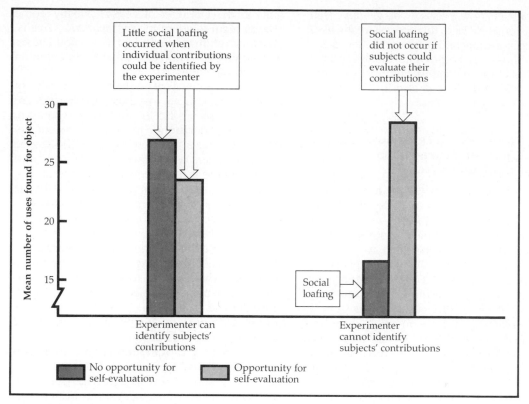

Figure 9.5 *Subjects produced more work when they thought their individual contributions could be identified by the experimenter than when they thought these could not be identified. Furthermore, subjects produced more work when there was an opportunity for them to evaluate their own work than when there was no such opportunity. Taken together, these results suggest that social loafing occurs when members of groups believe their individual contributions to a group effort cannot be individually identified or evaluated. Apparently, being "lost in the crowd" translates into poorer performance. (Source: Based on data from Szymanski and Harkins, 1987.)*

Lost in the crowd: One cause of lower performance by groups

One of the most important activities they perform, however, is **decision-making**. Governments, large corporations, military units, and virtually all other social entities entrust their key decisions to groups. As a result, most of the laws, policies, and business practices that affect our daily lives (or shape the future course of society) are determined by committees, boards of directors, and similar groups—*not* by single individuals. The rationale behind this approach is clear: most persons believe that groups, by pooling the expertise of their members, can often reach better decisions than individuals. Moreover, it is often assumed that because of the give-and-take that occurs during their deliberations, groups are less likely than individuals to "go off the deep end."

Are these assumptions accurate? Do groups actually make better (i.e., more accurate) decisions than individuals? In their efforts to answer this practical question, researchers concerned with group decisions have focused on three major topics: (1) how, precisely, do groups reach their decisions—what is this process really like? (2) do decisions reached by groups differ in any way from those reached by individuals? and (3) what accounts for the fact that groups occasionally make totally disastrous decisions—ones so bad they are hard to explain?

How Groups Reach Decisions: Social Decision Schemes and Social Transition Schemes

When groups first begin to discuss some issue, their members rarely voice unanimous agreement. Rather, they support a wide range of views and favor competing courses of action. After some period of discussion, however, a decision is usually reached. Of course, this is not always the case; juries do become "hung," and other decision-making groups, too, may deadlock. In most cases, though, *some* decision is ultimately reached. Is there any way of predicting this final outcome? In short, can we predict the decision a group is likely to reach from information about the views initially held by its members? Growing evidence suggests that we can (e.g., Davis, 1980; Kerr and MacCoun, 1985; Kaplan, 1987). In particular, it appears that the final decision reached by a group can often be predicted with a high degree of accuracy by means of relatively simple rules known as **social decision schemes**. These rules relate the initial distribution of member views or preferences to the group's final decision, and are quite straightforward. For example, one—the *majority-wins scheme*—suggests that in many cases the group will opt for whatever position is initially supported by a majority of its members. According to this rule, discussion serves mainly to confirm or strengthen the most popular view. In contrast, a second decision scheme—the *truth-wins rule*—suggests that the correct solution or decision will ultimately come to predominate, as its virtue is recognized by growing numbers of members. A third decision scheme, adopted by many juries, is the *two-thirds majority rule*. Here, juries tend to convict defendants if two-thirds of the jurors initially favor this decision. However, if this crucial majority is not reached, the likelihood that the jury will be "hung" is

quite high (David et al., 1984). Finally, some groups seem to adopt the *first-shift rule*. That is, they tend, ultimately, to adopt a decision consistent with the direction of the first shift in opinion shown by any member.

Surprising as it may seem, the results of many studies indicate that these simple rules are often quite successful in predicting even complex group decisions. Indeed, in recent research, they have been successful in this regard up to 80 percent of the time (e.g., Kerr, 1981). Of course, different rules seem to be more successful under some conditions than others. Thus, the majority-wins scheme seems best in situations involving *judgmental tasks*—ones that are largely a matter of opinion and for which no objectively correct decision exists. In contrast, the truth-wins rule seems best in predicting group decisions with respect to *intellective tasks*—ones for which there is a correct decision (Kirchler and Davis, 1986). These rules show that group decisions can be predicted with some accuracy.

The next logical question is how do groups move toward final agreement? This is a complex question; yet recent investigations have begun to shed considerable light even on this matter (e.g., Vinokur et al., 1985). One basic strategy in such research has been to focus on **social transition schemes**—rules indicating how groups move through different patterns of member views or positions en route to their final decisions (e.g., Kerr, 1981; Penrod and Hastie, 1980; Kerr et al., 1987; Laughlin, 1988). As an example of such research, and of the intriguing results it has yielded, we will consider a recent study by Kirchler and Davis (1986).

In this experiment, subjects took a test that supposedly measured decision-making ability. Then each person worked privately on a series of different problems, including an intellective task (whether a death was the result of murder or an accident) and a judgmental task (which of two job candidates to hire). After they were finished, the subjects were assembled in three-person groups to make group decisions about each of the problems. Before beginning to work together, however, feedback about performance on the decision-making ability test was announced publicly to each group. Some subjects received a (fictitious) score indicating low status; others received a score indicating moderate status; and the final third learned they had high status (they had, supposedly, scored high on the test; in fact, all feedback was assigned at random). We should also mention that the experimenters formed some groups where everyone was of equal status and others where some members had higher status than the others. This complex set of manipulations was used to examine the decision schemes the groups used and also whether status differences, together with the type of task, would influence which persons changed their decision preferences.

Observation of the final group decisions and changes in group member preferences revealed several results. First, consistent with our earlier comments, the final group decision about the intellective problem (which had a correct answer) was predicted by the truth-wins principle. On the judgmental problems, which were more a matter of opinion than facts, however, the majority-rules model predicted best. However, if one of the group members was of higher status than the others, a "power-wins" decision scheme—that is, the preference of the high-status member—best predicted the group outcome (see Figure 9.6).

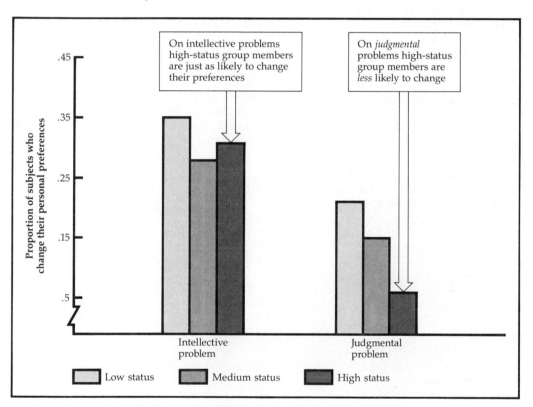

Figure 9.6 In group decisions about *intellective problems,* which have correct answers, high-status individuals are just as likely to change their initial preferences as are low- or moderate-status group members. But in the case of *judgmental problems,* which are more a matter of opinion than fact, high-status members are *less* likely to change. Thus, status does appear to have its privileges in groups, though only on certain types of issues. (Source: Data based on Kirchler and Davis, 1986.)

Changes in group members' preferences: Status and issue effects

Figure 9.6 is particularly revealing. You will note that the high-status subjects were just as likely to change their preference regarding the intellective task as were the low- and moderate-status subjects. However, in the case of judgmental tasks, higher-status individuals changed significantly less often. These results suggest that when there is a correct answer, status differences among group members make little difference: all members come to agree with the person(s) who devise the right answer, regardless of status. In contrast, when the problem is a matter of opinion—there is no single "correct" answer—status plays a greater role: high-status subjects are less likely to change their preferences and more likely to "get their way." The implication of these results is that to understand and predict who will change in a group discussion, we need to know not only the relative status of each person within the group, but also the type of issue under deliberation.

To conclude, research on social decision and social transition schemes suggests that the process by which groups move toward agreement is complex. Final group decisions are affected by where the group has been (i.e., previous patterns of views held by its members), the decision rules it uses, and the kinds of problems under deliberation and many other factors. Yet, the process is far from random. On the contrary, it appears quite orderly. Thus, while groups may not always arrive at the best or most accurate decisions, the roads they travel to them, at least, seem to be predictable.

The Nature of Group Decisions: Moderation or Polarization?

Recently, Mikhail Gorbachev, the premier of the Soviet Union, presented a plan for joint nuclear arms reduction to the President of the United States (see Figure 9.7). Did the President take the plan under advisement and reach a decision about its acceptance alone? Or did he confer with a group of close advisers before responding to the offer? As you can readily guess, the second course of action is closer to reality. Governments—even those headed by dic-

Figure 9.7 Even important leaders rarely make decisions without first conferring with a group of advisers. In part, this may stem from the widespread belief that groups are less likely than individuals to make serious errors.

Even very powerful leaders rarely make decisions without conferring with a group of advisers.

tators—rarely make important decisions without deliberation by *some* high-level group. As we noted earlier, an important reason behind this strategy is the widespread belief that groups are much less likely than individuals to make serious errors—to reach rash decisions or go straight "off the deep end." Is this really the case? Are groups really better at making decisions—or at least more conservative in this regard—than individuals? Research conducted by social psychologists offers some surprising answers.

Group Versus Individual Decisions: A Shift Toward Risk or a Shift Toward Polarization?
More than twenty years ago, a graduate student named James Stoner decided to examine this question in his master's thesis. In order to do so, he asked college students to play the role of advisers to imaginary persons supposedly facing the task of deciding between risky but attractive courses of action, and conservative but less attractive ones (Stoner, 1961). For example, in one of the situations, a fictitious character had to choose between a low-paying but secure job, and a higher-paying but less secure one (see Table 9.1 on page 229 for other examples of such *choice-dilemma* questions).

During the first phase of Stoner's study, each subject made recommendations about these situations alone. Then, they met in small groups and discussed each problem until a unanimous agreement was reached. In accordance with the comments above, Stoner expected that the decisions recommended by groups would be more conservative than those offered by their individual members. Surprisingly, however, just the opposite occurred. Groups actually recommended riskier decisions than individuals.

While the size of this difference was small, it had important implications. After all, if groups do indeed make riskier decisions than individuals, the strategy of entrusting important choices to committees, juries, and so on may be in error. In fact, it may be downright dangerous! Impressed by such implications, many researchers focused their attention on this effect, which soon became known as the **risky shift** (e.g., Burnstein, 1983; Lamm and Myers, 1978). Many of the experiments they conducted seemed to confirm

Stoner's initial findings; they, too, noted a shift toward risk within decision-making groups. In contrast, though, other studies failed to confirm such changes. Indeed, in a few cases, group discussion actually seemed to produce shifts toward *caution* rather than risk (e.g., Knox and Safford, 1976). How could this be? How could group discussion produce both shifts toward caution and shifts toward risk? Gradually, a compelling explanation emerged. What had at first seemed to be a shift toward risk was actually a more general phenomenon—a *shift toward polarization*. Group discussion, it appeared, led individual members to become more extreme—*not* simply more risky or more cautious. Thus, if they were mildly in favor of a particular course of action prior to the group discussion, they came to favor it even more strongly after these deliberations. And if they were mildly opposed to some action prior to the group discussion, they came to oppose it more strongly after the exchange of views. The shifts induced by group discussion, then, are quite general in scope. They represent shifts in the direction of greater extremity, hence the label **group polarization**. The basic nature of this process is illustrated in Figure 9.8.

As we noted earlier, the tendency for groups to become increasingly extreme in their views over time has important—and unsettling—implications. Thus, it is not surprising that this phenomenon has been the subject of a considerable amount of research (e.g., Isenberg, 1986). But why, precisely, does it occur? It is to this question that we turn next.

Group Polarization: Why Does It Occur?
While several different explanations for group polarization have been proposed, two have received the most attention: the *social comparison* and *persuasive arguments* views.

The social comparison approach suggests that prior to group discussion most individuals assume that they hold "better" views than the other members. That is, they assume that their views are more extreme, in the "right" or valued directions, than those of the people around them. Since it is obviously impossible for everyone to be above average in this respect, many

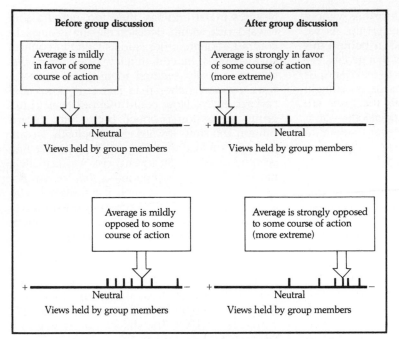

Figure 9.8 *After taking part in a group discussion, group members often shift to views that are more extreme (in the same general direction) than the ones held initially. Such shifts in views or decisions are known as group polarization effects.*

Group polarization: Its basic nature

group members soon experience a rude awakening: they learn that their own views are not nearly as extreme (in positive, valued directions) as they at first believed. Because most persons wish to maintain a positive self-image, and attempt to do so by comparing themselves favorably with others (through *social comparison*), this puts pressure on them to shift to more extreme positions. As they do, the group as a whole moves in this direction, and the polarization effect develops (e.g., Goethals and Zanna, 1979; Sanders and Baron, 1977).

This explanation for group polarization is supported by several interesting findings. For example, individuals do tend to perceive themselves as being more extreme, in the "right" direction, than the others (e.g., Wallach and Wing, 1968). Similarly, shifts toward extremity seem to occur in the total absence of group discussion,

when individuals simply learn that their views are not as far above average as they initially assumed (Myers et al., 1980). However, some evidence appears to be inconsistent with the social comparison view. Specifically, individuals sometimes recommended more extreme or risky decisions for strangers than for themselves (Laughlin and Earley, 1982). This result does not seem to agree with the notion that most persons wish to appear above average in boldness or related traits.

The *persuasive arguments view* offers a contrasting explanation for the occurrence of polarization. It contends that during group discussion, individual members present arguments that support their own views. Since some of these arguments, at least, will be ones not previously considered by other members, the persons hearing them for the first time may be persuaded to alter

Table 9.1   These items are similar to the ones used by Stoner (and many other researchers) to compare individual and group decisions. Subjects answer each item twice: once alone, and then again after engaging in group discussion. (Source: Adapted from Kogan and Wallach, 1964.)

Choice-dilemma items

1. Ms. F is currently a college senior who is very eager to pursue graduate study in chemistry leading to the Doctor of Philosophy degree. She has been accepted by University X and University Y. University X has a world-wide reputation for excellence in chemistry. While a degree from University X would signify that she is outstanding in this field, the standards are so very rigorous that only a fraction of the candidates actually receive the degree. University Y, on the other hand, has a lower reputation in chemistry, but almost everyone admitted is awarded the Doctor of Philosophy degree, though the degree has much less prestige than that from University X.

   Imagine that you are advising Ms. F. Listed below are several probabilities or chances that Ms. F would be awarded a degree at University X, with the greater prestige. Please check the *lowest* probability that you would consider acceptable to make it worthwhile for Ms. F to enroll in University X rather than University Y.

   _____ The chances are 9 in 10 that Ms. F would receive a degree from University X.
   _____ The chances are 7 in 10 that Ms. F would receive a degree from University X.
   _____ The chances are 5 in 10 that Ms. F would receive a degree from University X.
   _____ The chances are 3 in 10 that Ms. F would receive a degree from University X.
   _____ The chances are 1 in 10 that Ms. F would receive a degree from University X.
   _____ Place a check here if you think Ms. F should *not* enroll in University X, no matter what the probabilities.

2. Mr. A, an electrical engineer, who is married and has one child, has been working for a large electronics corporation since graduating from college five years ago. He is assured of a lifetime job with a modest, though adequate, salary, and good pension benefits upon retirement. On the other hand, it is very unlikely that his salary will increase much before he retires. While attending a convention, Mr. A is offered a job with a small, newly founded company that has a highly uncertain future. The new job would pay more to start and would offer the possibility of a share in the partnership if the company survived the competition with larger firms.

   Imagine that you are advising Mr. A. Listed below are several probabilities or chances of the new company's proving financially sound. Please check the *lowest* probability that you would consider acceptable to make it worthwhile for Mr. A to take the new job.

   _____ The chances are 1 in 10 that the company will prove financially sound.
   _____ The chances are 3 in 10 that the company will prove financially sound.
   _____ The chances are 5 in 10 that the company will prove financially sound.
   _____ The chances are 7 in 10 that the company will prove financially sound.
   _____ The chances are 9 in 10 that the company will prove financially sound.
   _____ Place a check here if you think Mr. A should *not* take the new job, no matter what the probabilities.

their views in these directions. Thus, over time the group will shift toward the point of view that is supported by the largest number of convincing arguments. In sum, the view that predominated at the start will enjoy stronger and stronger support, and polarization will develop (Vinokur and Bernstein, 1974).

This explanation, too, is supported by several research findings. First, it has been found that most arguments presented during group discussions do in fact support the initial views of most group members (Vinokur and Bernstein, 1974). Second, it appears that the greater the number and persuasiveness of the arguments favoring a particular point of view, the greater the shift in its direction as a result of group discussion (Ebbesen and Bowers, 1974; Hinsz and Davis, 1984). We should add, however, that other results do not support the accuracy of this interpretation. For example, polarization effects seem to occur even with respect to simple perceptual judgments. In such cases, arguments and persuasion should play little part (Baron and Roper, 1976).

Taking all available evidence into account, therefore, a clear choice between the two theories does not seem possible. In fact, such a choice may be unnecessary. Both social comparison *and* the exchange of information among individuals may play a role in the occurrence of group polarization. Regardless of the precise basis for group polarization, though, it has important implications. The occurrence of polarization may lead many decision-making groups to shift toward positions that are more and more extreme—and more and more dangerous. In this context, it is interesting to speculate about the potential role of such shifts in disastrous decisions by political or military groups who should, by all accounts, have known better (e.g., the decision by President Lyndon Johnson and his advisers to escalate American involvement in Vietnam or the decision by the Nazi high command to invade the Soviet Union during World War II). Did group polarization play a role in these events? At present, it is difficult to say. But evidence gathered in many separate experiments suggests this possibility is at least worth considering.

Decision-making by Groups: Some Special Problems

As we have just pointed out, the tendency of many decision-making groups to drift toward polarization can interfere with their ability to make accurate or effective choices. Unfortunately, this is not the only process that can develop during the course of group activities and produce such effects. Several others, too, can lead decision-making groups into disastrous courses of action. We will consider two of these here: groupthink and the inability of group members to *pool their unshared information.*

Groupthink: Why Groups Sometimes Lose Contact with Reality. Common sense seems to suggest that if a group is high in **cohesiveness** (that is, group members feel strong attachments to the group because they like one another and feel committed to the group's goals and activities), the group's performance should be enhanced, right? In fact, this reasoning can be wrong—dead wrong. When group attraction and commitment are coupled with several other factors—isolation of the group from outside information or influences, the presence of a dynamic, influential leader, and high stress from external threats—an unsettling process known as **groupthink** may be set in operation (Janis, 1982).

Groupthink is characterized by several trends, all of which severely hamper the decision-making capacity of a group. For example, when groupthink develops, group members begin to see themselves as invulnerable—they believe that they simply *can't* make mistakes! Second, they engage in collective rationalization, discrediting or ignoring any information counter to the group's current thinking. Third, pressure toward conformity becomes intense, so that few, if any, members, are willing to challenge the group's position or dissent from it in any way. The result of these and related tendencies is that the groups experiencing them (and groupthink) often head straight over the edge: they adopt extremely poor decisions, and then convince themselves, more and more firmly, that they are correct ones.

Unfortunately, groupthink does not seem to be a rare or unusual event. On the contrary, since many important decision-making groups enjoy high cohesiveness, face stressful situations in which rapid decisions are necessary, and are directed by strong, dynamic leaders, groupthink is a real danger in many contexts. Along with tendencies toward polarization, it helps explain why seemingly intelligent, rational groups of people sometimes reach decisions that are catastrophic in every respect.

The Inability of Groups to Exchange Unshared Information: Biased Sampling in Group Discussion. One of the major advantages often attributed to decision-making groups is their ability to pool the resources of their individual members. It is assumed that each member brings a unique pattern of skills and knowledge to the task at hand, so the group's final decision will benefit from the pooling of these intellectual resources. While this is a comforting belief, it has been called into serious question by Stasser and Titus (1985).

In actuality, when groups meet to consider various problems and reach important decisions, their discussions are often biased in ways that tend to reduce the potential benefits described above. First, studies show that groups tend to discuss *shared* rather than *unshared* information (Stasser and Titus, 1985; 1987). This is because shared information is more likely to be introduced by one or several members than unshared information. Second, their discussion is biased in favor of the current preferences of group members. Since each is likely to present information that supports his or her views, initial preferences are intensified, not corrected, by the give-and-take of group discussion. The final outcome, then, is *not* a sharing of information among group members so that all obtain a more complete and accurate picture of the situation than was true initially; rather, it is an intensification of initial preferences or views.

Clearly, this is disturbing. Fortunately, though, recent research suggests there are circumstances where the tendency to reiterate already shared information is reduced. Stasser and Titus (1987) proposed that group members *will*

share new information when little is available for discussion. This is because when there is little information on which to base the decision, people must resort to discussing all that is available. Information will also be shared in the discussion when there is little overlap in what each person knows. Recent research confirms that group members do indeed engage in more sharing when little information is initially held in common and when little information is available on which to base a decision (Stasser and Titus, 1987). Thus, at least under some circumstances, group members can obtain a more accurate and broader view of the problem under deliberation, through an exchange of information and views. Hopefully, this may lead them to wiser decisions. (See the "On the Applied Side" insert on pages 232–233 for some ideas about how innovations in modern technology may also influence group decision-making.)

LEADERSHIP:
Influence Within Groups

At different times during your life, you have belonged to many groups. Think back over some of these now. For each, can you recall one member who was more influential than the others? In all likelihood you can, for almost every group contains one person who wields more power than all the rest. Such individuals are usually labeled **leaders**; the process through which they exert influence over others and guide behavior is known as **leadership**.

As you can probably already realize, the impact of leaders on the groups they direct can be profound. Such persons often strongly affect the attitudes, behavior, and even perceptions of their followers. Indeed, in extreme cases they may induce subordinates to accept views that make little sense to others, or to engage in actions they would otherwise never perform. A case in point was the mass suicide of members of a religious cult when ordered to do so by their leader Jim Jones. Because of such effects, our discussion of groups and their impact on individuals would be incomplete without attention to this topic. In this final section, therefore, we

COMPUTERS AND THEIR EFFECTS ON GROUP DECISION-MAKING: WHERE TECHNOLOGY AND SOCIAL BEHAVIOR MEET

It is by now a cliche to say that we live in the "Computer Age." Computers are indeed bringing about many technological and societal changes because of their ability to process vast amounts of information at astounding speeds. It is hard to find business, government, or educational institutions that don't depend on computers for information storage and processing. The role of computers in communication is also expanding. For ex-

ample, computers have initiated electronic mail so people can send messages and data almost instantaneously from one computer to another—whether these are located just down the hall or across the world from one another. As it turns out, computers may also change the way groups traditionally have made decisions.

Increasingly, people in organizations are communicating and making group decisions through

computers (see Figure 9.9). With computer networks people can send messages and make decisions instantaneously, at low cost, and over long distances. But it should be obvious that computer-mediating decision-making is different from decision-making of the traditional kind in several ways. Computer communication is speedy but lacks the auditory and visual feedback of telephoning or face-to-face communication. Will

Figure 9.9 Traditionally, group decisions have been made through face-to-face discussion. Computer-mediated communication may change all of this, yet recent research suggests that the quality and quantity of group members' contributions may be lower in computer communication. Obviously, there is a need for more study of the effects of this technology and its impact on social behavior.

The computer: It may change the way groups make decisions

this affect the kinds of decisions people make?

Sara Kiesler and her colleagues (Kiesler, Siegel, and McGuire, 1984; McGuire, Kiesler, and Siegel, 1987) have observed that computer communication not only makes group members dependent on the computer text, but also eliminates important nonverbal cues relating to status and power. This may seem to be a positive effect of computer-mediated communication, but sometimes equal participation, objectivity, and efficiency can interfere with group outcomes. It may be necessary for some individuals to have greater power. Furthermore, groups commonly need emotional bonds to instill trust and personal commitment. As yet, we don't know whether computer communication can encourage such bonds.

One recent experiment compared decision-making by subjects who could communicate in a face-to-face manner or only by computer (McGuire, Kiesler, and Siegel, 1987). The subjects were a group of managers, and the decisions involved a series of investments. Interestingly, the researchers found that the managers who participated in the face-to-face discussions showed larger changes from their prediscussion preferences and came to greater agreement than those participating in the computer communication. This was apparently because the length, novelty, and fullness of discussion (remarks) in the face-to-face condition were greater than in the computer-mediated discussion. These results suggest that computer communication may encourage participants to take a hurried attitude toward sharing and elaborating arguments. Thus, while status cues may be minimized by computer communication, the dependence on computer text and the absence of nonverbal channels of communication may limit what people say and their personal engagement.

Needless to say, these findings are only preliminary. The suggestion, though, is that if computer-mediated discussions are used by managers, businesses, and others to make group decisions, those decisions may differ qualitatively from decisions reached through traditional face-to-face methods. As computers grow more powerful, more versatile, and less expensive, more and more people will be using them. And it is likely that many decisions that affect us will be made via computer communication. We need to be alert to the ways in which computers may change the dynamic of group decisions. In sum, computers are a powerful, versatile tool, but we must remain alert to their potential effects on social behavior and human relationships.

---

turn to the nature and impact of leadership. In particular, we will consider two important questions: (1) who becomes a leader—why do some persons but not others rise to positions of power and authority? (see Figure 9.10) and (2) what factors determine a leader's success once he or she has assumed this role?

Are Leaders Born or Made? The Role of Traits, Situations, and Followers

Are some persons born to lead? Common sense seems to suggest that this is so. Great leaders of the past such as Queen Elizabeth I, Alexander the Great, and George Washington do seem to differ from most persons in many ways. And even leaders lacking such worldwide fame seem different from their followers in certain respects. Top executives, many politicians, and sports stars often seem to possess a special "aura" that sets them apart from other persons. On the basis of such observations, early researchers interested in leadership formulated a view known as the **great person theory**. According to this approach, great leaders possess key traits that distinguish them from most other persons. Further, these traits remain stable across time and groups, so that all leaders share the same characteristics, regardless of where and when they live.

These are intriguing suggestions, but they have *not* been strongly confirmed. Decades of active research failed to yield a short, agreed-upon list of key traits shared by leaders (Geier, 1969). Indeed, so disappointing were overall results that most researchers came to the following conclusion: leaders simply do not differ from followers in clear and consistent ways.

While this conclusion is still accepted today, we should note a recent reawakening of interest in the possibility that leaders and followers *do* differ in some respects. Several types of evidence have contributed to this trend. Research suggests that persons possessing certain patterns

Figure 9.10 *Many considerations determine whether someone is perceived as a good leader. (Source: Drawing by Anthony; © 1988 The New Yorker Magazine, Inc.)*

Leadership: A complex phenomenon

of motives rise to leadership positions. For example, individuals with a high need for power plus a high degree of control are more successful as managers in business settings (McClelland and Boyatzis, 1982). Political leaders tend to be high in self-confidence and dominance (Costantini and Craik, 1980). In general, individuals high in dominance (Fleischer and Chertkoff, 1986; Nyquist and Spence, 1986) are more likely to be chosen as leaders in small groups. There is also evidence that individuals emerge as leaders over time who were both success-oriented and highly affiliative (Sorrentino and Field, 1986; Winter, 1987).

Such findings suggest that certain traits *can* play a role in determining who becomes a leader, at least in some contexts, and to some extent. But they certainly do *not* suggest that all leaders share key traits, or that possession of these is required for leadership in all times and all places.

At this point, you may be a bit puzzled. If leadership is not largely a function of the traits of leaders, what, precisely, does it involve? One answer is the **situational approach**, which recognizes that different situations often call for different types of leaders. For example, a football team may require a leader who is aggressive, competitive, and tough—as well as skilled in the game. In contrast, a negotiating team attempting to conclude a delicate agreement may need a leader who is calm, persuasive, and charming. Thus, according to the situational approach, full understanding of who becomes a leader involves careful attention *both* to the traits of potential leaders and to situational constraints (e.g., the tasks being performed, resources available, etc.; Bass, 1981). Selection of a leader, then, should involve a process of *matching*—one in which an individual whose particular mix of skills and characteristics is closely aligned with the requirements of the current situation.

Because it took account of many factors largely ignored by the great person theory, the situational approach represented an important advance over the earlier view. However, it, too, suffered from a major drawback: it devoted little or no attention to the role and impact of *followers*. Largely because of this weakness, it has recently been replaced by a third, and even more sophisticated, perspective: the **transactional approach**.

This view, which is currently accepted in one form or another by most social psychologists, recognizes an essential fact: while leaders certainly exert influence on their followers, these persons, in turn, frequently exert reciprocal influence on leaders (Hollander, 1978). Indeed, leaders are often strongly affected by their followers' attitudes, preferences, perceptions, and values. This makes eminent good sense; after all, leaders who pay little attention to the wishes of the persons they lead may soon find themselves without a following.

Consistent with this approach, research indicates that leaders do respond to the wishes and perceptions of their followers (e.g., Price and Garland, 1981; Sims and Manz, 1984), and may even shift leadership style to take account of follower characteristics (Scandura and Graen, 1984). For example, in one recent study (Leary et al., 1986), college students were led to believe they would be directing small groups. Some were told such groups need a leader who is mainly task-oriented; other subjects were told groups need a leader mainly interested in how group members get along (relationship-oriented). Then subjects were asked to fill out a questionnaire about their own characteristics, which supposedly would be distributed to the group members so they could learn what their leader was like.

Examination of the ratings (shown in Figure 9.11) shows that subjects who thought the optimal leader should be task-oriented rated themselves higher on task-oriented dimensions such as competence and efficiency. In contrast, subjects led to believe the optimal leader for the group should be relationship-oriented rated themselves higher on interpersonal attributes such as understanding and friendliness. Thus, it appears that leaders "manage" their impressions as a function of what the followers are perceived to require.

To conclude: because it emphasizes the social nature of leadership and directs attention to the complex interaction among leaders, situations, and followers, the transactional approach provides a more complex answer to the question, "Who becomes a leader?" than earlier views. Such complexity is well justified, however, for it also offers a more complete account of the leadership process.

Leadership Effectiveness: A Contingency Approach

All leaders are definitely not equal. Some are effective and contribute to high levels of performance and morale on the part of their followers, while others are much less successful in these respects. Why is this the case? This has been a central issue in much research concerned with leadership (e.g., House and Baetz, 1979; Vroom and Yetton, 1973). As an example of this work, we will consider an important theory proposed by Fiedler (e.g., Fiedler, 1978; Fiedler and Garcia, 1987).

Fiedler labels his model the **contingency theory**, and this term is certainly appropriate, for its central assumption is this: a leader's contribution to successful performance by his or her group is determined both by the leader's traits and by various features of the situation in which the group operates. To fully understand leader effectiveness, both types of factors must be considered.

With respect to the characteristics possessed by leaders, Fiedler identifies *esteem for least preferred co-worker* (LPC, for short) as most important. This refers to a leader's tendency to evaluate the person with whom he or she finds it most difficult to work either favorably or unfavorably. Leaders who perceive this person in negative terms (low LPC leaders) seem primarily concerned with attaining successful task performance. In contrast, those who perceive their least preferred co-worker in a positive light (high LPC leaders) seem mainly concerned with establishing good relations with their subordi-

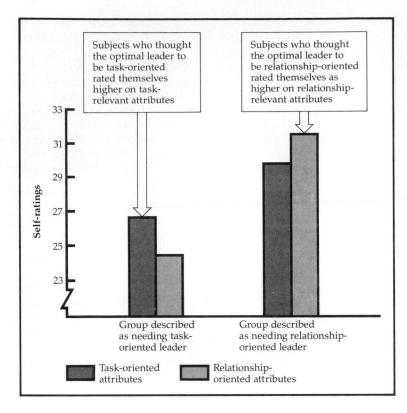

Figure 9.11 Subjects who believed that their group would need a leader who was task-oriented described themselves as more task-oriented than relationship-oriented. In contrast, subjects who were told their followers would need a relationship-oriented leader described themselves as relationship-oriented. Such results suggest that leaders present the image they think will facilitate their performance within their groups. Related evidence suggests that leaders also alter their actual behavior to be compatible with their followers. (Source: Based on data from Leary et al., 1986.)

Self-presentation by leaders

nates. Which of these types of leaders is more effective? Fiedler's answer is: it depends. And what it depends on are several situational factors.

Specifically, Fiedler suggests that whether low LPC or high LPC leaders are more effective depends on the degree to which the situation is favorable to the leader, or provides this person with *control* over other group members. This, in turn, is determined largely by three factors: (1) the nature of the leader's *relations with group members* (the extent to which she enjoys their support or loyalty), (2) the degree of *structure* in the task being performed (the extent to which task goals and roles are clearly defined), and (3) the leader's *position power* (his or her ability to enforce compliance by subordinates). Combining these three factors, the leader's situational control can range from very high (positive relations with group members, a highly structured task, high position power) to very low (negative relations, an unstructured task, low position power).

Now, to return to the central question: when are different types of leaders most effective? Fiedler proposes that low LPC leaders (ones who are task-oriented) are superior to high LPC leaders (ones who are people-oriented) when situational control is either low or high. In contrast, high LPC leaders have an edge when situational control falls within the moderate range (see Figure 9.12). The reasoning behind these predictions is as follows.

Under conditions of *low* situational control, groups need considerable guidance and direction to accomplish their goals. Since low LPC leaders are more likely to provide structure than high LPC leaders, they will usually be superior in such cases. Similarly, low LPC leaders also have an edge in situations that offer the leader a *high* degree of situational control. Here, low LPC leaders realize that conditions are good, and often adopt a relaxed "hands-off" style—one that is appreciated by their followers. In contrast, high LPC leaders, feeling that they already enjoy

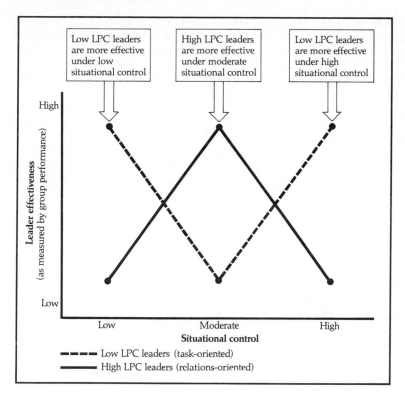

Figure 9.12 According to a theory proposed by Fiedler, low LPC leaders (ones who are primarily task-oriented) are more effective than high LPC leaders (ones who are primarily people-oriented) under very favorable and very unfavorable conditions (high or low situational control). In contrast, the opposite is true under moderately favorable or unfavorable conditions (moderate situational control).

The contingency model of leadership effectiveness

good relations with their subordinates, may shift their attention to task performance. Their efforts at providing guidance may then be perceived as needless meddling by their followers, and can, in fact, interfere with group performance. Turning to situations offering the leader *moderate* control, conditions are mixed, and attention to good interpersonal relations is often needed. High LPC leaders, with their strong interest in people, often have an important advantage in such cases. In contrast, low LPC leaders, who continue to focus on task performance, may adopt an autocratic, directive style, and so induce negative reactions among subordinates.

To repeat: Fiedler's theory predicts that low LPC (task-oriented) leaders will be more effective than high LPC (relations-oriented) leaders under conditions of either low or high situational control. In contrast, high LPC leaders will have the edge under conditions in which such control is moderate.

Contingency Theory: Its Current Status. Because it directs attention to characteristics of leaders, situational factors, and even the reactions of subordinates, Fiedler's theory is fully consistent with the modern, transactional approach described above. Where any scientific theory is concerned, though, the ultimate question must be: how does it fare when put to actual test? One review of more than 170 studies undertaken to test various aspects of Fiedler's framework indicates that most obtained positive results (Strube and Garcia, 1981). For example, Chemers et al. (1985) reasoned that leaders who were "out of match" with the conditions in their groups (e.g., low LPC leaders who enjoyed moderate control, or high LPC leaders who had high or low degrees of control) would experience greater job-related stress than leaders whose personal style matched these conditions (i.e., low LPC leaders with high or low control, high LPC with moderate control). Consistent with this reasoning, "out of match" university administrators and public school administrators reported higher levels of job stress and days missed from work (Chemers et al., 1985; Chemers, 1987).

At this point, we should note that not all findings have been consistent with the theory. In fact, a recent review suggests that while laboratory studies have tended to support Fiedler's view, field investigations (ones carried out with existing groups operating in a wide range of contexts) have not been as favorable in this respect (Peters, Hartke, and Pohlmann, 1985). Indeed, such investigations have sometimes yielded results contrary to what contingency theory would predict.

Taking all existing evidence into account, it appears that contingency theory can benefit from further development and refinement. At the same time, though, there is little doubt that it has added much to our understanding of leadership and leadership effectiveness (Chemers, 1987). In these respects, it certainly represents a major contribution, well worth considering.

SUMMARY

Groups often have very important effects on the attitudes and behaviors of their members. Perhaps the simplest type of this effect is **social facilitation**. This term refers to the effects of the presence of others on individuals' performance on various tasks. The presence of others increases arousal which, in turn, increases the tendency to perform our strongest responses to a given situation.

Groups working together sometimes outperform individuals and sometimes fail to equal individual performance. The type of task being performed (*additive, conjunctive,* or *disjunctive*) is crucial in determining what pattern emerges. When individuals' efforts are pooled, a phenomenon known as social loafing often results. Here, each individual puts out less effort than he or she would if contributing alone.

Groups make many key decisions. Often, these can be predicted by *social decision schemes*—simple rules relating the initial distribution of members' views to the final outcome.

The manner in which groups move toward agreement can be described by *social transition schemes,* which indicate the likelihood that group members will shift from one pattern of views to another. As a result of their deliberations, groups often demonstrate **group polarization**. That is, they shift toward more extreme positions. Decision-making groups are also subject to **groupthink**—a dangerous process in which group members perceive themselves as invulnerable and refuse to consider information contrary to their current views. An additional problem faced by decision-making groups is their apparent inability to pool unshared information.

Leaders are those members of a group who exert the most influence. At one time it was assumed that individuals rise to positions of leadership because they possess special traits (*great person theory*). Now it is realized that leadership stems from a complex interplay between leader characteristics, situational requirements, and follower preferences and perceptions (the *transactional view*). Many factors play a role in leader effectiveness. According to the *contingency theory* proposed by Fiedler, the most important of these involves a leader's personal style (whether he or she is mainly task- or relationship-oriented) and the degree of situational control enjoyed by the leader.

GLOSSARY

additive tasks Tasks for which group productivity represents the sum of individual members' efforts.

cohesiveness All the forces (positive and negative) that cause individuals to maintain their membership in specific groups. These include attraction to other group members and a close match between individuals' needs and the goals and activities of the group.

conjunctive tasks Tasks for which group productivity is determined by the effort or ability of the weakest member.

contingency theory of leader effectiveness A theory suggesting that leader effectiveness is determined both by characteristics of leaders and by several situational factors.

decision-making The process by which groups identify problems and attain solutions to them.

disjunctive tasks Tasks for which group performance is determined by the most competent or skilled member.

distraction-conflict theory of social facilitation An explanation for the occurrence of social facilitation effects. According to this view, the presence of others induces conflict between the tendencies to pay attention to these persons and to the task in hand. Such conflict increases arousal to perform dominant responses.

drive theory of social facilitation An explanation for the occurrence of social facilitation effects. According to this view, the mere presence of others induces arousal, which increases the tendency to perform dominant responses.

evaluation apprehension Concern over being evaluated by others. Such concern may increase arousal and may play an important role in social facilitation.

great person theory of leadership A theory suggesting that all great leaders share key traits that equip them for positions of power and authority.

group Two or more persons who interact with one another, share common goals, are interdependent, and recognize the existence of these relationships between them.

group influence The impact of groups on their members.

group polarization The tendency of group members to shift to more extreme positions than those they held initially, as a function of group discussion.

groupthink The tendency of members of highly cohesive groups led by dynamic leaders to adhere to shared views so strongly that they totally ignore external information inconsistent with these views.

leaders Those individuals in groups who exert the greatest influence on others.

leadership The process through which leaders exert their impact on other members.

risky shift The tendency for individuals to recommend riskier courses of action following group discussion than was true prior to such interaction.

situational approach to leadership The view that those members of a group most likely to become leaders are those who can best help it to reach its major goals.

social decision schemes Rules relating the initial distribution of member views to final group decisions.

social facilitation Effects on performance resulting from the presence of others.

social loafing The tendency of individuals performing a task to exert less effort on it when they work together with others than when they work alone.

social transition schemes Models describing the process through which groups move through different patterns of member views until they reach agreement or some decision.

transactional approach to leadership An approach suggesting that leadership involves a complex social relationship between leaders and followers in which each exerts influence on the other.

FOR MORE INFORMATION

FIEDLER, F. E., and GARCIA, J. E. (1987). *Leadership: Cognitive resources and performance.* New York: Wiley.

This book presents a thoughtful, well-written, and comprehensive overview of what we currently know about the complex process of leadership. Several topics that have only recently been studied in a systematic manner (e.g., the relationship between leaders' intelligence and group performance) are considered in detail. All in all, a valuable source to consult if you'd like to know more about this important process.

FORSYTH, D. R. (1983). *An introduction to group dynamics.* Monterey, Calif.: Brooks/Cole.

This excellent text examines many aspects of group functioning. The discussions of group performance and conformity are especially interesting.

HENDRICK, C. (Ed.). (1987). *Group processes.* Newbury Park, Calif.: Sage.

A collection of chapters covering specific topics on group process and group interaction. Each chapter is written by an expert and is quite up-to-date.

PRUITT, D. G., and RUBIN, J. Z. (1986). *Social conflict.* San Francisco: Random House.

A succinct overview of the psychological factors and processes that play a role in social conflict. The discussions of escalating or entrapping conflicts, and techniques for resolving ongoing disputes, are especially insightful.

Chapter Ten
Applying Social Psychology

HEALTH PSYCHOLOGY/The Social-Psychological Aspects of Health Care
The Development of Illness: The Role of Psychological Stress/Behavior That
Helps Prevent Illness/The Anatomy of an Illness Episode: From Symptoms
to Seeking Care/Once You're Ill: Interacting with Medical Personnel and
Undergoing Treatment

THE SOCIAL PSYCHOLOGY OF THE LEGAL SYSTEM
Eyewitness Testimony: The Whole Truth and Nothing but the Truth/The
Biasing Influence of Police, Attorneys, and the Judge/Defendants and Jurors:
Fairness and Unfairness Once Again

THE WORK SETTING/Organizational Behavior
Achieving Job Satisfaction and Assessing Its Effects/Performance Appraisal:
Attributions and Interventions/Increasing Productivity

Special Inserts
FOCUS ON RESEARCH/The Cutting Edge
    Coping with Surgery: Your Hospital Roommate Could Make a Difference
ON THE APPLIED SIDE
    Television in the Courtroom: A Controversial Issue
ON THE APPLIED SIDE
    The Effects of Quality Circles in Organizations: Does this Japanese Import
    Work Here?

As Dick entered the elevator with his parents, his father continued complaining as he had off and on for several days. "How could you have been dumb enough to go for a joyride in a stolen car with those hoodlum friends of yours? That Carl looks like a junky, and I'm not surprised the police stopped his car. They should have shot him and be done with it. And you, Mr. "A" student, with a case of beer on the floor and an open can in your fist! What kind of high school is it where you learn to act like this?"

Dick just shrugged and looked bored. His mother patted his arm and tried to calm down her husband. "Don't get excited, Joel. Let's all just wait to hear what the lawyer has to say."

The three of them got on the ninth floor and down the hallway to the offices of Morrison, Flanders, and Henson. The receptionist said that Mr. Henson was expecting them, and she led them to his book-lined office.

After introductions, the attorney asked many questions about the evening of the arrest and about the details of Dick's relationship with Carl. The most important element was Dick's assertion that he had no idea that the car in which he was riding had been stolen two days earlier. "I swear that I didn't know anything about any car theft. Carl told me he had saved up and bought it used."

The attorney looked at him steadily for several minutes. "I believe you, Dick, and I'll take the case. The next job is to convince a jury that you're telling the truth. We'll admit that you are guilty of consuming alcohol while below the legal drinking age in this state. The bigger problem is the charge of auto theft. That is a serious matter, and we'll have to fight it. Your 'friend' Carl has signed a statement implicating you."

Dick was clearly surprised and angry. "He's a liar."

"I think so, too, but we have a lot of work to do. Besides all of the information about what you were doing on the night of the theft, we have a rehabilitation project between now and the trial that will take place in three months."

"What do you mean?" Dick was puzzled.

"We have to overhaul your appearance. You will need to wear a suit and shine your shoes. You have to practice sitting up straight in your chair and saying 'yes, sir' and 'no, sir' when the judge and the prosecuting attorney ask you questions. The biggest task is to change your hair style. Punk may be popular among your friends, but the middle-aged jurors won't take kindly to spiked blond hair streaked with green dye. Take my word for it."

"Crud. What do my clothes or my hair have to do with whether I stole a car? Is it against the law to dress the way I want to?"

"Your clothes and hair have absolutely nothing to do with guilt or innocence. The issue is whether the jury, and to some extent the judge, believes you. If they like you and assume you are a polite, upstanding young man, they are more likely to believe you. Trust me when I say that they will respond much better to the image I suggested than to someone looking like a high school hood or refugee from a freak show. Your appearance and demeanor are crucial, though admittedly irrelevant, factors in their assessment of you."

"OK, if I have to."

Dick's father smiled for the first time in a long while.

Do you believe that Dick's clothes, manners, and hair style have anything to do with his credibility as a defendant? Throughout this book, we have discussed how first impressions, liking, and various interpersonal judgments are affected by a variety of factors. In this chapter, we will discuss how such reactions play a vital role in the courtroom and on the job. In addition, other quite different applications of social psychological research will be described.

As we have suggested throughout this book, social psychology does not begin or end in the laboratory. Nevertheless, when it is proposed that psychology can be applied to "real-world" problems, one of two reactions is frequently heard. Some think of psychological research as isolated from everyday concerns, and irrelevant, while others assume that applied psychology only involves psychotherapy with disturbed clients (Altmaier and Meyer, 1985). After reading the previous nine chapters, you know that neither perception is accurate.

Instead, basic research in social psychology leads rather naturally to application. Quite often, social psychologists wear two hats—one is that of the scientist who constructs theories based on empirical research, and the other is the hat of the behavioral engineer who uses his or her basic knowledge to solve practical problems outside the laboratory (Carroll, 1982). A sampling of some recent applied research appears in Table 10.1

Social psychologists exhibited an interest in application almost as soon as the field was established. For example, in 1899 William James pointed out how psychological findings could be utilized to improve education. In the 1930s and 1940s, Kurt Lewin (discussed in Chapter 1) was a strong advocate of **action research**—research that aims to understand and solve social problems. That tradition has continued, and many social psychologists devote their primary efforts to solving societal problems (Kiesler, 1985; Spielberger and Stenmark, 1985). Social psychology is useful in providing data relevant to issues as diverse as the improvement of day care for children and the evaluations of affirmative action policies (Shotland and Mark, 1985).

An increasing emphasis on application is reflected in the occupational shift of social psychologists away from academia and into applied settings. In the 1980s, a smaller portion of new Ph.D.s in social psychology are entering university positions (33 percent) than was true just a few years ago when 50 percent did so (Stapp and Fulcher, 1984). The majority of new social psychologists are now employed in hospitals, government agencies, business organizations, and other nonacademic institutions.

In this general context, we define **applied social psychology** as the utilization of social psychological principles and research methods in real-world settings in an attempt to solve societal problems (Weyant, 1986). The scope of this activity is sufficiently broad that we can cover only a small portion here. First, we will describe *health psychology* and the role of applied social psychology research in every aspect of health care from preventive medicine to coping with illness. Next, we will turn to the social psychology of the *legal system,* one of the earliest settings for applied research. Then we will examine the importance of psychology in the work setting as we discuss *organizational behavior.*

Table 10.1 *The findings of social psychologists have been applied to a wide variety of problems, as this brief sample indicates.*

The broad applications of social psychological knowledge

Questions to Which Applied Psychological Research Supplied Answers

What are the causes of overdrinking and other forms of substance abuse among adolescents? (Newcomb and Harlow, 1986)

Do newspaper crime stories increase the general fear of crime? (Heath, 1984)

Do hospital workers' attitudes about homosexuality affect their responses to AIDS patients? (O'Donnell et al., 1987)

Does crowding in prison influence the stressfulness and incidence of physical symptoms among inmates? (Ruback, Carr, and Hopper, 1986)

By emphasizing risk, can we increase automobile seatbelt use? (Weinstein, Grubb, and Vautier, 1986)

Does the way a persuasive appeal is phrased influence whether it encourages women to perform breast self-examination for early detection of malignant lumps? (Meyerowitz and Chaiken, 1987)

Does exclusion of jurors who are opposed to capital punishment create jurors who are "conviction-prone"? (Bersoff, 1987)

HEALTH PSYCHOLOGY: The Social-Psychological Aspects of Health Care

It is generally accepted that health and illness involve more than simply physical factors. We know, for example, that some personality variables may predispose an individual to having certain illnesses (Suls and Rittenhouse, 1987) and that the behavior of physicians can influence the course of recovery (Krantz, Grunberg, and Baum, 1985). **Health psychology** is the field that studies the psychological processes that affect the development, prevention, and treatment of physical illness (Taylor, 1985). Because health psychology is increasingly important, several graduate training programs have been developed with this specialized emphasis (Olbrisch et al., 1985). We now examine some of the ways in which social psychological research is relevant to medical issues.

The Development of Illness: The Role of Psychological Stress

In recent years it has become clear that life problems may take their toll not just on psychological well-being, but on physical health as well. In this section, we describe some recent contributions that health psychologists have made to understanding this process.

Life Stress and Illness. There is considerable evidence that life events that put a strain on a person's physical or psychological resources increase the subsequent risk of physical and psychological illness (Lazarus and Folkman, 1984). For example, the probability of becoming ill increases during the stress of exams (Dorian et al., 1982), following the death of a spouse (Schleifer et al., 1983), and as a consequence of other stressful events. Even minor everyday hassles (for example, commuter traffic, annoying co-workers) have negative effects on health (Weinberger, Hiner, and Tierney, 1987).

Stress may increase the chances of illness by several "routes." During stressful times, people are less likely to engage in preventive health measures such as maintaining a good diet or ex-

ercising (Wiebe and McCallum, 1986). Furthermore, there is growing evidence that the immune system which normally helps us to "fight off" infections is impaired when stress levels are high (Kiecolt-Glaser and Glaser, 1987; Stone et al., 1987). Such evidence has inspired a whole new interdisciplinary field—*psychoneuroimmunology*—which studies the relationships among stress, the mind, and the immune system. Below we consider some other psychological factors that influence a person's susceptibility to the illness-inducing effects of life stress.

Perceived Control and Pessimism. One of the reasons that negative life events can be so debilitating is that they threaten the basic human need to control events in one's life. People appear to have a need for **perceived control**. In Chapter Two we discussed how depression may result from feeling that important life events are beyond one's control. This also appears to be the case with physical illness; when events occur that are perceived as uncontrollable, subsequent illness is more likely to occur (McFarlane et al., 1983). As it turns out, some people more than others tend to perceive negative events as beyond their control and to believe that little can be done to improve the situation in the future. Persons with a pessimistic outlook report more symptoms subsequent to stressful events and also recover more slowly from heart bypass surgery (Scheier and Carver, 1987). Related studies also suggest that people with a pessimistic outlook tend to die at an earlier age than people with positive expectations (Peterson, Seligman, and Vaillant, 1988).

Type A Behavior and Heart Disease. Over the last thirty years, evidence has accumulated indicating that a certain behavioral style may increase a person's chances of developing heart disease (Friedman and Rosenman, 1959). This behavioral style, called the **Type A** coronary-prone behavior pattern, consists of excessive achievement-striving, competitiveness, hostility, and time urgency. In short, Type A individuals strive to achieve a lot, they like to win, and they become angry and impatient if their ambitious goals are frustrated. Individuals exhibiting this kind of behavior, especially the *anger compo-nent,* are twice as likely to suffer from heart dis-ease than their **Type B** counterparts, who show an absence of these behaviors (Dembroski and Costa, 1987; Matthews and Haynes, 1986).

What is it about a behavioral style emphasiz-ing competitiveness and hostility that increases the risk of heart disease? One possibility is that because of their commitment to work and achievement, Type A's ignore early symptoms of heart disease (such as chest pain) and don't re-lax or refer themselves for medical attention un-til it is too late. Another possibility is that Type A's are hyperreactive to life stresses or chal-lenges and this "reactivity" places a strain on the cardiovascular system. Consistent with this no-tion, research shows that Type A's tend to exhibit larger increases in blood pressure and heart rate in response to hard work and concentration or to angry provocation than do Type B individuals (Houston, 1983; Pittner, Houston, and Spiridi-gliozzi, 1983; Holmes, McGilley, and Houston, 1984). It should be clear to the reader that such evidence indicates there is a need to identify coronary-prone individuals and find ways to change this dangerous pattern of behavior.

Social Support and Coming to Terms with Past Trauma. Being in contact with friends or relatives—that is, having **social support**—can also make a difference in people's health. This seems to work in two ways (Cohen and Wills, 1985). First, people who have a social support network tend to be healthier in general, regard-less of whether stressful events have occurred or not. Second, when life problems do arise, friends provide needed resources to "buffer" the stress that often accompanies such problems. For example, if a person has been laid off or fired from his or her job, friends or relatives may provide material comforts as well as affection to help the person get through a bad time (Pilisuk, Boylan, and Acredolo, 1987; see Figure 10.1).

Confession or self-disclosure may also be good for health. Pennebaker (Pennebaker and Beall, 1986; Pennebaker, Hughes, and O'Heeron, 1987) proposes that failure to discuss traumatic or stressful events (for example, sexual abuse or divorce of parents) is physiologically harm-

Figure 10.1 Social support from friends and family provides significant health benefits. Their support is associated with better health in general and with "buffering" the effects of stress. In addition, confiding in others seems to be related to better health.

Friends: Valuable health resources

ful because holding back or inhibiting oneself about the event for fear of punishment or em-barrassment may place additional stress on the body. In several studies to test the "inhibition hypothesis," people who reported they never confided their traumas with anyone had more major and minor health problems (Pennebaker and O'Heeron, 1984). In a more direct test of the inhibition notion, subjects were asked to write about a personal traumatic event for twenty minutes daily for four days. Consistent with the inhibition hypothesis, the subjects who "con-fessed" reported fewer health visits and health problems in subsequent months than subjects who were not asked to confess (Pennebaker and Beall, 1986). These results suggest that the act of communicating one's problems may be beneficial.

Behavior That Helps Prevent Illness

It is obvious that preventing illness is preferable to treating illness. Though not all illnesses are preventable, many are. People are generally aware that exercise, avoidance of harmful substances—cigarettes, alcohol, hard drugs—and having timely medical checkups can help. Nevertheless, knowledge does not necessarily translate into behavior (as we saw in Chapter Four). Preventive behaviors take time and effort. As you may have observed, many people do not consistently make the effort to eat correctly, exercise, get regular medical checkups, or engage in other healthful activities (see Figure 10.2). Social psychologists have studied some of the reasons people do not perform preventive behaviors and how to lessen these maladaptive patterns.

Vulnerability and Effective Preventive Behavior. One reason that individuals may not engage in preventive behaviors is they tend to hold unrealistically optimistic beliefs about their health risks (Weinstein, 1987). For example, most people tend to feel that they themselves are less likely than their peers to suffer a heart attack or a drinking problem or that they could be a victim of a serious traffic accident. Furthermore, people have a tendency not to draw a connection between their behaviors—smoking, consumption of red meat or high cholesterol foods such as eggs—and the risk of a heart attack, for example. Thinking that one is invulnerable may be comforting over the short term, but, obviously, can have long-term negative effects if it discourages people from taking precautions.

The "illusion of invulnerability" may also partly be the result of the fact that health risks are ordinarily presented in very abstract statistical terms to people. As we saw in Chapter Three, people do not tend to use base-rate information of this kind. Instead, people may draw on

"I'll have an ounce of prevention."

Figure 10.2 An "ounce of prevention" can go a long way toward keeping people healthy. However, preventive health measures take time and effort. Despite what is depicted in this cartoon, they cannot be purchased. (Source: Drawing by Dana Fradon; © 1987 The New Yorker Magazine, Inc.)

Prevention: It can't be bought

personal experiences that challenge the medical evidence: "I know a man who smoked three packs of cigarettes a day and lived to be ninety-nine" (Rook, 1987). (The fallacy, of course, is that fifty other people smoked three packs a day and didn't live past fifty.)

Some Ways to Motivate Preventive Behavior: The Protection-Motivation Model. Fortunately, social psychologists are helping to find ways to motivate people to take preventive measures. In our society we see many public health messages on television and in the media. These have not always been effective, however, but one recent model, called **protection-motivation theory** (Rogers, 1983; Rippetoe and Rogers, 1987), proposes that persuasive appeals can increase preventive behavior if the message conveys four kinds of information. People should be informed that (1) the illness or disease is a severe one (*high threat*), (2) the individual is *vulnerable* to the threat, (3) specific behaviors are effective in preventing the occurrence of the threat (*high response efficacy*), and (4) the person can perform the preventive health behaviors (*self-efficacy*; see Figure 10.3). Rogers proposes that if a persuasive appeal contains these elements, the chances greatly increase that the individual will engage in relevant preventive behaviors.

In a study testing the protective motivation model's applicability for increasing physical exercise (Wurtele and Maddux, 1987), subjects read messages about the severity and potential threat of heart disease plus the health benefits of physical exercise. They then received instructions about how they could successfully maintain an exercise program. The results showed perceived vulnerability and self-efficacy were especially important factors contributing to subjects increasing their exercise levels. Similar results have been found for appeals to women to perform breast self-examination regularly in order to maximize the early detection of breast cancer (Rippetoe and Rogers, 1987). Thus, research using the protection-motivation model is helping to increase preventive behavior.

Preventing Cigarette Smoking Before It Starts. The evidence linking cigarette smoking and such diseases as lung cancer and heart disease is now well established, and most people are aware of the dangers of smoking (Eiser, 1983). Once the habit has formed, however, giving up an addictive substance is difficult, even when one firmly decides to quit (Abrams et al.,

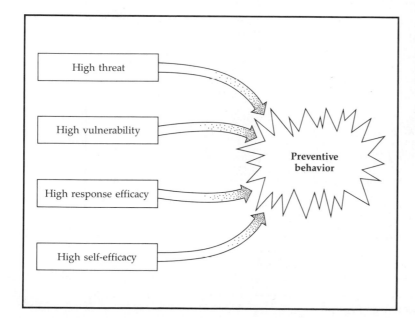

Figure 10.3 Rogers's protection-motivation model proposes that people are more likely to adopt preventive health measures if a persuasive appeal describes the four elements depicted in the diagram.

The protection-motivation model

High threat

High vulnerability

High response efficacy

High self-efficacy

Preventive behavior

1987; Shiffman and Jarvik, 1987). As a consequence, despite the importance of helping smokers give up the habit, it is perhaps even more important to prevent smoking from ever starting.

Recent health campaigns encourage children to say "no" to cigarettes to prevent the development of the addictive habit. Even so, recent studies show that the vast majority of children or adolescents "experiment" or try at least one cigarette. Some portion of them go on to become regular smokers. To mount a prevention effort, then, social psychologists have tried to identify those factors that encourage a youngster to continue to smoke after trying it. Survey studies reveal that children who are rebellious, feel

very helpless when confronted by any failure experience, or have friends or parents who smoke are the ones most likely to smoke on a regular basis (Hirschman, Leventhal, and Glynn, 1984; Eiser and van der Pligt, 1984; Collins et al., 1987). Surveys also show that adolescents have a number of misconceptions about smoking which may contribute to the addictive process (Leventhal, Glynn, and Fleming, 1987). For example, they overestimate the extent to which their peers and adults are smoking (see Figure 10.4). Perhaps youngsters' most serious misconception is that many believe that all it takes to quit is a little will power. Many report that they intend to smoke until they become addicted, at which

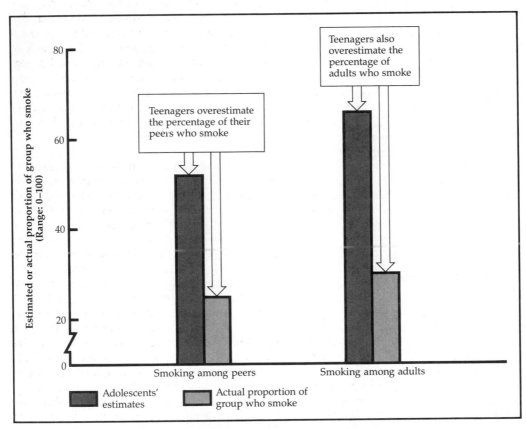

Figure 10.4 Adolescents tend to overestimate the proportion of their peers and adults who smoke. Such misconceptions contribute to the formation of the addictive habit. (Source: Based on data from Leventhal et al., 1987.)

Teenagers' misconceptions about smoking

point they will quit. But, "kicking the habit" takes considerable effort. On the basis of these findings, we think you can appreciate the need to provide youngsters with accurate information and skills to resist making cigarettes a habit.

In one prevention study, Canadian sixth-graders were selected as subjects on the basis of posing a high risk for becoming adult smokers (Flay et al., 1985). These young people either had powerful models for smoking behavior (parents or friends), or they were already smoking. The experimental group attended sessions that included information about the negative effects of smoking, training in skills designed to resist social influence, and encouragement to make a public no-smoking commitment to their classmates. A control group took part in a health educational program that omitted any consideration of smoking. The effectiveness of the program was evaluated after two and a half years had passed. Of the high-risk students who had not smoked at the beginning of the program, 75 percent in the experimental group had not smoked two and a half years later compared with 47 percent of the control group. These results suggest that learning how to resist pressures to smoke and receiving information about the effects of smoking can help prevent what some have called "slow motion suicide." While the success of such programs is a cause for optimism, we still have more to learn about to attain greater success.

The Anatomy of an Illness Episode: From Symptoms to Seeking Care

Almost all of us become ill from time to time. Though you may not think of psychological factors having much to do with your response to illness, processes of a psychological nature may be as important as the purely physical origins of the symptoms. We will examine aspects of the "psychology of symptoms" in the next section, and how it influences the decision to seek medical care.

Attending to Physical Symptoms. The degree to which we are conscious of internal bodily sensations varies widely. There are fa-

mous stories of soldiers severely wounded on the battlefield who were unaware of the apparent pain until they got back to the safety of their camp. Presumably, this is because their attention was on other things during the battle. In a less extreme vein, people who are introspective—who tend to think about themselves a lot—are more sensitive to internal sensations and tend to label even harmless physical sensations as potential signs of illness (Mcchanic, 1983). These individuals may represent the so-called "worried well" who use medical facilities unnecessarily because they overestimate the seriousness of minor symptoms and seek unneeded medical help (Wagner and Curran, 1984).

Mood may also influence our attention to symptoms. Depressed patients report a high frequency of physical symptoms. Even normal college students report more physical symptoms if they are placed in a negative mood by watching a sad or depressing film (Croyle and Uretsky, 1987). Presumably, a negative mood evokes memories for other negative states such as physical symptoms. These research studies suggest that attending to physical symptoms is obviously not purely a physical process.

Diagnosing Your Symptoms. Attention to physical changes is obviously the first step in diagnosis, but until such time as a person decides that symptoms indicate illness, he or she obviously will do nothing about seeking help. It appears that most people use a commonsense model of self-diagnosis (Leventhal, Nerenz and Steele, 1984). For example, a person who experiences a stomachache and vomiting may decide the problem is simply an intestinal virus that will soon go away. If the actual problem is more serious, such as a diseased appendix, the organ may burst before medical help is sought. Obviously, it is important to know the individual's commonsense model of symptoms to understand how he or she labels or interprets them.

Several examples of this mislabeling are found in recent research studies (Routh and Ernst, 1984). For example, a person's incorrect beliefs about a serious illness such as hypertension (chronically elevated blood pressure) can lead to avoidance of treatment altogether or to the failure to take medication (Meyer, Leventhal, and Gutman, 1985). Because there are no obvious detectable physical symptoms of this disorder, the person may decide the problem no longer exists. Mislabeling of symptoms has also been documented in elderly persons. One study (Prohaska et al., 1987) found that senior citizens associate some physical symptoms with simply getting old rather than as indicators of an underlying illness. As a result, they may fail to seek professional medical attention until it is too late to do anything about the disease.

Once You're Ill: Interacting with Medical Personnel and Undergoing Treatment

After a person decides he or she is ill and decides to seek treatment, it is necessary to undergo the frightening experience of visiting a physician and facing the possibility of painful procedures and a threatening diagnosis.

Doctor-Patient Interactions. Because of the anxiety and fear associated with medical visits, patients often forget to mention crucial symptoms and neglect to ask important questions: the result is dissatisfaction with the experience. This general problem can be overcome if patients are instructed to develop a series of questions before seeing a physician (Roter, 1984). After such preparation, they ask more questions, and as a result, are more likely to obtain more information about their care.

The behavior of physicians is also important. For example, research has found that doctors who are skilled in communicating and understanding their patients' nonverbal messages (see Chapter Two) tend to have patients who are more satisfied with their care and are more likely to comply with the doctors' recommendations (DiMatteo, Hays, and Prince, 1986). This is important because patients may not communicate all of their concerns in words. Physicians need to be able to "read" the patients' concern from their nonverbal gestures. Similarly, physicians need to be in control of their own nonverbal messages. After all, if a physician indicates undue anxiety, then the patient may "pick up" on it and become more upset than he or she is already. Evidence of this kind has inspired pro-

grams to teach physicians how to be more skilled in communicating and understanding nonverbal messages (Hays and DiMatteo, 1984).

Coping with Treatment. With many diagnostic and therapeutic procedures, the patient must undergo interventions that are intrusive, painful, and sometimes dangerous. The process of **coping** with such events refers to the behavior, feelings, and thoughts that make it possible to tolerate or even master the threat. Early in an illness, one of the best short-term strategies is to avoid thinking about the problem (Suls and Fletcher, 1985): stress is decreased if you don't admit that something is wrong. As the illness progresses, however, it is preferable to pay attention to it, to seek treatment, and to comply with treatment recommendations.

Perceived control plays as significant a role in coping with illness and treatment as it does in the development of illness. Apparently, one needs to find the appropriate balance. For example, Affleck et al. (1987) found that patients suffering from arthritis adapted better if they perceived that they had control over daily symptoms, *but* also perceived that their physicians had greater control over the long-term course of their disease. There are things patients can do on a daily basis to cope with their condition, so active participation makes sense. Patients are hardly in a position to evaluate what to do to obtain long-term improvement, however; in this instance, they must rely on the physician's expertise. So, patients' adaptation requires maintaining a balance between the need for a sense of control over their lives with their need to turn over treatment decisions to their health care providers.

Coping with intrusive medical procedures such as surgery can be facilitated by having health care professionals provide information beforehand about the procedures and sensations they will undergo (Johnson, 1984; Suls and Wan, 1988, in press). Such information provides a kind of "road map" for the patient and enables the patient to interpret the experience in a more accurate, less threatening manner. Even small children can cope with procedures that hurt if they know enough about what is going on (Jay et al., 1983). (Read the "Focus on Research" insert for discussion of some new research which

COPING WITH SURGERY: YOUR HOSPITAL ROOMMATE COULD MAKE A DIFFERENCE

Though no one wants to think about it, almost all of us will have to go to the hospital for surgery or undergo some invasive medical procedure in our lifetimes. As described earlier, providing information to patients about what to expect can be very helpful (Leventhal et al., 1988, in press; Suls and Wan, 1988, in press). These findings have been extended still further in an intriguing field experiment examining patients' recovery from coronary by-pass surgery. In general, hospital staff don't give a lot of thought to whom one has as a roommate before one goes into surgery. However, two social psychologists (Kulik and Mahler, 1987) proposed that one's preoperative roommate assignment could be important. They reasoned that patients would adapt better if they had a room-mate who had just gone through surgery rather than one who like themselves was also waiting to be operated on. The logic for this pre-diction was that patients would learn more information about what to expect through observation and interaction with some-one who had already undergone surgery.

In a study testing this hypothe-sis, the researchers studied the rate

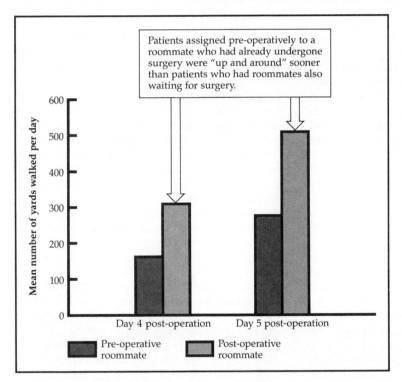

Figure 10.5   These results show that surgery patients who prior to surgery had been assigned to a roommate who had already gone through surgery walked more after surgery (a measure of recovery) than patients who had roommates who were also waiting for surgery. Other results indicate that having a postoperative roommate is associated with less anxiety, less medication, and an earlier departure from the hospital. The explanation provided is that the benefits come from learning about what to expect through observation and interaction with someone who has already gone through the operation. (Source: Based on data from Kulik and Mahler, 1987.)

Your hospital roommate can make a difference!

of recovery of patients who had been randomly assigned either to a room with someone like themselves waiting for surgery (preoperative roommate) or someone who had already been operated on (postoperative roommate). Several measures of adaptation were taken such as the patient's mood and amount of pain medication they used. On all of these indicators, the patients with *post-operative* roommates showed better adaptation after the surgery in terms of better mood, less anxiety, and decreased need for medication. The researchers also measured how much the patient walked after surgery (a measure of rate of recovery). As indicated in Figure 10.5, those with a postoperative roommate prior to surgery did more walking after surgery than those with a preoperative roommate. Perhaps most dramatically, the former group left the hospital on the average a day earlier.

Given that hospital costs are $1,000 or more a day, this study indicates that a simple change in roommate assignment could produce huge financial savings and simultaneously reduce the physical and psychological costs to the patient. This is just one example of how social psychological research on medical issues may advance knowledge and provide health benefits.

---

may lead to advances in the adaptation of surgery patients.)

It becomes clear from even a brief sampling of health psychology that psychological factors are involved in every aspect of health from preventive behavior to dealing with illness and its treatment. We will now turn from social psychological concerns with health to concerns with the legal system and what happens in the courtroom.

THE SOCIAL PSYCHOLOGY OF THE LEGAL SYSTEM

Our legal system is designed to yield objective, unbiased decisions based on a set of rules and procedures. Research in the field of **forensic psychology** indicates that human beings do not always conform to such idealistic principles. Whenever people interact, their behavior and their judgments are affected by factors such as attitudes, cognitions, and emotions (see Figure 10.6). We will describe how these variables affect the major participants in the courtroom—witnesses, police, judges, attorneys, and defendants.

Eyewitness Testimony: The Whole Truth and Nothing but the Truth

Anyone who has witnessed a crime, an accident, or any kind of event that is important in a trial swears to tell the truth about what he or she has seen or heard. Unfortunately, we have known for some time that even the most honest and well-meaning citizen may be extremely inaccurate when testifying (Wells and Murray, 1983). Even the ability to point out the guilty individual among others in a line-up (see Figure 10.7) is notoriously inadequate. In one experiment, for example, subjects were shown a televised film of a mock crime (Buckhout, 1980). Only 14.1 percent selected the correct person as the criminal in a line-up of six—a figure no greater than would be expected by chance. You may think that eyewitness inaccuracy is restricted to artificial laboratory settings and that people witnessing real crimes would do a better job. Sadly enough, accuracy is no better for a real than for a staged event (Murray and Wells, 1982). It should be acknowledged, however, that while witnesses tend not to be good at identifying the criminal, they do better in remembering other details of the crime (Yuille and Cutshall, 1986).

Both the courts and attorneys are aware that eyewitnesses are frequently in error. Nevertheless, the U.S. Supreme Court has ruled that eyewitnesses who express certainty about their testimony could be considered more credible than those who are uncertain. Unfortunately, research shows that the relationship between eyewitness confidence and eyewitness accuracy is relatively small (Bothwell, Deffenbacher, and Brigham, 1987; Fleet, Brigham, and Bothwell, 1987; Yarmey, 1986).

Given the consistent inaccuracy of eyewitness testimony, you might conclude that jurors

Figure 10.6 The legal system is designed to produce objective and fair judgments, but research shows that psychological factors act to interfere with objectivity and fairness at each step of the process. In this cartoon, the jurors appear to have perceived the trial as dramatic entertainment. (Source: Drawing by Cheney; © 1988 The New Yorker Magazine, Inc.)

Psychological factors can bias fair and objective judgments

"Your Honor, the jury finds the defendant weakly developed as a central character, overshadowed by the principal witness, unconvincingly portrayed as a victim of society, and guilty as charged."

Figure 10.7 Witnesses are often asked to identify the individual who committed a crime by selecting that person from a group assembled in a line-up. Such identifications are often quite inaccurate, but there are procedures that improve witness performance.

Identifying the guilty person in a line-up

have learned to ignore this type of evidence. Research by Lindsay et al. (1986) indicates, however, that such testimony has a striking effect on verdicts. In a mock jury situation, all aspects of a purse snatching were held constant, but in one condition, there was no eyewitness testimony, in another condition a single eyewitness identified the defendant as the thief, and in the third condition two eyewitnesses both identified the defendant as the guilty party. When there were two eyewitnesses, almost 50 percent of the jurors decided the defendant was guilty. When only one eyewitness identified him, a third of the jurors gave a guilty verdict. In contrast, only 10 percent of the jurors found the defendant guilty if there was no eyewitness testimony. Clearly, then, eyewitness testimony has a strong impact on judicial decisions.

Furthermore, if eyewitnesses act as though they are sure of their testimony (speak without hesitation, for example) or *say* they are confident in their testimony (despite the fact that we know, as mentioned earlier, that the relationship between confidence and accuracy is modest), jurors give them more credibility (Whitley and Greenberg, 1986).

Because correct identification of a criminal depends on accurately perceiving and then remembering the person's appearance, wrongdoers often attempt to alter how they look before appearing in a line-up. Research suggests that such tactics do confuse witnesses (Cutler, Penrod, and Martens, 1987). Furthermore, a witness may misidentify an innocent victim who happens to be wearing the same kind of clothing the suspect wore during the crime (Sanders, 1984a).

It is obviously very important to attempt to overcome the problem of inaccurate witnesses. One approach is to provide witnesses with practice and to sensitize them to the dangers of making incorrect decisions. The "training" of witnesses is accomplished by using a blank line-up before the actual identification must be made (Wells, 1984). Witnesses are shown a line-up composed entirely of innocent volunteers. Those who discover they have incorrectly identified one of these persons as the suspect are much more accurate when presented with the

actual line-up containing the suspect. This pretreatment seems to act as a learning experience that sharpens the witness's memory for the crucial characteristics of the suspect.

A second approach is to "reinstate the context" when the witness makes an identification. That is, subjects are exposed (via a series of photographs) to the victim and context surrounding the crime in an attempt to evoke sharper recall of the crime perpetrator. This approach, too, has had some success in increasing the identification accuracy (Cutler et al., 1987). (Before reading on, refer to the "On the Applied Side" insert for a discussion of a recent practice that may influence whether certain serious crimes ever come to trial.)

The Biasing Influence of Police, Attorneys, and the Judge

A trial is shaped in many ways by the behavior of the police, the opposing attorneys, and of the judge. The police gather evidence, help find witnesses, and, on occasion, testify themselves. Attorneys decide who will testify, what questions will be asked, and how the total case is to be summarized for the jury. The judge presides over the scene, rules on the admissibility of evidence, and explains the case and law to the jury. These various acts each serve to influence the decision of the jurors, as has been shown in applied social research.

The Police—Questions That Lead to Inaccuracy. One function that the police serve is to question eyewitnesses at the scene of the crime. The form these questions take could be important. Loftus (1980) has shown that questions can be worded in such a way as to mislead people by providing information that is inconsistent with what they actually witnessed. It was found that subjects who were asked **leading questions** tended during subsequent questioning to report false information contained in the leading questions. For example, an unbiased question might be, "Did the guy have a gun?" The leading version would be, "What did the guy's gun look like?" The latter is leading because it suggests that the individual definitely had a gun.

ON THE APPLIED SIDE

TELEVISION IN THE COURTROOM: A CONTROVERSIAL ISSUE

In recent years a number of states have passed legislation permitting courtroom trials to be televised. In part, this change was initiated so that the judicial process would be open to the public (Lindsay, 1984). Others have argued that electronic media coverage of the courtroom trials is simply another expression of freedom of the press. Nonetheless, concerns have been raised about the effects of bringing television into the courtroom. Some of these concerns were highlighted by the gang rape of a woman in Big Dan's Bar in New Bedford, Massachusetts. The subsequent rape trial became a media event when the Cable News Network broadcast the proceedings on national television.

Questions were raised about how media coverage might put undue strain on the victim and discourage other women from reporting a rape if they believe that television coverage would only add to the trauma of rape. On the other hand, the public might be-

lieve that televising the trial would raise people's awareness about rape and increase reporting.

Two social psychologists, Janet Swim and Eugene Borgida (1987), conducted a survey of a representative sample of residents of Minneapolis and St. Paul concerning beliefs about the television coverage of courtroom trials. The survey indicated that 85 percent of those surveyed disapproved of televising rape cases. These individuals were reluctant to extend freedom of the press to televised rape trials. They also felt that television disrupts the trial process and increases the victim's trauma. It appears, then, that people generally do not approve of the extension of television, at least, to certain kinds of courtroom cases.

Perhaps of greatest significance, 63 percent of the women polled said that knowledge that some rape trials are televised would discourage them from reporting a rape. Many also felt that television coverage would only cause a rape

victim additional trauma. Of probable relevance is the fact that the number of rapes reported to the police dropped from 30 to 0 percent in New Bedford during the televising of the trial.

It is noteworthy that since the New Bedford case, several states have prohibited coverage of rape trials. In still other states, television coverage is not permitted without the victim's consent. Nonetheless, it seems unlikely that more than a minority of rape victims know the law in their state prior to reporting rape. Public education efforts aimed at informing women about changes in how the legal system treats victims of sexual assault need to be expanded. In a more general way, the present example illustrates how social psychological research can expand our knowledge of the way in which legal and technological changes (such as electronic media coverage of court cases) are viewed by the public and in what ways these changes may alter their behavior.

In a study testing whether leading questions influence police interrogation, Smith and Ellsworth (1987) had subjects watch a videotape of a bank robbery; then they were questioned about the crime. One-half of the subjects were questioned by a confederate who was described as very knowledgeable about the crime (*knowledgeable questioner*). The other half were questioned by a confederate who was described as unfamiliar with the crime (*naive questioner*). In addition, half of each group were asked leading questions ("Where was the getaway car parked?") or nonleading questions ("Was there a getaway car?").

As shown in Figure 10.8, unbiased questions tended to produce relatively low error rates, regardless of whether a knowledgeable or naive questioner asked the questions. However, lead-

ing questions greatly reduced subjects' accuracy when the questioner was assumed to be knowledgeable about the crime. Apparently, interrogators may unintentionally plant information if witnesses believe their questioners are knowledgeable. This means that there is a real potential for increased witness inaccuracy in many situations. One practical application is that police officers should avoid suggesting to witnesses that they already know something about the crime. Under these circumstances, even if a misleading question is asked, the accuracy of the witness's report is less likely to suffer.

The Attorney: Advocate or Foe—and for Whom? Lawyers obviously play a crucial role in the courtroom. Psychological factors also influence their performance and effectiveness. For

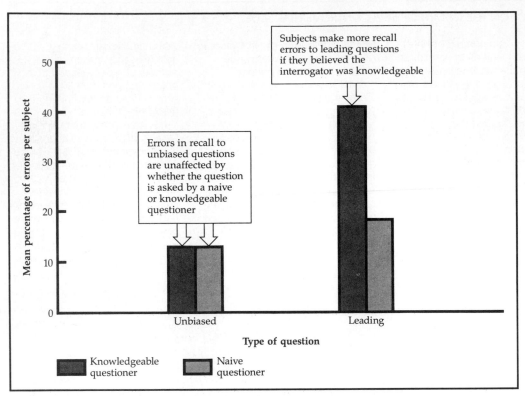

Figure 10.8 *When subjects were asked unbiased questions ("Was there a getaway car?"), they made approximately the same number of errors whether the questioner was knowledgeable or naive. However, when asked leading questions ("Where was the getaway car parked?"), subjects interrogated by the knowledgeable questioner made more errors than subjects interrogated by the naive questioner. Apparently, subjects only accept misleading information as accurate and modify their memories of the event when the questioner is considered credible. (Source: Based on data from Smith and Ellsworth, 1987.)*

Leading questions: A threat to eyewitness accuracy

example, just as police officers can increase witness inaccuracy by using leading questions, so can attorneys if witnesses are uncertain in their initial impressions (Loftus, 1980). Thus, if an attorney asks a witness a leading question such as, "What kind of hat was the thief wearing?" this may plant the idea that the thief wore a hat even if he or she didn't.

What is asked not only influences the witness, but also the perceptions of the jury. When questioning their own witnesses, attorneys tend to ask for direct information such as, "Tell me exactly what happened on the afternoon of September 20th." During cross-examination, witnesses for the other side tend to be asked closed questions such as, "You left the door open, didn't you" (McGaughey and Stiles, 1983). Jurors tend to perceive the witness as being less competent and less credible when closed questions are asked.

The Judge: An Impartial Referee? Judges as well as lawyers can behave in ways that affect the outcome of a trial. For example, during a trial the judge rules as to whether jurors may consider certain evidence—it may be admissible or inadmissible (Carretta and Moreland, 1983). Because judges have the final word in explaining the meaning of evidence to the jury, they can also influence the outcome at that point in the trial. For example, when judges attack the credibility of a key witness on one side or another, the final verdict can be affected (Cavoukian and Doob, 1980). Though these various problems can be solved by having totally objective and unbiased judges presiding over trials, it is difficult to imagine how anyone could truly fit that description.

In a much more subtle way, a judge is found to convey his or her attitudes about a defendant through tone of voice (Goleman, 1986). In a study of actual trials, when judges were aware of a defendant's past felonies (and the jurors were not), the final instructions to the jury were lacking in warmth, tolerance, and patience. Even though jurors were unaware of any biases held by the judges, the verdicts in these instances were twice as likely to be "guilty" as those for other defendants who had no felonies on their records.

There are also substantial differences among judges in the general levels of punishment they levy against defendants found guilty. In a study investigating factors associated with different levels of sentencing, Carroll et al. (1987) found that judges generally fall into one of two categories. One type believes that sentencing should be done in the interest of rehabilitation. Such judges also tend to emphasize the social or economic causes of crime and tend to be optimistic that government can correct social problems. The other type of judge believes sentencing should be done for punishment or retribution; they tend to perceive the individual as the cause of crime rather than societal conditions. Clearly, judges with the second orientation may tend to render harsher punishment than a judge who believes sentencing is primarily for rehabilitation and that societal conditions such as poverty are partially responsible for criminal behavior.

Defendants and Jurors: Fairness and Unfairness Once Again

When you read about research involving prejudice, attraction, attributions, and so forth, you might keep in mind that these variables are also operating in the courtroom. Though race, attitude similarity, attractiveness, and related factors have nothing to do with the merits of a given case, research shows that they nevertheless affect the outcome of both real and simulated trials.

The Defendants: Are They Treated Equally? A clear example of a powerful but supposedly irrelevant characteristic is the physical attractiveness of the person on trial. Attractive defendants tend to be acquitted more often than unattractive ones (Michelini and Snodgrass, 1980), and when found guilty, they receive lighter sentences (Stewart, 1980). Juries not only respond positively to an attractive victim, but they also are more sympathetic to an attractive defendant (Kerr, 1978a). Because attorneys are aware of such biases, they often advise their clients to go to great lengths to improve their appearance. Since the idea of a trial as a beauty contest is not a very appealing one, various suggestions have been made as to how to overcome these effects. Attractiveness has been found to be less powerful if a sufficient amount of factual information is presented to the jury (Baumeister and Darley, 1982), and if the judge explicitly reminds the jury of the basis on which the verdict should be reached (Weiten, 1980).

The race of a defendant is also found to affect the verdict that is reached. Many factors may play a role in affecting responses to blacks versus whites in the courtroom (prejudice, social class, differential crime rates, etc.), but the outcome is clearly one in which black defendants in the United States are at a disadvantage. Blacks are more likely to be convicted and more likely to receive a prison sentence than whites (Stewart, 1980). The race of the victim also plays a role. In the United States, criminals who kill white victims have a 11.1 percent chance of receiving a death sentence, while those who kill a black have only a 4.5 percent chance of such a sentence (Henderson and Taylor, 1985).

Jurors and Their Biases. One influence on the decisions of juries is the crime itself; another is the punishment for that crime. In effect, jurors may differ with the law about the seriousness of a given crime and about the appropriateness of a given punishment. When cases involve unpopular laws, such as Prohibition in the 1920s or anti-marijuana laws today, jurors tend to vote for acquittal. Decisions are also based on the severity of the punishment. Though many individuals seem to feel that crime can be discouraged by passing increasingly harsh laws, research shows that the more severe the prescribed punishment, the less likely jurors are to vote for conviction (Kerr, 1978b).

Personality differences also can affect the decisions of jurors. For example, jurors high in **dogmatism** tend to make different kinds of decisions than those low in dogmatism. Persons high in dogmatism have a strong respect for authority and an intolerance for the unconventional. Those low in dogmatism are less respectful of authority and more accepting of the unconventional. It might be expected that dogmatic jurors would generally tend to be severe in their verdicts, and indeed this seems to be the case (Mitchell and Byrne, 1973; Bartol, 1983). Recently, research has examined whether this tendency is only exhibited under certain circumstances.

Shaffer, Plummer, and Hammock (1986) had high and low dogmatic subjects (identified by an inventory) consider a transcript of a case concerning a defendant accused of a purse-snatching incident in which the legal evidence was heavily weighted toward guilt. One-half of the subjects learned that the defendant had suffered an injury (gunshot wound) during the incident (crime-relevant suffering), while the other half learned the incident occurred when the accused was out on bail awaiting the trial (crime-irrelevant suffering). The question was whether dogmatic subjects would take the defendant's suffering as a sign that he is a particularly unscrupulous person deserving of punishment and render an even harsher sentence, or whether the fact that he already had suffered as a result of the crime would prompt them to recommend a more lenient sentence.

As indicated in Figure 10.9, dogmatic and nondogmatic subjects did not disagree about the length of sentence when the accused's suffering was irrelevant to the crime. However, nondogmatic subjects were more lenient when he was injured at the crime scene. Presumably, this was because they saw the defendant as already suffering as a result of his actions. In contrast, the dogmatic subjects had less sympathy for the defendant when his suffering stemmed directly from his involvement in a crime. The severer punishment the dogmatic subjects recommended may reflect their seeing the accused's pretrial suffering at the crime as a sign of his unscrupulous nature deserving of extreme punishment. These results also may have an important practical implication. Some attorneys are known to use a defendant's pretrial suffering to play on jurors' sympathies. These results suggest, however, that such a tactic could lead to harsher treatment of the accused, at least from certain jurors.

An even more serious problem is the fact that in murder cases in states having the death penalty, juries are ordinarily selected so as to eliminate anyone who is opposed to that punishment. The jurors in such cases are termed "death-qualified." This creates a problem because psychological research has consistently shown that death-qualified jurors are more likely to convict a defendant than are jurors who oppose the death penalty (Turkington, 1986; Bersoff, 1987). The U.S. Supreme Court has decided that a defendant can have a fair trial, even when the jury is composed of individuals with a set of beliefs that are known to be associated with decisions favoring the prosecution. One counterproposal to eliminate this bias is to let the guilt or innocence of accused murderers be decided by juries that are *not* death-qualified. Afterward, decisions about how to punish the guilty could be made by jurors who accept that particular law.

In summary, applied research on the legal system provides convincing evidence that psychological factors influence witnesses, jurors, and responses to defendants, police, attorneys, and judges. One conclusion is that additional effort is needed to make our legal system as fair and objective as we wish it to be.

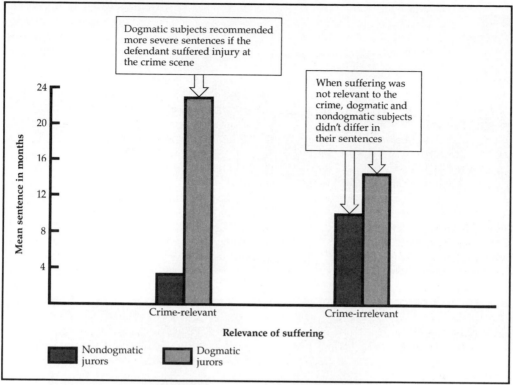

Figure 10.9 When a defendant experienced pretrial suffering (a gunshot wound) at the crime scene, dogmatic jurors recommended more severe prison sentences than did nondogmatic jurors. In contrast, when the suffering was not connected to the crime, both dogmatic and nondogmatic jurors recommended a moderate sentence. (Source: Based on data from Shaffer, Plummer, and Hammock, 1986.)

Juror dogmatism makes a difference

THE WORK SETTING: Organizational Behavior

As you might guess from earlier descriptions of social psychological research dealing with such topics as leadership (Chapter Nine), the applications of our field to behavior in organizations are widespread. A large portion of the lives of many adults is spent working at a job outside of the home, within organizations. Experiences working in organizations can provide important sources of satisfaction and dissatisfaction. Our behavior and the behavior of co-workers and supervisors can obviously have strong effects on us. Thus, the study of **organizational behavior** has broad consequences for both employees and employers (R. A. Baron, 1986b). This field seeks to understand and predict human behavior in organizational settings by means of the scientific study of individuals, groups, and the structure and function of organizations (see Figure 10.10). In the following sections, we will discuss how social psychological research has helped to understand and help to improve behavior in the work setting.

Figure 10.10   Most adults spend a large portion of their working hours at jobs outside of the home, within organizations. The photographs provide an indication of the diversity of some of these work situations. The study of organizational behavior involves learning about the factors that influence motivation of employees, job satisfaction, productivity, and other aspects of behavior within organizations.

On-the-job behavior

Achieving Job Satisfaction and Assessing Its Effects

A prospective employee's first contact with an organization occurs during the job interview. At that point, the employer desires to hire the employee most suitable for a particular position in that specific organization.

Selecting the Right Employee. The better the fit between employee and job, the greater will be that person's eventual job satisfaction and productivity (Hunter and Schmidt, 1983). As you might expect from the research on attraction (Chapter Six), the interpersonal decision to hire or not hire can be on the basis of liking rather than on logical grounds related to job suitability. For example, the applicant's physical attractiveness (Cash and Kilcullen, 1985; Jackson, 1983) and the interviewer's mood (R. A. Baron, 1986a) are factors that *should* be irrelevant but have been found to affect hiring decisions.

Of course, job-relevant characteristics also have an effect on which individuals are given jobs. For example, those who are most skilled at interpersonal communication are more likely to obtain high-level managerial positions than those who do not communicate well (Sypher and Sypher, 1983).

Increasing Job Satisfaction. It is generally accepted that **job satisfaction** is beneficial to the worker and perhaps to the organization. As you might suspect, perceptions of one's work as stressful or rewarding depend, in part, on actual job conditions (LaRocco, 1985). Satisfaction with work may not necessarily increase productivity (Musialowski, 1986; Nelkin and Brown, 1984), but it is nevertheless widely accepted that job satisfaction should ideally be maximized (Lawler, 1982). A general finding is that satisfaction is greater when employees possess an adequate amount of information about such matters as promotion policies and the way their performance is rated (Penley, 1982).

One possibility for increasing satisfaction is to make jobs more interesting by introducing variety into routine tasks and by giving the worker more control over what he or she does on the job. Such changes are known as **job enlarge-** ment. A widely known example of this approach was carried out in Sweden's Volvo plant. Both labor and management responded positively to job enlargement, and the quality of the product improved—however, overall productivity *decreased* (Gyllenhammer, 1977).

Another attempt to increase satisfaction is through the use of flexibile time schedules (**flexitime**). It is found that greater freedom in deciding when to work leads to a decrease in absenteeism, but job satisfaction is not necessarily improved (Narayanan and Nath, 1982).

Beyond the details of the job itself, satisfaction is positively related to the extent to which the individual feels **organizational commitment** (Coombs, 1979). An employee is committed to an organization to the extent that he or she feels involved, loyal, and able to identify with the company ("one of the family"; see Figure 10.11). Commitment increases when workers are high in the need to achieve and when they are given some degree of responsibility. Because of the success of Japanese firms in generating such commitment, many American firms have been trying to adopt their techniques. Thus, Japanese practices such as providing job security and encouraging identification (using company songs, wearing identifiable clothing or insignia, etc.) are being imported into the United States (Kupferberg, 1980). (For discussion of another employee-participation procedure imported from Japan and how well it works in the United States, read the "On the Applied Side" insert on page 263.)

Performance Appraisal: Attributions and Interventions

In the discussion of attribution theory in Chapter Two, we pointed out that people tend to explain the behavior of others in terms of external and internal causes. These same processes operate when another person's job performance is being evaluated. We will evaluate some of the factors affecting such judgments and some of the techniques used in the attempt to improve performance.

Judging How Well a Job Is Done. An obvious element influencing evaluations is how

"We're just like one big happy family here."

Figure 10.11 Employees feel committed to an organization to the degree they feel involved, loyal, and able to identify with a company. However, in this cartoon things were probably carried a bit too far (Source: Drawing by Richter; © 1987 The New Yorker Magazine, Inc.)

Organizational commitment: An extreme example

well an individual actually performs a task. For example, business managers tend to give the largest salary increases to those whose objective performances are best (Alexander and Barrett, 1982). No one finds fault with this criterion. The problem arises when subjective variables, such as attributions, come into play.

For example, the evaluator who has not had first-hand experience with the job in question may give undue credit to the employee who performs well and place undue blame on those who are having difficulty (Mitchell and Kalb, 1982). In general, a supervisor's blame for poor performance tends to rest on attributions about the worker (skill, motivation) rather than on the role of situational determinants of performance (Gioia and Sims, 1985). Heerwagen, Beach, and

Mitchell (1985) have shown that it is possible to alter attributions by stressing the importance of situational factors.

There is also a tendency to reward hard work and effort to a greater extent than skill (Knowlton and Mitchell, 1980). An employee is evaluated more highly if he or she is perceived as expending a lot of energy on the job than if perceived as being talented and taking it easy.

Effects of Initial Decisions on Subsequent Evaluations. In most organizations, performance is rated periodically—perhaps once or twice a year. Theoretically, this means that the evaluator must pay attention to performance during the intervening time period, judge that performance, and remember it accurately when

ON THE APPLIED SIDE

THE EFFECTS OF QUALITY CIRCLES IN ORGANIZATIONS:
DOES THIS JAPANESE IMPORT WORK HERE?

One employee-participation procedure widely practiced in Japan that is now being applied elsewhere is the concept of **quality circles** (Lawler and Mohrman, 1985; Marks, 1986). This idea was actually inspired by an American, H. Edwards Deming, who lectured in post–World War II Japan about ways to increase production quality. In this procedure, individuals who are engaged in similar work in an organization meet voluntarily once a week (or more) to discuss problems on the job and to suggest solutions (see Figure 10.12). At the heart of the quality circle (QC) concept is the assumption that the person who performs a job is the one who knows best how to identify and correct its problems. Thus, instead of the traditional American approach to management that relies on a special department to propose ways for workers to maintain or improve quality, the QC involves those persons closest to the particular work domain—the workers themselves.

Japanese industry has used the QC procedure with great success since the 1950s, and it has been credited, in part, for the rise of Japan as a major producer of manufactured goods for the rest of the world. Initially, American companies were reluctant to adopt QCs, but recession in the 1970s and loss of sales to Japanese products prompted reconsideration. In 1977 only five companies had QC programs, but the number of quality circles has grown to well over 25,000 in the United States (Barra, 1983), and the trend is increasing (Marks, 1986).

The question is whether QCs are actually effective: are employees who participate in QCs more satisfied with their jobs and more committed to the organization? And do QCs generate more useful solutions than the traditional organizational arrangements in which supervisors or special departments generate solutions to problems?

One recent review found that nearly one-half of the studies conducted to assess the effectiveness of QCs found uniformly positive results. QCs were associated with more and better solutions and with improved worker attitudes (Barrick and Alexander, 1987). But what about the failures? It appears that QCs take some time to become effective. QCs that last only a few months show few positive outcomes. There appear to be real gains, however, after the procedure has been implemented for four to eight months. These results suggest that managers would do well to take a long-term rather than a short-term perspective.

Of course, just like any other organizational change, QCs cannot be effective if they are not backed by genuine management commitment. For example, if management consistently refuses to accept the QC's recommendation or responds unenthusiastically, QC participants may become discouraged (Lawler and Mohrman, 1985). Also, QCs can become victims of their own success. Having dealt successfully with key problems, there may be no major problems left, so they decide to disband. But regardless of these cautions, by increasing employee participation, QCs do appear to have positive consequences. One expects that they will become an increasingly essential part of organizations into the next century.

Figure 10.12 Quality circles, such as the one depicted here, have been used in the United States with the hope that increased employee participation will increase satisfaction and productivity. The verdict is still "out" on how effective they can be in these respects.

Quality circles: Increasing employee participation

performance appraisal is required. In actual practice, appraisal is usually not a very salient issue most of the time, and anything that interferes with attention or memory will make the appraisal less accurate and less fair.

One major source of interference concerns the initial context in which the evaluator obtains performance information. Williams et al. (1986) found that if a rater initially is given the task of designating one worker out of a group for a special reward rather than rate all for deservingness, the rater tends to be unable to later recall differentiations among the nonselected workers. Failing to make distinctions between those lower in proficiency might lead to inaccurate feedback and also produce hard feelings on the part of some workers.

Responses to Performance Evaluation. In general, subordinates consider their own work performance as "above average" (Meyer, 1975) and rate themselves as higher in job performance than do their supervisors (Ilgen, Fisher, and Taylor, 1979). Hence, it should come as no surprise that employees prefer to receive and tend to believe positive feedback more than negative feedback (Bannister, 1979). Nonetheless, negative feedback can be debilitating (Larsen, 1986; see Figure 10.13).

Informal observation and recent research indicate that the manner in which negative feedback or criticism is given by supervisors is a major cause of conflicts in organizations (Weisinger and Lobsenz, 1981; Baron, 1988). Often, persons in authority criticize subordi-

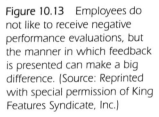

Figure 10.13 Employees do not like to receive negative performance evaluations, but the manner in which feedback is presented can make a big difference. (Source: Reprinted with special permission of King Features Syndicate, Inc.)

Negative performance evaluations

nates only when upset or angry. As a result, supervisors provide **destructive criticism**—feedback that tends to be vague (rather than focused on specific behaviors) and inconsiderate; they often attribute poor performance to internal causes such as lack of motivation or ability. This kind of feedback can be contrasted to **constructive criticism**—which, in reaction to the same worker performance, focuses on specific behaviors, is delivered in a considerate tone, and

attributes performance to external factors (such as task difficulty or working conditions).

In a study of the effects of constructive versus destructive feedback, Baron (1988) had subjects work on an ad campaign for a new product. Subsequently, subjects received either destructive or constructive feedback about their performance. As shown in Figure 10.14, subjects who received destructive criticism were angrier and rated their ability as lower than subjects who received

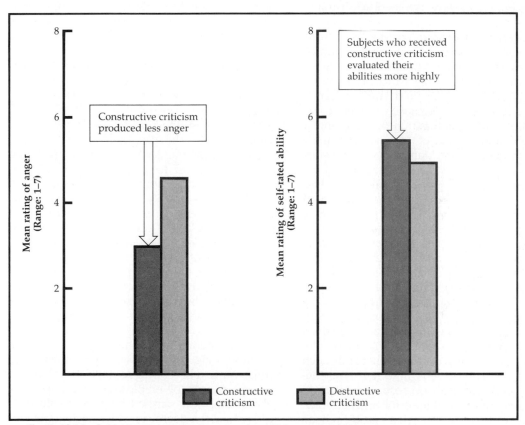

Figure 10.14 *Subjects who received constructive criticism about their work were less angry and evaluated their abilities more highly than subjects who received destructive criticism. Related results show that destructive criticism is also likely to lead employees to avoid their supervisors in the future and to set lower performance goals for the future. Given the negative effects of destructive criticism, managers should try to avoid this mode of communication. (Source: Based on data from Baron, 1988.)*

Destructive criticism: A poor way to communicate

constructive feedback. Other results show that workers receiving destructive feedback were more likely to report avoiding their supervisor in the future and reported lower future goals than were the workers who received constructive criticism. Such results suggest that use of destructive criticism can produce a variety of negative effects on its recipients. Thus, it is one type of communication that managers would do well to avoid.

Even feedback indicating that an employee is doing a "satisfactory job" can have a negative effect, depending on how the feedback is transmitted. In recent years, there has been an increasing trend for organizations to move from informal evaluations (usually taking the form of oral comments from the supervisor) to a system of more formal merit ratings which are used for all promotions, pay raises and layoffs (Carroll and Schneider, 1982). Because, as mentioned above, most workers think they are doing a "good job," the receipt of "satisfactory" merit ratings can alienate and demoralize employees (Meyer, 1975). One recent study examined reactions of employees in an agency that had switched from informal evaluations to formal performance ratings (Pearce and Porter, 1986). Satisfaction and morale showed a drop among workers receiving feedback that they were "satisfactory" or "meeting standards," after the introduction of formal appraisals. Of course, in organizations where only the most outstanding performers are retained after a trial period, a drop in attitude toward the organization probably would not be a cause for concern. However, for other organizations where turnover of adequate performers is costly or where all such members are considered important contributors, reactions of those who receive "adequate" ratings may present problems for organizational effectiveness. It seems clear that managers need to be concerned about how they present feedback and what purposes they want it to serve.

Increasing Productivity

Organizations employ a variety of ways to increase the productivity of their workers. A few of these will be considered here. Of course, the tra-

ditional way to motivate employees to work harder is through the promise of higher pay. There is often an incentive plan whereby appropriate compensation is increased after performance improves in a specified way (Caldwell, O'Reilly, and Morris, 1983; O'Malley, 1983). A key word here is "appropriate," because a salary increase that is perceived as either unjustified or inadequate can be extremely disruptive and counterproductive. But even when salary increases are appropriate, employees may still not be satisfied with their earnings. Because pay satisfaction tends to be related to increased productivity, we will focus on the determinants of salary satisfaction.

Satisfaction with Pay: Money Isn't Everything. As you might guess, a variety of considerations influence the degree of satisfaction one feels about one's salary. Four factors have received the most attention by researchers. First, *absolute value*—the magnitude of the economic benefits and the standard of living the individual enjoys because of his or her income—is important. A second factor concerns the degree to which earnings match what the employee thinks he or she deserves (Adams, 1965; Martin and Murray, 1983). This is referred to as *equity.* Another factor refers to the satisfaction with the intrinsic nature of the job. If a job provides *intrinsic satisfaction,* then an individual may be happy even with relatively low pay. Finally, pay satisfaction may be influenced by *social comparisons* of one's pay with what others are earning (Ronen, 1986).

In an attempt to examine the contribution of these different factors in pay satisfaction, Berkowitz and his colleagues (1987) interviewed a large sample of employees in a variety of jobs, asking how satisfied they were with their salaries and the degree to which each of the four factors contributed to their satisfaction. The findings showed that the material benefits afforded by one's salary, the degree to which salary was perceived to be deserved, and the intrinsic satisfaction the job provided were all important contributors to pay satisfaction. Of these three, feelings of deservingness (equity) had the strongest relationship with satisfaction. Surprisingly, social comparisons with other people's pay had little effect. Before dismissing this factor, however, it is possible that comparisons have an indirect effect by determining feelings of deservingness or judging one's standard of living. In any case, these and related findings (Ronen, 1986) suggest that feelings of deservingness may be more important than the absolute material benefits provided by a person's salary. Furthermore, having a job that is intrinsically enjoyable may increase satisfaction with even relatively low pay.

Information as a Motivator. Productivity can be enhanced when employees receive increased information about their jobs (Katzell and Guzzo, 1983). Thus, it is helpful to provide improved training with respect to job requirements, instructions about how to set realistic goals for performance, and training in decision-making. At a more general level, performance is improved when the worker possesses practical knowledge about how best to succeed in his or her career. Such information has been termed *tacit knowledge* (Wagner, 1987). These "rules of the game" are usually not openly expressed, but they have practical implications about how to succeed. In occupations as different as college professor and bank manager, the importance of tacit knowledge has been shown. It is beneficial in either field to know how to manage oneself (for example, arranging a daily schedule) and how to promote one's career (for example, awareness of which colleagues to ask for advice). Successful professionals possess this tacit knowledge to a greater extent than unsuccessful ones. Presumably, with the appropriate educational efforts, tacit knowledge could be more widely held.

This brief introduction to the application of social psychology to organizational behavior suggests once again that psychological factors are vital in every aspect of our lives. It is, in fact, difficult to imagine any human endeavor in which the findings of social psychology would be irrelevant and inapplicable. We hope you agree that the findings of social psychological research are widely generalizable and potentially useful to us all.

SUMMARY

Applied social psychology is the use of social-psychological research and practice in real-world settings as an attempt to solve a variety of social problems.

Health psychology refers to the application of psychological research to health problems. Perceiving that one has control over life events and the possession of a social support network can help to reduce the negative effects of life problems. Preventive health behaviors (involving diet, exercise, smoking, etc.) are also important if one can motivate people to perform them. The **protection motivation model** is an attempt to increase preventive behaviors. Several psychological factors influence whether people attend to symptoms and how they interpret them. Communication between physicians and doctors can be improved by attention to nonverbal messages.

The field of **forensic psychology** serves to link psychology with the legal process. Research on eyewitness testimony has documented the inaccuracy of witnesses in their testimony, though some procedures have been developed to increase the validity of such information. Police, attorneys, and judges have considerable influence on the way witnesses respond, whether such witnesses are perceived as credible, and on the jury's verdict. Many characteristics of the defendant (behavior, physical attractiveness, race, likability, etc.) affect a jury's decisions. In addition, jurors respond partly on the basis of their personality traits, partly on their beliefs, and partly on their attitudes about the particular crime in question.

The study of **organizational behavior** involves what people do in organizational settings. **Job satisfaction** is not always positively related to productivity, but it has various benefits for both employers and employees. Among the techniques developed in this regard are flexible time schedules, introducing variety into the tasks that are performed, and use of **quality circles**. Performance appraisal is crucial within an organization, and it is important to improve the process by eliminating irrelevant psychological influences. Productivity can be increased with pay raises, though satisfaction with salary is determined by several things in addition to the material benefits it provides.

GLOSSARY

action research Research which seeks to understand and solve social problems.

applied social psychology Social psychological research and practice in real-world settings directed toward the understanding of human social behavior and the attempted solution of social problems.

constructive criticism Feedback delivered in a considerate tone that focuses on specific behaviors and attributes poor job performance to external factors such as task difficulty or working conditions.

coping Those things a person does, feels, or thinks in order to master, tolerate, or decrease the negative effects of a threatening situation.

destructive criticism Feedback delivered in an inconsiderate tone that tends to be vague (rather than focused on specific behaviors) and attributes poor job performance to internal causes such as lack of effort or ability.

dogmatism Refers to a personality style which holds strong respect for authority and an intolerance of the unconventional.

flexitime Practice in organizational settings in which employees can work on flexible time schedules.

forensic psychology The study of the relationship between psychology and the law. This includes eyewitness reliability, and factors involving attorneys, judges, defendants, victims, and jurors.

health psychology The study and practice of the psychological origins, prevention, and treatment of physical illness.

job enlargement The practice of expanding the content of a job so as to include an increased number of different and varied tasks for each worker.

job satisfaction The extent to which a worker is content with his or her position in an organization, the work conditions, compensation, and general treatment relative to others in the organization.

leading questions Questions that are worded in such a way as to mislead people by providing information that is inconsistent with what they actually witnessed.

organizational behavior The study of human behavior in organizational settings. The focus includes individual processes, group processes, and organizational structure and function.

organizational commitment The extent to which an individual feels loyal to the organization for which he or she works and feels identified and involved with it.

perceived control The extent to which an individual believes he or she is able to influence the course of events.

protection-motivation model This model suggests that persuasive appeals can increase preventive behavior if they convey (1) the illness is a severe one, (2) the individual is vulnerable to it, (3) certain behaviors are effective in preventing the occurrence of the disease, and (4) the person is capable of performing the preventive health behaviors.

quality circle Procedure used in organizations whereby individuals engaged in similar work meet regularly to identify and correct any job problems. Thus, instead of relying on management or a special department to improve or maintain quality, the workers themselves develop solutions.

social support Refers to having friends or relatives upon whom one can rely. Having social support is associated with better physical health and being better able to resist the stressful effects of negative life events.

Type A Those individuals at the extreme of a personality dimension involving coronary-prone behavior, characterized by a hard-working, aggressive, time-pressured life-style.

Type B Those individuals at the low-risk extreme of the coronary-prone dimension. They are easygoing and relaxed, unconcerned about time pressures, and less likely than Type A's to develop cardiovascular disease.

FOR MORE INFORMATION

ALTMAIER, E. M., and MEYER, M. E. (Eds.). (1985). *Applied specialties in psychology*. New York: Random House.

This textbook spans the range of psychological applications to individual health, consumer behavior, business settings, and the courtroom. The chapter is written by experts representing each of the specific areas covered.

BARON, R. A. (1986). *Behavior in organizations: Understanding and managing the human side of work* (2d ed.). Boston: Allyn & Bacon.

A comprehensive and up-to-date introduction to the field of organizational behavior. It describes how certain basic psychological principles—such as learning, personality, attitudes, and motivation—are relevant to behavior in the organizational setting. Also covered in this well-written text are the work-related aspects of stress, communication, decision-making, group behavior, leadership, and various aspects of organizational structure and functioning.

TAYLOR, S. E. (1985). *Health psychology.* New York: Random House.

A very readable text describing the application of social psychological methods and research to health, illness, and the medical care system.

WEYANT, J. (1986). *Applied social psychology.* New York: Oxford University Press.

This brief, well-written text devotes each of its chapters to a different area to which social psychologists have concentrated their attention. Included are chapters on energy conservation, consumer behavior, the legal system, and education, to name just a few.

References

Abbott, A. R., & Sebastian, R. J. (1981). Physical attractiveness and expectations of success. *Personality and Social Psychology Bulletin, 7,* 481–486.

Abrams, D. B., Monti, P. M., Pinto, R. P., Elder, J. P., Brown, R. A., & Jacobus, S. I. (1987). Psychological stress and coping in smokers who relapse or quit. *Health Psychology, 6,* 289–304.

Abramson, L. Y., Seligman, M. E. P., & Teasdale, J. D. (1978). Learned helplessness in humans: Critique and reformulation. *Journal of Abnormal Psychology, 87,* 49–74.

Adams, G. R. (1977). Physical attractiveness research: Toward a developmental social psychology of beauty. *Human Development, 20,* 217–239.

Adams, J. S. (1965). Inequity in social exchange. In L. Berkowitz (Ed.), *Advances in experimental social psychology* (Vol. 2). New York: Academic Press.

Affleck, G., Tennen, H., Pfeiffer, C., & Fifield, J. (1987). Appraisals of control and predictability in adapting to a chronic disease. *Journal of Personality and Social Psychology, 53,* 273–279.

Aguero, J. E., Bloch, L., & Byrne, D. (1984). The relationships among sexual beliefs, attitudes, experience, and homophobia. *Journal of Homosexuality, 10,* 95–107.

Ajzen, I., & Fishbein, M. (1977). Attitude-behavior relations: A theoretical analysis and review of empirical research. *Psychological Bulletin, 84,* 888–918.

Alagna, F. J., Whitcher, S. J., & Fisher, J. D. (1979). Evaluative reactions to interpersonal touch in a counseling interview. *Journal of Counseling Psychology, 26,* 465–472.

Alexander, R. A. & Barrett, G. U. (1982). Equitable salary increase judgments based upon merit and non-merit considerations: A cross-national comparison. *International Review of Applied Psychology, 31,* 443–454.

Alicke, M. D., Smith, R. H., & Klotz, M. L. (1986). Judgments of physical attractiveness: The role of faces and bodies. *Personality and Social Psychology Bulletin, 12,* 381–389.

Allen, V. L., & Levine, J. M. (1971). Social support and conformity: The role of independent assessment of reality. *Journal of Experimental Social Psychology, 4,* 48–58.

Alloy, L. B., & Abramson, L. Y. (1979). Judgments of contingency in depressed and nondepressed students: Sadder but wiser. *Journal of Experimental Psychology: General, 108,* 441–485.

Alloy, L. B., & Ahrens, A. H. (1987). Depression and pessimism for the future: Biased use of statistically relevant information in predictions for self versus others. *Journal of Personality and Social Psychology, 52,* 366–378.

Allport, G. W. (1935). Attitudes. In C. Murchison (Ed.), *Handbook of social psychology.* Worcester, MA: Clark University Press.

Allyn, J., & Festinger, L. (1961). The effectiveness of unanticipated persuasive communications. *Journal of Abnormal and Social Psychology, 62,* 35–40.

Altmaier, E. M., & Meyer, M. E. (Eds.) (1985). *Applied specialties in psychology.* New York: Random House.

Amabile, T. M. (1983). Brilliant but cruel: Perceptions of negative evaluators. *Journal of Experimental Social Psychology, 19,* 146–156.

Anderson, C. A. (1987). Temperature and aggression: Effects on quarterly, yearly, and city rates of violent and nonviolent crime. *Journal of Personality and Social Psychology, 52,* 1161–1173.

Anderson, C. A., Lepper, M. R., & Ross, L. (1980). Perseverance of social theories: The role of explanation in the persistence of discredited information. *Journal of Personality and Social Psychology, 39,* 1037–1049.

Anderson, C. A., New, B. L., & Speer, J. R. (1985). Argument availability as a mediator of social theory perseverance. *Social Cognition, 3,* 235–249.

Anderson, C. A., & Sechler, E. S. (1986). Effects of explanation and counterexplanation on the development and use of social theories. *Journal of Personality and Social Psychology, 50,* 24–34.

Anderson, N. H. (1965). Primacy effects in personality impression formation using a generalized order effect paradigm. *Journal of Personality and Social Psychology, 2,* 1–9.

Anderson, S. M., & Klatsky, R. L. (1987). Traits and social stereotypes: Levels of categorization in person perception. *Journal of Personality and Social Psychology, 53,* 235–246.

Antill, J. K. (1983). Sex role complementarity versus similarity in married couples. *Journal of Personality and Social Psychology, 45,* 145–155.

Arkin, R. M., Gleason, J. M., & Johnston, S. (1976). Effects of perceived choice, expected outcome, and observed outcome of an action on the causal attributions of actors. *Journal of Experimental Social Psychology, 12,* 151–158.

Aronson, E., Bridgeman, D. L., & Geffner, R. (1978). Interdependent interactions and prosocial behavior. *Journal of Research and Development in Education, 12,* 16–27.

Asch, S. E. (1946). Forming impressions of personality. *Journal of Abnormal and Social Psychology, 41,* 258–290.

Asch, S. E. (1951). Effects of group pressure upon the modification and distortion of judgment. In H. Guetzkow (Ed.), *Groups, leadership, and men.* Pittsburgh: Carnegie.

Asch, S. E. (1957, April). An experimental investigation of group influence. In *Symposium on preventive and social psychiatry* (pp. 15–17). Walter Reed Army Institute of Research, Washington, DC: U.S. Government Printing Office.

Averill, J. R., & Boothroyd, P. (1977). On falling in love in conformance with the romantic ideal. *Motivation and Emotion, 1,* 235–247.

Axelrod, R., & Hamilton, W. D. (1981). The evolution of cooperation. *Science, 211,* 1390–1396.

Axsom, D., Yates, S., & Chaiken, S. (1987). Audience response as a heuristic cue in persuasion. *Journal of Personality and Social Psychology, 53,* 30–40.

Bandura, A. (1973). *Aggression: A social learning analysis.* Englewood Cliffs, NJ: Prentice-Hall.

Bandura, A. (1977). *Social learning theory.* Englewood Cliffs, NJ: Prentice-Hall.

Bandura, A. (1986). *Social foundations of thought and action.* Englewood Cliffs, NJ: Prentice-Hall.

Bandura, A., Ross, D., & Ross, S. (1961). Imitation of film-mediated aggressive models. *Journal of Abnormal and Social Psychology, 66,* 3–11.

Bannister, B. D. (1979). Performance outcome feedback and attributional feedback: Interactive effects on recipient responses. *Journal of Applied Psychology, 71,* 203–210.

Barden, R. D., Garber, J., Duncan, S. W., & Masters, J. C. (1981). Cumulative effects of induced affective states in children: Accentuation, inoculation, and remediation. *Journal of Personality and Social Psychology, 40,* 750–760.

Baron, R. A. (1972). Reducing the influence of an aggressive model: The restraining effects of peer censure. *Journal of Experimental Social Psychology, 8,* 266–275.

Baron, R. A. (1973). The "foot-in-the-door" phenomenon: Mediating effects of size of first request and sex of requester. *Bulletin of the Psychonomic Society, 2,* 113–114.

Baron, R. A. (1977). *Human aggression.* New York: Plenum.

Baron, R. A. (1979). Heightened sexual arousal and physical aggression: An extension to females. *Journal of Applied Social Psychology, 9,* 103–114.

Baron, R. A. (1981). The "costs of deception" revisited: An openly optimistic rejoinder. *IRB: A Review of Human Subjects Research, 3,* 8–10.

Baron, R. A. (1983). The control of human aggression: An optimistic perspective. *Journal of Social and Clinical Psychology, 1,* 97–119.

Baron, R. A. (1984) Reducing organizational conflict: An incompatible response approach. *Journal of Applied Psychology, 69,* 272–279.

Baron, R. A. (1986a). *Behavior in organizations: Understanding and managing the human side of work* (2nd ed.). Boston: Allyn and Bacon.

Baron, R. A. (1986b). Self-presentation in job interviews: When there can be "too much of a good thing." *Journal of Applied Social Psychology, 16,* 16–19.

Baron, R. A. (1987). Interviewer's moods and reactions to job applicants: The influence of affective states on applied social judgments. *Journal of Applied Social Psychology, 16,* 16–28.

Baron, R. A. (1988). Negative effects of destructive criticism: Impact on conflict, self-efficacy and task performance. *Journal of Applied Psychology, 73,* 199–207.

Baron, R. A., & Bell, P. A. (1977). Sexual arousal and aggression by males: Effects of type of erotic stimuli and prior provocation. *Journal of Personality and Social Psychology, 35,* 79–87.

Baron, R. S. (1986). Distraction-conflict theory: Progress and problems. In L. Berkowitz (Ed.), *Advances in experimental social psychology* (Vol. 20). New York: Academic Press.

Baron, R. S., Moore, D., & Sanders, G. S. (1978). Distraction as a source of drive in social facilitation research. *Journal of Personality and Social Psychology, 36,* 816–824.

Baron, R. S., & Roper, G. (1976). Reaffirmation of social comparison views of choice shifts: Averaging and extremity effects in an autokinetic situation. *Journal of Personality and Social Psychology, 33,* 521–530.

Barra, R. (1983). *Putting quality circles to work: A practical strategy for boosting productivity and profits.* New York: McGraw-Hill.

Barrick, M. R., & Alexander, R. A. (1987). A review of quality circle efficacy and the existence of positive-findings bias. *Personnel Psychology, 40,* 579–592.

Bar-Tal, D., & Kruglanski, A. (Eds.). 1988. *The social psychology of knowledge.* Cambridge: Cambridge University Press.

Bartol, C. R. (1983). *Psychology and American law.* Belmont, CA: Wadsworth.

Bartol, K. M., & Butterfield, D. A. (1976). Sex effects in evaluating leaders. *Journal of Applied Psychology, 61,* 446–454.

Bass, B. M. (1981). *Stogdill's handbook of leadership: A survey of theory and research.* New York: Free Press.

Batson, C. D., Cochran, P. J., Biederman, M. F., Blosser, J. L., Ryan, M. J., & Vogt, B. (1978). Failure to help when in a hurry: Callousness or conflict? *Personality and Social Psychology Bulletin, 4,* 97–101.

Batson, C. D., Duncan, B. D., Ackerman, P., Buckley, T., & Birch, K. (1981). Is empathic emotion a source of altruistic motivation? *Journal of Personality and Social Psychology, 40,* 290–302.

Batson, C. D., Fultz, J., & Schoenrade, P. A. (1987). Distress and empathy: Two qualitatively distinct vicarious emotions with different motivational consequences. *Journal of Personality, 55,* 19–40.

Batson, C. D., & Gray, R. A. (1981). Religious orientation and helping behavior: Responding to one's own or to the victim's needs? *Journal of Personality and Social Psychology, 40,* 511–520.

Batson, C. D., O'Quin, K., Fultz, J., & Vanderplas, M. (1983). Influence of self-reported distress and empathy on egoistic versus altruistic motivation to help. *Journal of Personality and Social Psychology, 45,* 706–718.

Bauman, D. J., Cialdini, R. B., & Kenrick, D. T. (1981). Altruism as hedonism: Helping and self-gratification as equivalent responses. *Journal of Personality and Social Psychology, 40,* 1039–1046.

Baumeister, R. F., & Covington, M. V. (1985). Self-esteem, persuasion, and retrospective distortion of initial attitudes. *Electronic Social Psychology, 1,* 1–22.

Baumeister, R. F., & Darley, J. M. (1982). Reducing the biasing effect of perpetrator attractiveness in jury simulation. *Personality and Social Psychology Bulletin, 8,* 286–292.

Baumeister, R. F., & Tice, D. M. (1984). Role of self-presentation and choice in cognitive dissonance under forced compliance: Necessary or sufficient causes? *Journal of Personality and Social Psychology, 46,* 5–13.

Baumgardner, A. H., Heppner, P. P., & Arkin, R. M. (1986). Role of causal attribution in personal problem solving. *Journal of Personality and Social Psychology, 50,* 636–643.

Baumrind, D. (1979). The costs of deception. *IRB: A Review of Human Subjects Research, 6,* 1–4.

Beaman, A. L., Cole, C. M., Preston, M., Klentz, B., & Steblay, N. M. (1983). Fifteen years of foot-in-the-door research: A meta-analysis. *Personality and Social Psychology Bulletin, 9,* 181–196.

Beck, S. B., Ward-Hull, C. I., & McLear, P. M. (1976). Variables related to women's somatic preferences of the male and female body. *Journal of Personality and Social Psychology, 34,* 1200–1210.

Beezley, D., Gantner, A. B., Bailey, D. S., & Taylor, S. P. (1987). Amphetamines and human physical aggression. *Journal of Research in Personality, 21,* 52–60.

Bem, D. J. (1972). Self-perception theory. In L. Berkowitz (Ed.), *Advances in experimental social psychology* (Vol. 6, pp. 18–30). New York: Academic Press.

Bem, D. J., & McConnell, H. K. (1970). Testing the self-perception explanation of dissonance phenomena: On the salience of premanipulation attitudes. *Journal of Personality and Social Psychology, 14,* 23–31.

Berger, S. M., Carli, L. C., Garcia, R., & Brady, J. J., Jr. (1982). Audience effects in anticipatory learning: A comparison of drive and practice-inhibition analyses. *Journal of Personality and Social Psychology, 42,* 378–386.

Berglas, S., & Jones, E. E. (1978). Drug choice as a self-handicapping strategy in response to noncontingent success. *Journal of Personality and Social Psychology, 36,* 405–417.

Berkowitz, L. (1974). Some determinants of impulsive aggression: Role of mediated associations with reinforcement for aggression. *Psychological Review, 81,* 165–176.

Berkowitz, L. (1978). Whatever happened to the frustration-aggression hypothesis? *American Behavioral Scientist, 8,* 691–708.

Berkowitz, L. (1984). Some effects of thoughts on anti-

and pro-social influences of media events: A cognitive-neoassociation analysis. *Psychological Bulletin, 95,* 410–427.

Berkowitz, L., & Donnerstein, E. (1982). External validity is more than skin deep: Some answers to criticisms of laboratory experiments. *American Psychologist, 37,* 245–257.

Berkowitz, L., & Embree, M. C. (1987). The effect of escape possibility on aversively stimulated aggression. *Journal of Research in Personality, 21,* 405–416.

Berkowitz, L., Fraser, C., Treasure, F. P., & Cochran, S. (1987). Pay, equity, job gratifications, and comparisons in pay satisfaction. *Journal of Applied Psychology, 72,* 544–551.

Berndt, T. J., & Heller, K. A. (1986). Gender stereotypes and social inferences: A developmental study. *Journal of Personality and Social Psychology, 50,* 889–898.

Bernstein, W. M., Stephenson, B. O., Snyder, M. L., & Wicklund, R. A. (1983). Causal ambiguity and heterosexual affiliation. *Journal of Experimental Social Psychology, 19,* 78–92.

Berscheid, E. (1985). Interpersonal attraction. In G. Lindzey & E. Aronson (Eds.), *Handbook of social psychology* (3rd ed.). New York: Random House.

Berscheid, E., Dion, K., Walster, E., & Walster, G. W. (1971). Physical attractiveness and dating choice: A test of the matching hypothesis. *Journal of Experimental Social Psychology, 7,* 173–189.

Bersoff, D. (1987). Social science data and the Supreme Court: Lockhart as a case in point. *American Psychologist, 42,* 52–58.

Bickman, L. (1971). The effect of another bystander's ability to help on bystander intervention in an emergency. *Journal of Experimental Social Psychology, 7,* 367–374.

Bickman, L., & Green, S. K. (1977). Situational cues and crime reporting: Do signs make a difference? *Journal of Applied Social Psychology, 7,* 1–18.

Bickman, L., & Rosenbaum, D. P. (1977). Crime reporting as a function of bystander encouragement, surveillance, and credibility. *Journal of Personality and Social Psychology, 35,* 577–586.

Bielass, M. (1987). Homosexism and nurses' knowledge about AIDS. Paper presented at the meeting of the Eastern Psychological Ass'n., New York.

Billig, M., & Tajfel, H. (1973). Social categorization and similarity in intergroup behavior. *European Journal of Social Psychology, 3,* 27–52.

Blake, R. R., & Mouton, J. S. (1979). Intergroup problem solving in organizations: From theory to practice. In W. G. Austin & S. Worchel (Eds.), *The so-cial psychology of intergroup relations.* Monterey, CA: Brooks/Cole.

Blankenship, V., Hnat, S. M., Hess, T. G., & Brown, D. R. (1984). Reciprocal interaction and similarity of personality attributes. *Journal of Social and Personal Relationships, 1,* 415–432.

Bodenhausen, G. V., & Lichtenstein, M. (1987). Social stereotypes and information-processing strategies: The impact of task complexity. *Journal of Personality and Social Psychology, 52,* 871–880.

Bodenhausen, G. V., & Wyer, R. S. (1985). Effects of stereotypes of decision making and information-processing strategies. *Journal of Personality and Social Psychology, 48,* 267–282.

Boggiano, A. K., Barrett, M., Weiher, A. W., McClelland, G. H., & Lusk, C. M. (1987). Use of maximal-operant principle to motivate children's intrinsic interest. *Journal of Personality and Social Psychology, 53,* 866–879.

Boggiano, A. K., Harackiewicz, J. M., Bessette, J. M., & Main, D. S. (1985). Increasing children's interest through performance-contingent reward. *Social Cognition, 3,* 400–411.

Boggiano, A. K., & Pittman, T. S. (Ed.). (in press). *Achievement and motivation: A social developmental perspective.* Cambridge: Cambridge University Press.

Bond, C. F. (1982). Social facilitation: A self-presentational view. *Journal of Personality and Social Psychology, 42,* 1042–1050.

Bornstein, R. F., Leone, D. R., & Galley, D. J. (1987). The generalizability of subliminal mere exposure effects: Influence of stimuli perceived without awareness on social behavior. *Journal of Personality and Social Psychology, 53,* 1070–1079.

Bothwell, R. K., Deffenbacher, K. A., & Brigham, J. C. (1987). Correlation of eyewitness accuracy and confidence: Optimality hypothesis revisited. *Journal of Applied Psychology, 72,* 691–695.

Bower, G. H., & Hilgard, E. R. (1981). *Theories of learning.* Englewood Cliffs, NJ: Prentice-Hall.

Bradley, G. W. (1978). Self-serving biases in the attribution process: A re-examination of the fact or fiction question. *Journal of Personality and Social Psychology, 36,* 56–71.

Bray, R. M., Johnson, D., & Chilstrom, J. T., Jr. (1982). Social influence by group members with minority opinions: A comparison of Hollander and Moscovici. *Journal of Personality and Social Psychology, 43,* 78–88.

Bray, R. M., & Sugarman, R. (1980). Social facilitation among interaction groups: Evidence for the evaluation-apprehension hypothesis. *Personality and Social Psychology Bulletin, 6,* 137–142.

Breckler, S. J. (1984). Empirical validation of affect, behavior, and cognition as distinct components of attitude. *Journal of Personality and Social Psychology, 47,* 1191–1205.

Brehm, J. W. (1966). *A theory of psychological reactance.* New York: Academic Press.

Brewer, M. B., & Silver, M. (1978). In-group bias as a function of task characteristics. *European Journal of Social Psychology, 36,* 219–243.

Briere, J. (1987). Predicting self-reported likelihood of battering: Attitudes and childhood experiences. *Journal of Research in Personality, 21,* 61–69.

Brigham, J. C. (1980). Limiting conditions of the "physical attractiveness stereotype": Attributions about divorce. *Journal of Research in Personality, 14,* 365–375.

Broome, B. J. (1983). The attraction paradigm revisited. Response to dissimilar others. *Human Communication Research, 10,* 137–151.

Brown, J. D., & Siegel, J. M. (1988). Attributions for negative life events and depression: The role of perceived control. *Journal of Personality and Social Psychology, 54,* 316–322.

Buck, R. (1984). *The communication of emotion.* New York: Guilford Press.

Buckhout, R. (1980). Nearly 2000 witnesses can be wrong. *Bulletin of the Psychonomic Society, 16,* 307–310.

Burger, J. M. (1986). Increasing compliance by improving the deal: The that's-not-all technique. *Journal of Personality and Social Psychology, 51,* 277–283.

Burger, J. M. (1987). Desire for control and conformity to a perceived norm. *Journal of Personality and Social Psychology, 53,* 355–360.

Burger, J. M., & Cooper, H. M. (1979). The desirability of control. *Motivation and Emotion, 3,* 381–393.

Burger, J. M., & Petty, R. E. (1981). The low-ball compliance technique: Task or person commitment? *Journal of Personality and Social Psychology, 6,* 89–95.

Burnstein, E. (1983). Persuasion as argument processing. In M. Brandstatter, J.H. Davis, and G. Stocker-Kreichgauer (Eds), *Group decision processes.* London: Academic Press.

Bushman, B. J. (1984). Perceived symbols of authority and their influence on compliance. *Journal of Applied Social Psychology, 14,* 501–508.

Buss, A. H. (1961). *The psychology of aggression.* New York: Wiley.

Byrne. D. (1971). *The attraction paradigm.* New York: Academic Press.

Byrne, D., Clore, G. L., & Smeaton, G. (1986). The attraction hypothesis: Do similar attitudes affect any-

thing? *Journal of Personality and Social Psychology, 51,* 1167–1170.

Byrne, D., Ervin, C. R., & Lamberth, J. (1970). Continuity between the experimental study of attraction and real life computer dating. *Journal of Personality and Social Psychology, 16,* 157–165.

Byrne, D., & Nelson, D. (1965). Attraction as a linear function of proportion of positive reinforcements. *Journal of Personality and Social Psychology, 1,* 659–663.

Cacioppo, J. T., & Petty, R. E. (1981). Effects of extent of thought on the pleasantness of P-O-X triads: Evidence for three judgmental tendencies in evaluating social situations. *Journal of Personality and Social Psychology, 40,* 1000–1009.

Cacioppo, J. T., Petty, R. E., Kao, C. F., & Rodriguez, R. (1986). Central and peripheral routes to persuasion: An individual difference perspective. *Journal of Personality and Social Psychology, 51,* 1032–1043.

Caldwell, D. F., O'Reilly, C. A., III, & Morris, J. H. (1983). Responses to an organizational reward: A field test of the sufficiency of justification hypothesis. *Journal of Personality and Social Psychology, 206,* 139–148.

Campbell, J. D. (1986). Similarity and uniqueness: The effects of attribute type, relevance, and individual differences in self-esteem and depression. *Journal of Personality and Social Psychology, 50,* 281–294.

Campbell, J. D., Tesser, A., & Fairey, P. J. (1986). Conformity and attention to the stimulus: Some temporal and contextual dynamics. *Journal of Personality and Social Psychology, 51,* 315–324.

Caplow, T., & Forman, R. (1950). Neighborhood interaction in a homogeneous community. *American Sociological Review, 15,* 357–366.

Carlson, M., & Miller, N. (1987). Explanation of the relation between negative mood and helping. *Psychological Bulletin, 102,* 91–108.

Carretta, T. R., & Moreland, R. L. (1983). The direct and indirect effects of inadmissible evidence. *Journal of Applied Social Psychology, 13,* 291–309.

Carroll, S. J. (1982). What is this thing called "Applied Social Psychology"? *Contemporary Psychology, 27,* 772–773.

Carroll, S. J., Perkowitz, W. T., Lurigio, A. J., & Weaver, F. M. (1987). Sentencing goals, causal attributions, ideology and personality. *Journal of Personality and Social Psychology, 50,* 107–118.

Carroll, S. J., & Schneider, C. E. (1982). *Performance appraisal and review systems.* Glenview, IL: Scott, Foresman.

Carver, C. S., Antoni, M., & Scheier, M. F. (1985). Self-consciousness and self-assessment. *Journal of Personality and Social Psychology, 48,* 117–124.

Carver, C. S., Ganellen, R., Froming, W., & Chambers, W. (1983). Modeling: An analysis in terms of category accessibility. *Journal of Experimental Social Psychology, 19,* 403–421.

Carver, C. S., & Scheier, M. F. (1981). *Attention and self-regulation: A control-theory approach to human behavior.* New York: Springer-Verlag.

Cash, T. F., & Duncan, N. C. (1984). Physical attractiveness stereotyping among black American college students. *Journal of Social Psychology, 122,* 71–77.

Cash, T. F., & Kilcullen, R. N. (1985). The age of the beholder: Susceptibility to sexism and beautyism in the evaluation of managerial applicants. *Journal of Applied Social Psychology, 15,* 591–605.

Cavoukian, A., & Doob, A. N. (1980). The effects of a judge's charge and subsequent recharge on judgments of guilt. *Basic and Applied Social Psychology, 1,* 103–114.

Chacko, T. I. (1982). Woman and equal employment opportunity: Some unintended effects. *Journal of Applied Psychology, 67,* 119–123.

Chaiken, S. (1987). The heuristic model of persuasion. In M. P. Zanna, J. M. Olson, & C. P. Herman (Eds.), *Social influence: The Ontario Symposium* (Vol. 5, pp. 3–39). Hillsdale, NJ: Erlbaum.

Chaiken, S., & Baldwin, M. W. (1981). Affective-cognitive consistency and the effect of salient behavioral information on the self-perception of attitudes. *Journal of Personality and Social Psychology, 34,* 605–614.

Chaiken, S., & Stangor, C. (1987). Attitudes and attitude change. *Annual Review of Psychology, 38,* 575–630.

Chapman, L. J., & Chapman, J. (1982). Test results are what you think they are. In D. Kahneman, P. Slovic, & A. Tversky (Eds.), *Judgment under uncertainty: Heuristics and biases* (pp. 239–248). New York: Cambridge University Press.

Chassin, L., Presson, C. C., Sherman, S. J., Corty, E., & Olshavsky, R. W. (1984). Self-images and cigarette-smoking in adolescence. *Personality and Social Psychology Bulletin, 7,* 670–676.

Chemers, M. M. (1987). Leadership processes: Intrapersonal, interpersonal and societal influences. In C. Hendrick (Ed.), *Group processes and interpersonal relations* (pp. 252–277). Newbury Park, CA: Sage.

Chemers, M. M., Hays, R. B., Rhodewalt, F., & Wysocki, J. (1985). A person-environment analysis of job stress: A contingency model explanation. *Journal of Personality and Social Psychology, 49,* 628–635.

Chidester, T. R. (1986). Problems in the study of interracial interaction: Pseudo-interracial dyad paradigm. *Journal of Personality and Social Psychology, 50,* 74–79.

Christy, P. R., Gelfand, D. M., & Hartmann, D. P. (1971). Effects of competition-induced frustration on two classes of modeled behavior. *Developmental Psychology, 5,* 104–111.

Cialdini, R. B. (1988). *Influence: Science and practice* (2nd ed.). Glenview, Il: Scott, Foresman.

Cialdini, R. B., Borden, R. J., Thorne, A., Walker, M. R., Freeman, S., & Sloan, L. R. (1976). Basking in reflected glory: Three (football) field studies. *Journal of Personality and Social Psychology, 34,* 366–375.

Cialdini, R. B., Cacioppo, J. T., Bassett, R., & Miller, J. A. (1978). Low-ball procedure for producing compliance: Commitment then cost. *Journal of Personality and Social Psychology, 36,* 463–476.

Cialdini, R. B., & Petty, R. (1979). Anticipatory opinion effects. In R. Petty, T. Ostrom, & T. Brock (Eds.), *Cognitive responses in persuasion.* Hillsdale, NJ: Erlbaum.

Cialdini, R. B., Schaller, M., Howlihan, D., Arps, K., Fultz, J., & Beaman, A. L. (1987). Empathy-based helping: Is it selfishly or selflessly motivated? *Journal of Personality and Social Psychology, 52,* 749–758.

Cialdini, R. B., Vincent, J. E., Lewis, S. K., Catalan, J., Wheeler, D., & Darby, B. L. (1975). Reciprocal concessions procedure for inducing compliance: The door-in-the-face technique. *Journal of Personality and Social Psychology, 31,* 1292–1294.

Clark, M. S., Milberg, S., & Erber, R. (1984). Effects of arousal on judgments of others' emotions. *Journal of Personality and Social Psychology, 46,* 551–560.

Clark, M., & Reis, H. (1988). Interpersonal processes in close relationships. *Annual Review of Psychology, 39,* 609–672.

Clore, G. L., & Byrne, D. (1974). A reinforcement-affect model of attraction. In T. L. Huston (Ed.), *Foundations of interpersonal attraction* (pp. 143–170). New York: Academic Press.

Clore, G. L., Wiggins, N. H., & Itkin, S. (1975). Gain and loss in attraction: Attributions from nonverbal behavior. *Journal of Personality and Social Psychology, 31,* 706–712.

Cohen, S., & Wills, T. A. (1985). Stress, social support, and the buffering hypothesis. *Psychological Bulletin, 98,* 310–357.

Collins, L. M., Sussman, S., Rauch, J. M., Dent, C. W., Johnson, C. A., Hansen, W. B., & Flay, B. R. (1987). Psychological predictors of young adolescent cigarette smoking: A sixteen-month, three-wave longitudinal study. *Journal of Applied Social Psychology, 17,* 554–573.

Conway, M., & Ross, M. (1984). Getting what you want by revising what you had. *Journal of Personality and Social Psychology, 47,* 738–748.

Cook, S. W. (1984a). Cooperative interaction in multiethnic contexts. In N. Miller & M. Brewer (Eds.), *Groups in contact: The psychology of desegregation* (pp. 155–185). New York: Academic Press.

Cook, S. W. (1984b). The 1954 social science statement and school desegregation: A reply to Gerard. *American Psychologist, 39,* 819–832.

Cook, S. W. (1985). Experimenting on social issues: The case of school desegregation. *American Psychologist, 40,* 452–460.

Coombs, L. C. (1979). The measurement of commitment to work. *Journal of Population, 2,* 203–223.

Cooper, J., & Fazio, R. H. (1984). A new look at dissonance theory. In L. Berkowitz (Ed.), *Advances in experimental social psychology,* vol. 17, (pp. 229–266). New York: Academic Press.

Cooper, J., Zanna, M. P., & Taves, P. A. (1978). Arousal as a necessary condition for attitude change following induced compliance. *Journal of Personality and Social Psychology, 36,* 1101–1106.

Costantini, E., & Craik, K. H. (1980). Personality and politicians: California party leaders, 1960–1976. *Journal of Personality and Social Psychology, 38,* 641–661.

Cottrell, N. B., Wack, D. L., Sekerak, G. L., & Rittle, R. H. (1968). Social facilitation of dominant responses by the presence of an audience and the mere presence of others. *Journal of Personality and Social Psychology, 9,* 245–250.

Cowan, G., Drinkard, J., & MacGavin, L. (1984). The effects of target, age and gender on use of power strategies. *Journal of Personality and Social Psychology, 47,* 1391–1398.

Cox, V. C., Paulus, P. B., & McCain, G. (1984). Prison crowding research: The relevance for prison housing standards and a general approach for crowding phenomena. *American Psychologist, 39,* 1148–1160.

Crocker, J., Thompson, L. L., McGraw, K. M., & Ingerman, C. (1987). Downward comparison, prejudice and evaluations of others: Effects of self-esteem and threat. *Journal of Personality and Social Psychology, 52,* 907–916.

Crosby, F. (1982). *Relative deprivation and working women.* New York: Oxford University Press.

Crouse, B. B., & Mehrabian, A. (1977). Affiliation of opposite-sexed strangers. *Journal of Research in Personality, 11,* 38–47.

Croyle, R., & Cooper, J. (1983). Dissonance arousal: Physiological evidence. *Journal of Personality and Social Psychology, 45,* 782–791.

Croyle, R., & Uretsky, M. B. (1987). Effects of mood on self-appraisal of health status. *Health Psychology, 6,* 239–254.

Crusco, A. H., & Wetzel, C. G. (1984). The Midas touch: The effects of interpersonal touch on restaurant tipping. *Personality and Social Psychology Bulletin, 10,* 512–517.

Crutchfield, R. A. (1955). Conformity and character. *American Psychologist, 10,* 191–198.

Cunningham, M. R. (1979). Weather, mood, and helping behavior: Quasi experiments with the sunshine Samaritan. *Journal of Personality and Social Psychology, 37,* 1947–1956.

Cunningham, M. R. (1981). Sociobiology as a supplementary paradigm for social psychological research. In L. Wheeler (Ed.), *Review of personality and social psychology* (Vol. 2). Beverly Hills, CA: Sage.

Cunningham, M. R. (1986). Measuring the physical in physical attractiveness: Quasi-experiments on the sociobiology of female facial beauty. *Journal of Personality and Social Psychology, 50,* 925–935.

Cunningham, M. R., Steinberg, J., & Grev, R. (1980). Wanting to and having to help: Separate motivations for positive mood and guilt induced helping. *Journal of Personality and Social Psychology, 38,* 181–192.

Curtis, R. C., & Miller, K. (1986). Believing another likes or dislikes you: Behaviors making the beliefs come true. *Journal of Personality and Social Psychology, 51,* 284–290.

Cutler, B. L., Penrod, S. D., & Martens, T. K. (1987). Improving the reliability of eyewitness identification: Putting content into context. *Journal of Applied Psychology, 72,* 629–637.

Daher, D. M., & Bankikiotes, P. G. (1976). Interpersonal attraction and rewarding aspects of disclosure content and level. *Journal of Personality and Social Psychology, 33,* 492–496.

Darley, J. M., & Batson, C. D. (1973). "From Jerusalem to Jericho": A study of situational and dispositional variables in helping behavior. *Journal of Personality and Social Psychology, 27,* 100–108.

Darley, J. M., & Fazio, R. (1980). Expectancy confirmation processes arising in the social interaction sequence. *American Psychologist, 35,* 867–881.

Darley, J. M., & Latane, B. (1968). Bystander intervention in emergencies: Diffusion of responsibility. *Journal of Personality and Social Psychology, 8,* 377–383.

Davis, J. H. (1980). Group decisions and procedural justice. In M. Fishbein (Ed.), *Progress in social psychology.* Hillsdale, NJ: Erlbaum.

Davis, J. H., Tindlae, R. S., Nagao, D. H., Hinsz, V. B., & Robertson, B. (1984). Order effects in multiple decisions by groups: A demonstration with mock juries and trial procedures. *Journal of Personality and Social Psychology, 47,* 1003–1012.

Deaux, K., & Lewis, L. L. (1984). Structure of gender components: Interrelationships among components and gender labels. *Journal of Personality and Social Psychology, 46,* 991–1004.

Deaux, K., & Major, B. (1987). Putting gender into context: An interactive model of gender-related behavior. *Psychological Review, 94,* 369–389.

DeBono, K. G. (1987). Investigating the social-adjustive and value-expressive functions of attitudes: Implications for persuasion processes. *Journal of Personality and Social Psychology, 52,* 279–287.

Deci, E. L., & Ryan, R. M. (1987). The support of autonomy and the control of behavior. *Journal of Personality and Social Psychology, 53,* 1024–1037.

DeJong, W., Marber, S., & Shaver, R. (1980). Crime intervention: The role of a victim's behavior in reducing situational ambiguity. *Personality and Social Psychology Bulletin, 6,* 113–118.

DeJong, W., & Musilli, L. (1982). External pressure to comply: Handicapped versus nonhandicapped requesters and the foot-in-the-door phenomenon. *Personality and Social Psychology Bulletin, 8,* 522–527.

Dembroski, T. M., & Costa, P. (1987). Coronary-prone behavior: Components of the Type A pattern and hostility. *Journal of Personality, 55,* 211–236.

Degerink, H. A., Schnedler, R. W., & Covey, M. K. (1978). Role of avoidance in aggressive responses to attack and no attack. *Journal of Personality and Social Psychology, 36,* 1044–1053.

DePaulo, B. M., & Pfeifer, R. L. (1986). On-the-job experience and skill at detecting deception. *Journal of Applied Social Psychology, 16,* 249–267.

DePaulo, B. M., Stone, J. L., & Lassiter, G. D. (1985). Deceiving and detecting deceit. In B. R. Schlenker (Ed.), *The self and social life* (pp. 323–370). New York: McGraw-Hill.

Diener, E. (1980). Deindividuation: The absence of self-awareness and self-regulation in group members. In P. B. Paulus (Ed.), *The psychology of group influence.* Hillsdale, NJ: Erlbaum.

DiMatteo, M. R., Hays, R. D., & Prince, L. M. (1986). Relationships of physicians' nonverbal communication skill to patient satisfaction, appointment noncompliance and physician workload. *Health Psychology, 5,* 581–594.

Dion, K. K., & Dion, K. L. (1975). Self-esteem and romantic love. *Journal of Personality, 43,* 39–57.

Dion, K. L., & Dion, K. K. (1987). Belief in a just world and physical attractive stereotyping. *Journal of Personality and Social Psychology, 52,* 775–780.

Dodge, K. A., & Coie, J. D. (1987). Social-information-processing factors in reactive and proactive aggression in children's peer groups. *Journal of Personality and Social Psychology, 53,* 1146–1158.

Dodge, K. A., Murphy, R. R., & Buschbaum, K. (1984). The assessment of intention-cue detection skills in children: Implications for developmental psychopathology. *Child Development, 55,* 163–173.

Dollard, J., Doob, L., Miller, N., Mowrer, O. H., & Sears, R. R. (1939). *Frustration and aggression.* New Haven: Yale University Press.

Donnerstein, E., Berkowitz, L., & Linz, D. (1987). In E. Donnerstein, D. Linz, & S. Penrod, *The question of pornography: Research findings and policy implications.* New York: Free Press.

Donnerstein, E., & Donnerstein, M. (1976). Research in the control of interracial aggression. In R. G. Geen & E. C. O'Neal (Eds.), *Perspectives on aggression.* New York: Academic Press.

Dorian, B. J., Keystone, E., Garfinkel, P. E., & Brown, J. M. (1982). Aberrations in lymphocyte subpopulations and function during psychological stress. *Clinical and Experimental Immunology, 50,* 132–138.

Dovidio, J. H., Evans, N., & Tyler, R. B. (1986). Racial stereotypes: The contents of their cognitive representations. *Journal of Experimental Social Psychology, 22,* 22–37.

Drachman, D., deCarufel, A., & Insko, C. A. (1978). The extra credit effect in interpersonal attraction. *Journal of Experimental Social Psychology, 14,* 458–465.

Driscoll, R., Davis, K. E., & Lipetz, M. E. (1972). Parental interference and romantic love: The Romeo and Juliet effect. *Journal of Personality and Social Psychology, 24,* 1–10.

Duck, S. (1985). Social and personal relationships. In S. R. Miller & M. L. Knapp (Eds.), *The handbook of interpersonal communication.* Beverly Hills, CA: Sage.

Duck, S., & Gilmour, R. (Eds.). (1981). *Personal relationships. 1: Studying personal relationships.* London: Academic Press.

Dutton, D. G., & Aron, A. P. (1974). Some evidence for heightened sexual attraction under conditions of high anxiety. *Journal of Personality and Social Psychology, 30,* 510–517.

Dutton, D. G., & Lake, R. A. (1973). Threat of own prejudice and reverse discrimination in interracial situations. *Journal of Personality and Social Psychology, 30,* 510–517.

Duval, S., & Wicklund, R. A. (1972). *A theory of objective self-awareness.* New York: Academic Press.

Eagly, A. H. (1987). *Sex differences in social behavior: A social-role interpretation.* Hillsdale, NJ: Erlbaum.

Eagly, A. H., & Carli, L. (1981). Sex of researchers and sex-typed communications as determinants of sex differences in influence ability: A meta-analysis of social influence studies. *Psychological Bulletin, 90,* 1–20.

Eagly, A. H., & Chaiken, S. (1984). Cognitive theories of persuasion. In L. Berkowitz (Ed.), *Advances in experimental social psychology* (Vol. 17, pp. 267–359). New York: Academic Press.

Eagly, A. H., & Steffen, V. J. (1984). Gender stereotypes stem from the distribution of women and men into social roles. *Journal of Personality and Social Psychology, 46,* 735–754.

Eagly, A. H., & Steffen, V. J. (1986). Gender stereotypes, occupational roles, and beliefs about part-time employees. *Psychology of Women Quarterly, 10,* 252–262.

Eagly, A. H., & Wood, W. (1982). Inferred sex differences in status as a determinant of gender stereotypes about social influence. *Journal of Personality and Social Psychology, 43,* 915–928.

Ebbesen, E. B., & Bowers, R. J. (1974). Proportion of risky to conservative arguments in a group discussion and choice shift. *Journal of Personality and Social Psychology, 29,* 316–327.

Ebbesen, E. B., Kjos, G. L., & Konecni, V. J. (1976). Spatial ecology: Its effects on the choice of friends and enemies. *Journal of Experimental Social Psychology, 12,* 505–518.

Eidelson, R. J. (1980). Interpersonal satisfaction and level of involvement: A curvilinear relationship. *Journal of Personality and Social Psychology, 39,* 460–470.

Eisen, S. V. (1979). Actor-observer differences in information inferences and causal attribution. *Journal of Personality and Social Psychology, 37,* 261–272.

Eisenberg, N., Cialdini, R. B., McCreath, H., & Shell, R. (1987). Consistency-based compliance: When and why do children become vulnerable? *Journal of Personality and Social Psychology, 52,* 1174–1181.

Eisenberg, N., & Miller, P. (1987). The relation of empathy to prosocial behavior and related behaviors. *Psychological Bulletin, 101,* 91–119.

Eiser, J. R. (1983). Smoking, addiction, and decision-making. *Journal of Applied Social Psychology, 32,* 11–28.

Eiser, J. R., & van der Plight, J. (1984). Attitudinal and social factors in adolescent smoking: In search of peer group influence. *Journal of Applied Social Psychology, 14,* 348–363.

Ekman, P., & Friesen, W. V. (1975). *Unmasking the face.* Englewood Cliffs, NJ: Prentice-Hall.

Ekman, P., Friesen, W., O'Sullivan, C. A., Diacoyanni-Tariatzis, H. K., Heider, K., Krause, R., LeCompte, W., Pitcairn, T., Ricci-Biti, P. E., Schener, K., Tomita, M., & Tzavaras, A. (1987). Universals and cultural differences in the judgments of facial expressions of emotion. *Journal of Personality and Social Psychology, 53,* 712–717.

Elkin, R. A., & Leippe, M. R. (1986). Physiological arousal, dissonance, and attitude change: Evidence for a dissonance-arousal link and a "don't remind me" effect. *Journal of Personality and Social Psychology, 51,* 55–65.

Ellis, S., Rogoff, B., & Cramer, C. C. (1981). Age segregation in children's social interactions. *Developmental Psychology, 17,* 399–407.

Ellsworth, P. C., & Carlsmith, J. M. (1973). Eye contact and gaze aversion in an aggressive encounter. *Journal of Personality and Social Psychology, 28,* 280–292.

Ellsworth, P. C., & Langer, E. J. (1976). Staring and approach: An interpretation of the stare as a non-specific activator. *Journal of Personality and Social Psychology, 33,* 117–122.

Elstein, A. S., Shulman, L. S., & Sprafka, S. A. (1978). *Medical problem solving: An analysis of clinical reasoning.* Cambridge, MA: Harvard University Press.

Erber, R., & Fiske, S. T. (1984). Outcome dependency and attention to inconsistent information. *Journal of Personality and Social Psychology, 47,* 709–726.

Eron, L. D. (1982). Parent-child interaction, television violence, and aggression of children. *American Psychologist, 37,* 197–211.

Eron, L. D. (1987). The development of aggressive behavior from the perspective of a developing behaviorism. *American Psychologist, 42,* 435–442.

Erwin, P. G., & Calev, A. (1984). Beauty: More than skin deep? *Journal of Social and Personal Relationships, 1,* 359–361.

Evans, M. C., & Wilson, M. (1949). Friendship choices of university women students. *Educational and Psychological Measurement, 9,* 307–312.

Fajardo, D. M. (1985). Author race, essay quality, and reverse discrimination. *Journal of Applied Social Psychology, 15,* 255–268.

Fazio, R. H. (1981). On the self-perception explanation of the over-justification effect. *Journal of Experimental Social Psychology, 17,* 417–426.

Fazio, R. H. (1988). On the power and functionality of attitudes. In A. R. Pratkanis, S. J. Breckler, & A. G. Greenwald (Eds.), *Attitude structure and function.* Hillsdale, NJ: Erlbaum.

Fazio, R. H., Chen, J., McDonel, E. C., & Sherman, S. J. (1982). Attitude accessibility, attitude-behavior consistency, and the strength of the object-evaluation association. *Journal of Experimental Social Psychology, 18,* 339–357.

Fazio, R. H., Lenn, T. M., & Effrein, E. A. (1984). Spontaneous attitude formation. *Social Cognition, 2,* 217–234.

Fazio, R. H., Powell, M. C., & Herr, P. M. (1983). Toward a process model of the attitude-behavior relation: Accessing one's attitude upon mere observation of the attitude object. *Journal of Personality and Social Psychology, 44,* 723–735.

Fazio, R. H., Sanbonmatsu, D. M., Powell, M. C., & Kardes, F. R. (1986). On the automatic activation of attitudes. *Journal of Personality and Social Psychology, 50,* 229–238.

Fazio, R. H., & Williams, C. J. (1986). Attitude accessibility as a moderator of the attitude-perception and attitude-behavior relations: An investigation of the 1984 presidential election. *Journal of Personality and Social Psychology, 51,* 505–514.

Fazio, R. H., & Zanna, M. P. (1978). Attitudinal qualities relating to the strength of the attitude-behavior relationship. *Journal of Experimental Social Psychology, 14,* 398–408.

Fazio, R. H., & Zanna, M. P. (1981). Direct experience and attitude-behavior consistency. In L. Berkowitz (Ed.), *Advances in experimental social psychology* (Vol. 14, pp. 161–202). New York: Academic Press.

Feinberg, R. A., Miller, F. G., & Ross, G. A. (1981). Perceived and actual locus of control similarity among friends. *Personality and Social Psychology Bulletin, 7,* 85–89.

Fenigstein, A., Scheier, M. F., & Buss, A. H. (1975). Public and private self-consciousness: Assessment and theory. *Journal of Consulting and Clinical Psychology, 43,* 522–527.

Ferguson, T. J., & Rule, B. G. (1983). An attributional perspective on anger and aggression. In R. G. Geen & E. I. Donnerstein (Eds.), *Aggression: Theoretical and empirical reviews* (Vol. 1, pp. 41–74). New York: Academic Press.

Feshbach, S. (1984). The catharsis hypothesis, aggressive drive, and the reduction of aggression. *Aggressive Behavior, 10,* 91–101.

Feshbach, S., & Singer, R. D. (1971). *Television and aggression.* San Francisco: Jossey-Bass.

Festinger, L. (1954). A theory of social comparison processes. *Human Relations, 7,* 117–140.

Festinger, L. (1957). *A theory of cognitive dissonance.* Evanston, IL: Row, Peterson.

Festinger, L., & Carlsmith, J. M. (1959). Cognitive consequences of forced compliance. *Journal of Abnormal and Social Psychology, 58,* 203–211.

Festinger, L., Schachter, S., & Back, K. (1950). *Social pressures in informal groups: A study of a housing community.* New York: Harper.

Fiedler, F. E. (1978). Contingency model and the leadership process. In L. Berkowitz (Ed.), *Advances in experimental social psychology* (Vol. 11). New York: Academic Press.

Fiedler, F. E., & Garcia, J. E. (1987). *Leadership: Cognitive resources and performance.* New York: Wiley.

Fincham, F. D., & Bradbury, T. N. (1987). Cognitive processes and conflict in close relationships: An attribution-efficacy model. *Journal of Personality and Social Psychology, 52,* 1106–1118.

Firestone, I. J., Lichtman, C. M., & Colamosca, J. V. (1975). Leader effectiveness and leadership conferral as determinants of helping in a medical emergency. *Journal of Personality and Social Psychology, 31,* 343–348.

Fiske, S. T., & Taylor, S. E. (1984). *Social cognition.* Reading, MA: Addison-Wesley.

Flay, B. R., Ryan, K. B., Best, J. A., Brown, K. S., Kersell, M. W., d'Avernas, J., & Zanna, M. P. (1985). Are social-psychological smoking prevention programs effective? *Journal of Behavioral Medicine, 8,* 37–60.

Fleet, M. L., Brigham, J. C., & Bothwell, R. K. (1987). The confidence—accuracy relationship: The effects of confidence assessment and choosing. *Journal of Applied Social Psychology, 17,* 171–187.

Fleischer, R. A., & Chertkoff, J. M. (1986). Effects of dominance and sex on leader selection in dyadic work groups. *Journal of Personality and Social Psychology, 50,* 94–99.

Fletcher, G. J. O., Fincham, F. D., Cramer, L., & Heron, N. (1987). The role of attributions in the development of dating relationships. *Journal of Personality and Social Psychology, 53,* 481–489.

Folkes, V. S. (1982). Forming relationships and the matching hypothesis. *Journal of Personality and Social Psychology, 8,* 631–636.

Forest, D., Clark, M. S., Mills, J., & Isen, A. M. (1979). Helping as a function of feeling state and nature of the helping behavior. *Motivation and Emotion, 3,* 161–170.

Forgas, J. P., & Bower, G. H. (1987). Mood effects on person-perception judgments. *Journal of Personality and Social Psychology, 53,* 53–60.

Forgas, J. P., Burnham, D. K., & Trimboli, C. (1988). Mood, memory, and social judgments in children. *Journal of Personality and Social Psychology, 54,* 697–703.

Forsterling, F. (1985). Attribution retraining: A review. *Psychological Bulletin, 98,* 495–512.

Franzoi, S. L., & Herzog, M. E. (1987). Judging physical attractiveness: What body aspects do we use? *Personality and Social Psychology Bulletin, 13,* 19–33.

Freedman, J. L. (1984). Effect of television violence on aggressiveness. *Psychological Bulletin, 96,* 227–246.

Freedman, J. L. (1986). Television violence and aggression: A rejoinder. *Psychological Bulletin, 100,* 372–378.

Freedman, J. L., & Fraser, S. C. (1966). Compliance without pressure: The foot-in-the-door technique. *Journal of Personality and Social Psychology, 4,* 195–202.

Freud, S. (1959). *Collected papers.* New York: Basic Books.

Frey, D. L., & Gaertner, S. L. (1987). Helping and the avoidance of inappropriate interracial behavior: A strategy that perpetuates a nonprejudiced self-image. *Journal of Personality and Social Psychology, 50,* 1083–1090.

Frick, R. W. (1985). Communicating emotion: The role of prosodic features. *Psychological Bulletin, 97,* 412–429.

Friedman, M., & Rosenman, R. H. (1959). Association of a specific overt behavior pattern with increases in blood cholesterol, blood clotting time, incidence of arcus senilis, and clinical coronary artery disease. *Journal of the American Medical Association, 169,* 1286–1296.

Friedrich-Cofer, L., & Huston, A. (1986). Television violence and aggression: The debate continues. *Psychological Bulletin, 100,* 364–371.

Fultz, J., Batson, C. D., Fortenbach, V. A., McCarthy, P. M., & Varney, L. L. (1986). Social evaluation and the empathy-altruism hypothesis. *Journal of Personality and Social Psychology, 50,* 761–769.

Gabrielcik, A., & Fazio, R. H. (1983). Priming and frequency estimation: A strict test of the availability heuristic. *Personality and Social Psychology Bulletin, 10,* 85–89.

Gaertner, S. L., & Dovidio, J. F. (1977). The subtlety of white racism, arousal, and helping behavior. *Journal of Personality and Social Psychology, 35,* 691–707.

Gastorf, J. W., Suls, J., & Sanders, G. S. (1980). Type A coronary-prone behavior pattern and social facilitation. *Journal of Personality and Social Psychology, 38,* 773–780.

Gavanski, I., & Hoffman, C. (1987). Awareness of influences on one's own judgments: The roles of covariation detection and attention to the judgment process. *Journal of Personality and Social Psychology, 52,* 453–463.

Geen, R. G. (1968). Effects of frustration, attack, and prior training in aggressiveness upon aggressive behavior. *Journal of Personality and Social Psychology, 9,* 316–321.

Geen, R. G. (1978). Some effects of observing violence upon the behavior of the observer. In B. A. Maher (Ed.), *Progress in experimental personality research* (Vol. 8). New York: Academic Press.

Geen, R. G. (1981). Behavioral and physiological reactions to observed violence: Effects of prior exposure to aggressive stimuli. *Journal of Personality and Social Psychology, 40,* 868–875.

Geen, R. G., & Donnerstein, E. (Eds.). (1983). *Aggression: Theoretical and empirical reviews.* New York: Academic Press.

Geen, R. G., & Gange, J. J. (1977). Drive theory of social facilitation: Twelve years of theory and research. *Psychological Bulletin, 84,* 1267–1288.

Geier, J. G. (1969). A trait approach to the study of leadership in small groups. *Journal of Communication, 17,* 316–323.

Geiselman, R. E., Haight, N. A., & Kimata, L. G. (1984). Context effects on the perceived physical attractiveness of faces. *Journal of Experimental Social Psychology, 20,* 409–424.

Georgoudi, M., & Rosnow, R. L. (1985). Notes toward a contextualist understanding of social psychology. *Personality and Social Psychology Bulletin, 11,* 5–22.

Gerard, H. B. (1983). School desegregation: The social science role. *American Pschologist, 38,* 869–877.

Gerard, H. B., Wilhelmy, R. A., & Conolley, E. S. (1968). Conformity and group size. *Journal of Personality and Social Psychology, 8,* 79–82.

Gerrard, M. (1987). Sex, sex guilt, and contraceptive use revisited: The 1980s. *Journal of Personality and Social Psychology, 52,* 975–980.

Gibbons, F. X. (1978). Sexual standards and reactions to pornography: Enhancing behavioral consistency through self-focused attention. *Journal of Personality and Social Psychology, 36,* 976–987.

Gilbert, D., & Jones, E. E. (1986). Perceiver-induced constraint: Interpretations of self-generated reality. *Journal of Personality and Social Psychology, 50,* 269–280.

Gillen, B. (1981). Physical attractiveness: A determinant of two types of goodness. *Personality and Social Psychology Bulletin, 7,* 277–281.

Gillis, J. S., & Avis, W. E. (1980). The male-taller norm in mate selection. *Personality and Social Psychology Bulletin, 6,* 396–401.

Gilovich, T., & Regan, D. T. (1986). The actor and the experiencer: Divergent patterns of causal attribution. *Social Cognition, 4,* 342–352.

Ginzel, L. E., Jones, E E., & Swann, W. B. (1987). How naive is the naive attributor: Discounting and augmentation in attitude attribution. *Social Cognition, 5,* 108–130.

Gioia, D. A., & Sims, H. P., Jr. (1985). Self-serving bias and actor-observer differences in organizations: An empirical analysis. *Journal of Applied Social Psychology, 15,* 547–563.

Glenn, N. D., & Weaver, C. N. (1979). Attitudes toward premarital, extramarital, and homosexual relations in the U.S. in the 1970s. *Journal of Sex Research, 15,* 108–118.

Glenn, N. D., & Weaver, C. N. (in press). The changing

relationship of marital status to reported happiness. *Journal of Marriage and the Family.*

Godfrey, D. K., Jones, E. E., & Lord, C. G. (1986). Self-promotion is not ingratiating. *Journal of Personality and Social Psychology, 50,* 106–115.

Goethals, G. R. (1986a). Social comparison theory: Psychology from the lost and found. *Personality and Social Psychology Bulletin, 12,* 261–278.

Goethals, G. R. (1986b). Fabricating and ignoring social reality: Self-serving estimates of consensus. In J. Olson, C. P. Herman, & M. P. Zanna (Eds.), *Relative deprivation and social comparison: The Ontario symposium on social cognition IV.* Hillsdale, NJ: Erlbaum.

Goethals, G. R., Cooper, J., & Naficy, A. (1979). Role of foreseen, foreseeable, and unforeseeable behavioral consequences in the arousal cognitive dissonance. *Journal of Personality and Social Psychology, 37,* 1179–1185.

Goethals, G. R., & Darley, J. M. (1987). Social comparison theory: Self-evaluation and group life. In B. Mullen & G. R. Goethals (Eds.), *Theories of group behavior.* New York: Springer-Verlag.

Goethals, G. R., & Zanna, M. P. (1979). The role of social comparison in choice shifts. *Journal of Personality and Social Psychology, 37,* 1469–1476.

Gold, J. A., Ryckman, R. M., & Mosley, N. R. (1984). Romantic mood induction and attraction to a dissimilar other: Is love blind? *Personality and Social Psychology Bulletin, 10,* 358–368.

Goldstein, J. H., David R. W., & Herman, D. (1975). Escalation of aggression: Experimental studies. *Journal of Personality and Social Psychology, 39,* 670–679.

Goleman, D. (1986, April 8). Studies point to power of nonverbal signals. *New York Times,* C-1, C-6.

Gonzales, M. Hope, David, J. M., Loney, G. L., Lukens, C. K., & Junghans, C. M. (1983). Interactional approach to interpersonal attraction. *Journal of Personality and Social Psychology, 44,* 1192–1197.

Gormly, A. V. (1979). Behavioral effects of receiving agreement or disagreement from a peer. *Personality and Social Psychology Bulletin, 5,* 405–408.

Gormly, J. B., & Gormly, A. V. (1981). Approach-avoidance: Potency in psychological research. *Bulletin of the Psychonomic Society, 17,* 221–223.

Gottlieb, J., & Carver, C. S. (1980). Anticipation of future interaction and the bystander effect. *Journal of Experimental Social Psychology, 16,* 253–260.

Gouaux, C. (1971). Induced affective states and interpersonal attraction. *Journal of Personality and Social Psychology, 20,* 37–43.

Gould, R., & Sigall, H. (1977). The effects of empathy and outcome on attribution: An examination of the divergent-perspectives hypothesis. *Journal of Experimental Social Psychology, 13,* 480–491.

Gouldner, A. (1960). The norm of reciprocity: A preliminary statement. *American Sociological Review, 25,* 161–178.

Granberg, D., & King, M. (1980). Cross-lagged panel analysis of the relation between attraction and perceived similarity. *Journal of Experimental Social Psychology, 16,* 573–581.

Graziano, W., Brothen, T., & Berscheid, E. (1978). Height and attraction: Do men and women see eye-to-eye? *Journal of Personality, 46,* 128–145.

Greco, R. S. (1983). Haiti and the stigma of AIDS. *Lancet,* 515–516.

Greedlinger, V., & Byrne, D. (1985). Propinquity and affiliative needs as joint determinants of classroom friendships. Unpublished manuscript.

Green, S. K., Buchanan, D. R., & Heuer, S. K. (1984). Winners, losers, and choosers: A field investigation of dating initiation. *Personality and Social Psychology Bulletin, 10,* 502–511.

Greenbaum, P., & Rosenfield, H. W. (1978). Patterns of avoidance in response to interpersonal staring and proximity: Effects of bystanders on drivers at a traffic intersection. *Journal of Personality and Social Psychology, 36,* 575–587.

Greenberg, J., & Musham, C. (1981). Avoiding and seeking self-focused attention. *Journal of Research in Personality, 15,* 191–200.

Greenberg, J., Pyszcynski, T., & Solomon, S. (1982). The self-serving attributional bias: Beyond self-presentation. *Journal of Experimental Social Psychology, 18,* 56–67.

Greenwald, A. G. (1968). Cognitive learning, cognitive response to persuasion, and attitude change. In A. Greenwald, T. Brock, & T. Ostrom (Eds.), *Psychological foundations of attitudes* (pp. 148–170). New York: Academic Press.

Greenwald, A. G. (1988). Why are attitudes important? In A. R. Pratkanis, S. J. Breckler, & A. G. Greenwald (Eds.), *Attitude structure and function.* Hillsdale, NJ: Erlbaum.

Greenwald, A. G., & Ronis, D. L. (1978). Twenty years of cognitive dissonance: Case study of the evolution of a theory. *Psychological Review, 85,* 53–57.

Griffitt, W. (1970). Environmental effects on interpersonal affective behavior: Ambient effective temperature and attraction. *Journal of Personality and Social Psychology, 15,* 240–244.

Griffitt, W., May, J., & Veitch, R. (1974). Sexual stimulation and interpersonal behavior: Heterosexual evaluative responses, visual behavior, and physical proximity. *Journal of Personality and Social Psychology, 30,* 367–377.

Groff, B. D., Baron, R. S., & Moore, D. L. (1983). Distraction, attentional conflict, and drivelike behavior. *Journal of Experimental Social Psychology, 19,* 359–380.

Gross, A. E., & Fleming, I. (1982). Twenty years of deception in social psychology. *Personality and Social Psychology Bulletin, 8,* 402–408.

Gully, K. J., & Dengerink, H. A. (1983). The dyadic interaction of persons with violent and nonviolent histories. *Aggressive Behavior, 9,* 13–20.

Gutek, B. A. (1985). *Sexism and the workplace.* San Francisco: Jossey-Bass.

Gyllenhammer, P. G. (1977, July–August). How Volvo adapts work to people. *Harvard Business Review,* pp. 102–113.

Hamilton, D. L., Dugan, P. M., & Troilier, T. K. (1985). The formation of stereotypic beliefs: Further evidence for distinctiveness-based illusory correlations. *Journal of Personality and Social Psychology, 48,* 5–17.

Hamilton, V. L. (1978). Obedience and responsibility: A jury simulation. *Journal of Personality and Social Psychology, 36,* 126–146.

Hansen, C. H., & Hansen, R. D. (1988). Finding the face-in-the-crowd: An anger superiority effect. *Journal of Personality and Social Psychology, 54,* 917–924.

Hansen, R. D., & Hill, C. H. (1985). Discounting and augmenting facilitative and inhibitory forces: The winner takes almost all. *Journal of Personality and Social Psychology, 49,* 1482–1493.

Harackiewicz, J. M., & Larson, J. R. (1986). Managing motivation: The impact of supervisor feedback on subordinate task interest. *Journal of Personality and Social Psychology, 51,* 547–570.

Harkins, S. G. (1987). Social loafing and social facilitation. *Journal of Experimental Social Psychology, 23,* 1–18.

Harkins, S. G., & Petty, R. E. (1987). Information utility and the multiple source effect. *Journal of Personality and Social Psychology, 52,* 260–268.

Harris, M. B., Harris, R. J., & Bochner, S. (1982). Fat, four-eyed, and female: Stereotypes of obesity, glasses, and gender. *Journal of Applied Social Psychology, 12,* 503–516.

Harvey, J. H., & Weary, G. (1985). *Attribution: Basic issues and applications.* San Diego: Academic Press.

Hatfield, E. (1983). Passionate love scale. Personal communication.

Hatfield, E., & Sprecher, S. (1986). *Mirror, mirror . . . The importance of looks in everyday life.* Albany, NY: State University of New York Press.

Hatfield, E., & Walster, G. W. (1981). *A new look at love.* Reading, MA: Addison-Wesley.

Hays, R. B. (1984). The development and maintenance of friendship. *Journal of Social and Personal Relationships, 1,* 75–98.

Hays, R., & DiMatteo, M. R. (1984). Toward a more therapeutic physician-patient relationship. In

S. Duck (Ed.), *Personal relationships:* Vol. 5. *Repairing personal relationships* (pp. 1–20). New York: Academic Press.

Hazan, C., & Shaver, P. (1987). Romantic love conceptualized as an attachment process. *Journal of Personality and Social Psychology, 52,* 511–524.

Heath, L. (1984). Impact of newspaper crime reports on fear of crime: Multimethodological investigation. *Journal of Personality and Social Psychology, 47,* 263–276.

Heerwagen, J. H., Beach, L. R., & Mitchell, T. R. (1985). Dealing with poor performance: Supervisor attributions and the cost of responding. *Journal of Applied Social Psychology, 15,* 638–655.

Heider, F. (1958). *The psychology of interpersonal relations.* New York: Wiley.

Heimberg, R. G., Acerra, M. C., & Holstein, A. (1985). Partner similarity mediates interpersonal anxiety. *Cognitive Therapy & Research, 9,* 443–453.

Helmreich, R. L., Spence, J. T., & Gibson, R. H. (1982). Sex-role attitudes: 1972–1980. *Personality and Social Psychology Bulletin, 8,* 656–663.

Hemstone, M., & Jaspars, J. (1982). Explanations for racial discrimination: The effects of group decision on intergroup attributions. *European Journal of Social Psychology, 12,* 1–16.

Henderson, J., & Taylor, J. (1985, November 17). Study finds bias in death sentences: Killers of whites risk execution. *Times Union,* p. A-19.

Hendrick, C. (Ed.). (1987). *Group processes.* Beverly Hills, CA: Sage.

Hendrick, C., & Constantini, A. F. (1970). Effects of varying trait inconsistency and response requirements on the primacy effect in impression formation. *Journal of Personality and Social Psychology, 15,* 158–164.

Hendrick, C., & Hendrick, S. (1986). A theory and method of love. *Journal of Personality and Social Psychology, 50,* 392–402.

Henley, N. M. (1973). The politics of touch. In P. Brown (Ed.), *Radical psychology.* New York: Harper & Row.

Herr, P. M. (1986). Consequences of priming: Judgment and behavior. *Journal of Personality and Social Psychology, 51,* 1106–1114.

Hertel, P. T., & Narvaez, A. (1986). Confusing memories for verbal and nonverbal communication. *Journal of Personality and Social Psychology, 50,* 474–481.

Higgins, E. T., Rholes, W. S., & Jones, C. R. (1977). Category accessibility and impression formation. *Journal of Experimental Social Psychology, 13,* 141–154.

Hill, C. A. (1987). Affiliation motivation: People who need people but in different ways. *Journal of Personality and Social Psychology, 52,* 1008–1018.

Hinsz, V. B., & Davis, J. H. (1984). Persuasive arguments theory, group polarization, and choice shifts. *Personality and Social Psychology Bulletin, 10,* 260–268.

Hirschman, R. S., Leventhal, H., & Glynn, K. (1984). The development of smoking behavior: Conceptualization and supportive cross-sectional survey data. *Journal of Applied Social Psychology, 14,* 184–206.

Hoffman, L. W. (1979). Maternal employment: 1979. *American Psychologist, 34,* 859–865.

Hoffman, M. L. (1981). Is altruism part of human nature? *Journal of Personality and Social Psychology, 40,* 121–137.

Hokanson, J. E., Burgess, M., & Cohen, M. E. (1963). Effects of displaced aggression on systolic blood pressure. *Journal of Abnormal and Social Psychology, 67,* 214–218.

Hollander, E. P. (1978). *Leadership dynamics: A practical guide to effective relationships.* New York: Free Press.

Holmes, D. S., McGilley, B. M., & Houston, B. K. (1984). Task-related arousal of Type A and Type B persons: Level of challenge and response specificity. *Journal of Personality and Social Psychology, 46,* 1322–1327.

Holtzworth-Munroe, A., & Jacobson, N. S. (1985). Causal attributions of married couples: When do they search for causes? What do they conclude when they do? *Journal of Personality and Social Psychology, 48,* 1398–1412.

Horvath, T. (1979). Correlates of physical beauty in men and women. *Social Behavior and Personality, 7,* 145–151.

House, R. J., & Baetz, M. L. (1979). Leadership: Some generalizations and new research directions. In B. M. Staw (Ed.), *Research in organizational behavior.* Greenwich, CT: JAI Press.

Houston, B. K. (1983). Psychophysiological responsivity and the Type A behavior pattern. *Journal of Research in Personality, 17,* 22–39.

Hovland, C. I. (1959). Reconciling conflicting results derived from experimental and survey studies of attitude change. *American Psychologist, 14,* 8–17.

Hovland, C. I., Lumsdaine, A., & Sheffield, F. (1949). Experiments on mass communication. In *Studies in social psychology in World War II.* Princeton, NJ: Princeton University Press.

Hovland, C. I., & Weiss, W. (1952). The influence of source credibility on communication effectiveness. *Public Opinion Quarterly, 15,* 635–650.

Huesmann, L. R. (1982). Television violence and aggressive behavior. In D. Pearl, L. Bouthilet, & J. Lazar (Eds.). *Television and behavior* (pp. 220–256). Washington, DC: National Institute of Mental Health.

Huff, C., & Cooper, J. (1987). Sex bias in educational software: The effect of designers' stereotypes on the software they design. *Journal of Applied Social Psychology, 17,* 519–532.

Hull, J. G. (1981). A self-awareness model of the causes and effects of alcohol consumption. *Journal of Abnormal Psychology, 90,* 586–600.

Hull, J. G., & Levy, A. S. (1979). The organizational functions of the self: An alternative to the Duval and Wicklund model of self-awareness. *Journal of Personality and Social Psychology, 37,* 756–768.

Hull, J. G., Van Treuren, R., Ashford, S. J., Propsom, P., & Andrus, B. W. (1988). Self-consciousness and the processing of self-relevant information. *Journal of Personality and Social Psychology, 54,* 452–466.

Hull, J. G., & Young, R. D. (1983). Self-consciousness, self-esteem, and success-failure as determinants of alcohol consumption in male social drinkers. *Journal of Personality and Social Psychology, 44,* 1097–1109.

Hull, J. G., Young, R. D., & Jouriles, E. (1986). Applications of the self-awareness model of alcohol consumption: Predicting patterns of use and abuse. *Journal of Personality and Social Psychology, 51,* 790–796.

Hunter, J. E., & Schmidt, F. L. (1983). Quantifying the effects of psychological interventions on employee job performance and work-force productivity. *American Psychologist, 38,* 473–478.

Huston, T. L., Ruggiero, M., Conner, R., & Geiss, G. (1981). Bystander intervention into crime: A study based on naturally-occurring episodes. *Social Psychology Quarterly, 44,* 14–23.

Ickes, W. (1984). Compositions in black and white: Determinants of interaction in interracial dyads. *Journal of Personality and Social Psychology, 47,* 330–341.

Ickes, W., Patterson, M. L., Rajecki, D. W., & Tanford, S. (1982). Behavioral and cognitive consequences of reciprocal versus compensatory responses to preinteraction expectancies. *Social Cognition, 1,* 160–190.

Ilgen, D., Fisher, C., & Taylor, S. (1979). Consequences of individual feedback on behavior in organizations. *Journal of Applied Psychology, 64,* 349–371.

Ingham, A. G., Levinger, G., Graves, J., & Peckham, V. (1974). The Ringelmann effect: Studies of group size and performance. *Journal of Experimental Social Psychology, 10,* 371–384.

Insko, C. A. (1985). Balance theory, the Jordan paradigm, and the Wiest tetrahedron. In L. Berkowitz (Ed.), *Advances in experimental social psychology.* New York: Academic Press.

Insko, C. A., Sedlak, A. J., & Lipsitz, A. (1982). A two-valued logic or two-valued balance resolution of the challenge of agreement and attraction effects in p-o-x triads, and a theoretical perspective on conformity and hedonism. *European Journal of Social Psychology, 12,* 143–167.

Isen, A. M. (1984). Toward understanding the role of affect in cognition. In R. S. Wyer, Jr. & T. K. Srull (Eds.), *Handbook of social cognition* (Vol. 3). Hillsdale, NJ: Erlbaum.

Isen, A. M. (1987). Positive affect, cognitive processes, and social behavior. In L. Berkowitz (Ed.), *Advances in experimental social psychology* (Vol. 20). New York: Academic Press.

Isen, A. M., Clark, M., & Schwartz, M. F. (1976). Duration of the effect of good mood on helping: "Footprints on the sands of time." *Journal of Personality and Social Psychology, 34,* 385–393.

Isen, A. M., Daubman, K. A., & Nowicki, G. P. (1987). Positive affect facilitates creative problem solving. *Journal of Personality and Social Psychology, 52,* 1122–1131.

Isen, A. M., Horn, N., & Rosenhan, D. L. (1973). Effects of success and failure on children's generosity. *Journal of Personality and Social Psychology, 27,* 239–247.

Isenberg, D. J. (1986). Group polarization: A critical review and meta-analysis. *Journal of Personality and Social Psychology, 50,* 1141–1151.

Istvan, J., Griffitt, W., & Weidner, G. (1983). Sexual arousal and the polarization of perceived sexual attractiveness. *Basic and Applied Social Psychology, 4,* 307–318.

Izard, C. (1977). *Human emotions.* New York: Plenum.

Izraeli, D. N., & Izraeli, D. (1985). Sex effects in evaluating leaders: A replication study. *Journal of Applied Psychology, 70,* 540–546.

Jackson, L. A. (1983). The influence of sex, physical attractiveness, sex role, and occupational sex-linkage on perceptions of occupational suitability. *Journal of Applied Social Psychology, 13,* 31–44.

Jamieson, D. W., Lydon, J. E., & Zanna, M. P. (1987). Attitude and activity preference similarity: Differential bases of interpersonal attraction for low and high self-monitors. *Journal of Personality and Social Psychology, 53,* 1052–1060.

Janis, I. L. (1954). Personality correlates of susceptibility to persuasion. *Journal of Personality, 22,* 504–518.

Janis, I. L. (1982). *Groupthink: Psychological studies of policy decisions and fiascoes* (2nd ed.). Boston: Houghton Mifflin.

Jay, S. M., Ozolins, M., Elliott, C. H., & Caldwell, S. (1983). Assessment of children's distress during painful medical procedures. *Health Psychology, 2,* 133–147.

Jellison, J. M., & Oliver, D. F. (1983). Attitude similarity and attraction: An impression management approach. *Personality and Social Psychology Bulletin, 9,* 111–115.

Jemmott, J. B. III, Croyle, R. T., & Ditto, P. H. (1988). Commonsense epidemiology: Self-based judgments from laypersons and physicians. *Health Psychology, 7,* 55–73.

Jemmott, J. B. III, Ditto, P. H., & Croyle, R. T. (1986). Judging health status: Effects of perceived prevalence and personal relevance. *Journal of Personality and Social Psychology, 50,* 899–905.

Johnson, J. E. (1984). Psychological interventions and coping with surgery. In A. Baum, S. E. Taylor, & J. E. Singer (Eds.), *Handbook of psychology and health* (Vol. 4, pp. 167–187). Hillsdale, NJ: Erlbaum.

Johnson, J. T., Jemmott, J. B., III, & Pettigrew, T. F. (1984). Causal attribution and dispositional inference: Evidence of inconsistent judgments. *Journal of Experimental Social Psychology, 20,* 567–585.

Johnson, T. E., & Rule, B. G. (1986). Mitigating circumstance information, censure, and aggression. *Journal of Personality and Social Psychology, 50,* 537–542.

Jones, E. E. (1964). *Ingratiation: A social psychological analysis.* New York: Appleton-Century-Crofts.

Jones, E. E. (1985). Major developments in social psychology during the past five decades. In G. Lindzey & E. Aronson (Eds.), *Handbook of social psychology* (3rd ed., Vol. 1) (pp. 1–46). New York: Random House.

Jones, E. E., & Berglas, S. (1978). Control of attributions about the self through self-handicapping strategies: The appeal of alcohol and the role of underachievement. *Personality and Social Psychology Bulletin, 4,* 200–206.

Jones, E. E., & Davis, K. E. (1965). From acts to dispositions: The attribution process in person perception. In L. Berkowitz (Ed.), *Advances in experimental social psychology* (Vol. 2). New York: Academic Press.

Jones, E. E., & Harris, V. (1967). The attribution of attitudes. *Journal of Experimental Social Psychology, 3,* 1–24.

Jones, E. E., & McGillis, D. (1976). Corresponding inferences and the attribution cube: A comparative reappraisal. In J. H. Harvey, W. J. Ickes, & R. F. Kidd (Eds.), *New directions in attribution research* (Vol. 1). Hillsdale, NJ: Erlbaum.

Jones, E. E., & Nisbett R. E. (1971). *The actor and the observer: Divergent perceptions of the causes of behavior.* Morristown, NJ: Erlbaum.

Josephson, W. L. (1987). Television violence and children's aggression: Testing the priming, social script, and disinhibition predictions. *Journal of Personality and Social Psychology, 53,* 882–890.

Kahneman, D., & Miller, D. T. (1986). Norm theory: Comparing reality to its alternatives. *Psychological Review, 93,* 136–153.

Kalick, S. M., & Hamilton, T. E., III (1986). The matching hypothesis reexamined. *Journal of Personality and Social Psychology, 51,* 673–682.

Kalick, S. M., & Hamilton, T. E. (1988). Closer look at a matching simulation. *Journal of Personality and Social Psychlogy, 54,* 447–452.

Kandel, D. B. (1978). Similarity in real-life adolescent friendship pairs. *Journal of Personality and Social Psychology, 36,* 306–312.

Kandel, D. B., Single, E., & Kessler, R. C. (1976). The epidemiology of drug use among New York State high school students: Distribution, trends, and change in rates of use. *American Journal of Public Health, 15,* 43–53.

Kaplan, M. F. (1987). The influencing process in group decision making. In C. Hendrick (Ed.), *Group processes.* Newbury Park, CA: Sage Publications.

Kaplan, M. F., & Miller, C. E. (1987). Group decision making and normative versus informational influence: Effects of type of issue and assigned decision rule. *Journal of Personality and Social Psychology, 53,* 306–313.

Katz, A. N. (1987). Self-reference in the encoding of creative-relevant traits. *Journal of Personality, 55,* 97–120.

Katz, D. (1960). The functional approach to the study of attitudes. *Public Opinion Quarterly, 24,* 163–204.

Katzell, R. A., & Guzzo, R. A. (1983). Psychological approaches to productivity improvement. *American Psychologist, 38,* 468–472.

Kaufman, M. T. (1980, Nov. 16). Love upsetting Bombay's view of path to altar. *New York Times,* p. 12.

Kelley, H. H. (1972). Attribution in social interaction. In E. E. Jones et al. (Eds.), *Attribution: Perceiving the causes of behavior.* Morristown, NJ: General Learning Press.

Kelley, H. H., & Michela, J. L. (1980). Attribution theory and research. *Annual Review of Psychology, 31,* 457–501.

Kelman, H. C. (1967). Human use of human subjects: The problem of deception in social psychological experiments. *Psychological Bulletin, 67,* 1–11.

Kenrick, D. T., Cialdini, R. B., & Linder, D. E. (1979). Misattribution under fear-producing circumstances: Four failures to replicate. *Personality and Social Psychology Bulletin, 5,* 329–334.

Kenrick, D. T., & Gutierres, S. E. (1980). Contrast effects and judgments of physical attractiveness: When beauty becomes a social problem. *Journal of Personality and Social Psychology, 38,* 131–140.

Kenrick, D. T., & Johnson, G. A. (1979). Interpersonal attraction in aversive environments: A problem for the classical conditioning paradigm? *Journal of Personality and Social Psychology, 37,* 572–579.

Kenrick, D. T., & MacFarlane, S. W. (1986). Ambient temperature and horn honking: A field study of the heat/aggression relationship. *Environment and Behavior, 18,* 179–191.

Kent, G. G., Davis, J. D., & Shapiro, D. A. (1981). Effect of mutual acquaintance on the construction of conversation. *Journal of Experimental Social Psychology, 17,* 197–209.

Kerber, K. W. (1984). The perception of nonemergency helping situations: Costs, rewards, and the altruistic personality. *Journal of Personality, 52,* 177–187.

Kernis, M. H., & Wheeler, L. (1981). Beautiful friends and ugly strangers: Radiation and contrast effects in perceptions of same-sex pairs. *Personality and Social Psychology Bulletin, 7,* 617–620.

Kerr, N. L. (1978a). Beautiful and blameless: Effects of victim awareness and responsibility on mock juror verdicts. *Personality and Social Psychology Bulletin, 4,* 479–482.

Kerr, N. L. (1978b). Severity of prescribed penalty and mock juror's verdicts. *Journal of Personality and Social Psychology, 36,* 1431–1442.

Kerr, N. L. (1981). Social transition schemes: Charting the group's road to agreement. *Journal of Personality and Social Psychology, 41,* 684–702.

Kerr, N. L. (1983). Social transition schemes: Model, method, and applications. In J. H. Davis & H. Brandstatter (Eds.), *Group decision making processes.* New York: Academic Press.

Kerr, N. L., & Brunn, S. E. (1983). Dispensability or member effort and group motivation losses: Free-ride effects. *Journal of Personality and Social Psychology, 44,* 78–94.

Kerr, N. L., & MacCoun, R. J. (1985). The effects of jury size and polling method on the process and product of jury deliberation. *Journal of Personality and Social Psychology, 48,* 349–363.

Kerr, N. L., MacCoun, R. J., Hansen, C. H., & Hymes, J. A. (1987). Gaining and losing social support: Momentum in decision-making groups. *Journal of Experimental Social Psychology, 23,* 119–145.

Kiecolt-Glaser, J. K., & Glaser, R. (1987). Psychosocial moderators of immune function. *Annals of Behavioral Medicine, 9,* 16–20.

Kiesler, C. A. (1985). Psychology and public policy. In E. M. Altmaier and M. E. Meyer (Eds.), *Applied specialties in psychology* (pp. 375–390). New York: Random House.

Kiesler, C. A., & Kiesler, S. B. (1969). *Conformity.* Reading, MA: Addison-Wesley.

Kiesler, S., Siegel, J., & McGuire, T. W. (1984). Social psychological aspects of computer-mediated communication. *American Psychologist, 39,* 1123–1134.

Kihlstrom, J. F., & Cantor, N. (1984). Mental representations of the self. In L. Berkowitz (Ed.), *Advances in experimental social psychology* (Vol. 17, pp. 1–47). New York: Academic Press.

Kilham, W., & Mann, L. (1974). Level of destructive obedience as a function of transmitter and executant roles in the Milgram obedience paradigm. *Journal of Personality and Social Psychology, 29,* 696–702.

Kipnis, D. (1984). *The powerholders.* Chicago: University of Chicago Press.

Kirchler, E., & Davis, J. H. (1986). The influence of member status differences and task type on group consensus and member position change. *Journal of Personality and Social Psychology, 51,* 83–91.

Kirkland, S. L., Greenberg, J., & Pyszczynski, T. (1987). Further evidence of the deleterious effects of overheard derogatory ethnic labels. *Personality and Social Psychology Bulletin, 13,* 216–227.

Kleinke, C. L. (1986). Gaze and eye contact: A research review. *Psychological Bulletin, 100,* 78–100.

Kleinke, C. L., Meeker, F. B., & LaFong, C. (1974). Effects of gaze, touch and use of name on evaluation of "engaged" couples. *Journal of Research in Personality, 7,* 368–373.

Kleinke, C. L., & Staneski, R. A. (1980). First impressions of female bust size. *Journal of Social Psychology, 110,* 123–134.

Klentz, B., & Beaman, A. L. (1981). The effects of type of information and method of dissemination on the reporting of a shoplifter. *Journal of Applied Psychology, 11,* 64–82.

Knapp, M. L. (1978). *Nonverbal communication in human interaction.* New York: Holt, Rinehart, & Winston.

Knight, G. P. (1980). Behavioral similarity, confederate strategy, and sex composition of dyad as determinants of interpersonal judgments and behavior in the prisoner's dilemma game. *Journal of Research in Personality, 14,* 91–103.

Knowlton, W. A., Jr., & Mitchell, T. R. (1980). Effects of causal attributions on a supervisor's evaluation of subordinate performance. *Journal of Applied Psychology, 65,* 459–466.

Knox, R. E., & Safford, R. K. (1976). Group caution at the race track. *Journal of Experimental Social Psychology, 12,* 317–324.

Kogan, N., & Wallach, M. A. (1964). *Risk taking: A study in cognition and personality.* New York: Holt, Rinehart, & Winston.

Kramer, J. F., & Stephens, L. (1983). Attributions and arousal as mediators of mitigation's effects on retaliation. *Journal of Personality and Social Psychology, 45,* 335–343.

Krantz, D. S., Grunberg, N. E., & Baum, A. (1985). Health psychology. In M. R. Rosenzweig & L. W. Porter (Eds.), *Annual review of psychology* (Vol. 36). Palo Alto, CA: Annual Reviews, Inc.

Kraut, R. E., & Poe, D. (1980). Behavioral roots of person perception: The deception judgments of customs inspectors and laymen. *Journal of Personality and Social Psychology, 39,* 784–798.

Kruglanski, A. E., & Mayscless, O. (1987). Motivational effects in the social comparison of opinions. *Journal of Personality and Social Psychology, 53,* 834–842.

Krulewitz, J. E., & Nash, J. E. (1980). Effects of sex role attitudes and similarity on men's rejection of male homosexuals. *Journal of Personality and Social Psychology, 38,* 67–74.

Kulik, J. A., & Brown, R. (1979). Frustration, attribution of blame, and aggression. *Journal of Experimental Social Psychology, 15,* 183–194.

Kulik, J. A., & Mahler, H. I. M. (1987). Effects of preoperative roommate assignment on preoperative anxiety and recovery from coronary-bypass surgery. *Health Psychology, 6,* 525–544.

Kunda, Z. (1987). Motivated inference: Self-serving generation and evaluation of causal theories. *Journal of Personality and Social Psychology, 53,* 636–647.

Kupferberg, S. (1980). The party line: Tupperware and capitalism. *The New Republic, 183* (24), 10–13.

Lamm, H., & Myers, D. G. (1978). Group-induced polarization of attitudes and behavior. In L. Berkowitz (Ed.), *Advances in experimental social psychology.* New York: Academic Press.

Landy, D. (1972). The effects of an overheard audience's reaction and attractiveness on opinion change. *Journal of Experimental Social Psychology, 8,* 276–288.

LaRocco, J. M. (1985). Effects of job conditions on worker perceptions: Ambient stimuli vs. group influence. *Journal of Applied Social Psychology, 15,* 735–757.

Larsen, J. R., Jr. (1986). Supervisors' performance feedback to subordinates: The impact of subordinate performance valence and outcome dependence. *Organizational Behavior and Human Decision Processes, 37,* 391–408.

Latané, B. (1981). The psychology of social impact. *American Psychologist, 36,* 343–356.

Latané, B., & Darley, J. M. (1970). *The unresponsive bystander: Why doesn't he help?* New York: Appleton-Century-Crofts.

Latané, B., & Rodin, J. (1969). A lady in distress: Inhibiting effects of friends and strangers on bystander intervention. *Journal of Experimental Social Psychology, 5,* 189–202.

Latané, B., Williams, K., & Harkins, S. (1979). Many

hands make light the work: The causes and consequences of social loafing. *Journal of Personality and Social Psychology, 37,* 822–832.

Latané, B., & Wolf, S. (1981). The social impact of majorities and minorities. *Psychological Review, 88,* 438–453.

Lau, S. (1982). The effect of smiling on person perception. *Journal of Social Psychology, 117,* 63–67.

Laughlin, P. R. (1980). Social combination processes of cooperative problem-solving groups on verbal intellective tasks. In M. Fishbein (Ed.), *Progress in social psychology.* Hillsdale, NJ: Erlbaum.

Laughlin, P. R. (1988). Collective induction: Group performance, social combination processes, and mutual majority and minority influence. *Journal of Personality and Social Psychology, 54,* 254–267.

Laughlin, P. R., & Earley, P. R. (1982). Social combination models, persuasive arguments theory, social comparison theory, and choice shift. *Journal of Personality and Social Psychology, 42,* 273–280.

Lavrakas, P. J. (1975). Female preferences for male physiques. *Journal of Research in Personality, 9,* 324–334.

Lawler, E. E., III (1982). Strategies for improving the quality of work life. *American Psychologist, 37,* 324–334.

Lawler, E. E., & Mohrman, S. A. (1985). Quality circles after the fad. *Harvard Business Review, 63,* 65–71.

Lazarus, R. S. (1984). On the primacy of cognition. *American Psychologist, 39,* 124–129.

Lazarus, R. S., & Folkman, S. (1984). *Stress, appraisal, and coping.* New York: Springer.

Leary, M. R., Robertson, R. B., Barnes, B. D., & Miller, R. S. (1986). Self-presentations of small group leaders: Effects of role requirements and leadership orientation. *Journal of Personality and Social Psychology, 51,* 742–749.

Lee, L. (1984). Sequences in separation: A framework for investigating endings of the personal (romantic) relationships. *Journal of Social and Personal Relationships, 1,* 49–73.

Lepper, M., & Greene, D. (Eds.). (1978). *The hidden costs of reward.* Hillsdale, NJ: Erlbaum.

Lerner, M. J. (1980). *The belief in a just world: A fundamental delusion.* New York: Plenum Press.

Lesnik-Oberstein, M., & Cohen, L. (1984). Cognitive style, sensation-seeking, and assortative mating. *Journal of Personality and Social Psychology, 46,* 112–117.

Leventhal, A., Nerenz, D. R., & Steele, D. J. (1984). Illness representations and coping with health threats. In A. Baum and J. Singer (Eds.), *Handbook of psychology and health* (pp. 219–252). Hillsdale, NJ: Erlbaum.

Leventhal, E. A., Leventhal, H., Shacham, S., & Easter-

ling, D. V. (in press). Active coping reduces reports of pain from childbirth. *Journal of Consulting and Clinical Psychology.*

Leventhal, H., Glynn, K., & Fleming, R. (1987). Is the smoking decision an "informed choice"? Effect of smoking risk factors on smoking. *Journal of American Medical Association, 257,* 3373–3376.

Leventhal, H., Singer, R., & Jones, S. (1965). The effects of fear and specificity of recommendation upon attitudes and behavior. *Journal of Personality and Social Psychology, 2,* 20–29.

Levinger, G. (1980). Toward the analysis of close relationships. *Journal of Experimental Social Psychology, 16,* 510–544.

Levitt, M. J. (1980). Contingent feedback, familiarization, and infant affect: How a stranger becomes a friend. *Developmental Psychology, 16,* 425–432.

Lewin, K., Lippitt, R., & White, R. K. (1939). Patterns of aggressive behavior in experimentally created "social climates." *Journal of Social Psychology, 10,* 271–299.

Leyens, J. P., Camino, L., Parke, R. D., & Berkowitz, L. (1975). Effects of movie violence on aggression in a field setting as a function of group dominance and cohesion. *Journal of Personality and Social Psychology, 32,* 346–360.

Liebert, R. M., & Baron, R. A. (1972). Some immediate effects of televised violence on children's behavior. *Developmental Psychology, 6,* 469–475.

Liebert, R., & Sprafkin, R. (1988). *The early window: Effects of television on children and youth,* (3rd ed.). New York: Pergamon.

Linder, D. E., Cooper, J., & Jones, E. E. (1967). Decision freedom as a determinant of the role of incentive magnitude in attitude change. *Journal of Personality and Social Psychology, 6,* 245–254.

Lindsay, R. C. L., Lim, R., Marando, L., & Culley, D. (1986). Mock-juror evaluations of eyewitness testimony: A test of metamemory hypotheses. *Journal of Applied Social Psychology, 16,* 447–459.

Lindsay, R. P. (1984). An assessment of the use of cameras in state and federal courts. *Georgia Law Reviews, 18,* 389–424.

Linville, P. W. (1982). The complexity-extremity effect and age-based stereotyping. *Journal of Personality and Social Psychology, 42,* 183–211.

Linz, D., Donnerstein, E., & Penrod, S. (1987). The findings and recommendations of the attorney general's commission on pornography: Do the psychological "facts" fit the political fury? *American Psychologist, 42,* 946–953.

Loftus, E. F. (1980). *Eyewitness testimony.* Cambridge, MA: Harvard University Press.

Lord, C. G., Ross, L., & Lepper, M. R. (1979). Biased assimilation and attitude polarization: The effects of prior theories on subsequently considered evidence. *Journal of Personality and Social Psychology, 37,* 2098–2109.

Lorenz, K. (1966). *On aggression.* New York: Harcourt, Brace & World.

Lorenz, K. (1974). *Civilized man's eight deadly sins.* New York: Harcourt, Brace, Jovanovich.

Loye, D., Gorney, R., & Steele, G. (1977). An experimental field study. *Journal of Communication, 27,* 206–216.

Mass, A., & Clark, R. D., III. (1984). Hidden impact of minorities: Fifteen years of minority influence research. *Psychological Bulletin, 95,* 428–450.

Major, B., Carrington, P. I., & Carnevale, P. J. D. (1984). Physical attractiveness and self-esteem: Attributions for praise from an other-sex evaluator. *Personality and Social Psychology Bulletin, 10,* 43–50.

Major, B., & Konar, E. (1984). An investigation of sex differences in pay expectations and their possible causes. *Academy of Management Journal, 27,* 777–792.

Major, B., Vanderslice, V., & McFarlin, D. B. (1985). Effects of pay expected on pay received: The confirmatory nature of initial expectations. *Journal of Applied Social Psychology, 14,* 399–412.

Malamuth, N. M. (1981). Rape proclivity among males. *Journal of Social Issues, 37,* 138–157.

Malamuth, N. M. (1984). Violence against women: Cultural and individual cases. In N. M. Malamuth & E. Donnerstein (Eds.), *Pornography and sexual aggression.* New York: Academic Press.

Malamuth, N. M., & Briere, J. (1986). Sexual violence in the media: Indirect effects on aggression against women. *Journal of Social Issues, 42,* 75–92.

Malamuth, N. M., & Check, J. V. P. (1981). The effects of mass media exposure on acceptance of violence against women. *Journal of Research in Personality, 15,* 436–446.

Malamuth, N. M., Check, J. V. P., & Briere, J. (1986). Sexual arousal in response to aggression: Ideological, aggressive, and sexual correlates. *Journal of Personality and Social Psychology, 50,* 330–340.

Mallick, S. K., & McCandless, B. F. (1966). A study of catharsis of aggression. *Journal of Personality and Social Psychology, 4,* 591–596.

Marks, G. (1984). Thinking one's abilities unique and one's opinions are common. *Personality and Social Psychology Bulletin, 10,* 203–208.

Marks, G., & Miller, N. (1982). Target attractiveness as a mediator of assumed attitude similarity. *Personality and Social Psychology Bulletin, 8,* 728–735.

Marks, G., & Miller, N. (1987). Ten years of research on the false-consensus effect: An empirical and theoretical review. *Psychological Bulletin, 102,* 72–90.

Marks, G., Miller, N., & Maruyama, G. (1981). Effect of targets' physical attractiveness on assumptions of similarity. *Journal of Personality and Social Psychology, 41,* 198–206.

Marks, M. L. (1986). The question of quality circles. *Psychology Today, 20,* pp. 36–38, 42, 44, 46.

Markus, H. (1977). Self-schemata and processing information about the self. *Journal of Personality and Social Psychology, 35,* 63–78.

Markus, H. (1978). The effect of mere presence on social facilitation: An unobtrusive test. *Journal of Experimental Social Psychology, 14,* 389–397.

Markus, H., Hamil, R., & Sentis, K. (1987). Thinking fat: Self-schemas for body weight and processing of weight relevant information. *Journal of Applied Social Psychology, 17,* 50–71.

Markus, H., & Kunda, Z. (1986). Stability and malleability of the self-concept. *Journal of Personality and Social Psychology, 51,* 858–866.

Markus, H., & Wurf, E. (1987). The dynamic self-concept: A social psychological perspective. *Annual Review of Psychology, 38,* 299–377.

Markus, H., & Zajonc, R. B. (1985). The cognitive perspective in social psychology. In G. Lindzey & E. Aronson (Eds.), *Handbook of social psychology.* New York: Random House.

Martens, R. (1969). Palmar sweating and the presence of an audience. *Journal of Experimental Social Psychology, 5,* 371–374.

Martin, C. L. (1987). A ratio measure of sex stereotyping. *Journal of Personality and Social Psychology, 52,* 489–490.

Martin, J., & Murray, A. (1983). Distributive injustice and unfair exchange. In D. M. Messick & K. S. Cook (Eds.), *Equity theory: Psychological and sociological perspectives.* New York: Praeger.

Maruyama, G., & Miller, N. (1981). Physical attractiveness and personality. In B. Maher (Ed.), *Advances in experimental research on personality* (Vol. 10). New York: Academic Press.

Maslach, C., Santee, R. T., & Wade, C. (1987). Individuation, gender role, and dissent: Personality mediators of situational forces. *Journal of Personality and Social Psychology, 53,* 1088–1094.

Maslach, C., Stapp, J., & Santee, R. T. (1985). Individuation: Conceptual analysis and assessment. *Journal of Personality and Social Psychology, 49,* 729–738.

Mason, A., & Blankenship, V. (1987). Power and affiliation motivation, stress, and abuse in intimate relationships. *Journal of Personality and Social Psychology, 52,* 203–210.

Mathes, E. W., Adams, H. E., & Davies, R. M. (1985). Jealousy: Loss of relationship rewards, loss of self-esteem, depression, anxiety, and anger. *Jour-*

nal of Personality and Social Psychology, 48, 1552–1561.

Matlin, M. W., & Zajonc, R. B. (1968). Social facilitation of word associations. *Journal of Personality and Social Psychology, 10,* 455–460.

Matthews, K. A., & Haynes, S. G. (1986). Type A behavior pattern and coronary-risk: Update and critical evaluation. *American Journal of Epidemiology, 123,* 923–960.

May, J. L., & Hamilton, P. A. (1980). Effects of musically evoked affect on women's interpersonal attraction and perceptual judgments of physical attractiveness of men. *Motivation and Emotion, 4,* 217–228.

Mayer, F. S., Duval, S., Holtz, R., & Bowman, C. (1985). Self-focus, helping request salience, felt responsibility, and helping behavior. *Journal of Personality and Social Psychology, 11,* 133–144.

McAllister, H. A., & Bregman, N. J. (1983). Self-disclosure and liking: An integration theory approach. *Journal of Personality, 51,* 202–212.

MacArthur, L. A. (1972). The how and what of why: Some determinants and consequences of causal attribution. *Journal of Personality and Social Psychology, 22,* 171–193.

McClelland, D. C., & Boyatzis, R. E. (1982). Leadership motive pattern and long-term success in management. *Journal of Applied Psychology, 67,* 737–743.

McFarlane, A. H., Norman, G. R., Streiner, D. L., & Roy, R. G. (1983). The process of social stress: Stable, reciprocal, and mediating relationships. *Journal of Health and Social Behavior, 24,* 160–173.

McFarland, C., & Ross, M. (1987). The relation between current impressions and memories of self and dating partners. *Personality and Social Psychology Bulletin, 13,* 228–238.

McGaughey, K. J., & Stiles, W. B. (1983). Courtroom interrogation of rape victims: Verbal response mode use by attorneys and witnesses during direct examination vs. cross-examination. *Journal of Applied Social Psychology, 13,* 78–87.

McGovern, L. P., Ditzian, J. L., & Taylor, S. P. (1975). The effect of one positive reinforcement on helping with cost. *Bulletin of the Psychonomic Society, 5,* 421–423.

McGrath, J. E. (1984). *Groups: Interaction and performance.* Englewood Cliffs, NJ: Prentice-Hall.

McGraw, K. M. (1987). Outcome valence and base rates: The effects on moral judgments. *Social Cognition, 5,* 58–75.

McGuire, W. J. (1969). The nature of attitudes and attitude change. In G. Lindzey and E. Aronson (Eds.), *Handbook of social psychology* (Vol. 2). Reading, MA: Addison-Wesley.

McGuire, T., Kiesler, S., & Siegel, J. (1987). Group and computer-mediated discussion effects in risk decision making. *Journal of Personality and Social Psychology, 52,* 917–930.

Mechanic, D. (1983). Adolescent health and illness behavior: Hypotheses for the study of distress in youth. *Journal of Human Stress, 9,* 4–13.

Mehlman, R. C., & Snyder, C. R. (1985). Excuse theory: A test of the self-protective role of attributions. *Journal of Personality and Social Psychology, 49,* 994–1001.

Mehrabian, A. (1968). Relationship of attitude to seated posture, orientation, and distance. *Journal of Personality and Social Psychology, 10,* 26–30.

Meindl, J. R., & Lerner, M. J. (1985). Exacerbation of extreme responses to an out-group. *Journal of Personality and Social Psychology, 47,* 71–84.

Metalsky, G. I., Halberstadt, L. J., & Abramson, L. Y. (1987). Vulnerability to depressive mood reactions: Toward a more powerful test of the diathesis-stress and causal mediation components of the reformulated theory of depression. *Journal of Personality and Social Psychology, 52,* 386–393.

Meyer, D., Leventhal, H., & Gutman, M. (1985). Common-sense models of illness: The example of hypertension. *Health Psychology, 4,* 115–135.

Meyer, H. H. (1975). The pay-for-performance dilemma. *Organizational Dynamics, 3,* 39–50.

Meyer, J. P., & Mulherin, A. (1980). From attribution to helping: An analysis of the mediating effects of affect and expectancy. *Journal of Personality and Social Psychology, 39,* 201–210.

Meyer, J. P., & Pepper, S. (1977). Need compatibility and marital adjustment in young married couples. *Journal of Personality and Social Psychology, 35,* 331–342.

Meyerowitz, B. E., & Chaiken, S. (1987). The effect of message framing on breast self-examination attitudes, intentions and behavior. *Journal of Personality and Social Psychology, 52,* 500–510.

Michelini, R. L., & Snodgrass, S. R. (1980). Defendant characteristics and juridic decisions. *Journal of Research in Personality, 14,* 340–350.

Middlemist, R. D., Knowles, E. S., & Matter, C. F. (1976). Personal space invasions in the lavatory: Suggestive evidence for arousal. *Journal of Personality and Social Psychology, 33,* 541–546.

Milardo, R. M., Johnson, M. P., & Huston, T. L. (1983). Developing close relationships: Changing patterns of interaction between pair members and social networks. *Journal of Personality and Social Psychology, 44,* 964–976.

Milgram, S. (1963). Behavioral study of obedience. *Journal of Abnormal and Social Psychology, 69,* 137–143.

Milgram, S. (1965). Liberating effects of group pressure. *Journal of Personality and Social Psychology, 1,* 127–134.

Milgram, S. (1974). *Obedience to authority.* New York: Harper.

Milgram, S., Liberty, H. J., Toledo, R., & Wackenhut, J. (1986). Response to intrusion into waiting lines. *Journal of Personality and Social Psychology, 51,* 683–689.

Miller, C. T. (1986). Categorization and stereotypes about men and women. *Personality and Social Psychology Bulletin, 12,* 502–512.

Miller, D. T., & McFarland, C. (1986). Counterfactual thinking and victim compensation. *Personality and Social Psychology Bulletin, 12,* 513–519.

Miller, D. T., & Ross, M. (1975). Self-serving biases in the attribution of causality: Fact or fiction? *Psychological Bulletin, 82,* 313–325.

Miller, N., & Brewer, M. (1984). *Groups in contact: The psychology of desegregation.* New York: Academic Press.

Miller, N., Maruyama, G., Beaber, R. J., & Valone, K. (1976). Speed of speech and persuasion. *Journal of Personality and Social Psychology, 34,* 615–624.

Miller, S. M., Lack, E. R., & Asroff, S. (1985). Preference for control and the coronary-prone behavior pattern: "I'd rather do it myself." *Journal of Personality and Social Psychology, 49,* 492–499.

Mischel, W. (1968). *Personality and assessment.* New York: Wiley.

Mitchell, H. E., & Byrne, D. (1973). The defendant's dilemma: Effects of jurors' attitudes and authoritarianism on juridic decision. *Journal of Personality and Social Psychology, 25,* 123–129.

Mitchell, T. R., & Kalb, L. S. (1982). Effects of job experience on supervisor attributions for a subordinate's poor performance. *Journal of Applied Psychology, 67,* 181–188.

Monson, T. C., & Hesley, J. W. (1982). Causal attributions for behaviors consistent or inconsistent with an actor's personality traits: Differences between those offered by actors and observers. *Journal of Personality and Social Psychology, 18,* 416–432.

Moreland, R. L., & Zajonc, R. B. (1982). Exposure effects in person perception: Familiarity, similarity, and attraction. *Journal of Experimental Social Psychology, 18,* 395–415.

Morgan, C. J. (1978). Bystander intervention: Experimental test of a formal model. *Journal of Personality and Social Psychology, 36,* 43–55.

Morganthau, T. (1983, August 8). Gay American in transition. *Newsweek,* pp. 30–40.

Moriarty, T. (1975). Crime, commitment, and the responsive bystander: Two field experiments. *Journal of Personality and Social Psychology, 31,* 370–376.

Morris, D., Collett, P., Marsh, P., & O'Shaughnessy, M. (1979). *Gestures: Their origins and distribution.* London: Cape.

Morris, W. N., & Miller, R. S. (1975). The effects of consensus-breaking and consensus-preempting partners on reduction of conformity. *Journal of Personality and Social Psychology, 11,* 215–223.

Morris, W. N., Miller, R. S., & Spangenberg, S. (1977). The effects of dissenter position and task difficulty on conformity and response to conflict. *Journal of Personality and Social Psychology, 45,* 251–266.

Morris, W. N., Worchel, S., Bois, J. L., Pearson, J. A., Rountree, C. A., Samaha, G. M., Wachtler, J., & Wright, S. L. (1976). Collective coping with stress: Group reactions to fear, anxiety, and ambiguity. *Journal of Personality and Social Psychology, 33,* 674–679.

Moscovici, S. (1985). Social influence and conformity. In G. Lindzey and E. Aronson (Eds.), *Handbook of social psychology* (Vol. III). New York: Random House.

Moscovici, S., & Faucheux, C. (1972). Social influence, conforming bias, and the study of active minorities. In L. Berkowitz (Ed.), *Advances in experimental social psychology* (Vol. 6, pp. 149–202). New York: Academic Press.

Moscovici, S., & Lage, E. (1976). Studies in social influence III: Majority versus minority influence in a group. *European Journal of Social Psychology, 6,* 149–174.

Moss, M. K., & Page, R. A. (1972). Reinforcement and helping behavior. *Journal of Applied Social Psychology, 2,* 360–371.

Mueser, K. T., Grau, B. W., Sussman, S., & Rosen, A. J. (1984). You're only as pretty as you feel: Facial expression as a determinant of physical attractiveness. *Journal of Personality and Social Psychology, 46,* 469–478.

Mugny, G. (1975). Negotiations, image of the other and the process of minority influence. *European Journal of Social Psychology, 5,* 209–229.

Mullen, B. (1983). Operationalizing the effect of the group on the individual. *Journal of Experimental Social Psychology, 19,* 295–322.

Mullen, B. (1986a). Atrocity as a function of lynch mob composition: A self-attention perspective. *Personality and Social Psychology Bulletin, 12,* 187–197.

Mullen, B. (1986b). Stuttering, audience size, and the other-total ratio: A self-attention perspective. *Journal of Applied Social Psychology, 16,* 139–149.

Mullen, B. (1987). Self-attention theory: The effects of group composition on the individual. In B. Mullen & G. R. Goethals (Eds.), *Theories of group behavior* (pp. 125–146). New York: Springer-Verlag.

Mullen, B., Atkins, J. L., Champion, D. S., Edwards, C.,

Hardy, D., Story, J. E., & Vanderklok, M. (1985). The false consensus effect: A meta-analysis of 115 hypothesis tests. *Journal of Experimental Social Psychology, 21,* 262–283.

Mullen, B., & Baumeister, R. F. (1987). Group effects on self-attention and performance: Social loafing, social facilitation, and social impairment. In C. Hendrick (Ed.), *Group processes and intergroup relations* (pp. 189–206). Newbury Park, CA: Sage Publications.

Mullen, B., & Goethals, G. R. (Eds). (1987). *Theories of group behavior.* New York: Springer-Verlag.

Mullen, B., & Hu, L. (1987). Perceptions of ingroup and outgroup variability: A meta-analytic integration. Unpublished manuscript, Syracuse University.

Murnen, S., Byrne, D., & Przybyla, D. (1981). Arousal and attraction: Anxiety reduction, misattribution, or response strength? Paper presented at Eastern Psychological Association meeting, 1982, New York City.

Murray, D. M., & Wells, G. L. (1982). Does knowledge that a crime was staged affect eyewitness performance? *Journal of Applied Social Psychology, 12,* 42–53.

Murray, H. A. (1962). *Explorations in personality.* New York: Science Editions. (Originally published 1938)

Murstein, B. I. (1972). Physical attractiveness and marital choice. *Journal of Personality and Social Psychology, 22,* 8–12.

Murstein, B.I. (1980). Love at first sight: A myth. *Medical Aspects of Human Sexuality, 14,* 34, 39–41.

Musialowski, D. (1986). Quality of worklife, disease prevention, and productivity. Unpublished manuscript, State University of New York at Albany.

Myers, D. G., Burggink, J. B., Kersting, R. C., & Schlosser, B. S. (1980). Does learning others' opinions change one's opinions? *Personality and Social Psychology Bulletin, 6,* 253–260.

Nahemow, L., & Lawton, M. P. (1975). Similarity and propinquity in friendship formation. *Journal of Personality and Social Psychology, 32,* 205–213.

Narayanan, V. K., & Nath, R. (1982). A field test of some attitudinal and behavioral consequences of flexitime. *Journal of Applied Psychology, 67,* 214–218.

Nelkin, D., & Brown, M. S. (1984). *Workers at risk: Voices from the workplace.* Chicago: University of Chicago Press.

Nemeth, C. J. (1986). Differential contributions of majority and minority influence. *Psychological Review, 93,* 23–32.

Newcomb, M. D., & Harlow, L. L. (1986). Life events and substance use among adolescents: Mediating effects of perceived loss of control and meaningfulness in life. *Journal of Personality and Social Psychology, 51,* 564–577.

Newcomb, T. M. (1961). *The acquaintance process.* New York: Holt, Rinehart and Winston.

Neuberg, S. L., & Fiske, S. T. (1987). Motivational influences on impression formation: Outcome dependency, accuracy-driven attention, and individuating processes. *Journal of Personality and Social Psychology, 53,* 431–444.

Nisbett, R. E., & Kunda, Z. (1985). Perception of social distributions. *Journal of Personality and Social Psychology, 48,* 297–311.

Nisbett, R. E., & Ross, L. (1980). *Human inference: Strategies and shortcomings of social judgment.* Englewood Cliffs, NJ: Prentice-Hall.

Nisbett, R. E., & Wilson, T. D. (1977). Telling more than we can know: Verbal reports on mental processes. *Psychological Review, 84,* 231–259.

Nyquist, L. V., & Spence, J. T. (1986). Effects of dispositional dominance and sex role expectations on leadership behaviors. *Journal of Personality and Social Psychology, 50,* 87–93.

O'Donnell, L., O'Donnell, C. R., Pleck, J. R., Sharey, J., & Rose, R. M. (1987). Psychosocial responses of hospital workers to acquired immune deficiency syndrome (AIDS). *Journal of Applied Social Psychology, 17,* 269–285.

O'Grady, K. E. (1982). Sex, physical attractiveness, and perceived risk for mental illness. *Journal of Personality and Social Psychology, 43,* 1064–1071.

Ohbuchi, K., & Izutsu, T. (1984). Retaliation by male victims: Effects of physical attractiveness and intensity of attack of female attacker. *Personality and Social Psychology Bulletin, 10,* 216–224.

Ohbuchi, K., & Ogura, S. (1984). The experience of anger (1): The survey for adults and university students with Averill's questionnaire (Japanese). *Japanese Journal of Criminal Psychology, 22,* 15–35.

Olbrisch, M. E., Weiss, S. M., Stone, G. C., & Schwartz, G. E. (1985). Report of the National Working Conference on Education and Training in Health Psychology. *American Psychologist, 40,* 1038–1041.

Olson, J. M., Herman, C. P., & Zanna, M. P. (Eds.). (1986). *Relative deprivation and social comparison: The Ontario Symposium* (Vol. 4). Hillsdale, NJ: Erlbaum.

O'Malley, M. N. (1983). Interpersonal and intrapersonal justice: The effect of subject and confederate outcomes on evaluations of fairness. *Journal of Experimental Social Psychology, 13,* 121–128.

O'Malley, M. N., & Andrews, L. (1983). The effect of mood and incentives on helping: Are there some things money can't buy? *Motivation and Emotion, 7,* 179–189.

O'Malley, M. N., & Becker, L. A. (1984). Removing the egocentric bias: The relevance of distress cues to evaluation of fairness. *Personality and Social Psychology Bulletin, 10,* 235–242.

Orbuch, P., & McKinney, K. (1984). Asking questions in bars: The girls (and boys) may not get prettier at closing time and other interesting results. *Psychology and Social Psychology Bulletin, 10,* 482–488.

Ortega, D. F., & Pipal, J. E. (1984). Challenge seeking and the Type A coronary-prone behavior pattern. *Journal of Personality and Social Psychology, 46,* 1328–1334.

Oskamp, S., & Spacapan, S. (Eds.). (1987). *Interpersonal processes.* Newbury, Park, CA: Sage.

O'Sullivan, C. S., & Durso, F. T. (1984). Effects of schema-incongruent information on memory for stereotypical attributes. *Journal of Personality and Social Psychology, 47,* 1328–1334.

Pallak, M. S., Cook, D. A., & Sullivan, J. J. (1980). Commitment and energy conservation. *Applied Social Psychology Annual, 1,* 235–253.

Palmer, J., & Byrne, D. (1970). Attraction toward dominant and submissive strangers: Similarity versus complementarity. *Journal of Experimental Research in Personality, 4,* 108–115.

Palys, T. S. (1986). Testing the common wisdom: The social content of video pornography. *Canadian Psychology, 27,* 22–35.

Park, B., & Rothbart, M. (1982). Perception of outgroup homogeneity and levels of social categorization: Memory for the subordinate attributes of ingroup and outgroup members. *Journal of Personality and Social Psychology, 42,* 1051–1068.

Parke, R. D., Berkowitz, L., Leyens, J. P., West, S. G., & Sebastian, R. J. (1977). Some effects of violent and nonviolent movies on the behavior of juvenile delinquents. In L. Berkowitz (Ed.), *Advances in experimental social psychology* (Vol. 10). New York: Academic Press.

Parsons, J. E., Alder, T., & Meece, J. L. (1984). Sex differences in achievement: A test of alternate theories. *Journal of Personality and Social Psychology, 46,* 26–43.

Patch, M. E. (1986). The role of source legitimacy in sequential request strategies of compliance. *Personality and Social Psychology Bulletin, 12,* 199–205.

Pearce, J. L., & Porter, L. W. (1986). Employee responses to formal performance appraisal feedback. *Journal of Applied Psychology, 71,* 211–218.

Pendleton, M. G., & Batson, C. D. (1979). Self-presentation and the door-in-the-face technique for inducing compliance. *Personality and Social Psychology Bulletin, 5,* 77–81.

Penley, L. E. (1982). An investigation of the information processing framework of organizational communication. *Human Communication Research, 8,* 348–365.

Pennebaker, J. W., & Beall, S. (1986). Confronting a traumatic event: Toward an understanding of inhibition and disease. *Journal of Abnormal Psychology, 95,* 274–281.

Pennebaker, J. W., Hughes, C. F., & O'Heeron, R. C. (1987). The psychophysiology of confession: Linking inhibitory and psychosomatic processes. *Journal of Personality and Social Psychology, 52,* 781–793.

Pennebaker, J. W., & O'Heeron, R. C. (1984). Confiding in others and illness rate among spouses of suicide and accidental death victims. *Journal of Abnormal Psychology, 93,* 473–476.

Penrod, S., & Hastie, R. (1980). A computer simulation of jury decision making. *Psychological Review, 87,* 133–159.

Perloff, L. S., & Fetzer, B. K. (1986). Self-other judgments and perceived vulnerability of victimization. *Journal of Personality and Social Psychology, 50,* 502–510.

Peters, L. H., Hartke, D. D., & Pohlmann, J. T. (1985). Fiedler's contingency theory of leadership: An application of the meta-analysis procedures of Schmidt and Hunter. *Psychological Bulletin, 97,* 274–285.

Peters, L. H., O'Conner, E. J., Weekley, J., Pooyan, A., Frank, B., & Erenkrantz, B. (1984). Sex bias and managerial evaluations: A replication and extension. *Journal of Applied Psychology, 69,* 349–352.

Peterson, C., & Barrett, L. C. (1987). Explanatory style and academic performance among university freshmen. *Journal of Personality and Social Psychology, 53,* 603–607.

Peterson, C., Seligman, M. E. P., & Vaillant, G. (1988). Pessimistic explanatory style is a risk factor for physical illness: A thirty-five year longitudinal study. *Journal of Personality and Social Psychology, 55,* 23–27.

Petty R. E., & Cacioppo, J. T. (1979). Issue involvement can increase or decrease persuasion by enhancing message-relevant cognitive responses. *Journal of Personality and Social Psychology, 37,* 1915–1926.

Petty, R. E., & Cacioppo, J. T. (1981). *Attitudes and persuasion: Classic and contemporary approaches.* Dubuque, IA: Wm. C. Brown.

Petty, R. E., & Cacioppo, J. T. (1985). *Communication and persuasion: Central and peripheral routes to attitude change.* New York: Springer-Verlag.

Petty, R. E., & Cacioppo, J. T. (1986). The elaboration likelihood model of persuasion. In L. Berkowitz (Ed.), *Advances in experimental social psychology* (Vol. 19, pp. 123–205). New York: Academic Press.

Petty, R. E., Harkins, S. G., Williams, K. D., & Latané, B. (1980). The effects of group size on cognitive effort and evaluation. *Personality and Social Psychology Bulletin, 3,* 579–582.

Petty, R. E., Ostrom, T. M., & Brock, T. C. (Eds.). (1981). *Cognitive responses in persuasion.* Hillsdale, NJ: Erlbaum.

Phillips, D. P. (1983). The impact of mass media violence on U.S. homicides. *American Sociological Review, 48,* 560–568.

Piliavin, J. A., Callero, P. L., & Evans, D. E. (1982). Addiction to altruism? Opponent-process theory and habitual blood donation. *Journal of Personality and Social Psychology, 43,* 1200–1213.

Piliavin, J. A., Dovidio, J. F., Gaertner, S. L., & Clark, R. D., III. (1981). *Emergency intervention.* New York: Academic Press.

Pilisuk, M., Boylan, R., & Acredolo, C. (1987). Social support, life stress, and subsequent medical care utilization. *Health Psychology, 6,* 273–288.

Pines, A., & Aronson, E. (1983). Antecedents, correlates, and consequences of sexual jealousy. *Journal of Personality, 51,* 108–136.

Pittner, M. S., Houston, B.K., & Spiridigliozzi, G. (1983). Control over stress, Type A behavior pattern, and response to stress. *Journal of Personality and Social Psychology, 44,* 627–637.

Pliner, P., Hart, H., Kohl, J., & Saari, D. (1974). Compliance without pressure: Some further data on the foot-in-the-door technique. *Journal of Experimental Social Psychology, 10,* 17–22.

Powers, P. C., & Geen, R. S. (1972). Effects of the behavior and the perceived arousal of a model on instrumental aggression. *Journal of Personality and Social Psychology, 23,* 175–184.

Price, K. H., & Garland, H. (1981). Compliance with a leader's suggestions as a function of perceived leader/members competence and potential reciprocity. *Journal of Applied Psychology, 66,* 329–336.

Price, K. H., & Vandenberg, S. G. (1979). Matching for physical attractiveness in married couples. *Personality and Social Psychology Bulletin, 5,* 398–400.

Prohaska, T. R., Keller, M. L., Leventhal, E. A., & Leventhal, H. (1987). Impact of symptoms and aging attribution on emotions and coping. *Health Psychology, 6,* 495–514.

Pryor, J. B., Gibbons, F. X., Wicklund, R. A., Fazio, R. H., & Hood, R. (1977). Self-focused attention and self-report validity. *Journal of Personality, 45,* 514–527.

Przybyla, D. P. J., Murnen, S., & Byrne, D. (1985). Arousal and attraction: Anxiety reduction, misattribution, or response strength? Unpublished manuscript, State University of New York at Albany.

Pursell, S. A., & Banikiotes, P. G. (1978). Androgyny and initial interpersonal attraction. *Personality and Social Psychology Bulletin, 4,* 235–243.

Rajecki, D. W., Kidd, R. F., & Ivins, B. (1976). Social fa-cilitation in chickens: A different level of analysis. *Journal of Experimental Social Psychology, 37,* 1902–1914.

Ramirez, J., Bryant, J., & Zillmann, D. (1983). Effects of erotica on retaliatory behavior as a function of level of prior provocation. *Journal of Personality and Social Psychology, 43,* 971–978.

Raps, C. S., Peterson, C., Reinhard, K. E., Abramson, L. Y., & Seligman, M. E. P. (1982). Attributional style among depressed patients. *Journal of Abnormal Psychology, 91,* 102–108.

Read, S. J. (1987). Constructing causal scenarios: A knowledge structure approach to causal reasoning. *Journal of Personality and Social Psychology, 52,* 288–302.

Reardon, R., & Rosen, S. (1984). Psychological differentiation and the evaluation of juridic information: Cognitive and affective consequences. *Journal of Research in Personality, 18,* 195–211.

Reed, D., & Weinberg, M. S. (1984). Premarital coitus: Developing and establishing sexual scripts. *Social Psychology Quarterly, 47,* 129–138.

Reeder, G. D., & Coovert, M. D. (1986). Revising an impression of morality. *Social Cognition, 4,* 1–17.

Reeder, G. D., & Brewer, M. B. (1979). A schematic model of dispositional attribution in interpersonal perception. *Psychological Review, 86,* 61–79.

Regan, D. T. (1971). Effects of a favor and liking on compliance. *Journal of Experimental Social Psychology, 7,* 627–639.

Reis, H. T., Nezlek, J., & Wheeler, L. (1980). Physical attractiveness in social interaction. *Journal of Personality and Social Psychology, 38,* 604–617.

Reiss, M., Rosenfeld, R., Melburg, V., & Tedeschi, J. T. (1981). Self-serving attributions: Biased private perceptions and distorted public descriptions. *Journal of Personality and Social Psychology, 41,* 224–231.

Research and Forecasts, Inc. (1981). *The Connecticut Mutual Life report on American values in the '80s: The impact of belief.* Hartford: Connecticut Mutual Life Insurance Co.

Rhodewalt, F., & Davidson, J., Jr. (1983). Reactance and the coronary-prone behavior pattern: The role of self-attribution in response to reduced behavioral freedom. *Journal of Personality and Social Psychology, 44,* 220–228.

Rice, R. W., Instone, D., & Adams, J. (1984). Leader sex, leader success, and leadership process: Two field studies. *Journal of Applied Psychology, 69,* 12–31.

Riordan, C. (1978). Equal-status interracial court: A review and revision of a concept. *International Journal of Intercultural Relations, 2,* 161–185.

Riordan, C. A., & Tedeschi, J. T. (1983). Attraction in aversive environments: Some evidence for classical conditioning and negative reinforcement.

Journal of Personality and Social Psychology, 44, 683–692.

Rippetoe, P. A., & Rogers, R. W. (1987). Effects of components of protection-motivation theory on adaptive and maladaptive coping with a health threat. *Journal of Personality and Social Psychology, 52,* 596–604.

Riskind, J. H., Rholes, W. C., Brannon, A. M., & Burdick, C. A. (1987). Attributions and expectations: A confluence of vulnerabilities in mild depression in a college student population. *Journal of Personality and Social Psychology, 52,* 349–354.

Riskind, J. H., & Wilson, D. W. (1982). Interpersonal attraction for the competent person: Unscrambling the competition paradox. *Journal of Applied Social Psychology, 12,* 444–452.

Rittle, R. H. (1981). Changes in helping behavior: Self-versus situational perceptions as mediators of the foot-in-the-door effect. *Personality and Social Psychology Bulletin, 7,* 431–437.

Roberts, M. C., Wurtele, S. K., Boone, R., Metts, V., & Smith, V. (1981). Toward a reconceptualization of the reciprocal imitation phenomenon: Two experiments. *Journal of Research in Personality, 15,* 447–459.

Robles, R., Smith, R., Carver, C. S., & Wellens, A. R. (1987). Influence of subliminal visual images on the experience of anxiety. *Personality and Social Psychology Bulletin, 13,* 399–410.

Rodgers, J. L., Billy, J. O. B., & Udry, J. R. (1984). A model of friendship similarity in mildly deviant behaviors. *Journal of Applied Social Psychology, 14,* 413–425.

Rodrigues, A., & Newcomb, T. M. (1980). The balance principle: Its current state and its integrative function in social psychology. *Interamerican Journal of Psychology, 14,* 85–136.

Rofe, Y. (1984). Stress and affiliation: A utility theory. *Psychological Review, 91,* 235–250.

Rogers, M., Miller, N., Mayer, F. S., & Duvall, S. (1982). Personal responsibility and salience of the request for help: Determinants of the relation between negative affect and helping behavior. *Journal of Personality and Social Psychology, 43,* 956–970.

Rogers, R. W. (1980). Subjects' reactions to experimental deception. Unpublished manuscript, University of Alabama.

Rogers, R. W. (1983). Cognitive and physiological processes in fear appeals and attitude change: A revised theory of protection motivation. In J. R. Cacioppo & R. E. Petty (Eds.), *Social psychophysiology: A sourcebook* (pp. 153–176). New York: Guilford.

Rogers, R. W., & Ketcher, C. M. (1979). Effects of anonymity and arousal on aggression. *Journal of Psychology, 102,* 13–19.

Rogers, T. B., Kuiper, N. A., & Kirker, W. S. (1977). Self-reference and the encoding of personal information. *Journal of Personality and Social Psychology, 35,* 677–688.

Ronen, S. (1986). Equity perception in multiple comparisons: A field study. *Human Relations, 39,* 333–346.

Rook, K. S. (1987). Effect of case history versus abstract information on health attitudes and behavior. *Journal of Applied Social Psychology, 17,* 533–554.

Rose, S. M. (1984). How friendships end: Patterns among young adults. *Journal of Social and Personal Relationships, 1,* 267–277.

Rosenbaum, M. E. (1986). The repulsion hypothesis: On the nondevelopment of relationships. *Journal of Personality and Social Psychology, 51,* 1156–1166.

Rosenfield, D., Folger, R., & Adelman, H. F. (1980). When rewards reflect competence: A qualification of the overjustification effect. *Journal of Personality and Social Psychology, 39,* 368–376.

Rosenfield, D., Greenberg, J., Folger, R., & Borys, R. (1982). Effect of an encounter with a black panhandler on subsequent helping for blacks: Tokenism or conforming to a negative stereotype? *Personality and Social Psychology Bulletin, 8,* 664–671.

Rosenhan, D. L., Salovey, P., & Hargis, K. (1981). The joys of helping: Focus of attention mediates the impact of positive affect on altruism. *Journal of Personality and Social Psychology, 40,* 899–905.

Ross, L., Amabile, T. M., & Steinmetz, J. L. (1977). Social rules, social control, and biases in social perception. *Journal of Personality and Social Psychology, 35,* 485–494.

Ross, L., Greene, D., & House, P. (1977). The "false consensus effect": An egocentric bias in social perception and attribution processes. *Journal of Experimental Social Psychology, 13,* 279–301.

Ross, L., Lepper, M. R., & Hubbard, M. (1975). Perseverance in self-perception and social perception: Biased attributional process in the debriefing paradigm. *Journal of Personality and Social Psychology, 32,* 880–892.

Ross, M., & Sicoly, F. (1979). Egocentricity biases in availability and attribution. *Journal of Personality and Social Psychology, 37,* 322–336.

Roter, D. L. (1984). Patient question asking in physician-patient interaction. *Health Psychology, 3,* 395–409.

Rotton, J., & Frey, J. (1985). Air pollution, weather, and violent crimes: Concomitant time-series analysis of archival data. *Journal of Personality and Social Psychology, 49,* 1207–1220.

Routh, D. K., & Ernst, A. R. (1984). Somatization disorder in relatives of children and adolescents with functional abdominal pain. *Journal of Pediatric Psychology, 50,* 427–437.

Ruback, R. B., Carr, T. S., & Hopper, C. H. (1986). Perceived control in prison: Its relation to reported crowding, stress, and symptoms. *Journal of Applied Social Psychology, 16,* 375–386.

Rubin, Z. (1974). From liking to loving: Patterns of attraction in dating relationships. In T. L. Huston (Ed.), *Foundation of interpersonal attraction.* New York: Academic Press.

Rubin, Z. (1980). *Children's friendships.* Cambridge, MA: Harvard University Press.

Rubin, Z. (1985). Deceiving ourselves about deception: Comment on Smith and Richardson's "Amelioration of deception and harm in psychological research." *Journal of Personality and Social Psychology, 48,* 252–253.

Rule, B. G., Taylor, B. R., & Dobbs, A. R. (1987). Priming effects of heat on aggressive thoughts. *Social Cognition, 5,* 131–143.

Rusbult, C. E. (1980). Commitment and satisfaction in romantic associations: A test of the investment model. *Journal of Experimental Social Psychology, 16,* 172–186.

Rusbult, C. E. (1983). A longitudinal test of the investment model: The development (and deterioration) of satisfaction and commitment in heterosexual involvements. *Journal of Personality and Social Psychology, 45,* 101–117.

Rusbult, C. E., Johnson, D. J., & Morrow, G. D. (1986). Impact of couple patterns of problem solving on distress and nondistress in dating relationships. *Journal of Personality and Social Psychology, 50,* 744–753.

Rusbult, C. E., Musante, L., & Solomon, M. (1982). The effects of clarity of decision rule and favorability of verdict on satisfaction with resolution of conflicts. *Journal of Applied Social Psychology, 12,* 304–317.

Rusbult, C. E., & Zembrodt, I. M. (1983). Responses to dissatisfaction in romantic involvements: A multidimensional scaling analysis. *Journal of Experimental Social Psychology, 19,* 274–293.

Russ, R. C., Gold, J. A., & Stone, W. F. (1980). Opportunity for thought as a mediator of attraction to a dissimilar stranger: A further test of an information seeking interpretation. *Journal of Experimental Social Psychology, 16,* 562–572.

Russell, D. W., McAuley, E., & Tarico, V. (1987). Measuring causal attributions for success and failure: A comparison of methodologies for assessing causal dimensions. *Journal of Personality and Social Psychology, 52,* 1248–1257.

Rutkowski, G. K., Gruder, C. L., & Romer, D. (1983). Group cohesiveness, social norms, and bystander

intervention. *Journal of Personality and Social Psychology, 44,* 545–552.

Sadalla, E. K., Kenrick, D. T., & Vershure, B. (1987). Dominance and heterosexual attraction. *Journal of Personality and Social Psychology, 52,* 730–738.

Saegert, S., Swap, W., & Zajonc, R. B. (1973). Exposure, context, and interpersonal attraction. *Journal of Personality and Social Psychology, 25,* 234–242.

Salovey, P., & Rodin, J. (1986). The differentiation of social-comparison jealousy and romantic jealousy. *Journal of Personality and Social Psychology, 50,* 1100–1112.

Sanbonmatsu, D. M., Sherman, S. J., & Hamilton, D. L. (1987). Illusory correlation in the perception of individuals and groups. *Social Cognition, 5,* 1–25.

Sanders, G. S. (1983). An attentional process model of social facilitation. In A. Hare, H. Blumberg, V. Kent, & M. Davies (Eds.), *Small groups.* London: Wiley.

Sanders, G. S. (1984a). Effects of context cues on eyewitness identification responses. *Journal of Applied Social Psychology, 14,* 386–397.

Sanders, G. S. (1984b). Self-presentation and drive in social facilitation. *Journal of Experimental Social Psychology, 20,* 312–322.

Sanders, G. S., & Baron, R. S. (1977). Is social comparison irrelevant for producing choice shifts? *Journal of Experimental Social Psychology, 13,* 303–314.

Sanders, G. S., Baron, R. S., & Moore, D. L. (1978). Distraction and social comparison as mediators of social facilitation effects. *Journal of Experimental Social Psychology, 14,* 291–303.

Sanders, G. S., & Mullen, B. (1983). Accuracy in perception of consensus: Differential tendencies of people with majority and minority positions. *European Journal of Social Psychology, 13,* 57–70.

Sansone, C. (1986). A question of competence: The effects of competence and task feedback on intrinsic interest. *Journal of Personality and Social Psychology, 51,* 918–931.

Santee, R. T., & Maslach, C. (1982). To agree or not to agree: Personal dissent amid social pressure to conform. *Journal of Personality and Social Psychology, 42,* 690–700.

Scandura, T. A., & Graen, G. B. (1984). Moderating effects of initial leader-member exchange status on the effects of a leadership intervention. *Journal of Applied Psychology, 69,* 428–436.

Schachter, S. (1951). Deviation, rejection, and communication. *Journal of Abnormal and Social Psychology, 46,* 190–207.

Schachter, S. (1959). *The psychology of affiliation.* Stanford, CA: Stanford University Press.

Schachter, S., & Singer, J. (1962). Cognitive, social, and physiological determinants of the emotional state. *Psychological Review, 69,* 379–399.

Schank, R. C., & Abelson, R. P. (1977). *Scripts, plans, goals, and understanding: An inquiry into human knowledge structures.* Hillsdale, NJ: Erlbaum.

Scheier, M. F., & Carver, C. S. (1983). Two sides of the self: One for you and one for me. In J. Suls and A. G. Greenwald (Eds.), *Psychological perspectives on the self* (Vol. 2, pp. 123–158). Hillsdale, NJ: Erlbaum.

Scheier, M. F., & Carver, C. S. (1987). Dispositional optimism and physical well-being: The influence of generalized outcome expectancics in health. *Journal of Personality, 55,* 169–210.

Scheier, M. F., & Carver, C. S. (1986). A model of self-regulation: Translating intention into action. In L. Berkowitz (Ed.), *Advances in experimental social psychology* (Vol. 20). New York: Academic Press.

Schleifer, S. J., Keller, S. E., Camerino, M., Thornton, J. C., & Stein, M. (1983). Suppression of lymphocyte function following bereavement. *Journal of American Medical Association, 250,* 374–377.

Schlenker, B. R. (1982). Self-contemplations. *Contemporary Psychology, 27,* 615–616.

Schmitt, B. H., Gilovich, T., Goore, N., & Joseph, L. (1986). Mere presence and social facilitation: One more time. *Journal of Experimental Social Psychology, 22,* 242–248.

Schullo, S. A., & Alperson, B. L. (1984). Interpersonal phenomenology as a function of sexual orientation, sex, sentiment, and trait categories in long-term dyadic relationships. *Journal of Personality and Social Psychology, 47,* 983–1002.

Schwarzwald, J., Bizman, A., & Raz, M. (1983). The foot-in-the-door paradigm: Effects of second request size on donation probability and donor generosity. *Personality and Social Psychology Bulletin, 9,* 443–450.

Schwarzwald, J., Raz, M., & Zvibel, M. (1979). The applicability of the door-in-the-face technique when established behavioral customs exist. *Journal of Applied Social Psychology, 9,* 576–586.

Sears, D. O. (1986). College sophomores in the laboratory: Influences of a narrow data base on social psychology's view of human nature. *Journal of Personality and Social Psychology, 51,* 515–530.

Segal, M. W. (1974). Alphabet and attraction: An unobtrusive measure of the effect of propinquity in a field setting. *Journal of Personality and Social Psychology, 30,* 654–657.

Shaffer, D. R., & Graziano, W. G. (1983). Effects of positive and negative moods on helping tasks having pleasant or unpleasant consequences. *Motivation and Emotion, 7,* 269–278.

Shaffer, D. R., Plummer, D., & Hammock, G. (1986). Hath he suffered enough? Effects of jury dogmatism, defendant similarity and defendant's pretrial suffering on juridic decisions. *Journal of Personality and Social Psychology, 50,* 1059–1067.

Shaffer, D. R., Rogel, M., & Hendrick, C. (1975). Intervention in the library: The effect of increased responsibility on bystanders' willingness to prevent a theft. *Journal of Applied Social Psychology, 5,* 303–319.

Shanab, M. E., & Yahya, K. A. (1977). A behavioral study of obedience in children. *Journal of Personality and Social Psychology, 35,* 530–536.

Shelton, M. L., & Rogers, R. W. (1981). Fear-arousing and empathy-arousing appeals to help: The pathos of persuasion. *Journal of Applied Social Psychology, 11,* 366–378.

Sherif, M. (1935). A study of some social factors in perception. *Archives of Psychology,* No. 187.

Sherif, M., Harvey, O. J., White, B. J., Hood, W. E., & Sherif, C. W. (1961). *Intergroup conflict and cooperation: The Robbers cave experiment.* Norman, OK: Institute of Group Relations.

Sherman, S. J. (1980). On the self-erasing nature of errors of prediction. *Journal of Personality and Social Psychology, 16,* 388–403.

Sherman, S. J., Presson, C. C., & Chassin, L. (1984). Mechanisms underlying the false consensus effect: The special role of threats to the self. *Personality and Social Psychology Bulletin, 10,* 127–138.

Sherman, S. J., Presson, C. C., Chassin, L., Bensenberg, M., Corty, E., & Olshavsky, R. W. (1982). Smoking intentions in adolescents: Direct experience and predictability. *Personality and Social Psychology Bulletin, 8,* 376–383.

Sherman, S. J., Presson, C. C., Chassin, L., Corty, E., & Olshavsky, R. (1983). The false consensus effect in estimates of smoking prevalence: Underlying mechanisms. *Personality and Social Psychology Bulletin, 9,* 197–207.

Shiffman, S., & Jarvik, M. E. (1987). Situational determinants of coping in smoking relapse crises. *Journal of Applied Social Psychology, 17,* 3–15.

Shotland, R. L., & Heinold, W. D. (1985). Bystander response to arterial bleeding: Helping skills, the decision-making process, and differentiating the helping response. *Journal of Personality and Social Psychology, 49,* 347–356.

Shotland, R. L., & Mark, M. M. (1985). *Social science and social policy.* London: Sage.

Sigelman, C. K., Thomas, D. B., Sigelman, L., & Robich, F. D. (1986). Gender, physical attractiveness, and electability: An experimental investigation of voter biases. *Journal of Applied Social Psychology, 16,* 229–248.

Simon, B., & Brown, R. (1987). Perceived intragroup homogeneity in minority-majority contexts. *Journal of Personality and Social Psychology, 53,* 703–711.

Simpson, J. A. (1987). The dissolution of romantic relationships: Factors involved in relationship stability and emotional stress. *Journal of Personality and Social Psychology, 53,* 683–692.

Sims, H. P., & Manz, C. C. (1984). Observing leader verbal behavior: Toward reciprocal determinism in leadership theory. *Journal of Applied Psychology, 69,* 222–232.

Sistrunk, F., & McDavid, J. W. (1971). Sex variable in conforming behavior. *Journal of Personality and Social Psychology, 17,* 200–207.

Sivacek, J., & Crano, W. D. (1982). Vested interest as a moderator of attitude-behavior consistency. *Journal of Personality and Social Psychology, 43,* 210–221.

Sloan, L. R., Love, R. E., & Ostrom, T. M. (1974). Political heckling: Who really loses? *Journal of Personality and Social Psychology, 30,* 518–525.

Slusher, M. P., & Anderson, C. A. (in press). Belief perseverance and self-defeating behavior. In R. Curtis (Ed.), *Self-defeating behavior: Experimental research, clinical impressions, and practical implications.* New York: Plenum.

Smeaton, G., & Byrne, D. (1987). The effects of R-rated violence and erotica, individual differences, and victim characteristics on acquaintance rape proclivity. *Journal of Research in Personality, 21,* 171–184.

Smith, A. J. (1957). Similarity of values and its relation to acceptance and the projection of similarity. *Journal of Psychology, 43,* 251–260.

Smith, D. E., Gier, J. A., & Willlis, F. N. (1982). Interpersonal touch and compliance with a marketing request. *Basic and Applied Social Psychology, 3,* 35–38.

Smith, M. B., Bruner, J. S., & White, R. W. (1956). *Opinions and personality.* New York: Wiley.

Smith, S. S., & Richardson, D. (1983). Amelioration of deception and harm in psychological research: The important role of debriefing. *Journal of Personality and Social Psychology, 5,* 1075–1082.

Smith, S. S., & Richardson, D. (1985). On deceiving ourselves about deception: Reply to Rubin. *Journal of Personality and Social Psychology, 48,* 254–255.

Smith, V. I., & Ellsworth, P. C. (1987). The social psychology of eyewitness accuracy: Misleading questions and communicator expertise. *Journal of Applied Psychology, 72,* 294–300.

Snyder, C. R., & Fromkin, H. L. (1980). *Uniqueness: The human pursuit of difference.* New York: Plenum.

Snyder, C. R., Higgins, R. L., & Stucky, R. J. (1983). *Excuses: Masquerades in search of grace.* New York: Wiley-Interscience.

Snyder, C. R., Lassegard, M., & Ford, C. E. (1986). Distancing after group success and failure: Basking in reflected glory and cutting off reflected failure. *Journal of Personality and Social Psychology, 51,* 382–389.

Snyder, M. (1974). The self-monitoring of expressive behavior. *Journal of Personality and Social Psychology, 30,* 526–537.

Snyder, M. (1987). *Public appearances, private realities: The psychology of self-monitoring.* New York: Freeman.

Snyder, M., & Cummingham, M. R. (1975). To comply or not to comply: Test the self-perception explanation of the "foot-in-the-door" phenomenon. *Journal of Personality and Social Psychology, 31,* 64–67.

Snyder, M., & DeBono, K. G. (1988). Understanding the functions of attitudes: Lessons from personality and social behavior. In A. R. Pratkanis, S. J. Breckler, & A. G. Greenwald (Eds.), *Attitude structure and function.* Hillsdale, NJ: Erlbaum.

Snyder, M., & Kendzierski, D. (1982). Acting on one's attitudes: Procedures for linking attitude and behavior. *Journal of Experimental Social Psychology, 18,* 165–183.

Solomon, R. C. (1981, October). The love lost in cliches. *Psychology Today,* pp. 83–85, 87–88.

Sorrentino, R. M., & Field, N. (1986). Emergent leadership over time: The functional value of positive motivation. *Journal of Personality and Social Psychology, 50,* 1091–1099.

Spears, R., van der Pligt, J., & Eiser, J. R. (1985). Illusory correlation in the perception of group attitudes. *Journal of Personality and Social Psychology, 48,* 863–875.

Spielberger, C. D., & Stenmark, D. E. (1985). Community psychology. In E. M. Altmaier & E. Meyer (Eds.), *Applied specialties in psychology* (pp. 75–97). New York: Random House.

Sprecher, S., DeLamater, J., Neuman, N., Neuman, M., Kahn, P., Orbuch, D., & McKinney, K. (1984). Asking questions in bars: The girls (and boys) may not get prettier at closing time and other interesting results. *Personality and Social Psychology Bulletin, 10,* 482–488.

Srull, T. K., & Wyer, R. S. (1979). The role of category accessibility in the interpretation of information about persons: Some determinants and implications. *Journal of Personality and Social Psychology, 37,* 1660–1672.

Stapp, J., & Fulcher, R. (1984). The employment of 1981 and 1982 doctorate recipients in psychology. *American Psychologist, 39,* 1408–1423.

Stasser, G., & Titus, W. (1985). Pooling of unshared

information in group decision making: Biased information sampling during discussion. *Journal of Personality and Social Psychology, 48,* 1467–1478.

Stasser, G., & Titus, W. (1987). Effects of information load and percentage of shared information on the dissemination of unshared information during group discussion. *Journal of Personality and Social Psychology, 53,* 81–93.

Steck, L., Levitan, D., McLane, D., & Kelley, H. H. (1982). Care, need, and conceptions of love. *Journal of Personality and Social Psychology, 43,* 481–491.

Steffen, V. J., & Eagley, A. H. (1985). Implicit theories about influence style: The effects of status and sex. *Personality and Social Psychology Bulletin, 11,* 191–205.

Steinberg, R., & Shapiro, S. (1982). Sex differences in personality traits of female and male master of business administration students. *Journal of Applied Psychology, 67,* 306–310.

Steiner, I. D. (1972). *Group process and productivity.* New York: Academic Press.

Steiner, I. D. (1976). Task-performing groups. In J. W. Thibaut, J. T. Spence, & R. C. Carson (Eds.), *Contemporary topics in social psychology.* Morristown, NJ: General Learning Press.

Stephan, W. (1985). Intergroup relations. In G. Lindzey and E. Aronson (Eds.), *Handbook of social psychology* (3rd ed., Vol. 2, pp. 599–648). New York: Random House.

Sternberg, R. J. (1986). A triangular theory of love. *Psychological Review, 93,* 119–135.

Stewart, J. E., II (1980). Defendant's attractiveness as a factor in the outcome of criminal trials: An observational study. *Journal of Applied Social Psychology, 10,* 348–361.

Stone, A. A., Cox, D. S., Valdimarsdotti, H., Jandorf, L., & Neale, J. M. (1987). Evidence that secretory IgA antibody is associated with daily mood. *Journal of Personality and Social Psychology, 52,* 988–993.

Stone, A. A., & Neale, J. M. (1984). Effects of severe daily events on mood. *Journal of Personality and Social Psychology, 46,* 137–144.

Stone, L. (1977). *The family, sex, and marriage in England: 1500–1800.* New York: Harper.

Stoner, J. A. F. (1961). A comparison of individual and group decisions involving risk. Unpublished master's thesis, School of Industrial Management, MIT.

Straus, M. A., Gelles, R. J., & Steinmetz, S. K. (1980). *Behind closed doors: Violence in the American family.* Garden City, NJ: Anchor Books.

Streeter, L. A., Krauss, R. M., Geller, V., Olson, C., & Apple, W. (1977). Pitch changes during attempted deception. *Journal of Personality and Social Psychology, 35,* 345–350.

Strom, J. C., & Buck, R. W. (1979). Staring and participants' sex: Physiological and subjective reactions. *Personality and Social Psychology Bulletin, 5,* 114–117.

Strube, M. J., & Garcia, J. E. (1981). A meta-analytic investigation of Fiedler's contingency model of leadership effectiveness. *Psychological Bulletin, 90,* 307–321.

Strube, M. J., Miles, M. E., & Finch, W. H. (1981). The social facilitation of a simple task: Field tests of alternative explanations. *Personality and Social Psychology Bulletin, 7,* 701–707.

Suls, J. (Ed.). (1982). *Psychological perspectives on the self* (Vol. 1). Hillsdale, NJ: Erlbaum.

Suls, J., & Fletcher, B. (1983). Social comparison in the social and physical sciences: An archival study. *Journal of Personality and Social Psychology, 44,* 575–580.

Suls, J., & Fletcher, B. (1985). The relative efficacy of avoidant and nonavoidant coping strategies: A meta-analysis. *Health Psychology, 4,* 249–288.

Suls, J., & Greenwald, A. G. (Eds.). (1983). *Psychological perspectives on the self* (Vol. 2). Hillsdale, NJ: Erlbaum.

Suls, J., & Greenwald, A. G. (Eds.). (1986). *Psychological perspective on the self* (Vol. 3). Hillsdale, NJ: Erlbaum.

Suls, J., & Miller, R. L. (Eds.). (1977). *Social comparison processes: Theoretical and empirical perspectives.* Washington, DC: Hemisphere.

Suls, J., & Rittenhouse, J. D. (1987). Personality and physical health. *Journal of Personality, 55,* 155–168.

Suls, J., & Rosnow, J. (1988). Concerns about artifacts in behavioral research. In J. Morawski (Ed.), *The rise of experimentation in American psychology* (pp. 163–187). New Haven, CT: Yale University Press.

Suls, J., & Wan, C. K. (1987). In search of the false uniqueness phenomenon: Fear and estimates of social consensus. *Journal of Personality and Social Psychology, 52,* 211–217.

Suls, J., & Wan, C. K. (in press). The effects of sensory and procedural information on coping with stressful medical procedures and pain: A meta-analysis. *Journal of Consulting and Clinical Psychology.*

Suls, J., Wan, C. K., & Sanders, G. S. (1988). False consensus and false uniqueness in estimating the prevalence of health-protective behaviors. *Journal of Applied Social Psychology, 18,* 66–79.

Sunnafrank, M. J., & Miller, G. R. (1981). The role of initial conversations in determining attraction to similar and dissimilar strangers. *Human Communication Research, 8,* 16–25.

Swann, W. B., Jr., Griffin, J. J., Jr., Predmore, S. C., & Gaines, B. (1987). Cognitive-affective crossfire: When self-consistency meets self-enhancement.

Journal of Personality and Social Psychology, 52, 881–889.

Swap, W. C. (1977). Interpersonal attraction and repeated exposure to rewarders and punishers. *Personality and Social Psychology Bulletin, 3,* 248–251.

Sweeney, P. D., Anderson, K., & Bailey, S. (1986). Attributional style in depression: A meta-analytic review. *Journal of Personality and Social Psychology, 50,* 974–991.

Sweeney, P. D., & Gruber, K. L. (1984). Selective exposure: Voter information preferences and the Watergate affair. *Journal of Personality and Social Psychology, 46,* 1208–1221.

Swim, J., & Borgida, E. (1987). Public opinion on the psychological and legal aspects of televising rape trials. *Journal of Applied Social Psychology, 17,* 507–518.

Sypher, B. D., & Sypher, H. E. (1983). Perceptions of communication ability: Self-monitoring in an organizational meeting. *Personality and Social Psychology Bulletin, 9,* 297–304.

Szymanski, K., & Harkins, S. G. (1987). Social loafing and self-evaluation with a social standard. *Journal of Personality and Social Psychology, 53,* 891–897.

Tajfel, H. (1970, November). Experiments in intergroup discrimination. *Scientific American,* pp. 96–102.

Tanford, S., & Penrod, S. (1984). Social influence model: A formal integration of research on majority and minority influence processes. *Psychological Bulletin, 95,* 189–225.

Taormina, R. J., & Messick, D. M. (1983). Deservingness for foreign aid: Effects of need, similarity, and estimated effectiveness. *Journal of Applied Social Psychology, 13,* 371–391.

Taylor, S. E. (1985). *Health psychology.* New York: Random House.

Taylor, S. E., & Brown, J. D. (1988). Illusion and well-being: A social psychological perspective on mental health. *Psychological Bulletin, 103,* 193–210.

Tedeschi, J. T., Smith, R. B. III, & Brown, R. C., Jr. (1974). A reinterpretation of research on aggression. *Psychological Bulletin, 81,* 540–562.

Tesser, A. (1986). Some effects of self-evaluation maintenance on cognition and action. In R. Sorrentino & E. T. Higgins (Eds.), *The handbook of motivation and cognition: Foundations of social behavior* (pp. 435–464). New York: Guilford Press.

Tesser, A., & Campbell, J. (1983). Self-definition and self-evaluation maintenance. In J. Suls & A. Greenwald (Eds), *Psychological perspectives on the self* (Vol. 2, pp. 1–31). Hillsdale, NJ: Erlbaum.

Tesser, A., Campbell, J., & Smith M. (1984). Friendship choice and performance: Self-evaluation mainte-

nance in children. *Journal of Personality and Social Psychology, 46,* 561–574.

Tesser, A., Millar, M., & Moore, J. (1988). Some affective consequences of social comparison and reflection processes: The pain and pleasure of being close. *Journal of Personality and Social Psychology, 54,* 49–61.

Tesser, A., & Paulhus, D. L. (1976). Toward a causal model of love. *Journal of Personality and Social Psychology, 46,* 561–574.

Tetlock, P. E., & Kim, J. I. (1987). Accountability and judgment processes in a personality prediction task. *Journal of Personality and Social Psychology, 52,* 700–709.

Thelen, M H., Frautschi, N. M. Roberts, M. C., Kirkland, K. D., & Dollinger, S. J. (1981). Being imitated, conformity, and social influence: An integrative review. *Journal of Research in Personality, 15,* 403–426.

Thomas, G. C., Batson, C. D., & Coke, J. S. (1981). Do good Samaritans discourage helpfulness? Self-perceived altruism after exposure to highly helpful others. *Journal of Personality and Social Psychology, 40,* 194–200.

Thomas, M. H. (1982). Physiological arousal, exposure to a relatively lengthy aggressive film, and aggressive behavior. *Journal of Research in Personality, 16,* 72–81.

Thompson, R. A., & Hoffman, M. L. (1980). Empathy and the development of guilt in children. *Developmental Psychology, 16,* 155–156.

Thompson, W. C., Cowan, C. L., & Rosenhan, D. L. (1980). Focus of attention mediates the impact of negative affect on altruism. *Journal of Personality and Social Psychology, 38,* 291–300.

Toch, H. (1985). The catalytic situation in the violence equation. *Journal of Applied Social Psychology, 15,* 105–123.

Toi, M., & Batson, C. D. (1982). More evidence that empathy is a source of altruistic motivation. *Journal of Personality and Social Psychology, 43,* 281–292.

Triplett, N. (1898). The dynamogenic factors in pacemaking and competition. *American Journal of Psychology, 9,* 507–533.

Troilier, T. K., & Hamilton, D. L. (1986). Variables influencing judgments of correlational relations. *Journal of Personality and Social Psychology, 50,* 879–888.

Turkington, C. (1986, February). High court weighs value of research by social scientists. *APA Monitor, 17,* 1, 30.

Turner, J. C., Hogg, M. A., Oakes, P. J., Reicher, S., & Wetherell, M. S. (1987). *A self-categorization theory of group behavior.* Oxford: Blackwell.

Tversky, A., & Kahneman, D. (1971). The belief in the "law of small numbers." *Cognitive Psychology, 5,* 207–232.

Tversky, A., & Kahneman, D. (1973). Availability: A heuristic for judging frequency and probability. *Cognitive Psychology, 5,* 207–232.

Tversky, A., & Kahneman, D. (1982). Judgment under uncertainty: Heuristics and biases. In D. Kahneman, P. Slovic, & A. Tversky (Eds.), *Judgment under uncertainty* (pp. 3–20). New York: Cambridge University Press.

Tyler, T. R., & Cook, F. L. (1984). The mass media and judgment of risk: Distinguishing impact on personal and societal level judgments. *Journal of Personality and Social Psychology, 47,* 693–708.

Umberson, D., & Hughes, M. (1984, August). The impact of physical attractiveness on achievement and psychological well-being. Paper presented at the meeting of the American Sociological Association, San Antonio, Texas.

Utne, M. K., Hatfield, E., Traupmann, J., & Greenberger, D. (1984). Equity, marital satisfaction, and stability. *Journal of Social and Personal Relationships, 1,* 323–332.

Vallacher, R. R., & Wegner, D. M. (1987). What do people think they're doing? Action identification and human behavior. *Psychological Review, 94,* 3–15.

Veitch, R., & Griffitt, W. (1976). Good news, bad news: Affective and interpersonal effects. *Journal of Applied Social Psychology, 6,* 69–75.

Verbrugge, L. (1983). Multiple roles and physical health of women and men. *Journal of Health and Social Behavior, 24,* 16–29.

Vinokur, A., & Burnstein, E. (1974). Effects of partially shared persuasive arguments on group-induced shifts: A group problem-solving approach. *Journal of Personality and Social Psychology, 29,* 305–315.

Vinokur, A., Burnstein, E., Sechrest, L., & Wortman, P. M. (1985). Group decision making by experts: Field study of panels evaluating medical technologies. *Journal of Personality and Social Psychology, 49,* 70–84.

Vroom, V. H., & Yetton, P. W. (1973). *Leadership and decision-making.* Pittsburgh, PA: University of Pittsburgh Press.

Wagner, P. J., & Curran, P. (1984). Health beliefs and physician identified "worried well." *Health Psychology, 3,* 459–474.

Wagner, R. K. (1987). Tacit knowledge in everyday intelligent behavior. *Journal of Personality and Social Psychology, 52,* 1236–1248.

Wallach, M. A., & Wing, C. W. (1968). Is risk a value? *Journal of Personality and Social Psychology, 9,* 101–106.

Walster, E., & Festinger, L. (1962). The effectiveness of "overheard" persuasive communications. *Journal of Abnormal and Social Psychology, 65,* 395–402.

Warner, R. B., & Sugarman, D. B. (1986). Attributions of personality based on physical appearance, speech, and handwriting. *Journal of Personality and Social Psychology, 50,* 792–799.

Watts, B. L. (1982). Individual differences in circadian activity rhythms and their effects on roommate relationships. *Journal of Personality, 50,* 374–384.

Weinberger, M., Hiner, S. L., & Tierney, W. M. (1987). In support of hassles as a measure of stress in predicting health outcomes. *Journal of Behavioral Medicine, 10,* 19–32.

Weiner, B. (1980). A cognitive (attribution) emotion-action model of motivated behavior: An analysis of judgments of helpgiving. *Journal of Personality and Social Psychology, 39,* 186–200.

Weinstein, N. D. (1987). Unrealistic optimism about susceptibility to health problems: Conclusions from a community-wide sample. *Journal of Behavioral Medicine, 10,* 481–500.

Weinstein, N. D., Grubb, P. D., & Vautier, J. S. (1986). Increasing automobile seat belt use: An intervention emphasizing risk susceptibility. *Journal of Applied Psychology, 71,* 285–290.

Weisinger, H., & Lobsenz, N. M. (1981). *Nobody's perfect: How to give criticism and get results.* New York: Warner Books.

Weiten, W. (1980). The attraction-leniency effect in jury research: An examination of external validity. *Journal of Applied Social Psychology, 10,* 340–347.

Wells, G. L. (1984). The psychology of lineup identification. *Journal of Applied Social Psychology, 14,* 89–103.

Wells, G. L., & Murray, D. M. (1983). What can psychology say about the "Neil v. Biggers" criteria for judging eye-witness accuracy? *Journal of Applied Psychology, 68,* 347–362.

Wells, G. L., Taylor, B. R., & Turtle, J. W. (1987). The undoing of scenarios. *Journal of Personality and Social Psychology, 53,* 421–430.

Werner, C., & Parmalee, P. (1979). Similarity of activity preferences among friends: Those who play together stay together. *Social Psychology Quarterly, 42,* 62–66.

Weyant, J. M. (1986). *Applied social psychology.* New York: Oxford University Press.

Weyant, J. M., & Smith, S. L. (1987). Getting more by asking for less: The effects of request size on donations for charity. *Journal of Applied Social Psychology, 17,* 392–400.

White, G. L. (1980a). Inducing jealousy: A power perspective. *Personality and Social Psychology Bulletin, 6,* 222–227.

White, G. L. (1980b). Physical attractiveness and courtship progress. *Journal of Personality and Social Psychology, 39,* 660–668.

White, G. L. (1981). Some correlates of romantic jealousy. *Journal of Personality, 49,* 129–146.

White, P. A. (1987). Causal report accuracy: Retrospect and prospect. *Journal of Experimental Social Psychology, 23,* 311–315.

White, R. K. (1977). Misperception in the Arab-Israeli conflict. *Journal of Social Issues, 33,* 190–221.

Whitley, B. E., & Greenberg, M. S. (1986). The role of eyewitness confidence in juror perceptions of credibility. *Journal of Applied Social Psychology, 16,* 387–409.

Wicker, A. W. (1969). Attitudes versus actions: The relationship of verbal and overt behavioral responses to attitude objects. *Journal of Social Issues, 25,* 41–78.

Wiebe, D. J., & McCallum, D. M. (1986). Health practices and hardiness as mediators in the stress-illness relationship. *Health Psychology, 5,* 425–438.

Wiggins, J. S., Wiggins, N., & Conger, J. C. (1968). Correlates of heterosexual somatic preference. *Journal of Personality and Social Psychology, 10,* 253–268.

Wilder, D. A. (1977). Perception of groups, size of opposition, and social influence. *Journal of Experimental Social Psychology, 13,* 253–268.

Wilder, D. A. (1984). Intergroup contact: The typical member and the exception to the rule. *Journal of Experimental Social Psychology, 20,* 177–194.

Williams, J. E., & Best, D. L. (1982). *Measuring sex stereotypes: A third-nation study.* Beverly Hills, CA: Sage.

Williams, K., DeNisi, A. S., Meglino, B. M., & Cafferty, T. P. (1986). Initial decisions and subsequent performance ratings. *Journal of Applied Psychology, 71,* 189–195.

Williams, K., Harkins, S., & Latané, B. (1981). Identifiability as a deterrent to social loafing: Two cheering experiments. *Journal of Personality and Social Psychology, 40,* 303–311.

Wills, T. A. (1981). Downward comparison principles in social psychology. *Psychological Bulletin, 90,* 245–271.

Wilson, T. D., & Linville, P. W. (1982). Improving the academic performance of college freshmen: Attribution therapy revisited. *Journal of Personality and Social Psychology, 42,* 367–376.

Wilson, T. D., & Stone, J. I. (1985). Limitation of self-knowledge: More on telling more than we can know. In P. Shaver (Ed.), *Review of Personality and Social Psychology* (Vol. 6).

Winer, D. L., Bonner, T. O., Jr., Blaney, P. H., & Murray, E. J. (1981). Depression and social attraction. *Motivation and Emotion, 5,* 153–166.

Winter, D. G. (1987). Leader appeal, leader performance, and the motive profiles of leaders and followers: A study of American presidents and elections. *Journal of Personality and Social Psychology, 52,* 196–202.

Wispe, L. (1986). The distinction between sympathy and empathy: To call forth a concept, a word is needed. *Journal of Personality and Social Psychology, 50,* 314–321.

Wolf, S. (1985). Manifest and latent influence of majorities and minorities. *Journal of Personality and Social Psychology, 48,* 899–908.

Wolfe, B. M., & Baron, R. A. (1971). Laboratory aggression related to aggression in naturalistic social situations: Effects of an aggressive model on the behavior of college students and prisoner observers. *Psychonomic Science, 24,* 193–194.

Wood, W. (1982). Retrieval of attitude-relevant information from memory: Effects on susceptibility to persuasion and on intrinsic motivation. *Journal of Personality and Social Psychology, 42,* 798–810.

Wood, W., Polek, D., & Aiken, C. (1985). Sex differences in group task performance. *Journal of Personality and Social Psychology, 48,* 63–71.

Worchel, S. (1974). The effect of three types of arbitrary thwarting on the instigation to aggression. *Journal of Personality, 42,* 301–318.

Wortman, C. B., & Linsenmeier, J. A. W. (1977). Interpersonal attraction and techniques of ingratiation in organizational settings. In B. M. Staw & G. R. Salancik (Eds.), *New directions in organizational behavior.* Chicago: St. Clair Press.

Wu, C., & Shaffer, D. R. (1987). Susceptibility to persuasive appeals as a function of source credibility and prior experience with the attitude object. *Journal of Personality and Social Psychology, 52,* 677–688.

Wurtele, S. K., & Maddux, J. E. (1987). Relative contributions of protection motivation theory components in predicting exercise intentions and behavior. *Health Psychology, 6,* 453–466.

Wyer, R. W., & Srull, T. K. (1986). Human cognition in its social context. *Psychological Review, 93,* 322–359.

Yandrell, B., & Insko, C. A. (1977). Attributions of attitudes to speakers and listeners under assigned-behavior conditions: Does behavior engulf the field? *Journal of Experimental Social Psychology, 13,* 269–278.

Yarmey, D. A. (1986). Verbal, visual and voice identification of a rape suspect under different levels of illumination. *Journal of Applied Psychology, 71,* 363–370.

Yarnold, P. R., & Grimm, L. G. (1982). Time urgency

among coronary-prone individuals. *Journal of Abnormal Psychology, 91,* 175–177.

Yuille, J. C., & Cutshall, J. L. (1986). A case study of eyewitness memory of a crime. *Journal of Applied Psychology, 71,* 291–301.

Zaccaro, S. J. (1984). Social loafing: The role of task attractiveness. *Personality and Social Psychology Bulletin, 10,* 99–106.

Zajonc, R. B. (1965). Social facilitation. *Science, 149,* 269–274.

Zajonc, R. B. (1968). Attitudinal effects of mere exposure. *Journal of Personality and Social Psychology Monographs Supplement, 9,* 1–27.

Zajonc, R. B. (1984). On the primacy of affect. *American Psychologist, 39,* 117–123.

Zajonc, R. B., Heingartner, A., & Herman, E. M. (1969). Social enhancement and impairment of performance in the cockroach. *Journal of Personality and Social Psychology, 13,* 83–92.

Zajonc, R.B., & Sales, S. M. (1966). Social facilitation of dominant and subordinate responses. *Journal of Experimental Social Psychology, 2,* 160–168.

Zaller, J. R. (1987). Diffusion of political attitudes. *Journal of Personality and Social Psychology, 53,* 821–833.

Zanna, M. P., & Hamilton, D. L. (1977). Further evidence for meaning change in impression formation. *Journal of Experimental Social Psychology, 13,* 224–238.

Zanna, M. P., & Olson, J. M. (1982). Individual differences in attitudinal relations. In M. P. Zanna, E. T. Higgins, & C. P. Herman (Eds.), *Consistency in social behavior: The Ontario Symposium* (Vol. 2). Hillsdale, NJ: Erlbaum.

Zanna, M. P., Olson, J. M., & Herman, C. P. (Eds.). (1987). *Social influence: The Ontario Symposium* (Vol. 5). Hillsdale, NJ: Erlbaum.

Zillmann, D. (1983a). Transfer of excitation in emotional behavior. In J. T. Cacioppo & R. E. Petty (Eds.), *Social psychophysiology.* New York: Guilford Press.

Zillmann, D. (1983b). Arousal and aggression. In R. G. Geen and E. Donnerstein (Eds.), *Aggression: Theoretical and empirical reviews.* New York: Academic Press.

Zillmann, D. (1979). *Hostility and aggression.* Hillsdale, NJ: Erlbaum.

Zillmann, D., Katcher, A. H., & Milavsky, B. (1972). Excitation transfer from physical exercise to subsequent aggressive behavior. *Journal of Experimental Social Psychology, 8,* 247–259.

Zola, I. K. (1966). Culture and symptoms—an analysis of patients' presenting complaints. *American Sociological Review, 31,* 615–630.

Zuckerman, M., DePaulo, B., & Rosenthal, R. (1981). Verbal and nonverbal communication of deception. In L. Berkowitz (Ed.), *Advances in experimental social psychology* (Vol. 14, pp. 1–59). New York: Academic Press.

Zuckerman, M., Koestner, R., & Alton, A. D. (1984). Learning to detect deception. *Journal of Personality and Social Psychology, 46,* 519–528.

Zuckerman, M., Miserandino, M., & Bernieri, F. (1983). Civil inattention exists—in elevators. *Personality and Social Psychology Bulletin, 9,* 578–586.

Zimbardo, P. G. (1977). *Shyness: What it is and what you can do about it.* Reading, MA: Addison-Wesley.

Name Index

Subject Index

Photo Credits

Chapter One 1, Billy E. Barnes/Southern Light; 5 (left), Wide World; 5 (center), Susan Van Etten; 5 (right), Peter Menzell/Stock, Boston; 23, Jeffrey W. Myers/Stock, Boston.

Chapter Two 27, Robert Harbison; 30 (top), Paul Conklin; 30 (bottom), A. Collins/Monkmeyer Press Photos; 31, 33, Susan Van Etten; 45, Jean-Claude Lejeune/Stock, Boston.

Chapter Three 53, Greg Plachta/Southern Light; 58, 64, Susan Van Etten.

Chapter Four 79, Mike Mazzaschi/Stock, Boston; 81, 84, Paul Conklin; 85, Courtesy, Benetton, Inc.; 98, Wide World.

Chapter Five 103, Melanie Stetson Freeman; 105, 110, Wide World; 112 (left), La Belle jarniere, 1939, Berne Kunstmuseum/Art Resource; 112 (right), Etude pour l'improvisation, Paris, Galerie Moeght/Art Resource; 113, Wide World; 119, Frank Siteman/The Picture Cube; 120, Courtesy, The Bloom Agency/McCann-Erickson; 124, Paul Conklin/Monkmeyer Press Photos.

Chapter Six 127, 129, 135, Paul Conklin; 139, Courtesy, © 1988, Republic Pictures Corporation.

Chapter Seven 155, Robert Harbison; 158, Wide World; 159 (left), Eric Kroll/Taurus; 159 (right), The New York University Film Library; 163, Paul Conklin; 164, William Vandivert.

Chapter Eight 181, Jerry Howard/Stock, Boston; 183 (left), Scott Photo Service and Susan Van Etten; 183 (right), Rhoda Sidney/Southern Light; 187, supplied by authors; 191, Bandura, Ross and Ross, 1963; Copyright American Psychological Association, 1963; 200, Bohdan Hrynewych/Southern Light.

Chapter Nine 213, Bruce Davidson/Magnum Photo; 215 (top left), Frank Siteman/The Picture Cube; 215 (top right), Paul Conklin; 215 (middle), David S. Strickler/The Picture Cube; 215 (bottom), Peter Menzel/Stock, Boston; 221 (top), Susan Van Etten; 221 (middle), Michael Kagan/Monkmeyer Press Photos; 221 (bottom), Jean-Claude Lejeune/Stock, Boston; 226, Wide World; 232 (top), Peter Menzell/Stock, Boston; 232 (bottom), Paul Conklin.

Chapter Ten 341, Billy E. Barnes/Southern Light; 245, Susan Van Etten; 253, Ted Cordingley; 260 (top), David A. Krathwohl/Stock, Boston; 260 (bottom left), Charles Gupton/Southern Light; 260 (bottom right), Paul Conklin; 263, Paul Conklin.